THE GLOSSARY OF
COLOR
THEORY

Compiled & Edited By:
Manohar Giri

Rhythm

Independent
Publication

THE GLOSSARY OF COLOR THEORY

Compiled & Edited By:
Manohar Giri

ISBN:9798862448290

9798862448290

Published by:

Rhythm Independent Publication,

Jinkethimmanahalli, Varanasi, Bengaluru, Karnataka, India - 560036

For all types of correspondence, send your mails to the provided address above.

The information presented herein has been collated from a diverse range of sources, comprehensive perspective on the subject matter.

Abundance (Gold)

Abundance (Gold) is a color used in color theory and color symbolism in design. It is a warm, metallic hue that combines the richness of yellow with the elegance and sophistication of gold. As a symbol of abundance, this color represents wealth, opulence, and prosperity. In color theory, abundance (gold) is classified as a tertiary color, created by mixing primary colors yellow and orange with secondary color green. This color is often associated with precious metals like gold, giving it a sense of luxury and value.

Accessibility Color Testing Tools

Accessibility color testing tools are integral in the field of color theory and color symbolism in design. These tools help designers and developers ensure that the color selections and combinations they use are accessible to all individuals, including those with visual impairments or color vision deficiencies. Color theory is the study of how colors interact with one another and how they can be used to communicate specific messages or emotions. It plays a crucial role in design, as the right combination of colors can evoke certain feelings or convey a particular brand identity. However, it's important to remember that not all individuals perceive colors in the same way. Color symbolism in design refers to the use of specific colors to convey deeper meanings or associations. Different cultures and societies may interpret colors differently, adding another layer of complexity to the design process. Furthermore, individuals with color vision deficiencies may struggle to differentiate between certain colors, which can impact their ability to perceive the intended symbolism. Accessibility color testing tools address these challenges by providing designers with the means to evaluate color choices and ensure that they are accessible to all users. These tools typically include features such as color contrast analyzers, color blindness simulators, and color palette generators. Color contrast analyzers are especially important in ensuring accessibility. They measure the contrast between foreground and background colors and provide a numerical value that indicates whether the contrast meets accessibility standards. This is crucial for individuals with low vision or contrast sensitivity, as insufficient contrast can make it difficult or impossible to read text or distinguish important elements on a website or application. Color blindness simulators simulate different types of color vision deficiencies, allowing designers to see how their color selections may appear to individuals with these conditions. This helps ensure that important information or visual cues are not solely reliant on color differentiation, as individuals with color vision deficiencies may not be able to discern between certain colors. Color palette generators assist designers in creating harmonious color combinations while considering accessibility. These tools provide a range of color options that are aesthetically pleasing and also meet accessibility guidelines, helping designers strike the right balance between visual appeal and inclusivity. In conclusion, accessibility color testing tools are essential resources for designers and developers working with color theory and color symbolism in design. These tools enable the creation of visually appealing and inclusive designs by evaluating color contrast and accounting for the varying perceptions of colors among different individuals, ultimately enhancing overall accessibility and user experience.

Accessibility Color Testing

Accessibility color testing is a crucial aspect of color theory and design that aims to ensure that the use of colors in a design is inclusive and does not pose any barriers for individuals with various visual impairments or color vision deficiencies. It involves evaluating the color choices and combinations used in a design to ensure they meet accessibility standards and guidelines. In color theory, colors are classified based on their hue, value, and saturation. Each color has its own psychological and emotional impact, and understanding color symbolism is fundamental in design. Different cultures and contexts attribute symbolic meanings to various colors, which can influence how they are perceived and interpreted by viewers. Therefore, when conducting accessibility color testing, it is essential to consider both the physiological and psychological aspects of color perception. Color blindness, also known as color vision deficiency, is one of the most common visual impairments. People with color vision deficiencies have difficulty distinguishing certain colors or perceiving color differences accurately. The most common type of color blindness is red-green color blindness, where individuals have difficulty differentiating between shades of red and green. This condition affects a significant portion of the population, and designers need to be mindful of their color choices to ensure inclusivity. To conduct accessibility color testing, designers use various tools and techniques. One commonly used method is to simulate different types of color blindness using digital applications or online tools. By doing so, designers can see how their designs appear to individuals with color vision deficiencies and make necessary adjustments to enhance accessibility. Additionally, designers can check the contrast ratios between foreground and background colors to ensure readability, as low contrast can pose challenges for individuals with vision impairments. In conclusion, accessibility color testing is an essential component of design that considers both color theory and color symbolism. It ensures that colors are chosen in a way that does not exclude individuals with visual impairments or color vision deficiencies. By conducting color testing and making necessary adjustments, designers ensure more inclusive and accessible designs for all users.

Accessible Color Design Tools

Accessible color design tools refer to digital resources or software applications that aid designers in creating visually appealing and inclusive color schemes. These tools aim to ensure that the choice of colors complies with color theory principles and provides accessibility for individuals with visual impairments or color vision deficiencies. In the realm of color theory, accessible color design tools help designers select colors that harmonize well together and convey the intended message or emotion. These tools take into account fundamental concepts such as hue, saturation, and value, as well as the relationships between colors, such as complementary, analogous, or triadic combinations. By following these principles, designers can create visually balanced and aesthetically pleasing color palettes. Moreover, accessible color design tools also consider the significance of color symbolism in design. Colors often carry cultural or psychological meanings that can greatly impact the perception and interpretation of a design. For instance, red may signify passion or danger, while blue can evoke feelings of calmness or trust. By leveraging these symbolic associations, designers can effectively convey their intended message and elicit specific emotions from viewers. However, the accessibility of color choices is equally crucial in the design process. Accessibility refers to the ability of individuals with disabilities to perceive, understand, navigate, and interact with digital content. Accessible color design tools aid designers in complying with accessibility guidelines, such as the Web Content Accessibility Guidelines (WCAG). These guidelines provide recommendations for creating inclusive designs, particularly in terms of color contrast, which ensures that text and images remain readable for individuals with visual impairments or color vision deficiencies. By utilizing accessible color design tools, designers can enhance their understanding and application of color theory and color symbolism while simultaneously prioritizing accessibility. These tools promote the creation of designs that are visually appealing, meaningful, and inclusive, catering to a wider audience and fostering a more inclusive digital environment.

Achievement (Bronze)

Achievement (Bronze) in the context of color theory and color symbolism in design refers to a color that conveys a sense of accomplishment or success at a basic level. Bronze, as a color, is often associated with third place or third-tier achievement, representing a step below gold and silver. In color theory, bronze is created by combining shades of yellow and brown. It has a warm, earthy tone with a slight metallic shimmer. Its composition and appearance can vary depending on the specific shade or tone used, but it generally exudes a sense of grounding and stability.

Achromatic Colors

Achromatic colors, also known as neutral colors, are colors that have no hue or chroma, meaning they lack any specific color or pigment. They are devoid of any color and are commonly represented by shades of gray, black, and white. In the context of color theory, achromatic colors are considered to be neutral because they do not have a dominant wavelength. They are created by mixing equal parts of all primary colors, resulting in a colorless or grayscale appearance. On the color wheel, achromatic colors are located at the center, between the warm and cool colors.

Action (Crimson)

Action (Crimson) refers to a vibrant and intense shade of red that holds significant meaning in color theory and color symbolism in design. It is a color that commands attention and evokes strong emotions, making it a powerful tool in visual communication. In color theory, crimson falls under the red color family, specifically in the range of darker, deeper reds. It is often associated with energy, passion, and strength. The intensity of crimson grabs the viewer's attention, making it suitable for highlighting important elements or creating focal points in design compositions. Its bold and assertive nature can convey a sense of urgency or prompt the viewer to take action. Furthermore, crimson holds symbolic meanings that can vary across different cultures and contexts. In Western societies, it is commonly associated with love, desire, and romance. Its association with blood has also led crimson to symbolize power, courage, and vitality. From a psychological perspective, crimson is known to stimulate appetite and increase heart rate, which is why it is often used in food branding or advertising. When applied in design, the use of action (crimson) should be considered carefully to align with the intended message and desired emotional response. Excessive use may overwhelm the viewer or create a sense of urgency that is inappropriate for the context. Combining crimson with other colors can create various visual effects and enhance its impact. For example, pairing it with neutrals like black or white can create a bold and dramatic contrast, while incorporating shades of crimson's complementary color, such as green, can create a more balanced and harmonious composition. In summary, action (crimson) is a deep and lively shade of red that captures attention and conveys powerful emotions. Its significance in color theory and symbolism makes it a valuable tool in design for emphasizing important elements, creating a sense of urgency, or evoking passion and desire. Careful consideration should be given to its application to ensure it aligns with the intended message and desired emotional response.

Action (Maroon)

Action (Maroon) is a color that falls within the category of red, often associated with intense energy, power, and passion. As a deep and rich shade, it symbolizes strength, confidence, and determination. In the context of color theory, maroon is created by mixing red with varying amounts of brown. This combination gives it a warm and earthy feel, setting it apart from other shades of red. Its name originates from the French word 'marron', which means chestnut, further emphasizing its deep and natural undertones.

Adobe Capture App

Adobe Capture App is a digital tool designed to assist designers and artists in capturing, refining, and utilizing colors for their creative projects, taking into account color theory and symbolism in design. Color theory is a fundamental principle in design that explores the relationships and interactions between colors. It encompasses the understanding of the color wheel, color harmonies, and how different colors convey various emotions and messages. Adobe Capture App simplifies the process of working with colors by providing creative professionals with a convenient and efficient way to capture, identify, and manipulate colors through their mobile devices.

Adobe Capture

Adobe Capture is a digital tool that allows designers to capture and save colors from the world around them, enabling easy integration of these colors into various design projects. In the context of color theory and color symbolism in design, Adobe Capture serves as a valuable resource for understanding and implementing color concepts.Color theory explores how colors interact with each other and how they can be used to evoke emotions, convey messages, and create visual harmony. It involves the study of color combinations, color schemes, and the psychological effects of different colors on viewers. Adobe Capture assists designers in applying these color theory principles by enabling them to capture colors from real-life scenes or inspiration sources and saving them as customizable color swatches.

3

Adobe Color CC Website

The Adobe Color CC website is a powerful online tool that provides designers and artists with a comprehensive range of color options, helping them explore, create, and implement harmonious color schemes in their designs. As a platform based on color theory and color symbolism in design, Adobe Color CC offers a user-friendly interface that allows users to experiment with color combinations, choose from a vast database of pre-selected color palettes, and even create their custom color schemes. The website operates on the principles of color theory, which is the study of how colors interact with each other, how they are perceived by the human eye, and how they can be combined to create aesthetically pleasing and visually balanced designs. Through the Adobe Color CC website, users can easily explore the various color relationships such as complementary, analogous, triadic, and more, understanding how these combinations can influence the overall mood and impact of their designs.

Adobe Color CC

Adobe Color CC is a web-based tool developed by Adobe that allows designers and artists to explore, create, and share color schemes based on principles of color theory and symbolism in design. Color theory is the study of how colors relate to one another and the effects they have on humans. It provides a framework for understanding the visual impact and emotional responses that colors can evoke. Understanding color theory is crucial for designers as it helps them create harmonious and visually pleasing compositions. Color symbolism, on the other hand, refers to the cultural and psychological associations that people attribute to different colors. These associations can vary across cultures and individuals, and designers often use color symbolism to communicate specific messages or evoke particular emotions in their designs. Adobe Color CC provides a range of features that aid designers in working with color theory and symbolism. One of its key tools is the color wheel, which allows users to select colors based on various color harmonies such as complementary, analogous, or triadic schemes. By choosing colors that are aesthetically compatible, designers can create balanced and visually cohesive designs. In addition to the color wheel, Adobe Color CC also offers the ability to create custom color palettes. Users can experiment with different color combinations and save their preferred palettes for future use. This feature is especially helpful in maintaining consistent branding or design themes across multiple projects. Another useful aspect of Adobe Color CC is its integration with other Adobe Creative Cloud applications such as Photoshop and Illustrator. Designers can easily import color palettes created in Adobe Color CC into these applications, streamlining the design process and ensuring color consistency throughout a project. In conclusion, Adobe Color CC is a powerful tool that aids designers in working with color theory and symbolism in design. By providing a range of features such as the color wheel and custom palettes, it enables designers to create harmonious and visually impactful compositions. Its integration with other Adobe applications further enhances the efficiency and consistency of the design process. Overall, Adobe Color CC is an invaluable resource for designers seeking to elevate their use of color in their work.

Adobe Color Wheel

The Adobe Color Wheel is a digital tool that aids in selecting and harmonizing colors in design projects. It is based on color theory, which encompasses the principles and guidelines for combining and using colors effectively. In color theory, the color wheel is a visual representation of the relationships between colors. It consists of 12 hues that are evenly spaced around the wheel. These hues can be categorized into three main color groups: primary (red, blue, and yellow), secondary (orange, green, and purple), and tertiary (the six colors created by mixing a primary and a secondary color). The Adobe Color Wheel allows designers to explore and experiment with various color combinations. It provides different color rules or schemes, such as complementary, analogous, triadic, and tetradic, which help create visually pleasing and harmonious designs. For example, complementary colors are located opposite each other on the color wheel, creating a high contrast and vibrant effect when used together. Analogous colors, on the other hand, are adjacent to each other, resulting in a harmonious and calming visual experience. Beyond color theory, colors also carry symbolism and meaning in design. Different cultures, traditions, and contexts attribute specific emotions, values, and associations to certain colors. For instance, red can signify passion, energy, or danger, while blue often conveys calmness, trust, or professionalism. Understanding color symbolism and incorporating it

4

into design can enhance communication and evoke specific reactions from the audience. The Adobe Color Wheel provides designers with a range of predefined color palettes, also referred to as color themes or color sets. These palettes are created by professional designers and artists and can be filtered by various themes, moods, or colors. Designers can use these palettes as a starting point or inspiration for their own projects, ensuring their color choices align with their intended aesthetic and message. Overall, the Adobe Color Wheel is a valuable tool for designers, allowing them to leverage color theory and symbolism to create visually appealing and meaningful designs. By exploring color relationships and experimenting with different combinations, designers can effectively communicate their messages and capture the desired emotions and responses from their target audience.

Adobe Kuler Tool

Adobe Kuler Tool is a digital application that serves as a valuable resource for color theory and color symbolism in the field of design. It provides designers with an efficient and systematic way to explore, create, and utilize colors in their projects. In the realm of color theory, Adobe Kuler Tool enables designers to comprehend the relationships and interactions between different colors. It offers various color models such as RGB, CMYK, and HSB to facilitate the understanding of color spaces. By utilizing this tool, designers can experiment with different combinations of colors, assess their harmony and contrast, and make informed decisions based on the principles of color theory. In the context of color symbolism, Adobe Kuler Tool assists designers in conveying specific meanings and emotions through color choices. It offers a vast library of color themes created by artists, designers, and other professionals, each associated with different feelings or concepts. By exploring these themes, designers can select colors that align with the desired mood or message of their design, enhancing its visual impact and effectiveness. Furthermore, Adobe Kuler Tool provides designers with the flexibility to create their own color schemes. Through the use of a color wheel, designers can fine-tune the hues, saturation, and brightness of each color, achieving precise customization. This empowers designers to tailor their color palettes to suit the specific requirements of their projects and audience. The tool also enables designers to obtain color values in various formats, including hexadecimal, RGB, and CMYK. This flexibility ensures seamless integration with different design software and platforms, allowing designers to implement their chosen colors accurately and consistently across multiple mediums. In conclusion, Adobe Kuler Tool serves as an invaluable tool for designers in the exploration and application of color theory and color symbolism. By providing a comprehensive understanding of color relationships and offering a wide range of color palettes, it enhances designers' ability to create visually compelling and impactful designs.

Adobe Kuler

Adobe Kuler, also known as Adobe Color, is a web-based application that assists designers and artists in generating color schemes for their creative projects. It utilizes concepts from color theory to facilitate the selection and combination of colors that evoke desired emotions, convey specific messages, and create harmonious visual compositions. In the realm of color theory, Adobe Kuler provides a platform for the exploration of color relationships, enabling users to grasp the fundamental principles governing the interaction between colors. Through the app's intuitive interface, designers gain access to a wide variety of color schemes, such as complementary, analogous, triadic, and monochromatic, allowing them to experiment with different combinations and better understand the ways colors interact and visually impact one another. Colors hold immense symbolism and convey meaning beyond their aesthetic appeal. Adobe Kuler acknowledges this aspect by facilitating color symbolism exploration in design. The application enables users to associate specific emotions, moods, or concepts with particular colors, empowering designers to communicate effectively through their color choices. By offering a diverse selection of pre-existing color themes, as well as the ability to create custom schemes, Adobe Kuler encourages designers to select colors that align with the desired symbolism of their projects. By incorporating Adobe Kuler into their design workflow, artists and designers gain access to a powerful tool that harnesses the principles of color theory and color symbolism. The application grants the ability to create visually cohesive designs that evoke specific emotions, messages, and impressions. Through the careful selection and combination of colors, designers can effectively communicate their intended narratives and engage audiences on a deeper level.

Adventure (Apricot)

5

Adventure (Apricot) is a hue within the color spectrum that holds significant meaning and symbolism in the context of color theory and design. This vibrant shade falls under the orange category, combining the warmth of orange with the delicacy and softness of peach. In color theory, Adventure (Apricot) is associated with enthusiasm, energy, and excitement. It exudes a sense of spontaneity and a zest for life, making it an excellent choice for designs that aim to evoke feelings of adventure and liveliness.

Adventure (Orange)

The color orange is a vibrant hue that falls between red and yellow on the color spectrum. In color theory, orange is considered a warm color, evoking feelings of energy, enthusiasm, and excitement. It is often associated with the sun, autumn leaves, and citrus fruits. In design, the color orange can be used to create a sense of adventure and stimulate positive emotions. Its energetic and playful nature makes it an excellent choice for designs that aim to captivate and engage the audience.

Adventure (Salmon)

The color salmon is a shade that falls within the red color family, specifically a light, pinkish-orange hue. It is often characterized by its subtlety and softness, which make it a popular choice in various design contexts. In color theory, salmon is considered a warm color due to its association with the red spectrum, and it is known to evoke feelings of warmth, comfort, and happiness. These emotional qualities can have a significant impact on the overall visual experience of a design. Salmon is frequently used to create a sense of tranquility and serenity, making it suitable for calming and relaxing environments. When used in design, salmon can convey different meanings and symbolisms depending on the overall context and the other colors it is paired with. This color is often associated with femininity and can add a touch of delicacy and grace to a design. It is commonly used in branding and packaging for products targeted towards women, such as cosmetics and fashion accessories. Salmon can also be used to create a sense of vibrancy and playfulness in a design. When combined with brighter, contrasting colors, it can create a visually striking and energetic composition. This makes it a popular choice for designs intended to attract attention and engage viewers, such as advertising materials. Furthermore, salmon is frequently used in nature-themed designs to depict a variety of elements, including sunsets, flowers, and coral reefs. Its light and warm qualities help capture the essence of natural beauty and can enhance the overall visual appeal of the design. In summary, salmon is a light pinkish-orange shade within the red color family. In color theory and design, it is often associated with warmth, tranquility, femininity, vibrancy, and natural elements. It is a versatile color that can evoke different emotions and communicate various meanings depending on how it is used in combination with other colors and within the overall design context.

Adventure (Tangerine)

Adventure (Tangerine) is a vibrant and energetic color commonly used in color theory and color symbolism in design. It is a shade of orange that leans towards red, giving it a warm and lively appearance. In color theory, adventure (tangerine) falls within the warm color palette, known for its stimulating and uplifting effects. It is often associated with enthusiasm, creativity, and excitement. This color evokes feelings of adventure, encouraging exploration and risk-taking. It can also symbolize a sense of vitality and an appetite for new experiences.

Aesthetic Color Choices

Aesthetic color choices in the context of color theory and color symbolism in design refer to deliberate selections of colors that evoke specific emotions, create desired atmospheres, and convey intended messages in visual compositions and designs. In color theory, aesthetic color choices are based on an understanding of the color wheel and the relationships between different colors. This includes concepts such as complimentary colors, analogous colors, and color harmonies. By carefully selecting colors that work well together, designers can create visually pleasing and harmonious compositions. Aesthetic color choices in this context involve considering factors such as color temperature, hue intensity, and contrast to create a balanced and visually appealing design. Color symbolism plays an important role in aesthetics as well.

Different colors are often associated with specific meanings and emotions, and designers can leverage this symbolism to enhance the message or mood of their designs. For example, warm colors such as red and orange are often associated with energy and passion, while cool colors such as blue and green can evoke feelings of calmness and tranquility. Aesthetic color choices in this context involve carefully selecting colors that align with the intended symbolism or convey the desired emotional response. Additionally, cultural and contextual factors also influence aesthetic color choices. Colors may have different meanings or associations across different cultures, and designers need to consider these cultural nuances when selecting colors for a specific audience or context. For example, the color white is often associated with purity and innocence in Western cultures, while it can symbolize mourning in some Asian cultures. Aesthetic color choices in this context require sensitivity and awareness of cultural diversity. In conclusion, aesthetic color choices in design involve the deliberate selection of colors based on color theory, color symbolism, and cultural factors. By understanding the relationships between colors and their meanings, designers can create visually appealing compositions that effectively communicate messages and evoke desired emotions. The careful consideration of color choices adds depth and richness to the overall aesthetic of a design.

Aesthetic Color Selection Guides

An aesthetic color selection guide is a tool used in color theory and design to help in the selection of colors that are visually pleasing and align with the desired aesthetic of a particular design or artwork. This guide takes into consideration various principles of color theory, such as the color wheel, color harmony, and color symbolism, to create a cohesive and visually appealing color palette. Color theory is the study of how colors interact with each other and how they are perceived by the human eye. It is based on the understanding that colors can evoke different emotions and have symbolic meanings. By understanding the principles of color theory, designers can create visually captivating designs that effectively communicate their intended message or evoke a specific response from the viewer.

Affection (Pink)

The color pink is a vibrant and delicate hue that is often associated with affection, sweetness, and femininity in the context of color theory and color symbolism in design. In color theory, pink is classified as a tint of red, created by mixing red with white. It is considered a warm color due to its close association with red, but it has a softer and more gentle effect than its intense counterpart. Pink is often used to create a calming and comforting atmosphere, making it a popular choice for bedrooms, nurseries, and spaces where a sense of tranquility and affection is desired. In design, the color pink is commonly used to convey a range of emotional and symbolic meanings. Its association with affection and sweetness makes it a popular choice for branding and design elements targeting a female audience, such as beauty products, fashion, and children's products. Pink is also frequently used in romantic and intimate contexts, as it is often associated with love, compassion, and tenderness. Furthermore, pink is known to have a soothing and calming effect on people, making it an ideal color choice for areas aimed at promoting relaxation and happiness. Its gentle and nurturing quality can create an inviting and warm atmosphere, making it a favorable color for healthcare and wellness-related spaces. Additionally, pink is also associated with innocence and youth, making it a popular choice for children's products and spaces. Overall, the color pink evokes a sense of affection, warmth, and femininity in both color theory and design. Its softness, calming effect, and association with love and compassion make it a versatile and widely used color choice across various industries and design contexts.

Ambition (Maroon)

Ambition is a color within the Maroon hue, which is classified as a deep, reddish-brown shade. In color theory, Maroon is achieved by mixing red and brown pigments, resulting in a tone that is both dark and rich in appearance. In terms of color symbolism in design, Maroon is often associated with ambition. This hue conveys a sense of determination, drive, and a strong desire to achieve goals. It represents a person's motivation and the relentless pursuit of success.

Ambition (Orange)

7

Ambition, in the context of color theory and color symbolism in design, is represented by the color orange. Orange is a warm and vibrant color that combines the energy of red with the happiness of yellow. It is often associated with ambition, creative expression, and enthusiasm. In color theory, orange is considered a secondary color, created by mixing red and yellow. Its position on the color wheel is between red and yellow, symbolizing a balance between the intensity of red and the cheerfulness of yellow. This balance reflects the idea of ambition, which requires both drive and positivity.

Ambition (Purple)

The color purple in color theory and color symbolism in design represents ambition. Purple is a blend of blue and red, combining the calmness and stability of blue with the energy and power of red. This blend creates a color that is often associated with ambition, determination, and creativity. In color theory, purple is considered a secondary color, meaning it is created by combining two primary colors. This composition adds to the symbolism of ambition as it suggests that ambition is not a standalone trait but rather a combination of different qualities and characteristics. It signifies the drive to achieve goals, the motivation to take action, and the persistence to overcome obstacles.

Analogous Color Scheme Generator

An analogous color scheme generator is a tool used in color theory and design to create a visually harmonious color palette by selecting colors that are adjacent to each other on the color wheel. This color scheme is based on the concept that colors that are close to each other on the color wheel harmonize well together, creating a sense of unity and balance in design. In color theory, the color wheel is a visual representation of the visible spectrum of colors. It is divided into twelve segments, each representing a different hue. The analogous color scheme is created by selecting colors that are located next to each other on the color wheel, typically within a range of three to five colors. These colors have a similar wavelength and are therefore visually harmonious. Analogous color schemes are often used in design to create a sense of harmony and coherence. They are considered to be easy on the eyes and can create a soothing and peaceful atmosphere. This color scheme is commonly used in various design fields, such as graphic design, interior design, and fashion design. In addition to their visual harmony, colors in an analogous color scheme can also convey symbolic meanings. Each color carries its own symbolism, and when combined in a design, they can evoke specific emotions and associations. For example, using shades of blue, green, and purple in an analogous color scheme can create a calming and tranquil atmosphere, while using shades of red, orange, and yellow can evoke a sense of warmth and energy. Analogous color scheme generators allow designers to easily explore different combinations and variations of analogous color schemes. These generators typically provide a visual interface where users can select a base color, and the generator will automatically generate a range of analogous colors based on that base color. This tool saves time and effort for designers, allowing them to quickly experiment with different color schemes and find the one that best conveys the desired message or mood. In conclusion, an analogous color scheme generator is a valuable tool in color theory and design, allowing designers to create harmonious and visually appealing color palettes. It takes advantage of the natural relationships between colors on the color wheel to create a sense of unity and balance in design. Additionally, the colors selected in an analogous color scheme can carry symbolic meanings, further enhancing the impact of the design.

Analogous Color Scheme Generators

Analogous color scheme generators are tools that assist designers in selecting and creating color palettes based on the concept of analogous colors. In color theory, analogous colors are colors that are adjacent to each other on the color wheel. These colors share a similar hue and are often used together to create a harmonious and unified design. Color symbolism plays a significant role in design, as colors can evoke specific emotions and convey messages. An analogous color scheme is commonly associated with feelings of harmony, balance, and tranquility, making it a popular choice for creating visually pleasing designs in various industries such as fashion, interior design, and graphic design.

Analogous Colors

8

Analogous colors refer to a group of colors that are closely related to each other on the color wheel. They are created by selecting colors that are adjacent to each other. In color theory, the color wheel is a visual representation of the organization of colors. It consists of primary, secondary, and tertiary colors, arranged in a circular format. Analogous colors are found next to each other on the color wheel. Analogous colors are often used in design to create harmonious and visually appealing compositions. When used together, they create a sense of unity and balance. The colors blend well with each other and create a smooth transition, avoiding sharp contrasts. In terms of color symbolism, analogous colors can evoke specific emotions and moods. Each color has its own psychological associations and using analogous colors can enhance those feelings. For example, using analogous warm colors such as red, orange, and yellow can create a sense of excitement and energy. On the other hand, using analogous cool colors such as blue, green, and purple can evoke a calming and soothing effect. When working with analogous colors, it is important to consider the balance of hues within the composition. Utilizing a dominant color and incorporating smaller amounts of the adjacent colors can create a focal point and visual interest. Additionally, adding neutral or contrasting colors can help to enhance the overall design and prevent the analogous colors from becoming overwhelming.

Anger (Red)

Anger, represented by the color red, is a powerful emotional response associated with feelings of intense displeasure, frustration, and aggression. In the context of color theory and symbolism in design, red is often used to evoke strong and passionate reactions. As one of the primary colors, red is considered a highly energetic color that demands attention and immediately draws the viewer's eye. It has the highest visibility and stands out in any visual composition, making it a popular choice for creating focal points in design. The eye-catching nature of red can bring energy and vitality to a design, making it an effective tool for grabbing attention and conveying urgency. Red is frequently associated with fire and blood, further intensifying its connotations of anger. In color psychology, red is believed to increase heart rate and blood pressure, evoking intense emotions and a sense of urgency. This makes it a suitable choice for designs addressing topics such as danger, conflict, or urgency. Red can also be used to represent physical strength and power, making it appropriate for designs related to sports, warfare, or activism. In addition to its association with anger, red is often seen as a symbol of love and passion. It is commonly used in designs targeting romantic or sensual themes. Red has the ability to stimulate strong emotions and create a sense of excitement and desire. However, the use of red should be approached with caution as its strong and intense nature can also be overwhelming if used excessively. In design, red is typically used as an accent color to add emphasis and draw attention. When used sparingly in combination with neutral or complementary colors, red can create a visually stimulating and engaging composition. In conclusion, red represents anger in the context of color theory and symbolism in design. It is a powerful color that evokes intense emotions and draws attention. It can be used to symbolize passion, love, power, and urgency, but should be used judiciously to avoid overwhelming the viewer.

Apps For Color Combinations

Color theory is an essential aspect of design that deals with the principles of combining colors in a harmonious and aesthetically pleasing manner. It involves understanding the various relationships between colors, their effects on emotions, and their symbolic meanings. In the field of design, color combinations play a crucial role in conveying messages and evoking specific feelings or moods. Color combinations are particularly important as they can define the overall look and feel of a design. Different color harmonies, such as complementary, analogous, or monochromatic, can be used to create visual interest, balance, and contrast. These harmonies rely on the relationships between colors on the color wheel, which helps designers select colors that work well together. Apps for color combinations are digital tools that assist designers and individuals in exploring, experimenting, and creating harmonious color schemes. These apps provide various functionalities to assist users in selecting, combining, and visualizing colors. They often allow users to generate color palettes, save and organize combinations, and even extract colors from images. One of the key benefits of using color combination apps is the convenience they offer. Designers can access a vast range of colors and harmonies without spending hours manually experimenting with different shades and combinations. This not only saves time but also ensures that the chosen combinations are visually appealing and aligned

9

with the intended message or emotion. Moreover, color combination apps often provide additional features that enhance the design process. Users can preview how colors will appear in different contexts, such as web or printed materials, ensuring the selected combinations are suitable for the intended platform. Some apps even offer color blindness simulators, allowing designers to account for accessibility in their designs. In addition to their practical functionality, color combination apps also empower designers to explore the symbolic meanings associated with different colors. Each color holds cultural and psychological connotations, which may influence the perception and interpretation of a design. By understanding the symbolism of colors, designers can effectively communicate their intended message or evoke specific emotions within their audience. Overall, color combination apps are powerful tools that support designers in creating visually appealing and meaningful designs. By leveraging the principles of color theory and the symbolism of colors, designers can effectively engage their audience and convey messages that resonate deeply. These apps simplify and streamline the process of selecting harmonious color combinations, saving valuable time and ensuring the overall success of a design.

Attractiveness (Gold)

Attractiveness (Gold) is a color in the context of color theory and color symbolism in design. It is a warm, metallic hue that is often associated with luxury, wealth, and prestige. Gold is created by combining yellow, a primary color, with a small amount of brown or red pigments. In color theory, attractiveness (gold) is considered a high-value color due to its luminosity and brightness. It is often used to draw attention and create a focal point in design. Gold is highly reflective, creating a sense of opulence and grandeur. It is commonly used in design elements such as logos, typography, and backgrounds to add a touch of elegance and sophistication. The color gold is also associated with success, achievement, and prosperity, making it a popular choice for branding and marketing material. In terms of symbolism, gold represents wealth, opulence, and extravagance. It is often associated with power and authority, and is commonly used to depict kings, queens, and other figures of high status. Gold also signifies wisdom and enlightenment, and is used to represent the divine and spiritual aspects in art and design. When used in combination with other colors, gold can have different effects. Pairing gold with black creates a dramatic and elegant look, while combining it with white or pale colors adds a sense of purity and innocence. Gold can also be used as a contrasting color against darker shades to create a vibrant and striking effect. In conclusion, attractiveness (gold) is a warm, metallic color that conveys luxury, wealth, and prestige. It is a high-value color in terms of luminosity and brightness, often used to draw attention and create a focal point in design. Gold is associated with power, authority, and success, and is commonly used in branding and marketing. It represents wealth, opulence, and enlightenment, and can be combined with other colors to create different effects.

Authority (Black)

Authority is a color that belongs to the black hue in color theory. In the context of color symbolism in design, authority represents power, control, and dominance. Black, as a color, is often associated with formality, sophistication, and elegance. It is a hue that is commonly used to convey authority and to create a sense of seriousness and importance. In the realm of design, black is frequently employed to establish a strong, commanding presence.

Autumn (Orange)

Autumn, also known as orange, is a color commonly associated with warmth, energy, and the changing of seasons. In color theory, orange is located between red and yellow on the color wheel, making it a warm color. It is created by mixing red and yellow pigments. In the context of color symbolism in design, orange is often used to convey feelings of enthusiasm, creativity, and excitement. It is a vibrant and attention-grabbing color that can evoke a sense of vitality and positivity. Orange is frequently used in call-to-action buttons and advertisements to draw attention and stimulate action.

Awareness (Indigo)

Awareness refers to a deep understanding or knowledge of something. In the context of color theory and color symbolism in design, awareness is associated with the color indigo. Indigo is a deep, rich shade of blue with a hint of purple, often described as a color between blue and violet. In color theory, indigo is considered a cool color. Cool colors are typically associated with calmness, tranquility, and stability. They are known to have a calming effect on the viewer and are often used to create a sense of relaxation or introspection. Indigo's cool nature allows it to evoke a sense of serenity and peace. In terms of color symbolism, indigo is often associated with qualities such as intuition, spirituality, and higher consciousness. It is believed to enhance awareness and perception, making it a popular choice for designs intended to promote mindfulness or self-reflection. Indigo is also associated with wisdom, knowledge, and deep understanding, making it a suitable choice for designs related to education or intellectual pursuits. Indigo's symbolic associations and psychological effects can be utilized in various design applications. For example, in branding and logo design, indigo may be used to convey a sense of trustworthiness, integrity, and reliability. In web design, indigo can be employed to create a sense of calmness and focus, making it suitable for websites related to wellness, meditation, or spirituality. Overall, awareness in the context of color theory and color symbolism is represented by the color indigo. Indigo is a cool color associated with calmness, spirituality, and deep understanding. It can be used in design to evoke a sense of relaxation and introspection or to convey qualities such as wisdom and trustworthiness. By understanding the symbolic associations and psychological effects of indigo, designers can effectively communicate specific messages and evoke desired emotions in their design compositions.

Balance (Aqua)

Balance in color theory refers to the distribution of visual weight within a design or composition. It is a principle used to create harmony and unity, ensuring that no single color dominates or overpowers the others. The color aqua, a shade of blue with green undertones, can be used to achieve balance in design through its characteristics and symbolism. Aqua is known for its calming and soothing qualities, evoking a sense of tranquility and serenity. When used in design, it can help create a balanced and harmonious visual experience for the viewer. Its association with water and the sea further enhances its calming effect and can be particularly effective in designs aimed at promoting relaxation or a sense of well-being.

Balance (Copper)

Balance in color theory refers to the equilibrium and harmony achieved when different colors are used in a design. In the context of copper, balance implies the proportional use of copper as a color and its harmonious relationship with other colors in a composition. Copper, a warm and vibrant metallic color, holds various symbolic meanings in design. It represents wealth, abundance, and prosperity. Copper is also associated with the earth element, embodying stability, grounding, and durability. When used in design, it can evoke feelings of warmth, comfort, and authenticity.

Balance (Gray)

Balance (Gray) refers to a concept in color theory and color symbolism in design which pertains to the visual equilibrium achieved by incorporating shades of gray within a composition. It involves the harmonious distribution and interaction of light and dark grays to create a sense of equilibrium, stability, and unity. In color theory, balance is an essential principle that ensures a composition feels visually pleasing and stable. A balanced color scheme in design is achieved through the careful arrangement of colors, including the use of grays. Gray, being a neutral color, plays a crucial role in achieving balance as it can help bring together other colors without overpowering or dominating them. Grays are often used to balance out vibrant and intense colors in a design. They can be used as a background color or as a gradient transition between two contrasting colors. The use of gray helps to tone down the intensity of other colors and create a sense of calm and neutrality, allowing the eye to rest and focus on other elements within the composition. Balance (Gray) also has symbolic implications in design. Gray is often associated with tranquility, neutrality, and stability. It can evoke a sense of sophistication, elegance, and timelessness. Its balanced nature makes it a versatile color choice for conveying a sense of calmness and serenity in a design, making it suitable for various contexts and purposes. When used effectively, gray can serve as a bridge between different color elements, creating harmony and cohesion within a design. It can help establish hierarchy, provide contrast, and enhance the overall visual balance. Furthermore, the integration of gray in a composition can evoke emotional responses such as peace, maturity, and subtlety. In conclusion, Balance (Gray) is a fundamental concept in color theory and color symbolism in design, ensuring visual equilibrium and harmony. Grays, with their neutral and balanced nature, play an important role in achieving balance within a composition. By incorporating shades of gray strategically, designers can create visually pleasing, stable, and unified designs that evoke emotions of tranquility and sophistication.

Balance (Green)

Balance is a fundamental principle in color theory and color symbolism in design. It refers to the equal distribution of visual weight and harmony in a design composition using the color green. Green represents balance as it is the merging of the warm color yellow and the cool color blue, symbolizing equilibrium and harmony. Balance in color theory can be broadly categorized into two types: symmetrical balance and asymmetrical balance. Symmetrical balance occurs when elements are mirrored or positioned evenly on both sides of a central axis, creating a sense of stability and equilibrium. In the context of the color green, symmetrical balance can be achieved by using an equal amount of green on either side of the composition or by creating a symmetrical pattern with green as the dominant color. This creates a visually balanced and harmonious design. On the other hand, asymmetrical balance is achieved when unequal visual elements are arranged in a way that still creates a sense of balance and harmony. This can be done by strategically placing larger or darker green elements on one side of the composition and lighter or smaller green elements on the other side. The difference in visual weight is compensated by the placement and arrangement of other elements in the design, resulting in an overall balanced composition. In color symbolism, green is not only associated with balance but also with nature, growth, and renewal. It symbolizes freshness, fertility, and abundance. In design, the use of green to represent balance can evoke a sense of tranquility, stability, and groundedness. It provides a calming effect and promotes a feeling of relaxation and harmony in the viewer. Overall, balance in the context of the color green is the even distribution of visual weight and harmony in a design composition. It can be achieved through symmetrical or asymmetrical arrangements of green elements to create a sense of stability and equilibrium. The color green, associated with nature and growth, symbolizes balance and harmony in design, providing a sense of tranquility and groundedness to the viewer.

Balance (Mint)

The concept of balance in color theory and color symbolism in design refers to the visual harmony achieved through the distribution of colors and their relative intensity within a composition. It is the equilibrium or stability created by the combination of different colors, tones, and hues. In color theory, balance is achieved when the visual weight of colors is evenly distributed within a design. This means that no single color dominates or overpowers the others. Each color contributes to the overall balance, creating a sense of unity and coherence.

Balance (Teal)

Balance, in the context of color theory and color symbolism in design, refers to the distribution of visual weight and visual elements within a composition. It is a fundamental principle of design that helps create harmony, stability, and an overall sense of equilibrium. In color theory, balance is achieved through the careful arrangement of colors, both in terms of their intensity and their placement within the composition. There are three main types of balance: symmetrical balance, asymmetrical balance, and radial balance. Symmetrical balance, also known as formal balance, occurs when elements are arranged equally on both sides of a central axis. This type of balance creates a sense of stability and order. It is often used in traditional and formal designs, where the goal is to create a sense of symmetry and harmony. Asymmetrical balance, on the other hand, is achieved through the careful arrangement of different visual elements of varying size, shape, and color. It involves a more dynamic and informal composition, where the visual weight is distributed unequally. Asymmetrical balance creates a sense of movement and energy, and is often used in modern and contemporary designs. Radial balance is characterized by a central focal point from which different elements radiate outwards. It is achieved by arranging elements in a circular or spiral pattern. This type of balance creates a sense of movement and flow, and is often used in designs that aim to convey a sense of energy or motion, such as logos or icons.

Balance also plays a significant role in color symbolism in design. Different colors have different visual weights, and the careful balance of colors can evoke specific emotions and create specific effects. For example, a balanced composition of warm colors, such as reds and yellows, can convey a sense of energy and excitement, while a balanced composition of cool colors, such as blues and greens, can create a calm and soothing atmosphere. In conclusion, balance in color theory and color symbolism in design is the distribution of visual weight and visual elements within a composition. It helps create harmony, stability, and an overall sense of equilibrium. Whether achieved through symmetrical, asymmetrical, or radial arrangements, balance is a fundamental principle of design that contributes to the effectiveness and impact of a visual composition.

Balance (Turquoise)

Balance (Turquoise) is a color that holds significant meaning in color theory and color symbolism in design. In color theory, balance refers to the distribution of visual weight in a composition or design. It is a key principle used to create a sense of harmony, stability, and equilibrium. Turquoise, a color often associated with calmness and serenity, adds a unique element to the concept of balance. In design, balance can be achieved through various techniques, such as the arrangement of colors, shapes, and elements on a page. Turquoise, as a color, contributes to achieving balance by providing a sense of coolness and tranquil energy. It is commonly used as an accent color to create contrast and draw attention to specific elements without overpowering the overall composition.

Beauty (Lavender)

The color lavender is a pale tint of purple that is often associated with beauty, femininity, and elegance in the context of color theory and color symbolism in design. In color theory, lavender is created by adding white to pure purple, resulting in a lighter and softer hue. It is considered a cool color, as it contains more blue undertones than red undertones. This coolness gives lavender a calming and soothing effect, making it a popular choice for creating an atmosphere of relaxation and tranquility in interior design, spas, and beauty-related products.

Blood (Red)

In the context of color theory, blood (red) is a primary color that is highly saturated and has a wavelength of approximately 620-750 nanometers. It is known as a warm color and is often associated with strong emotions, power, energy, and passion. The color red has a high visual impact and can capture attention easily, making it a powerful tool in design. In color symbolism, red is often associated with love, romance, and desire. It can also signify courage, strength, and determination. Additionally, red is frequently used to evoke a sense of urgency or danger. The vibrant and intense nature of this color makes it very versatile in design, as it can be used to create both bold and dynamic visuals, as well as to convey more subtle and nuanced emotions. Red is often used as an accent color to highlight and draw attention to important elements within a composition.

Boldness (Crimson)

Color theory is a field of study that explores the visual effects and psychological aspects of color. In the realm of color symbolism in design, boldness refers to the quality or characteristic of a color that exudes confidence, strength, and intensity. Within color theory, red is often associated with boldness. Specifically, the shade crimson is known for its vibrancy and powerful presence. Its deep red hue commands attention and can elicit feelings of excitement and passion. Crimson is a striking color that demands to be noticed and can be used to make a bold statement in design.

Books On Color Psychology

Color psychology is a branch of psychology that focuses on how colors can affect human behavior, emotions, and perceptions. In the context of color theory and color symbolism in design, color psychology explores the impact that different colors have on individuals and how they can be used to evoke specific responses or create desired effects. Understanding color psychology is essential in design as colors can greatly influence the overall mood and

13

perception of a design. Different colors are associated with various emotions and meanings, which designers can utilize to create a specific atmosphere or convey a particular message.

Boredom (Gray)

Boredom (Gray) refers to a specific shade of gray within the context of color theory and color symbolism in design. In color theory, gray is often associated with neutrality and balance. It is created by mixing equal amounts of black and white, resulting in a lack of chromatic intensity. Gray is considered achromatic, meaning it lacks any hue or colorfulness. Boredom (Gray), in this context, represents a specific shade of gray that is associated with feelings of boredom, monotony, and dullness.

Brand Color Guidelines Documents

Brand Color Guidelines Documents are essential components of a comprehensive brand identity system. They provide a formal definition of the colors that represent a brand, outlining their specific usage and guidelines for consistency. These documents are rooted in color theory and symbolism in design, which play significant roles in shaping the perception and communication of a brand's message. Color theory is the study of how colors interact and how they can be combined harmoniously in design. It explores concepts such as color harmony, contrast, and saturation to create visually appealing and impactful compositions. In the context of brand color guidelines, color theory helps in selecting a set of colors that work well together and accurately reflect the brand's values, personality, and intended audience. Color symbolism, on the other hand, refers to the cultural and psychological associations that colors may evoke. Different colors can elicit specific emotions, moods, and meanings, which can be leveraged in brand design to effectively communicate a desired message. By understanding color symbolism, brand color guidelines can ensure that the chosen colors align with the brand's intended image and effectively resonate with its target market. Brand Color Guidelines Documents typically include the following elements: - Primary Colors: These are the core colors that represent the brand and are used prominently in all brand assets. They are carefully chosen to convey the brand's essence and establish recognition. - Secondary Colors: These additional colors support the primary colors and provide flexibility in design. They may be used in various contexts to complement the primary colors and enhance the brand's visual identity. - Color Variations: This section defines different variations of the brand colors, such as light or dark versions, to ensure consistent usage across different applications and mediums. - Color Usage Rules: These guidelines specify where and how each color should be used across different brand touchpoints, including logo design, typography, marketing materials, and digital platforms. - Color Palettes: Brand color guidelines may include curated color palettes consisting of primary and secondary colors, as well as additional accent colors. These palettes help maintain consistency and provide designers with a comprehensive set of approved colors. In summary, Brand Color Guidelines Documents are formal definitions that follow color theory principles and consider color symbolism to establish a consistent and impactful visual identity for a brand. By providing clear instructions on color selection and usage, these documents ensure that the brand's colors effectively communicate its message, resonate with its target audience, and establish a strong brand presence.

Brand Color Guidelines

Brand Color Guidelines refer to a set of rules and recommendations that outline the specific colors to be used in a brand's visual identity. These guidelines are based on the principles of color theory and color symbolism in design. Color theory is the study of how colors can be combined and used harmoniously in a design context. It explores the effects that colors have on the aesthetic and emotional experience of the viewer. By understanding color theory, designers can create visually appealing and meaningful compositions that effectively communicate a brand's message. Color symbolism, on the other hand, refers to the psychological and cultural associations that specific colors evoke. Different colors have different meanings and can elicit specific emotions or convey certain concepts. For example, red is often associated with passion and energy, while blue can represent trust and calmness. By leveraging color symbolism, designers can enhance the overall perception and understanding of a brand. Brand Color Guidelines take into consideration both color theory and color symbolism to ensure consistency and cohesiveness in a brand's visual identity. They establish a defined color palette that represents the brand's personality, values, and overall message. These guidelines typically specify primary colors, secondary colors, and sometimes even tertiary colors that can be used in different design applications, such as logos, typography, packaging, and marketing materials. By adhering to Brand Color Guidelines, businesses can create a recognizable and memorable visual identity that resonates with their target audience. Consistency in color usage across different touchpoints helps build brand recognition and establishes a sense of trust and reliability. Additionally, these guidelines enable designers and marketers to effectively leverage color psychology to evoke the desired emotions and associations in their audience.

Brightness (Gold)

Brightness, in the context of color theory and color symbolism in design, refers to the perceived intensity or luminosity of a color. It is one of the three dimensions of color, along with hue and saturation, that helps describe and differentiate colors. In color theory, brightness is often used interchangeably with value or lightness. It represents how light or dark a color appears relative to a neutral gray or white. Colors with high brightness appear closer to white, while colors with low brightness appear closer to black. For example, pastel colors have high brightness, while deep or dark colors have low brightness.

CMYK Color Model

CMYK (Cyan, Magenta, Yellow, and Key) is a color model used in color theory and design to achieve a wide range of colors by combining different percentages of these four primary colors. It is primarily used in the printing industry, where different colors are produced by depositing tiny dots of these four inks onto a white paper or surface. The CMYK color model works by subtracting colors from white light, which is the absence of color. Starting with a white canvas, each ink color is added in different amounts to create the desired hue. Cyan, which is a blue-green color, absorbs red light; magenta, which is a pink-purple color, absorbs green light; yellow absorbs blue light, and the key color (usually black) provides depth and detail to the resulting printed image. By overlapping these inks in various combinations, a wide spectrum of colors can be achieved. In design, the CMYK color model is essential for creating printed materials such as brochures, flyers, and posters. It ensures that the colors seen on the computer screen accurately match the final printed output. Designers must convert their digital RGB (Red, Green, Blue) colors into CMYK before sending their files to the printer for production. This conversion is necessary because RGB colors are created by emitting light, while CMYK colors are created by subtracting light. The CMYK color model also carries symbolism in design. Each of the four colors can evoke different emotions and convey specific meanings. For example, cyan often represents tranquility, calmness, or a sense of coolness. Magenta is associated with love, passion, and femininity. Yellow symbolizes happiness, positivity, and energy. Black, as the key color, is used for stability, elegance, and formality. Understanding the CMYK color model is crucial for designers, as it allows them to create visually appealing and meaningful designs with the right combination of colors. By manipulating the percentages of each ink color, they can achieve desired effects, set the mood, and communicate specific messages to their audience through the use of color.

Calibrated Color Devices

Calibrated color devices are tools or instruments used in the field of color theory and design to accurately measure and reproduce colors. These devices are designed to produce consistent and accurate color representations, ensuring that colors appear the same across different devices, media, and viewing conditions. In color theory, colors can have different meanings and symbolisms. Understanding and effectively working with color symbolism is essential in design, as colors can evoke specific emotions, communicate messages, and create visual impact. Calibrated color devices play a crucial role in achieving this, as they allow designers to precisely control and reproduce colors according to their intended meaning and symbolism.

Calm (Blue)

The color blue is often associated with a sense of calmness and serenity in color theory and color symbolism in design. As one of the primary colors, blue stands out as a versatile and universally appealing hue. Its calming nature can evoke feelings of relaxation, tranquility, and peace, making it a popular choice in various design applications. In color theory, blue is classified as a cool color, along with green and purple. Cool colors are known to recede, creating a sense of distance and depth. This property makes blue an ideal choice for creating the illusion of space in design compositions. Whether used as a dominant color or as an accent, blue can help establish a sense of depth and openness within a design.

Calm (Pink)

Pink is a color within the red color family that is often associated with calmness, tranquility, and peace. In color theory, pink is created by mixing red and white, resulting in a lighter and less intense version of red. Its soft and delicate appearance makes it visually soothing and gentle to the eye. In the context of color symbolism in design, pink is often used to convey a sense of calm and relaxation. It is commonly associated with femininity, sensitivity, and nurturing qualities. Pink is often used in designs aimed at promoting self-care, wellness, and emotional well-being. Its serene and peaceful nature makes it suitable for creating a relaxing ambiance in various design applications.

Calm (White)

Calm (White) - In color theory and color symbolism in design, white is often associated with a sense of calmness and tranquility. This pure and sharp color is known for its ability to create a peaceful and soothing atmosphere. White is the absence of color and is commonly seen as a neutral color. It is often used to create a sense of spaciousness and openness in interior design. In color psychology, white is believed to be a color that promotes a sense of purity, freshness, and innocence.

Calming (Lavender)

Calming (Lavender) is a color that is derived from a combination of blue and red, with a higher proportion of blue. It is associated with relaxation, tranquility, and peace. In color theory, lavender is considered a cool color, as it has a soothing effect on the viewer. Lavender is often used in design to create a sense of calmness and serenity. It is frequently utilized in spaces that require a peaceful and relaxing atmosphere, such as bedrooms, spas, and wellness centers. The color lavender has the ability to promote a restful environment and can help to reduce stress and anxiety.

Calming (Teal)

Calming (Teal) is a color in the context of color theory and color symbolism in design that represents a soothing and serene aesthetic. It falls under the blue-green color family and is often described as a medium to dark shade of cyan. This color conveys a sense of tranquility, balance, and stability. In color theory, teal is a combination of blue and green pigments. Blue is known for its calming properties, while green is associated with nature, growth, and harmony. The amalgamation of these colors creates an even more subdued and peaceful hue, making teal a popular choice for creating an atmosphere of relaxation and calmness.

Catalogs Of Color Swatches

A catalog of color swatches in the context of color theory and color symbolism in design is a collection of representative samples or patches of different colors. It serves as a reference tool for designers, artists, and other professionals in visually exploring, understanding, and expressing the potential color choices for their creative works. Color swatches in a catalog are carefully organized and grouped together based on various categorizations such as hue, saturation, value, complementary or analogous colors, and color harmonies. This categorization allows users to quickly locate and compare different colors within a cohesive system. By providing a range of color options, catalogs of color swatches assist designers in making informed decisions about incorporating specific colors into their projects. They enable designers to consider the emotional, psychological, and cultural associations attached to different colors and choose the ones that best align with their intended message or concept. Color theory plays a significant role in understanding and utilizing color swatches. It provides the foundation that guides the selection and combination of colors in design. Color swatch catalogs, therefore, uphold the principles of color theory by offering a comprehensive selection of colors that adhere

16

to concepts such as color relationships, color schemes, and color contrast. In the realm of color symbolism, catalogs of color swatches help designers tap into the symbolic meanings associated with different colors. Colors have the ability to evoke specific emotions, convey certain moods, and communicate distinct messages. By exploring the various color swatches available in a catalog, designers can discover colors that align with the intended symbolism of their design, whether it be in branding, advertising, or artistic expression. In summary, catalogs of color swatches serve as essential tools for designers and artists. They provide a comprehensive collection of representative color samples, organized based on categorizations and principles of color theory, and enable the exploration of color symbolism in design.

Caution (Red)

Caution (Red) represents an intense and powerful color in color theory. It is classified as a warm color, located at the end of the visible light spectrum, with a high wavelength and low frequency. Red evokes strong emotions and is often associated with love, passion, and energy. In color symbolism, caution is commonly expressed through the use of the color red. Red has a significant role in design as it has the ability to capture attention and create a sense of urgency. Its bold and dynamic nature makes it an ideal choice for expressing warning signs or indicating alerts. The combination of caution and the color red helps to communicate potential dangers or hazards that require immediate attention or careful consideration.

Caution (Yellow)

Caution (Yellow) is a hue within the color spectrum that is commonly associated with color theory and color symbolism in design. It is a vibrant and highly noticeable color that exudes a sense of warning, alertness, and attention. In color theory, yellow is considered a warm color, as it is closely related to the vibrant energy of sunshine and fire. This warmth contributes to the dynamic nature of caution yellow and its ability to capture attention and convey messages. Caution yellow is widely used in various design contexts to communicate warnings, precautions, and potential hazards. Its brightness and visibility make it an ideal choice for signage, road markings, and safety equipment. In these applications, the color serves as a visual cue to prompt individuals to be cautious and aware of potential dangers or risks in their surroundings.

Change (Orange)

Orange is a secondary color in color theory, created by mixing red and yellow. It is considered a warm color because it evokes feelings of energy and excitement. In the context of color symbolism in design, orange is often associated with attributes such as enthusiasm, creativity, and warmth. This vibrant color is frequently used in design to draw attention and create a sense of liveliness. It is commonly employed to evoke feelings of optimism and playfulness, making it suitable for designs that aim to create a friendly and inviting atmosphere.

Charm (Lavender)

Charm (Lavender) is a color in the purple color family that falls within the color theory and color symbolism in design. It is a pale, light shade of purple with a high amount of white added to the base color. In color theory, charm lavender is achieved by combining blue and a small amount of red with a large amount of white. The addition of white creates a soft and delicate hue that is often associated with femininity and elegance. It is a cool color that is calming and soothing to the eye. When used in design, charm lavender can convey various meanings and emotions. It is commonly associated with romance, luxury, and sophistication. Its soft and gentle nature makes it an ideal color for creating a sense of tranquility and serenity in a design. It can also evoke feelings of nostalgia and sentimentality. In branding and marketing, charm lavender can be used to target a specific audience, particularly those who appreciate beauty, grace, and refinement. It can be used to promote products and services related to beauty, fashion, and luxury. Its association with romance also makes it a popular choice for wedding-related designs. Charm lavender can be used effectively in combination with other colors. It pairs well with neutrals such as white, gray, and beige, creating a soft and elegant color palette. It can also be combined with other shades of purple, creating a monochromatic scheme that is both visually pleasing and harmonious. Overall, charm lavender is a color that represents elegance, femininity, and luxury. Its delicate and soothing nature makes it a popular choice in design, particularly in areas that

17

aim to evoke a sense of grace and beauty.

Charts For Color Conversion

A chart for color conversion is a visual representation of different color models and their corresponding color values. It is used in color theory and color symbolism in design to provide a systematic way of converting colors between different color spaces and creating harmonious color palettes. In color theory, colors are often represented using different color models such as RGB (Red, Green, Blue), CMYK (Cyan, Magenta, Yellow, Black), and HSB/HSV (Hue, Saturation, Brightness/Value). Each color model has its own set of primary colors and color mixing rules. A color conversion chart allows designers to easily translate colors between these models. For example, if a designer wants to convert an RGB color to its CMYK equivalent for print, they can refer to a color conversion chart to find the corresponding CMYK values. In addition to color models, color conversion charts can also include information about color symbolism. Color symbolism refers to the meaning and associations attributed to different colors in various cultures and contexts. For example, in Western culture, red is often associated with passion, love, and energy, while green is associated with nature, growth, and health. By incorporating color symbolism into their designs, designers can evoke specific emotions or convey certain messages to their audience. A color conversion chart can provide designers with a quick reference for the symbolic meanings of different colors, allowing them to make informed choices about color palettes and create visually impactful designs. In conclusion, a chart for color conversion is a valuable tool in color theory and design. It helps designers convert colors between different color models and incorporate color symbolism into their designs, enhancing the visual impact and meaning of their creations.

Charts For Mixing Colors

Color mixing is an essential aspect of color theory and plays a significant role in color symbolism in design. Charts for mixing colors are graphical representations that visually demonstrate how different hues can be combined to create new shades and tones. In color theory, colors are often classified as primary, secondary, and tertiary colors. Primary colors are the building blocks of color mixing and cannot be created by mixing other colors. They include red, blue, and yellow. Secondary colors, namely orange, green, and purple, are obtained by blending two primary colors. Tertiary colors, such as pink, turquoise, and brown, are created by mixing a primary color with a secondary color. Charts for mixing colors showcase various combinations and ratios of different hues. They provide a visual reference for designers, artists, and individuals interested in understanding the color blending process. These charts typically display primary colors on one axis and secondary colors on another axis, creating a grid-like structure. By intersecting two primary colors, the resulting secondary color can be identified on the chart. Color mixing extends beyond the primary and secondary colors, incorporating intermediate hues created by blending primary and secondary colors. Charts for mixing colors often include a spectrum of shades and tones, allowing users to explore a vast range of color possibilities. By locating a specific hue on the chart, individuals can determine the combination of colors required to produce that shade. Color symbolism in design further emphasizes the significance of color mixing charts. Different colors convey various meanings and emotions, influencing the psychological impact of a design. By utilizing color mixing charts, designers can experiment with different color combinations to evoke specific feelings or associations. For example, blending warm colors like red and yellow creates oranges, which are often associated with energy, vitality, and enthusiasm. Conversely, combining cool colors such as blue and green produces tranquil and calming tones, often associated with serenity and peace. In conclusion, charts for mixing colors are essential tools in color theory and color symbolism in design. They provide a visual representation of how different hues can be blended to create new shades and tones. By understanding the principles of color mixing and utilizing these charts, designers can effectively convey emotions, meanings, and associations through their color choices.

Cheerfulness (Yellow)

Cheerfulness, represented by the color yellow, plays a significant role in color theory and symbolism within design. In color theory, yellow is categorized as a warm color that sits between green and orange on the color wheel. It is often associated with feelings of happiness, optimism, and energy. In design, yellow is frequently used to create a sense of cheerfulness and positivity.

It is a vibrant and lively color that easily attracts attention, making it an excellent choice for grab the viewer's eye and convey a message of optimism. By incorporating yellow into a design, it can evoke feelings of happiness and joy, helping to create a visually appealing and engaging experience.

Chroma

Chroma, in the context of color theory and color symbolism in design, refers to the intensity or purity of a color. It is one of the three properties that define a color, alongside hue and value. Chroma determines how vibrant or dull a color appears. Higher chroma indicates a more vivid and saturated color, while lower chroma results in a duller or more muted color. In color theory, the chroma of a color is determined by the amount of gray added to it. Adding gray or reducing the intensity of a color decreases its chroma, resulting in a less saturated shade. Conversely, removing or reducing gray from a color increases its chroma and makes it more vibrant. The purest form of a color with the highest chroma is often referred to as "fully saturated." Chroma plays a significant role in color symbolism in design. Different colors with varying chroma levels evoke different emotional and psychological responses. Colors with high chroma, such as bright red or electric blue, are associated with energy, excitement, and intensity. They can create a sense of urgency or grab attention in design compositions. On the other hand, colors with low chroma, like pastel shades or muted tones, are often linked to calmness, tranquility, and subtlety. They can create a more relaxed or soothing atmosphere in design. Low-chroma colors are often used in minimalist or minimalist-inspired designs to convey a sense of elegance and simplicity. Designers strategically use chroma to convey specific messages, evoke emotions, and create visual interest. They consider the chromatic intensity of colors in relation to the overall design concept, target audience, and desired visual impact. By manipulating chroma, designers can establish a mood, emphasize focal points, guide visual hierarchy, and communicate brand identity effectively.

Clarity (Gold)

Clarity (Gold) is a term used in color theory and color symbolism in design to describe a shade of gold that represents transparency, purity, and brightness. It is often associated with concepts such as illumination, enlightenment, and perfection. In color theory, gold is a warm color that falls under the yellow hue. It is often associated with the sun and has been historically used to represent wealth, luxury, and power. Gold has a natural shine and radiance that captures attention and evokes a sense of prestige and elegance.

Clarity (Lemon)

Clarity (Lemon) is a color in color theory that is characterized by its vibrant, bright yellow hue. It is often associated with qualities such as freshness, energy, and positivity. In color symbolism in design, clarity (lemon) is often used to convey feelings of happiness, warmth, and cheerfulness. It is a color that is commonly associated with summer, sunshine, and outdoor activities. Its brightness and vibrancy make it a popular choice for designs that aim to grab attention and create a lively and energetic atmosphere.

Clarity (Turquoise)

Clarity (Turquoise) is a color commonly used in color theory and design, representing a shade of blue-green that exudes a sense of clarity, purity, and freshness. It belongs to the blue color family, characterized by its blend of blue and green pigments, resulting in a vibrant yet soothing hue. In color theory, clarity (turquoise) is often associated with a range of meanings and symbolisms. It is known to symbolize serenity, tranquility, and calmness. It evokes feelings of relaxation and peacefulness when used in design. The shade is reminiscent of clear tropical waters and pristine skies, creating a sense of openness and expansiveness.

Cleanliness (White)

Cleanliness is a color principle in color theory and a symbol in design that is represented by the color white. In color theory, white is considered the absence of color as it contains all colors in the visible light spectrum, showcasing purity and lightness. It is achieved by the combination of red, green, and blue light at full intensity, resulting in a color that has a high light value and low

19

saturation. In design, white is synonymous with cleanliness, sterility, and hygiene. It's often associated with clarity, simplicity, and a sense of spaciousness. Using white as a dominant color can create a minimalist aesthetic, presenting a clean and uncluttered design. White spaces within layouts establish a sense of organization and order. It provides a blank canvas for other colors and elements to stand out, making it an ideal choice for highlighting important information or creating contrast.

Cleansing (Aqua)

Cleansing (Aqua) refers to a color in the context of color theory and color symbolism in design. Aqua is a shade of blue-green that represents cleansing and purification. In color theory, aqua is classified as a cool color, as it is predominantly blue with a hint of green. Cool colors are often associated with calmness, tranquility, and relaxation. Aqua's cool undertones evoke a sense of serenity and can create a soothing atmosphere in design. Symbolically, aqua is often associated with water and the sea. Water is a universal symbol of cleansing and renewal, and aqua represents the revitalizing and purifying qualities of water. It is often used to convey a sense of freshness and purity in design. The color aqua is commonly used in various design contexts, including graphic design, interior design, and fashion design. In graphic design, aqua can be used to create a visually appealing contrast against warmer colors or to communicate a sense of calmness and clarity. When used in interior design, aqua can add a refreshing touch to a space and create a tranquil atmosphere. In fashion design, aqua is often used to create eye-catching and vibrant looks, especially during warmer seasons. Overall, aqua's association with cleansing and purification makes it a versatile color choice in design. Its cool undertones and symbolic representation of water allow it to create harmonious and serene visual experiences. Whether used subtly or boldly, aqua can add a sense of clarity and rejuvenation to any design.

Collections Of Color Fans

A collection of color fans, in the context of color theory and color symbolism in design, refers to a set of color swatches or samples organized in a fan-shaped format. These fans are created to help designers, artists, and enthusiasts explore and select colors for their projects based on their understanding of color theory and the symbolism associated with different colors. Color fans typically consist of a range of hues, shades, and tints, often arranged according to a specific color system such as the color wheel or a specific color model like RGB or CMYK. Each color is represented by a small swatch or chip, allowing users to easily compare and contrast different colors within the fan.

Color Accessibility Tools

Color accessibility tools are tools that are used in the field of design to ensure that the colors chosen for a project are both visually appealing and inclusive for all users, especially those with visual impairments or color vision deficiencies. These tools focus on the principles of color theory and color symbolism to create harmonious and meaningful color palettes that meet accessibility guidelines. Color theory is the study of how colors interact with each other and with the human eye. It involves understanding concepts such as the color wheel, color harmony, and color contrast. By applying color theory principles, designers can create color palettes that are visually appealing and have a balanced distribution of colors. Color symbolism, on the other hand, refers to the interpretation of colors and their meanings in different cultures and contexts. Certain colors may evoke specific emotions or convey particular messages, and understanding color symbolism helps designers to use colors effectively to communicate their intended message.

Color Aesthetics

Color aesthetics refers to the study of the visual perception and interpretation of colors in the context of color theory and color symbolism in design. It involves understanding the psychological and emotional effects that different colors evoke, as well as their symbolic meanings and cultural associations. Color theory is the study of how colors interact with one another and how they can be combined to create visually appealing and harmonious compositions. It encompasses concepts such as the color wheel, color harmony, color contrast, and color temperature. Understanding color theory is essential for designers to effectively use colors to convey specific messages, create desired moods, and visually communicate ideas or information. Color symbolism, on the other hand, explores the meaning and interpretation of colors in different cultures and contexts. Colors often carry symbolic meanings that can vary widely across cultures and even within different industries or fields. For example, red typically symbolizes passion, love, or danger in Western cultures, but it represents luck and prosperity in Chinese culture. Designers must consider these cultural associations and choose colors deliberately to align with the intended message or concept. Color aesthetics in design involves the thoughtful and intentional use of colors to create a desired visual impact. It requires an understanding of how colors can affect emotions, moods, and perceptions. Warm colors like red, orange, and yellow tend to evoke feelings of energy, vibrancy, and warmth, while cool colors like blue, green, and purple can create a sense of calmness, tranquility, or professionalism. The choice of color palette in design can greatly influence the user experience, brand perception, and overall visual appeal. Colors must be selected based on their appropriateness to the intended message, the target audience, and the context in which they will be seen. Color aesthetics play a crucial role in creating visual hierarchy, attracting attention, establishing brand recognition, and enhancing the overall visual impact of a design.

Color Analysis Applications

A color analysis application is a tool or software that is used to analyze and interpret colors within the context of color theory and color symbolism in design. It helps designers, artists, and other professionals understand the psychological and emotional impact of different colors and how they can be used effectively in their work. In the field of color theory, the application allows users to explore the color wheel, which is a visual representation of the relationships between colors. By selecting different colors on the wheel or inputting specific color values, the application can provide information on complementary or analogous colors, helping users create harmonious color schemes. It can also provide data on color harmonies, such as triadic or split-complementary, which can guide the selection of colors that work well together. Furthermore, a color analysis application can provide information on the psychological and emotional associations of different colors. It can provide insight into how specific colors are perceived and the emotions they can evoke in viewers. For example, the application might indicate that red is associated with passion and energy, while blue is associated with tranquility and trust. This information can inform design choices and help designers create specific moods or atmospheres through color selection. Additionally, the application may include features for color symbolism analysis. Color symbolism refers to the cultural or contextual meanings that colors can carry. For example, in many Western cultures, white is associated with purity and innocence, while black is associated with darkness and mourning. By considering these cultural associations, designers can use colors to reinforce or subvert certain messages or themes in their work. The application can provide information on the symbolism of different colors in various cultures and contexts, allowing designers to make informed decisions about color usage.

Color Analysis Software

Color analysis software is a tool used in the context of color theory and color symbolism in design. It is a computer program that works by analyzing various aspects of color, such as hue, saturation, and brightness, to provide meaningful insights and aid in the creation and selection of color palettes. In the world of design, color is a powerful tool that can evoke emotions, convey messages, and create visual harmony. The use of appropriate colors is crucial in capturing the essence of a brand, expressing the intended mood, and engaging the target audience. However, selecting the right colors can be a challenging task for designers and artists, especially when considering the complexities of color theory and the significance of color symbolism. Color analysis software simplifies the process of color selection by offering a range of tools and features that assist in understanding color relationships and their impact on visual perception. By inputting specific color values or samples, the software can provide detailed analysis and recommendations based on established color theories and principles. One of the key functionalities of color analysis software is the ability to generate color harmonies. Color harmony is the arrangement of colors in a way that is aesthetically pleasing to the eye. The software can generate harmonious color combinations by analyzing the relationship between colors, such as complementary, analogous, and triadic. This helps designers create cohesive and visually appealing color schemes that reinforce the desired message or mood. Furthermore, color analysis software can assist in understanding color symbolism, which refers to the associations and meanings assigned to certain colors. Different colors hold various cultural, psychological, and personal interpretations, and understanding these connotations is vital for effective visual communication. The software can provide insights into the symbolism of different colors, allowing designers to make informed decisions and create designs that resonate with their intended audience.

Color Analysis Tools

Color analysis tools refer to software or digital resources that are used in the field of color theory and design to analyze and understand the various aspects of color, such as its properties, symbolism, and psychological effects. These tools provide designers with valuable insights and guidance in creating visually appealing and effective color palettes for their projects. Color theory is a fundamental principle in the field of design that studies the interaction and harmony between different colors. It explores how colors can be combined, contrasted, and used to evoke particular emotions or communicate specific messages. Understanding color theory is crucial for designers as it helps them make informed decisions about color choices and achieve the desired visual impact in their designs. Color analysis tools assist designers in this process by offering a range of features and functionalities. These tools often include color pickers, which allow designers to select and extract colors from images or websites. They can also generate color schemes based on predefined rules or principles, such as complementary, analogous, or triadic color schemes. By providing designers with a visual representation of different color combinations, these tools help them evaluate the harmony and balance of their designs. In addition to color scheme generation, color analysis tools also provide information about the symbolism and psychological effects associated with specific colors. They can give designers insights into cultural, historical, and contextual meanings of colors, enabling them to communicate messages and evoke emotions effectively. For example, red is often associated with passion and energy, while blue is linked to calmness and trust. By understanding these associations, designers can create designs that align with the desired message and audience. Overall, color analysis tools play a crucial role in helping designers make informed decisions about color choices in their designs. By providing insights into color theory, symbolism, and psychological effects, these tools contribute to the creation of visually appealing and effective designs that resonate with the target audience.

Color Analysis

Color analysis, in the context of color theory and color symbolism in design, refers to the study and interpretation of colors and their impact on human perception, emotions, and visual communication. It involves understanding how different colors interact, their psychological effects, and the symbolic meanings they carry in various cultures and contexts. In color theory, colors are classified into different categories, such as primary, secondary, and tertiary colors. These colors are further grouped into warm and cool colors, based on their placement on the color wheel. Understanding these color relationships is crucial in creating visually appealing and harmonious designs. Color analysis helps designers make informed decisions about color combinations, contrasts, and the overall mood or atmosphere the design is intended to evoke. Color symbolism, on the other hand, examines the cultural or contextual associations and meanings attributed to different colors. These symbolic meanings can vary across cultures and have the power to evoke specific emotions, convey messages, or represent concepts. For example, red is often associated with passion, energy, and danger, while blue is commonly associated with calmness, trust, and stability. Additionally, colors can be used to convey cultural or gender-specific meanings, such as white symbolizing purity in some cultures or pink representing femininity. Effective color analysis in design includes considering the target audience and the intended message or purpose of the design. By understanding the psychological and symbolic significance of colors, designers can create impactful visuals that resonate with viewers, convey the desired message, and elicit the desired emotional response. Color analysis is not limited to a single discipline but expands to various creative fields such as graphic design, fashion, interior design, and branding, where colors play a crucial role in shaping visual identity and perception.

Color Association

Color association refers to the connection or link between colors and their meanings or emotions

22

in the context of color theory and color symbolism in design. It is based on the understanding that colors have the ability to evoke specific emotions or convey certain messages, which can be used strategically in design to enhance the overall impact and effectiveness of a visual composition. In color theory, colors are often classified into different categories, such as warm colors (e.g., red, orange, yellow) and cool colors (e.g., blue, green, purple). Each color category is associated with particular emotions, moods, or psychological effects. For example, warm colors are often viewed as energetic, stimulating, and attention-grabbing, while cool colors are seen as calming, soothing, and relaxing. Color symbolism, on the other hand, explores the specific meaning or cultural significance assigned to certain colors. Different cultures and societies may associate different emotions or concepts with particular colors. For instance, red can symbolize love, passion, or danger in Western cultures, while it may be associated with luck, celebration, or prosperity in Eastern cultures. Understanding these cultural color associations is important when designing for specific target audiences or international markets. Color association plays a crucial role in design as it allows designers to communicate visually without the need for words. By choosing and combining colors strategically, designers can evoke specific emotions, create visual hierarchy, guide attention, and deliver messages more effectively. For example, using warm, vibrant colors like red and orange in a call-to-action button can help grab users' attention and encourage them to take an action. Similarly, using cool, calming colors like blue and green in a healthcare website can promote a sense of trust, tranquility, and well-being. However, it is important to note that color associations can be influenced by personal experiences, cultural backgrounds, and individual preferences. Therefore, it is crucial for designers to conduct research and test their color choices with their target audience to ensure that the intended associations are conveyed accurately and effectively.

Color Balance

Color balance, in the context of color theory and color symbolism in design, refers to the harmonious distribution of colors in a composition or visual element. It involves the arrangement and proportion of different colors to create a sense of equilibrium, visual interest, and emotional impact. Color balance plays a crucial role in creating aesthetically pleasing and effective designs. By carefully selecting and arranging colors, designers can evoke specific emotions, convey messages, and enhance the overall visual experience for the viewer.

Color Blindness Correction Tools

Color blindness correction tools refer to various methods and technologies that aim to assist individuals with color vision deficiencies in perceiving and distinguishing colors accurately. In the context of color theory and color symbolism in design, these tools are particularly relevant as they help address the challenges faced by colorblind individuals in interpreting and utilizing color in their visual creations. Color blindness, also known as color vision deficiency, is a condition where the ability to perceive certain colors is impaired. It is caused by abnormalities in the photopigments in the cones of the retina, resulting in the inability to differentiate between specific wavelengths of light. This condition can affect the way individuals perceive and interpret colors, leading to difficulties in navigating color-coded information and experiencing limitations in various everyday activities. Color blindness correction tools can be categorized into two main types: digital and physical. Digital color blindness correction tools mainly involve software and applications that manipulate colors in real-time, making them more distinguishable for colorblind individuals. These tools typically employ algorithms that modify color combinations, enhance contrast, or convert certain colors into shades that can be more easily perceived by individuals with specific color vision deficiencies. On the other hand, physical color blindness correction tools encompass different aids and devices that individuals can use in real-world situations. For example, color filtering glasses and lenses can help enhance the perception of specific colors by selectively blocking certain wavelengths of light. These glasses work by altering the light spectrum before it reaches the wearer's eyes, allowing them to differentiate between colors that may appear similar or indistinguishable without the aid of the filters. Overall, color blindness correction tools play a crucial role in facilitating equal access to information, communication, and design for individuals with color vision deficiencies. By using these tools, colorblind individuals can overcome limitations and effectively navigate color-coded environments, explore the nuances of color symbolism, and participate fully in the world of design and visual expression.

Color Blindness Simulation Software

A color blindness simulation software is a digital tool that allows designers to experience and replicate the visual perception of individuals with color vision deficiencies. This software works by altering the colors of digital images or design elements to simulate how individuals with different types and severities of color blindness would perceive them. In the context of color theory, color blindness simulation software is useful for ensuring accessibility and inclusivity in design. It helps designers understand how their color choices may be perceived by individuals with color vision deficiencies, allowing them to create designs that are more visually distinct and identifiable for a wider range of users. By simulating the experience of color blindness, designers can anticipate potential visibility issues and adapt their designs accordingly. In the realm of color symbolism, color blindness simulation software helps designers consider how their use of color may impact the intended message or meaning of their design. Different colors are often associated with specific emotions, concepts, or cultural contexts. However, these associations may not hold true for individuals with color vision deficiencies. With the use of simulation software, designers can test how their color choices communicate and whether they remain effective for users with color vision deficiencies. By revealing the limitations and challenges faced by individuals with color vision deficiencies, color blindness simulation software promotes inclusive design practices. It encourages designers to prioritize contrast, shape, and other visual cues beyond color to enhance accessibility. This software empowers designers to create designs that are more equitable, making information and experiences accessible to everyone, regardless of their color vision abilities. In conclusion, color blindness simulation software plays a vital role in color theory and color symbolism in design. By simulating different types and degrees of color blindness, it helps designers understand how their color choices may affect the visibility, user experience, and overall meaning of their designs for individuals with color vision deficiencies. Through the insights gained from this software, designers can create more inclusive and impactful designs that cater to a wider audience.

Color Blindness Simulation Tools

Color Blindness Simulation Tools are digital tools used in the context of color theory and color symbolism in design to replicate the experience of individuals with color vision deficiencies. These tools help designers, artists, and developers gain a better understanding of how their work appears to individuals who are colorblind. Color blindness, or color vision deficiency, is a condition that affects a person's ability to perceive certain colors. It can range from mild to severe, and the most common type is red-green color blindness. This means that individuals with this condition have difficulty distinguishing between shades of red and green, or they may see these colors differently. Other types of color blindness include blue-yellow color blindness and total color blindness. In the context of color theory, color blindness simulation tools enable designers to view their designs from the perspective of someone with color vision deficiencies. This allows them to assess the accessibility and usability of their work for individuals with different types of color blindness. By using these tools, designers can identify any potential issues with color contrast, color combinations, and overall color palette choices that may make their designs challenging to perceive for those with color vision deficiencies. Moreover, in the context of color symbolism, color blindness simulation tools can help designers understand how color choices may affect the intended message or emotion conveyed in their designs. Colors often carry symbolic meanings and evoke specific emotions in design. However, if these colors are not distinguishable for individuals with color vision deficiencies, the intended message or emotional response may be lost. By simulating color blindness, designers can ensure that their color choices remain effective and meaningful for a wider audience. Overall, color blindness simulation tools are invaluable resources in the field of design. They allow designers to create more inclusive and accessible designs, as well as ensure that the desired message and emotions are effectively conveyed, regardless of an individual's color vision capabilities.

Color Blindness Simulator

A color blindness simulator is a tool used in color theory and design to mimic the vision of individuals with color vision deficiencies. These simulators enable designers to experience and understand how people with different types of color blindness perceive colors in order to create designs that are accessible and inclusive to all users. Color blindness, also known as color vision deficiency, is the inability to perceive certain colors accurately. This condition occurs when

24

the cells in the retina, called cones, responsible for detecting different colors are either absent or not functioning properly. As a result, individuals with color blindness may have difficulty seeing specific colors or may mistake them for others. In color theory, colors are known to evoke emotions, convey messages, and create visual appeal in designs. Different colors have various meanings and symbolize different things in different cultures. For example, red often represents passion or danger, while blue is often associated with calmness or trust. Understanding color symbolism is crucial for designers to effectively communicate their intended messages and emotions through their designs. When designing for individuals with color vision deficiencies, it is important to consider how they perceive colors. This is where color blindness simulators come into play. These simulators allow designers to preview their designs through the eyes of individuals with different types of color blindness, such as red-green color blindness or blue-yellow color blindness. By experiencing how colors appear to individuals with color vision deficiencies, designers can make informed decisions about color combinations, contrasts, and color symbolism to ensure that their designs are accessible and meaningful to all users. By using a color blindness simulator, designers can make adjustments to their color choices to improve the legibility and usability of their designs for individuals with color vision deficiencies. This includes selecting colors that have a high contrast ratio, avoiding relying solely on color to convey important information, and incorporating other visual cues, such as patterns or textures, to enhance the clarity of the design. In conclusion, a color blindness simulator is a valuable tool for designers to understand and address the needs of individuals with color vision deficiencies. By simulating the perception of color blind individuals, designers can create designs that are accessible, inclusive, and effectively communicate their intended messages and emotions to all users.

Color Blindness Simulators

Color blindness simulators are tools used in the field of color theory and design to mimic the experience of individuals with different types of color vision deficiencies, commonly known as color blindness. These simulators are intended to help designers and other professionals understand how individuals with color vision deficiencies perceive colors and make informed decisions in creating accessible and inclusive designs. Color theory is the study of how colors interact and affect human perception. It explores the properties and relationships of colors, including attributes such as hue, saturation, and brightness. Understanding color theory is crucial in various design disciplines, such as graphic design, web design, and interior design, as it helps create visually pleasing and meaningful compositions. In the context of color symbolism, colors often convey specific meanings and emotions that vary across cultures and contexts. For instance, red can symbolize passion and love, while blue can connote peace and tranquility. Designers use color symbolism to enhance the message and impact of their designs, considering the psychological and emotional responses that colors elicit from viewers. Color blindness, or color vision deficiency, is a condition that affects the perception of colors. People with color vision deficiencies may have difficulty distinguishing between certain colors or perceiving them as intended. The most common type of color blindness is red-green color blindness, which affects the ability to differentiate between red and green hues. Other forms include blue-yellow color blindness and total color blindness (achromatopsia). Color blindness simulators allow designers and other professionals to view their designs as individuals with color vision deficiencies would see them. By simulating the various types of color blindness, these tools enable designers to assess the accessibility and inclusivity of their designs. They help identify potential issues that may arise for color blind individuals and inform adjustments to color choices, contrasts, and visual hierarchies. In conclusion, color blindness simulators are valuable resources in the field of color theory and design. They provide a way to empathize with individuals with color vision deficiencies and ensure that designs are accessible and inclusive. By using these simulators, designers can create visually appealing compositions that effectively convey intended messages, while considering the varying perceptions of color by different people.

Color Blindness

Color blindness refers to a visual impairment that affects an individual's ability to perceive and differentiate between certain colors. It is a condition that occurs when the cells of the retina, which are responsible for detecting light and color, do not function properly. This impairment primarily affects the perception of red, green, and blue colors, resulting in difficulties distinguishing between them. In the context of color theory, color blindness has a significant impact on the way colors are perceived and understood. Color theory is the study of how colors interact, blend, and create visual effects. It forms the foundation for various design fields, including graphic design, interior design, and fashion design, where color symbolism plays a crucial role. Color symbolism refers to the cultural and psychological associations that individuals attach to specific colors. Different colors evoke different emotions, evoke particular moods, and convey symbolic meanings. However, for individuals with color blindness, the ability to perceive and interpret these symbolic associations may be limited or altered. For example, in color theory, red is often associated with passion, energy, and danger. However, for someone with red-green color blindness, distinguishing between shades of red and green may be challenging or impossible. This can lead to misinterpretation or miscommunication of the intended symbolism in design. Moreover, color blindness also affects the visual hierarchy in design. The use of contrasting colors assists in creating focal points, directing attention, and organizing visual information. However, those with color blindness may not perceive these contrasts as intended, which can result in a loss of clarity and hierarchy in the design. Designers, therefore, need to consider the potential limitations of color blindness when creating visual materials. Utilizing color palettes that include a range of hues with distinct brightness and saturation levels helps individuals with color blindness perceive differences more easily. Additionally, incorporating other visual cues, such as patterns or texture, can aid in conveying messages and establishing a clear visual hierarchy.

Color Calibration Devices

Color calibration devices are tools used to ensure accurate and consistent color reproduction across various devices, such as computer monitors, printers, and scanners. They are essential in the field of color theory and symbolism in design, as they help designers achieve precise and reliable color representation in their work. Color theory is the study and application of color and its effects on human perception. It involves understanding the properties of color, such as hue, saturation, and brightness, and how they interact with each other. Color symbolism, on the other hand, refers to the cultural and psychological associations that people have with specific colors. In design, it is crucial to create visuals that accurately reflect the intended color palette, as colors can evoke specific emotions and convey symbolic meanings. However, different devices and printing methods can display colors differently, leading to inconsistencies in the final output. This is where color calibration devices come in. Color calibration devices typically consist of a colorimeter or spectrophotometer, which measures and analyzes the colors emitted or reflected by a device. These measurements are then compared to standardized color profiles to determine the device's color accuracy. Calibration software is used to adjust the device's settings and bring its color output in line with the desired standard. By calibrating their devices, designers can ensure that the colors they choose will be reproduced accurately on various mediums. This is especially important when working with clients or collaborating with other designers, as it allows for consistent color communication and prevents misunderstandings. Calibration devices also play a significant role in color theory, as they allow designers to explore and experiment with different color combinations. By accurately reproducing colors, designers can evaluate how certain hues, saturations, and brightness levels interact to create specific effects. This empirical understanding of color theory helps designers make informed decisions when creating compositions and selecting color palettes. In conclusion, color calibration devices are essential tools for designers working with color theory and symbolism. They enable accurate and consistent color reproduction across devices, ensuring that intended palettes are faithfully represented. By using calibration devices, designers can create visuals that evoke the desired emotions and effectively communicate symbolic meanings.

Color Calibration Instruments

Color Calibration Instruments are tools used in the field of color theory and design to measure and adjust colors accurately and consistently. These instruments are particularly crucial in maintaining color consistency across various devices, such as computer monitors, printers, cameras, and projectors. Color theory deals with the study and understanding of colors, their properties, and how they interact with one another. It is essential for designers, artists, and photographers to have accurate representations of colors in their work. However, colors can appear differently on different devices due to variations in color profiles, settings, and manufacturing processes. Color Calibration Instruments enable professionals to calibrate and standardize colors, ensuring that they are reproduced accurately on each device or medium. These tools typically consist of a colorimeter or spectrophotometer, which measures the color properties of an object or display and provides information about its color accuracy and consistency. In the context of color symbolism in design, Color Calibration Instruments play a crucial role in conveying the intended meaning and emotions through colors. Different colors have different symbolic associations and can evoke specific psychological responses. For example, red is often associated with energy, passion, and intensity, while blue is associated with calmness, trust, and stability. Using Color Calibration Instruments, designers can ensure that the colors chosen for a design accurately reflect the desired symbolism and emotional impact. By calibrating colors precisely, designers can avoid unintended variations that may dilute the intended meaning or evoke unintended responses from viewers. In conclusion, Color Calibration Instruments are essential tools for professionals working with colors in the field of design and color theory. These instruments enable accurate and consistent color reproduction across different devices and mediums, ensuring that the intended meaning and emotions associated with colors are effectively communicated to the viewer.

Color Calibration

Color calibration is a process in color theory and design that aims to achieve consistent and accurate colors on various devices and mediums. The purpose of color calibration is to ensure that colors appear the same and convey the intended meaning and emotions across different platforms, such as computer screens, printers, and other digital or physical media. In color theory, colors have symbolic meanings and evoke certain emotions or associations. For example, warm colors like red and orange are often associated with energy, passion, and warmth, while cool colors like blue and green are associated with calmness, tranquility, and nature. Therefore, it is crucial to maintain the accuracy and consistency of colors to convey the desired messages and create the intended visual impact.

Color Code Conversion Tools

Color code conversion tools are essential resources used in color theory and color symbolism in the field of design. These tools allow designers to convert color codes between different color systems, facilitating the accurate selection and representation of colors in various design projects. Color theory is the science and art behind colors and their visual effects on human perception. It encompasses concepts such as color harmony, contrast, and the emotional responses triggered by different colors. In the design industry, understanding and applying color theory principles is crucial for creating visually appealing and impactful designs. Color symbolism, on the other hand, refers to the cultural and psychological meanings associated with specific colors. Different colors can evoke various emotions, moods, and connotations, making them powerful tools for conveying messages or creating certain atmospheres within a design. Color codes, also known as color models or color systems, are standardized methods of representing colors numerically. They enable designers to specify and reproduce colors accurately across different mediums and devices. Some popular color models include RGB (Red Green Blue), CMYK (Cyan Magenta Yellow Key/Black), HSL (Hue Saturation Lightness), and HEX (Hexadecimal). However, while working on design projects, it is not uncommon to encounter situations where color codes need to be converted from one system to another. This is where color code conversion tools come into play. These tools provide designers with a simple and efficient way to transform color codes from RGB to CMYK, HSL to HEX, or any other combination, ensuring consistency and accuracy in color representation. By using color code conversion tools, designers can overcome compatibility issues between different color models. They can easily translate colors from one system to another without jeopardizing the integrity of their designs. This is particularly important when transitioning between digital and print-based projects, as digital mediums primarily use RGB while print requires CMYK. Moreover, color code conversion tools aid in the exploration and experimentation of color choices. Designers can quickly and effortlessly compare colors in different systems, allowing them to make informed decisions based on the desired emotional or symbolic impact of a particular color. In conclusion, color code conversion tools are vital resources in the realm of color theory and color symbolism in design. They enable designers to accurately represent and communicate their intended color choices while considering the emotional and symbolic meanings associated with different colors. By utilizing these tools, designers can ensure consistency and precision in their color selections, ultimately enhancing the visual impact of their designs.

Color Code Converters

A color code converter is a tool used in color theory and design that allows users to convert colors from one color code representation to another. Color codes are numerical or alphanumeric representations of colors, used to specify colors in various design applications such as graphic design, web design, and computer programming. Different color code systems have been developed over time, each with its own set of codes and conventions. Color code converters provide a convenient way to convert colors between different code systems. For example, they can convert colors from RGB (Red, Green, Blue) to CMYK (Cyan, Magenta, Yellow, Black) or from hexadecimal codes to Pantone colors. In color theory, different color code systems are used to describe and manipulate color in different contexts. For instance, RGB is a commonly used color model in digital design, where colors are displayed on screens using varying intensities of red, green, and blue light. CMYK, on the other hand, is primarily used in printing, where colors are created by mixing varying amounts of cyan, magenta, yellow, and black ink. Color symbolism is an important aspect of design, where colors are used to convey meaning and evoke emotions. Different cultures and contexts attach different meanings to different colors. For example, red is often associated with passion and energy, while blue is associated with serenity and calmness. Color code converters can help designers ensure that the colors they use convey the desired symbolism. By providing a way to convert between different color code representations, designers can experiment with different color combinations and easily adapt their designs to different platforms and mediums.

Color Combination Apps

Color combination apps refer to software applications or online tools that assist designers and artists in determining harmonious color palettes for their projects. These apps utilize principles of color theory and symbolism to provide users with a wide range of color combinations that are visually appealing and convey desired emotions or messages. Color theory is the study of how colors interact and harmonize with each other. It is based on the color wheel, which organizes colors in a circular fashion, with primary colors (red, blue, and yellow) at the center, secondary colors (orange, green, and purple) in between, and tertiary colors formed by mixing primary and secondary colors in outer rings. Analogous colors are located next to each other on the wheel and create a sense of harmony, while complementary colors are opposite each other and provide strong contrast. In design, color symbolism is the use of specific colors to evoke certain emotions or convey particular messages. Each color carries its own symbolism and associations. For example, red can represent passion and love, while blue is often associated with calmness and trust. Understanding color symbolism is essential when creating a design that effectively communicates its intended message and resonates with the target audience. Color combination apps take these principles into account by offering a vast array of pre-selected color palettes or allowing users to create their own combinations. These apps typically provide various color schemes, such as monochromatic (different shades of a single color), analogous (colors next to each other on the color wheel), complementary (colors opposite each other), and triadic (three colors equidistant on the color wheel). Additionally, advanced color combination apps may offer features such as color blindness simulation, which helps designers ensure their palettes are accessible to individuals with color vision deficiencies. Some apps even integrate machine learning algorithms to analyze color preferences and trends, providing personalized recommendations based on user input and current design practices.

Color Combination Resources

Color combination resources are tools or references used in the field of color theory and design to assist in selecting and creating aesthetically pleasing color combinations. These resources are essential for designers, artists, and professionals in various creative fields as they provide guidance and inspiration for selecting colors that work well together. In the realm of color theory, color combination resources help in understanding and implementing the principles of color harmony, balance, and contrast. They provide a wide range of color palettes, schemes, and variations that adhere to these principles. By utilizing these resources, designers can create color combinations that evoke different emotions, convey specific meanings, or cater to specific design goals. Color combination resources also account for the symbolism associated with different colors. The use of color symbolism in design allows designers to communicate and evoke specific emotions, concepts, or cultural references through color choices. For example, the color red may symbolize passion, power, or urgency, while blue may represent calmness, trust, or stability. By using color combination resources, designers can consider these symbolic meanings and create designs that effectively convey their intended message. These resources typically offer a wide range of color palettes pre-generated by experts or curated from various sources. They provide collections of colors that complement each other and can be used together harmoniously. Some resources may suggest monochromatic color schemes, where different shades and tints of a single color are used. Others may offer complementary color schemes, where colors that lie opposite each other on the color wheel are combined for maximum contrast. Additionally, resources may provide analogous color schemes, where colors that are adjacent to each other on the color wheel are utilized for a sense of harmony. Color combination resources can be found in various forms, such as color swatch libraries, color palette generators, or online platforms dedicated to sharing and exploring color combinations. They may also include tools and functionalities for adjusting color values, exploring color variations, or simulating color combinations in different design contexts. In summary, color combination resources are essential tools for designers and artists, as they provide guidance and inspiration for creating aesthetically pleasing and meaningful color combinations. By leveraging these resources, designers can effectively communicate their intended emotions, concepts, and messages through carefully selected and harmonious colors.

Color Combination Websites

Color combination websites are online platforms or tools that provide designers with a range of color combinations based on color theory and color symbolism. These websites are specifically designed to assist designers in selecting appropriate color schemes for their projects by offering a curated selection of color palettes. In the context of color theory, color combination websites take into consideration the principles of color harmony and balance. They provide a variety of color schemes that adhere to these principles, such as complementary, analogous, triadic, and monochromatic color schemes. By offering a wide array of pre-selected color combinations, designers can easily experiment with different harmonious color schemes without having to manually select and test each color individually. Moreover, color combination websites also consider the significance of color symbolism in design. Colors have the power to evoke certain emotions, convey specific messages, and create certain visual effects. These websites take into account the psychological impact of colors and offer a selection of color combinations that align with the intended message or atmosphere of the design project. By utilizing color combination websites, designers can save time and effort in the color selection process. These platforms provide a collection of color palettes that have been thoughtfully curated by experts and are ready to be used in various design contexts. Designers can easily browse through the available color combinations, select the ones that resonate with their design goals, and directly incorporate them into their projects. In conclusion, color combination websites play a vital role in the design process by providing designers with a curated selection of color palettes based on color theory and symbolism. These platforms save designers time and effort by offering a range of harmonious color schemes that align with the intended message or atmosphere of a design project. Utilizing color combination websites can greatly enhance the overall visual impact and effectiveness of a design.

Color Combination

Color Combination: Color combination refers to the arrangement or pairing of different colors in a design or artwork. It plays a crucial role in color theory and has a significant impact on the overall visual appeal and meaning conveyed by the design. Color combinations are an important aspect of graphic design, fashion design, interior design, and other creative fields. Color theory identifies various color combinations that can be used to achieve different visual effects and evoke specific emotions or messages. These combinations are based on principles such as color harmony, contrast, and symbolism. Understanding color combinations allows designers to create aesthetically pleasing and effective designs that resonate with their intended audience. Color harmony refers to the pleasing arrangement of colors that work well together. It is achieved by combining colors that are related or complementary to each other on the color wheel. Examples of color harmony include analogous colors (colors that are adjacent to each other on the color wheel), complementary colors (colors that are opposite to each other on the color wheel), and triadic colors (colors that are evenly spaced on the color wheel). Contrasting color combinations involve pairing colors that have a noticeable difference in hue, value, or saturation. This creates visual interest and can be used to draw attention to specific elements in a design. For example, using a combination of a bright color with a neutral color can create a bold and eye-catching design. Color symbolism also plays a role in color combination. Different colors have different associations and can convey specific meanings. For example, the combination of red and white is often associated with passion and purity, while the combination of blue and yellow is often associated with trust and happiness. Designers can utilize these symbolic associations to enhance the message or mood expressed by their designs.

Color Combinations

Color combinations refer to the various ways in which different colors can be used together in a harmonious or contrasting manner in design. In the context of color theory, color combinations are based on the principles of how colors interact and influence each other visually and emotionally. Color symbolism is an important aspect of design that explores the meaning and associations of different colors. Each color has its own symbolic connotations, and when combined with other colors, these symbolic meanings can be enhanced or altered. Understanding color combinations and their symbolism allows designers to convey specific messages and evoke certain emotions through their creations.

Color Combiners

A color combiner in the context of color theory and color symbolism in design refers to the process of blending two or more colors together to create a new color. It is an essential tool for designers and artists as it allows them to achieve the desired visual effects and convey specific meanings or emotions through their work. When combining colors, it is important to understand the principles of color theory, which include the primary, secondary, and tertiary colors, as well as their relationships on the color wheel. Primary colors, such as red, blue, and yellow, cannot be created by mixing other colors together. Secondary colors, such as purple, green, and orange, are created by combining two primary colors. Tertiary colors are formed by mixing a primary color with a neighboring secondary color. The choice of colors to combine is not random but is guided by the desired aesthetic or symbolic message. Each color has its own meaning and symbolism, which can vary across cultures and contexts. For example, red is often associated with passion, energy, and power, while blue symbolizes tranquility, trust, and reliability. Therefore, a designer may choose to combine these colors to create a visual representation of strength and stability. In addition to considering the symbolic meanings of colors, designers also need to take into account the color harmonies and contrasts. Color harmonies include complementary colors, which are opposite each other on the color wheel and create a vibrant contrast when combined. Analogous colors, on the other hand, are adjacent on the color wheel and create a harmonious and calming effect when used together. Designers can also experiment with other color schemes, such as monochromatic, split-complementary, or triadic, to achieve different visual effects. Overall, color combiners play a crucial role in the world of design as they enable creators to communicate their intended messages through the careful selection and blending of colors. By understanding the principles of color theory, symbolism, and harmonies, designers can effectively use color combinations to evoke emotions, convey meaning, and create visually appealing compositions.

Color Composition

Color composition refers to the deliberate arrangement and combination of colors in a design, based on principles of color theory and symbolism, to create visually harmonious and meaningful compositions. It involves the careful selection and positioning of colors to achieve a desired aesthetic, emotional, or psychological effect. Color composition plays a crucial role in the overall impact and message of a design, as colors have the power to evoke specific emotions, convey symbolism, and influence viewer perception. In color theory, color composition encompasses various principles and techniques that guide designers in selecting and combining colors effectively. Some of these principles include color harmony, color contrast, and color balance. Color harmony focuses on creating pleasing color combinations by using colors that are aesthetically complementary, such as analogous colors (colors that are adjacent on the color wheel) or complementary colors (colors that are opposite each other on the color wheel). Color contrast involves using colors that are different in terms of hue, value, or saturation to create visual interest and emphasize certain elements within a design. Color balance aims to distribute colors evenly throughout a composition to achieve a sense of equilibrium and prevent any one color from overpowering the others. In addition to color theory, color composition also considers the symbolic associations and cultural connotations of colors. Different colors carry different meanings and can evoke specific emotions or associations. For example, warm colors like red and orange are often associated with energy, passion, and excitement, while cool colors like blue and green are often associated with calmness, tranquility, and nature. Understanding color symbolism allows designers to use colors strategically to enhance the intended message or mood of a design. Furthermore, color composition can also take into account the psychological effects and physiological responses that certain colors elicit, such as the calming effect of blue or the stimulating effect of red.

Color Contrast Analysis Software

Color contrast analysis software is a tool that aids in the evaluation and assessment of the contrast between different colors used in design, taking into consideration color theory and symbolism. It is specifically designed to ensure that the chosen colors have sufficient contrast to meet accessibility guidelines and to enhance the overall effectiveness and impact of the design. Color theory is an important aspect of design that explores the relationships and interactions between colors. It helps designers understand how different colors affect each other, visually and psychologically. The choice of colors can evoke specific emotions, symbolize concepts, and create harmony or contrast within a design. In design, color contrast refers to the difference between two or more colors used together. It plays a crucial role in enhancing readability, legibility, and overall user experience. Insufficient contrast can make it difficult for users to distinguish between text and background, leading to accessibility issues for individuals with visual impairments. Color symbolism, on the other hand, adds an additional layer of meaning to the chosen colors. Different colors are associated with specific emotions, cultural references, or symbolic representations. For example, red is often associated with passion or danger, while blue may symbolize tranquility or trust. Understanding color symbolism can help designers effectively communicate their intended message or evoke desired responses from the audience. Color contrast analysis software simplifies the process of evaluating color contrast. It typically utilizes algorithms and color models, such as RGB or HSL, to calculate the contrast ratio between two colors. These algorithms take into account factors such as brightness, saturation, and hue to determine the level of contrast between the colors. By using color contrast analysis software, designers can ensure that their color choices adhere to accessibility guidelines, such as the Web Content Accessibility Guidelines (WCAG). These guidelines provide specific contrast ratio requirements to ensure that text can be easily read by individuals with varying levels of visual acuity. In conclusion, color contrast analysis software is a valuable tool for designers in evaluating and optimizing the contrast between colors used in design. It helps ensure accessibility, readability, and overall effectiveness of the design, while considering the principles of color theory and symbolism.

Color Contrast Analyzer Software

A Color Contrast Analyzer Software is a tool that is used in design to analyze and evaluate the contrast between different colors. It is based on color theory and symbolism, which are fundamental concepts in design. Color theory is the study and application of color in design and art. It involves understanding the properties of colors, such as hue, saturation, and brightness, as well as their relationships in the color wheel. Color theory helps designers create harmonious color combinations and create a visual hierarchy by using contrasting colors.

Color Contrast Analyzer Tools

Color contrast analyzer tools are essential resources used in the field of design to assess the level of contrast between different colors. They provide objective measurements and analysis of the contrast between foreground and background colors, aiding designers in creating visually balanced and harmonious compositions. In the realm of color theory, contrast refers to the variance between colors in terms of their lightness, darkness, and saturation. Color contrast is crucial in design as it ensures readability, legibility, and accessibility. Insufficient contrast can make it difficult for individuals with visual impairments or color vision deficiencies to perceive content, hindering their ability to navigate and interact with the design effectively. Moreover, color symbolism plays a significant role in design, where colors hold specific meanings and

31

associations. Different cultures and societies attribute unique interpretations to various colors, making color symbolism a powerful tool for designers to convey messages, evoke emotions, and communicate concepts. Color contrast analyzer tools assist designers in analyzing the contrast ratio between colors, allowing them to evaluate the readability and accessibility of their designs. These tools utilize algorithms and color models such as RGB (Red, Green, Blue) or L*a*b* (Lightness, a-axis, b-axis) to determine the contrast ratio between foreground and background colors. By inputting the color values of elements like text and backgrounds, designers can obtain precise measurements of the contrast ratio. The contrast ratio typically ranges from 1:1 (no contrast) to 21:1 (maximum contrast), with specific guidelines and regulations governing contrast accessibility for different applications. Analyzing the contrast ratio enables designers to adhere to accessibility standards, ensuring that their designs are inclusive and readable by as many individuals as possible. Additionally, these tools allow designers to experiment with various color combinations, helping them find the ideal contrast to convey the desired message, evoke appropriate emotions, and align with the intended symbolism. In conclusion, color contrast analyzer tools serve as valuable aids for designers in assessing and optimizing the contrast between colors in their designs. By ensuring sufficient contrast, designers can enhance the accessibility, readability, and overall impact of their creations, while also leveraging the power of color symbolism to effectively communicate messages and evoke emotions.

Color Contrast Analyzers

Color Contrast Analyzers are tools that are used in the field of design to measure the contrast between different colors. These tools help designers ensure that there is enough contrast between elements in their designs to make them visually distinguishable. In color theory, contrast refers to the difference in luminance or color between two or more elements. It is a fundamental principle in design as it helps create visual interest and enhance legibility. The use of contrast is especially important when it comes to text and other important elements in a design, as poor contrast can make it difficult for users to read or understand. Color Contrast Analyzers allow designers to analyze and evaluate the contrast between different colors in their designs. These tools typically measure the contrast ratio between two colors, which is a numeric value that represents the difference in brightness or hue. The higher the contrast ratio, the greater the difference between the colors. In the context of color symbolism in design, contrast can also play a role in conveying meaning and evoking emotions. Different colors have different symbolic associations and can elicit different responses from viewers. By using contrasting colors strategically, designers can create visual emphasis and help communicate the intended message more effectively. For example, using a bold, saturated color against a neutral background can attract attention and create a sense of importance or urgency. In contrast, using harmonious colors with similar hues can create a more calming and soothing effect. Color Contrast Analyzers can help designers ensure that their use of contrast aligns with the intended symbolism and message of their design. By providing objective measurements of color contrast, these tools can guide designers in making informed decisions about color choices and arrangements. In conclusion, Color Contrast Analyzers are important tools in the field of design that help measure and evaluate the contrast between different colors. They assist designers in creating visually appealing and readable designs, while also allowing for the strategic use of contrast to convey meaning and evoke emotions.

Color Contrast Analyzing Tools

The color contrast analyzing tools are tools used in the field of color theory and design to assess and evaluate the contrast between different colors in a design composition. These tools aid in determining the visual impact and legibility of the color combinations used, ensuring accessibility and effective communication of the design. In color theory, contrast refers to the difference in visual properties of colors. It plays a crucial role in design as it helps create emphasis, hierarchy, and organization in visual compositions. The use of contrasting colors can evoke certain emotions and messages, making them a powerful tool in design communication. However, not all color combinations yield the desired results, and that's where contrast analyzing tools come into play.

Color Contrast

Color contrast refers to the difference in hue, value, and saturation between two or more colors.

In the context of color theory, it is an important concept as it helps create visual interest, enhance readability, and communicate specific messages in design. In design, color contrast is used to ensure that the elements on a page or screen stand out and are easily distinguishable from one another. This can be achieved by using colors from opposite ends of the color wheel, such as complementary or analogous colors. Complementary colors, which are located directly opposite each other on the color wheel, provide the highest level of contrast. They bring out the best in each other, making each color appear more vibrant and intense. Analogous colors, on the other hand, are adjacent to each other on the color wheel and create a softer, more harmonious contrast. Color contrast is not only important in terms of aesthetics but also for accessibility purposes. The contrast between foreground and background colors is crucial in ensuring that text is legible, especially for individuals with visual impairments. This is particularly important when designing for digital platforms, where color contrast guidelines are often provided to meet accessibility standards. Additionally, color contrast can also carry symbolic meanings in design. Certain color combinations can evoke specific emotions or convey particular messages. For example, the contrast between black and white is often associated with clarity, simplicity, and sophistication. Similarly, the contrast between red and green is commonly used to indicate danger or caution. Designers can leverage these symbolic associations to enhance the visual impact and storytelling of their designs.

Color Conversion Charts

Color Conversion Charts are essential tools in color theory and color symbolism in design. These charts provide a systematic way to convert colors from one color space to another, allowing designers to accurately communicate and reproduce their vision across different mediums. Color theory serves as the foundation for understanding the interaction of colors and their psychological impact on the viewer. It explores the relationships between colors, their harmonies, and their perceived emotional and cultural associations. Color symbolism, on the other hand, delves deeper into the meanings and interpretations assigned to specific colors in different contexts and cultures. In design, the choice of color can greatly affect the overall message and visual impact of a project. However, various devices and mediums display colors differently, making it crucial for designers to accurately convert colors from one color space to another. This is where color conversion charts prove their significance. Color conversion charts typically include conversion formulas and numerical values that allow designers to translate colors between different color models, such as RGB (Red, Green, Blue), CMYK (Cyan, Magenta, Yellow, Key/Black), HSL (Hue, Saturation, Lightness), and HSV (Hue, Saturation, Value). By providing clear guidelines, these charts enable designers to maintain consistency and accuracy in reproducing colors across various platforms, such as digital screens, print media, and even fabrics. Moreover, color conversion charts assist designers in understanding the visual effects of color harmonies and contrasts. For instance, they can help determine complementary colors, which lie opposite to each other on the color wheel and create a vibrant contrast. Analogous colors, which are adjacent to each other on the color wheel, can also be identified using these charts. This knowledge allows designers to create visually appealing and balanced compositions by utilizing the full potential of color relationships. In summary, color conversion charts play a crucial role in color theory and color symbolism in design. They provide designers with the necessary tools to convert colors accurately between different color models, ensuring consistency and effectiveness across various mediums. Additionally, these charts assist in the exploration of color harmonies and contrasts, enabling designers to create visually captivating and meaningful compositions.

Color Conversion Guides

Color conversion guides are tools or resources that provide assistance in converting colors between different color models, enabling designers to effectively communicate their desired color choices across various platforms and media. In the realm of color theory, color conversion guides serve as essential references to help designers understand and navigate the intricacies of color representation. They allow designers to seamlessly translate colors from one color model to another, such as converting RGB (Red, Green, Blue) values to CMYK (Cyan, Magenta, Yellow, Black) values. By providing the corresponding values for each color model, these guides ensure consistency and accuracy in color reproduction across different types of devices and printing processes. Beyond color theory, color conversion guides also play a significant role in the realm of color symbolism within design. Different colors carry various meanings and associations, evoking specific emotions and perceptions in viewers. When designing for different cultures, industries, or purposes, it is crucial to understand the intended symbolism behind colors and ensure that they are accurately conveyed. Color conversion guides aid designers in translating symbolic colors from one color model to another without losing their intended connotations. For example, if a designer wants to ensure that a particular shade of blue, representing trust and loyalty, is consistently perceived across different mediums, they can refer to a color conversion guide to convert the RGB values to CMYK or hexadecimal values. This way, the intended symbolism behind the color remains intact, regardless of the output medium. Overall, color conversion guides serve as indispensable tools for both understanding the technical aspects of color representation and maintaining the symbolic meaning of colors within design. These guides enable designers to communicate their color choices effectively and consistently, ensuring that their designs accurately reflect their intentions and resonate with the intended audience.

Color Conversion Software

Color conversion software is a computer program designed to facilitate the transformation of colors between different color models or color spaces. In the context of color theory and color symbolism in design, color conversion software plays a crucial role in ensuring accurate color representation and communication. Color theory is the study of how colors interact and influence each other. It is a fundamental aspect of design as it helps designers create visually appealing and harmonious compositions. Color symbolism, on the other hand, refers to the use of specific colors to convey certain meanings or emotions. Understanding and using color theory and color symbolism effectively can greatly enhance the visual impact and overall message of a design. Color conversion software allows designers to convert colors from one color model or color space to another. The RGB (Red, Green, Blue) color model is commonly used in digital design, while the CMYK (Cyan, Magenta, Yellow, Key) color model is widely used in print design. Additionally, there are other color models or color spaces, such as HSB (Hue, Saturation, Brightness), LAB (Lightness, Green-Red, Blue-Yellow), and Pantone, which are used in specific contexts or industries. By using color conversion software, designers can accurately convert colors between different color models or color spaces, ensuring consistency and accuracy when translating digital designs to print or when working with different devices or software that use different color models. This is particularly important because different color models have different color gamuts, which determine the range of colors that can be represented. Furthermore, color conversion software allows designers to explore various color combinations and harmonies by providing tools to manipulate and adjust colors easily. Designers can experiment with different color schemes, such as complementary, analogous, or triadic, to create visually pleasing and meaningful designs that effectively communicate the intended message or evoke specific emotions. In conclusion, color conversion software is an essential tool for designers, enabling them to convert colors between different color models or color spaces accurately. It helps ensure consistent color representation across various mediums and devices and allows designers to explore and utilize color theories and symbolism effectively in their designs.

Color Conversion Tools

A Color Conversion Tool is a tool used in color theory and design to convert colors from one color model to another. It allows designers to translate colors between different color systems, such as RGB (Red, Green, Blue), CMYK (Cyan, Magenta, Yellow, Key), HSL (Hue, Saturation, Lightness), and HEX (Hexadecimal). Color theory is the study of how colors interact and how they can be combined to create visually pleasing designs. Understanding color models and their conversions is essential for effective color selection and communication. Different color models serve different purposes, and a color conversion tool helps designers translate colors accurately between these models. In design, colors carry symbolic meanings that can evoke emotions, set moods, and convey messages. For example, red often represents passion and excitement, while blue is associated with calmness and tranquility. The ability to convert colors allows designers to explore various color options and select the most appropriate hues for their intended purposes. With a color conversion tool, designers can ensure consistency across different media types, such as print and digital. Since color models have different gamuts (ranges of available colors), conversions are necessary to maintain color accuracy when transitioning between mediums. For example, a color that appears vibrant on a computer screen may appear dull when printed on paper. By converting colors from RGB to CMYK, designers can ensure that the printed output matches their digital design. In summary, a Color Conversion Tool is a valuable resource for designers working with colors. It enables the conversion of colors between different color models, facilitating effective color selection and communication. By using a color conversion tool, designers can maintain color consistency across various media types and explore different symbolic meanings in their designs.

Color Conversion Websites

Color conversion websites are online tools or platforms that facilitate the process of converting colors between different color models or systems. In the context of color theory and color symbolism in design, these websites are valuable resources for designers and artists to ensure accurate and consistent color representation across various mediums and devices. Color theory is the study of how colors interact, harmonize, and convey different emotions or meanings. It encompasses concepts such as color models, color mixing, and color symbolism. Different color models, such as RGB (Red, Green, Blue), CMYK (Cyan, Magenta, Yellow, Black), and HSL/HSV (Hue, Saturation, Lightness/Value), represent colors in different ways, and each model has its own advantages and limitations. Color conversion websites allow designers to seamlessly convert colors between these different models. For example, if a designer is working on an RGB-based design but needs to have the colors printed using the CMYK model, they can use a color conversion website to accurately convert the RGB values to CMYK values, ensuring that the printed colors closely match the intended design. In addition to facilitating technical color conversions, these websites also aid in exploring and understanding color symbolism. Color symbolism refers to the emotions, moods, and meanings associated with different colors in various cultures and contexts. Designers often use color symbolism to evoke specific reactions or convey certain messages through their designs. Color conversion websites often provide comprehensive color palettes, color schemes, and color symbolism guides. These resources help designers effectively select and utilize colors that align with the desired mood, message, or brand identity of their designs. By exploring these websites, designers can discover the cultural or psychological associations linked to specific colors, allowing them to make informed decisions that enhance the overall impact and meaning of their designs.

Color Converters

A color converter, in the context of color theory and color symbolism in design, refers to a tool or process that allows for the transformation of colors between different color models or color spaces. The goal of color conversion is to accurately represent a color in a different color model, ensuring consistent and harmonious color choices in various design applications. Color theory, the study of color relationships and their impact on human perception, plays a crucial role in design. Different color models, such as RGB (Red, Green, Blue) or CMYK (Cyan, Magenta, Yellow, Key/Black), are used to define and represent colors in digital and print media. However, these color models may not always be compatible or suitable for a particular design project. The use of a color converter allows designers to seamlessly convert colors from one color model to another, ensuring consistency and accuracy across different devices and mediums. For example, if a design project requires colors to be printed in CMYK, but the initial color choices were made in RGB, a color converter can transform the RGB values to their corresponding CMYK equivalents, minimizing any color discrepancies between the digital and print versions of the design. In addition to translating colors between different color models, color converters can also be used to convert colors to their corresponding color harmonies or color symbolism schemes. Color symbolism refers to the meanings and associations assigned to different colors, and it is often used in design to convey specific messages or evoke particular emotions. By using a color converter that incorporates color symbolism, designers can select colors that align with the intended message or atmosphere of a design. For example, if a design project aims to create a calming and soothing environment, a color converter with color symbolism capabilities can suggest or convert colors associated with tranquility and serenity, such as cool blues and soft greens.

Color Coordination

Color coordination refers to the deliberate arrangement of colors in design to create visual harmony and convey specific meanings or emotions. It is an essential aspect of color theory and color symbolism, two underlying principles that guide the effective use of color in various design disciplines. Color theory, based on the study of the color wheel, explores the relationships between different colors and their effects on human perception. It provides guidelines for combining and contrasting colors in ways that are visually pleasing and engaging. Color coordination, therefore, involves utilizing these principles to create harmonious color schemes that resonate with the intended message or mood of the design.

Color Correction

Color correction is a technique used in design and color theory to adjust and enhance the colors of an image or design to achieve a desired color balance, visual appearance, or symbolic representation. It involves altering the tones, hues, saturation, and brightness of the colors to create a more visually appealing and harmonious composition. In the context of color theory, color correction plays a crucial role in achieving the desired emotional or psychological impact of a design. Colors have the ability to evoke specific emotions and convey symbolic meanings. Different colors have varying connotations and associations, and color correction allows designers to manipulate these characteristics to effectively communicate their intended message.

Color Depth

Color depth refers to the number of distinct colors that can be displayed or represented in an image, graphics display system, or computer screen. It is an important concept in color theory and plays a significant role in color symbolism in design. Color depth is typically measured in bits, which determines the maximum number of possible colors. For example, a color depth of 8 bits allows for 2^8 or 256 different colors, while a color depth of 24 bits allows for 2^{24} or over 16 million colors. The higher the color depth, the more realistic and vibrant the images or graphics can appear.

Color Exploration Apps

Color exploration apps are digital tools that facilitate the exploration and study of color theory and color symbolism in design. These apps are designed to provide users with a platform for experimenting with different color combinations, understanding the psychological effects of colors, and creating harmonious color palettes. Color theory is a study of how colors interact with each other and how they are perceived by the human eye. It is a fundamental concept in design that helps in creating visually appealing and effective compositions. Color exploration apps enable users to experiment with different color combinations by providing them with a range of color options and tools to mix and match colors. Users can explore various color schemes such as complementary, analogous, triadic, and monochromatic, and understand how different colors interact and create visual harmony. In addition to exploring color combinations, color exploration apps also allow users to study the psychological effects of colors. Colors have the power to evoke emotions, influence moods, and convey messages. For example, red is often associated with passion and energy, while blue is associated with calmness and trust. These apps provide information on the symbolism and cultural significance of different colors, helping users make informed choices in their design projects. Furthermore, color exploration apps can assist designers in creating harmonious color palettes. A color palette is a selection of colors that are used consistently in a design project to create a cohesive visual identity. These apps offer features such as color scheme generators, color wheel tools, and color harmonies to assist users in creating balanced and aesthetically pleasing palettes. By exploring different color combinations and understanding color relationships, designers can create harmonious and impactful designs. Overall, color exploration apps serve as valuable tools for designers and artists to study and experiment with colors. They provide a platform for understanding color theory, exploring color symbolism, and creating harmonious color palettes. By utilizing these apps, designers can enhance their understanding of the visual language of colors and create visually compelling designs that effectively communicate their intended messages.

Color Exploration Tools

Color Exploration Tools refer to a set of resources and techniques used in the field of color theory and design to analyze, experiment with, and understand the various aspects and potential applications of colors. These tools provide designers with a systematic approach to selecting and combining colors for their creative projects, be it graphic design, web design, interior design, or any other artistic endeavor that involves the use of color. In the realm of color theory, color exploration tools help designers explore and comprehend the visual properties and characteristics of colors. They enable designers to examine different color palettes, combinations, and variations, allowing them to understand how colors interact with one another and how they can create certain visual effects and moods. These tools often include color wheels, color charts, and color matching systems, which aid in selecting harmonious color schemes, identifying complementary colors, and exploring color relationships such as analogous and triadic color schemes. Furthermore, color exploration tools also play a crucial role in understanding and utilizing color symbolism in design. Colors carry symbolic meanings and emotions that can evoke particular feelings and associations. For instance, red may represent passion and energy, while blue may convey calmness and trust. By using color exploration tools, designers can delve into the symbolism behind different colors and choose colors that align with the intended message or branding of their designs. These tools allow designers to experiment with different color combinations and see how they affect the overall perception and interpretation of their designs. In conclusion, color exploration tools offer designers a systematic and analytical approach to understand, experiment with, and utilize colors effectively in their designs. These tools help designers analyze color properties, select harmonious color schemes, and explore the symbolism and emotional impact of colors. By employing color exploration tools, designers can create visually pleasing and emotionally resonant designs that effectively communicate their intended message.

Color Exploration Websites

Color exploration websites are online platforms that allow users to explore, learn about, and experiment with different colors in the context of color theory and color symbolism in design. These websites provide a range of tools and resources to help users better understand the impact and meaning of colors in various design disciplines. In the field of color theory, these websites offer interactive color wheels or palettes that allow users to analyze and visualize color relationships, such as complementary, analogous, or monochromatic colors. Users can experiment with these color combinations to gain a deeper understanding of how different colors interact with each other and how they can be used to create visually harmonious or contrasting designs. Through these tools, users can also learn about color harmonies and the different emotions and moods that different color combinations can evoke. Color exploration websites also provide resources and information about color symbolism in design. They may include libraries or databases of color meanings and associations, allowing users to explore how different cultures, industries, or contexts interpret and use colors in symbolic ways. By understanding these associations, designers can make informed color choices that align with the intended messages and goals of their projects. Furthermore, these websites often showcase real-world examples of color usage in design, such as website designs, logo designs, or branding campaigns. By examining these examples, users can gain inspiration and insights into how colors are effectively used to communicate specific messages or represent certain values in different design contexts. Additionally, these websites may offer tutorials, articles, or case studies that provide further guidance and knowledge on color usage in design.

Color Extraction Applications

Color extraction applications refer to software programs or tools that analyze images or design elements to identify and extract specific colors present within them. These applications play a significant role in color theory and color symbolism in design, as they enable designers to select and work with particular colors in their creative process. In color theory, color extraction applications assist in understanding and applying the principles of how colors interact with one another. By extracting the colors used in images or designs, these applications facilitate the creation of aesthetically pleasing and harmonious color palettes. Designers can analyze the extracted colors to determine their relationships, such as complementary, analogous, or triadic, and use this knowledge to create visually balanced compositions. Moreover, color extraction applications are also valuable when considering color symbolism in design. Colors carry symbolic meanings and can evoke emotions and attitudes in viewers. By extracting the colors from images, illustrations, or other visual elements, designers can ensure that the chosen colors align with the intended message or concept. They can evaluate the extracted colors' symbolism

37

and make informed decisions regarding their inclusion or exclusion in the final design. These applications often provide additional features that allow designers to modify and refine the extracted colors. For example, they may offer options to adjust the brightness, saturation, or contrast of the extracted colors, enabling designers to fine-tune the desired aesthetic or symbolic qualities. Overall, color extraction applications serve as indispensable tools for designers, enabling them to analyze, extract, and manipulate colors to create visually appealing and conceptually relevant designs. By incorporating the principles of color theory and color symbolism, designers can effectively communicate their intended messages and elicit desired emotional responses from their audience.

Color Extraction Software

Color extraction software refers to a specialized tool used in the field of color theory and color symbolism in design. It is a computer program that is designed to analyze digital images and extract the colors present within those images. This software helps designers and artists identify and collect specific colors they want to use in their creative works. Color theory is a field that explores the principles and effects of color in various artistic contexts. It examines how colors interact with each other and how they can be used to create particular moods, convey symbolism, and enhance visual experiences. Understanding color theory is crucial for designers as it helps them make informed decisions about color combinations, contrasts, and harmonies in their designs. Color symbolism, on the other hand, deals with the interpretation and meaning associated with different colors. Colors can communicate specific messages and evoke certain emotions or cultural associations. For example, red is often associated with passion and power, while blue is commonly linked to calmness and trust. Designers often use color symbolism to evoke desired responses from their audience. Color extraction software plays a significant role in color theory and color symbolism in design by simplifying the process of identifying and collecting colors from images. This software uses advanced algorithms to analyze the pixel data of an image and identify the dominant and complementary colors present in it. Designers can use color extraction software to create color palettes for their projects. By extracting and collecting the colors present in an image, they can build a harmonious and cohesive color scheme that aligns with their intended message or theme. This helps designers save time and effort in manually sampling and selecting colors. In addition to aiding designers, color extraction software also offers benefits for marketers, advertisers, and brand strategists. They can use this software to extract colors from competitor logos, advertisements, or product images, helping them gain insights into their competitors' color choices and strategies. This information can then be leveraged to develop unique and differentiated color schemes for their own branding and marketing efforts.

Color Extraction Tools

Color extraction tools are software or algorithms that analyze digital images and extract the dominant or representative colors present in the image. In the context of color theory and color symbolism in design, these tools are used to identify and extract key colors from an image, which can then be applied in various design applications. Color theory is the study of how colors interact, blend, and evoke emotions. It is an essential aspect of designing visuals, as colors have the power to influence how a viewer perceives an image or design. Understanding color theory helps designers create visually appealing and harmonious compositions. Color symbolism, on the other hand, refers to the use of colors to convey meanings and emotions. Different colors are associated with specific emotions and concepts, and designers often utilize these associations to enhance the message or purpose of their design. Color extraction tools play a crucial role in these areas by providing designers with a convenient and efficient way to identify colors from images. These tools analyze the pixels in an image, determine the most frequently occurring or dominant colors, and present them in a format that can be easily used in design applications. By using color extraction tools, designers can extract the primary colors from an image and use them as a starting point for their design. These extracted colors can serve as a color palette that captures the overall mood and atmosphere of the image. Designers can then build upon these colors to create a cohesive and visually engaging design. Furthermore, color extraction tools can also help designers in understanding the color relationships within an image. By analyzing the extracted colors and their distribution, designers can gain insights into the color proportions and combinations used in the original image. This information can guide their color choices in creating harmonious and balanced designs. In conclusion, color extraction tools are invaluable assets for designers working with color theory and color symbolism. These tools enable designers to extract the dominant colors from an image, providing them with a starting point for their design process and facilitating the creation of visually appealing and meaningful designs.

Color Extraction Utilities

Color extraction utilities in the context of color theory and color symbolism in design refer to software or tools that help extract or identify colors used in various visual elements such as images, logos, or webpages. These utilities are designed to capture the specific colors within an image or design, providing users with essential information about the color's attributes, such as its RGB or HEX values. Color plays a crucial role in design as it can evoke emotions, convey meanings, and create visual harmony or contrast. By understanding the colors used in a design, designers can make informed decisions about color combinations, ensuring that the overall aesthetic and message align with the intended goal. Color extraction utilities enable designers to simplify the process of identifying and working with specific colors. They save time and effort by automatically detecting and providing information about the colors present, eliminating the need for manual color sampling or guesswork. Designers can utilize these utilities to analyze existing designs, identify color palettes, or extract colors for future use or reference. In the field of color theory, these extraction utilities facilitate the exploration and application of specific color schemes. For example, a designer may want to explore the analogous colors used in a photograph, or identify the complementary colors that create visual contrast. By utilizing color extraction utilities, designers can extract the relevant colors and apply them to their own designs to achieve desired visual effects. Furthermore, color symbolism encompasses the cultural and psychological associations assigned to specific colors. Different cultures or contexts perceive colors differently, and certain colors may evoke specific emotions or convey particular meanings. Color extraction utilities assist in identifying these symbolic colors, enabling designers to align their designs with the intended message or cultural context. Overall, color extraction utilities serve as valuable tools in the design process, helping designers analyze and replicate colors used in existing designs, explore and apply color schemes, and understand the symbolic significance of different colors. By utilizing these utilities, designers can create visually appealing and meaningful designs that effectively communicate their intended messages.

Color Extractor Software

A color extractor software is a tool used in the field of design and color theory to extract and analyze colors from various sources such as images, websites, or documents. It helps designers and artists to identify and utilize specific color palettes for their projects, considering both the aesthetic and symbolic aspects of colors. In the realm of color theory, colors are not just visual elements but also carriers of meaning and symbolism. Different colors evoke various emotions, convey messages, and have cultural or personal associations. For designers, understanding the symbolic significance of colors is vital as it allows them to create visual communication in a more intentional and effective way. The color extractor software plays a pivotal role in this process by providing an efficient means of color analysis. By using advanced algorithms, it can accurately identify and extract colors from different sources, breaking them down into their individual components such as hue, saturation, and brightness. This information is crucial for designers to recreate and work with specific color schemes. One of the essential aspects of design is choosing colors that align with the intended message or purpose of a project. Color symbolism significantly contributes to this decision-making process. For example, red can symbolize passion, love, or danger, while blue can convey serenity or sadness. By analyzing colors and their symbolism, designers can make informed choices that enhance the visual impact and strengthen the intended message of their work. In addition to color symbolism, the color extractor software aids in creating harmonious color combinations. The tool can generate complementary, analogous, or monochromatic color schemes based on the extracted colors. Harmonious color schemes help convey a sense of unity and balance in design and can greatly enhance the overall aesthetic appeal. Overall, a color extractor software is a valuable tool for designers and artists in analyzing and utilizing colors effectively. By understanding color theory and symbolism, it allows for intentional color choices that align with the intended message, evoke emotions, and create visually captivating designs.

Color Extractors

A color extractor is a tool or software that enables the extraction of color information from various sources such as images, websites, or digital designs. In the context of color theory and color symbolism in design, color extractors play a crucial role in understanding the visual aspects and emotional impact of colors. Color theory refers to the principles and guidelines that govern the use and combination of colors. It helps designers create harmonious and aesthetically pleasing compositions. By extracting colors from different sources, color extractors provide designers with a starting point for choosing a color palette that matches their design objectives. Color symbolism, on the other hand, is the use of specific colors to convey certain meanings or evoke particular emotions. Color extractors assist designers in identifying the dominant colors present in an image or design, enabling them to align the color choices with the intended symbolism. With the help of color extractors, designers can effortlessly analyze images or designs by determining the RGB or hexadecimal values of specific colors. These tools allow for quick identification of primary, secondary, and accent colors, providing designers with valuable insight into the overall color schemes. In design, colors evoke emotions and create moods. For example, warm colors like red and orange tend to convey energy, passion, and excitement, while cool colors like blue and green evoke feelings of calmness and serenity. Using a color extractor, designers can identify the dominant colors and choose the appropriate color palette to achieve the desired emotional impact. Moreover, color extractors also facilitate the creation of complementary and analogous color schemes. Complementary colors are located opposite each other on the color wheel and create a vibrant and dynamic contrast when used together. Analogous colors, on the other hand, are adjacent to each other on the color wheel and create a harmonious and cohesive composition. In conclusion, color extractors are indispensable tools for designers in the realm of color theory and color symbolism. By extracting color information from various sources, they enable designers to make informed decisions regarding color choices, harmonies, and the emotional impact of their designs. These tools facilitate the creation of visually appealing compositions and help convey the desired messages or meanings through the strategic use of color.

Color Fan Collections

Color fan collections refer to a curated set of color swatches or samples that are organized in a fan-like format. These collections are commonly used in the fields of color theory and design, serving as a practical tool for color selection and representation. In the realm of color theory, color fan collections aid in understanding and applying the principles of color harmonies, such as complementary, analogous, and triadic color schemes. By providing a comprehensive range of colors, these collections allow designers to explore various color combinations and make informed decisions based on the desired mood or message of their design. Color symbolism, on the other hand, involves the use of specific colors to convey certain meanings or evoke particular emotions. Color fan collections help designers identify and utilize colors that align with the intended symbolism of their design. For example, warm tones like red and orange may be chosen to evoke passion or energy, while cool blues and greens may be used to create a sense of calmness or tranquility. Color fans typically consist of individual color swatches that are attached or bound together at one end, allowing them to be easily flipped through or fanned out. Each swatch is labeled with the corresponding color name or code, enabling designers to accurately communicate their color choices with others involved in the design process. These collections often come in a variety of themes or color systems, including Pantone, CMYK, RGB, and more. They can be purchased commercially or created by designers themselves, depending on their specific needs and preferences. Overall, color fan collections are a valuable resource for designers, providing them with a tangible and organized way to explore, select, and communicate colors for their projects. By understanding the principles of color theory and incorporating color symbolism, designers can effectively utilize color fan collections to create visually appealing and emotionally impactful designs.

Color Fan Decks For Reference

Color fan decks are physical tools used in color theory and design to provide a comprehensive reference of colors and their symbolic meanings. These decks typically consist of a collection of color swatches arranged in a systematic order. In color theory, color fan decks serve as a visual representation of the color spectrum, helping designers and artists to identify and compare different hues, shades, and tints. The deck usually organizes colors in a logical progression, such as by hue, saturation, or value. By examining the swatches in a fan deck, individuals can easily observe the relationships between colors and make informed decisions about color combinations and contrasts in their design work. Beyond its use in color theory, color fan decks also play a crucial role in understanding color symbolism. Colors carry symbolic meanings that vary across different cultures and contexts. The fan decks provide a condensed resource for designers to grasp these symbolic associations and incorporate them into their designs. For example, certain colors may evoke specific emotions or convey particular messages. Red, often associated with passion and power, can create a sense of urgency or excitement. Blue, on the other hand, is commonly linked to calmness and trust, making it suitable for conveying stability and reliability. By referencing a color fan deck, designers can select hues that align with their intended emotional or symbolic goals. Moreover, color fan decks help designers maintain consistency in their color choices. By referring to a set of predefined colors, designers can create a unified color palette that enhances overall visual harmony and brand recognition. In addition, the fan decks often provide tips and guidelines for color usage, aiding designers in making informed decisions regarding color combinations, contrasts, and harmonies. In conclusion, color fan decks are invaluable tools in color theory and design. Not only do they provide a visual reference for exploring the color spectrum, but they also serve as a guide for understanding the symbolic meanings and emotional associations of various colors. By utilizing these decks, designers can make informed decisions about color choices, maintain consistency, and effectively communicate their intended messages through their designs.

Color Fan Decks

A color fan deck is a collection of individual color samples arranged in a sequential manner, typically organized by a color system or model such as the Pantone Matching System (PMS) or the Munsell Color System. Each color sample is represented by a small, rectangular chip, allowing designers, artists, or anyone working with colors to have a physical representation of the colors within a particular color system. Color fan decks are commonly used in color theory and design to aid in the selection and coordination of colors. They provide a reliable and consistent reference for accurately communicating color choices and harmonizing color schemes. By utilizing a color fan deck, designers can easily compare and contrast different color options, ensuring accurate color matching and enhancing their understanding of color relationships.

Color Forecasting

Color forecasting is a process within the field of color theory and design that involves the prediction and analysis of emerging color trends and their symbolic meanings. It aims to predict the colors that will be popular and relevant in future design, fashion, and consumer products. This process helps designers, marketers, and manufacturers make informed decisions about color palettes and product development. Color forecasting is based on a deep understanding of color theory and psychology, as well as an awareness of cultural, social, and technological influences. It takes into consideration the evolving tastes, preferences, and lifestyles of consumers, as well as the broader socio-cultural and economic trends shaping society. By analyzing these factors, color forecasters can identify emerging color trends and predict their impact on design and consumer behavior.

Color Gamut

A color gamut refers to the range of colors that can be produced by a given device or medium, such as a display, printer, or paint set. It represents the full spectrum of colors that can be perceived by the human eye within the constraints of a particular system. In the field of color theory, understanding and working with color gamuts is essential for designers and artists. It allows them to predict how colors will appear in different contexts and mediums, and to make informed decisions about color choices and combinations.

Color Generators

A color generator in the context of color theory and color symbolism in design refers to a tool or system that aids in the creation or selection of colors. These generators can be digital or physical, and they provide designers with a range of colors to choose from or help them generate new color combinations. Color generators are based on the principles of color theory, which involve understanding the relationships between colors and how they interact with one another. They take into account concepts such as color harmony, contrast, and the psychological effects of colors to assist designers in creating visually appealing and effective color palettes.

Color Gradient Generator Software

A color gradient generator software is a tool used in the context of color theory and color symbolism in design. It allows users to create smooth transitions between two or more colors, commonly referred to as color gradients or color ramps. Color theory is the study of how colors interact with each other and how they are perceived by the human eye. It plays a crucial role in various design fields, including graphic design, web design, and visual arts. Understanding color theory helps designers create visually appealing compositions that evoke certain emotions and convey specific messages. Color symbolism, on the other hand, refers to the cultural and emotional associations tied to different colors. For example, red is often associated with passion, love, or anger, while blue may symbolize trust, calmness, or sadness. Designers often use color symbolism strategically to enhance the visual impact and effectively communicate the intended message of their designs. A color gradient generator software assists designers by providing a user-friendly interface to create color gradients. These gradients can be customized to suit specific design needs, such as creating a smooth transition between two complementary colors or simulating a lighting effect. The software typically allows users to select colors from a wide range of color models, including RGB (red, green, blue), CMYK (cyan, magenta, yellow, black), or HSL (hue, saturation, lightness). Once the colors are chosen, the software calculates and generates the intermediate colors between the selected endpoints to create a visually pleasing gradient. The generated gradient can then be applied to various design elements, such as backgrounds, text, or shapes, to add depth, visual interest, and convey specific emotions or messages. By providing designers with the ability to experiment with different color combinations and gradients, a color gradient generator software facilitates the creative process and empowers designers to effectively apply color theory and symbolism in their designs. Whether it's creating a calming atmosphere for a website or evoking a sense of energy in a logo, the software enables designers to harness the power of color gradients to create visually compelling and emotionally resonant designs.

Color Gradient Generator Tools

A color gradient generator tool is a software or online application that allows designers to create custom color gradients for use in various design projects. Color gradients are created by transitioning smoothly between two or more colors, resulting in a visually pleasing and harmonious effect. In the context of color theory, color gradients are often used to add depth, dimension, and visual interest to designs. They can be used to create a sense of movement or transition, as well as convey emotions and moods. The choice of colors in a gradient can greatly impact the overall aesthetic and meaning of a design. Color symbolism is the use of specific colors to represent ideas, emotions, or concepts. Different colors are often associated with specific meanings or feelings. For example, red is commonly associated with passion or danger, while blue is often associated with calmness or trust. When using color gradients, designers can leverage these color associations to enhance the intended message or symbolism of their designs. Color gradient generator tools provide a convenient and efficient way for designers to experiment with different color combinations and create custom gradients that align with their design goals. These tools typically offer a range of options and controls, such as choosing the number of colors in the gradient, adjusting the hue, saturation, and brightness levels, and controlling the gradient direction. By allowing designers to easily experiment with different color combinations and variations, color gradient generator tools empower them to create unique and visually engaging designs. These tools save time and effort, as designers no longer need to manually create gradients or guess the desired color mixtures. In conclusion, color gradient generator tools are essential for designers looking to incorporate visually appealing and meaningful color gradients into their designs. These tools enable the exploration of color theory and symbolism, helping designers create impactful and aesthetically pleasing designs.

Color Gradient Generators

Color gradient generators are tools used in color theory and design to create smooth transitions between two or more colors. They are essential for creating visually appealing designs and applying color symbolism. In color theory, a gradient is a gradual transition from one color to another. It can be implemented in various ways, such as a linear gradient, radial gradient, or angular gradient. A linear gradient consists of a straight transition between colors, while a radial gradient creates a circular or elliptical transition. An angular gradient allows for a smooth transition in a specific direction. Color symbolism refers to the use of colors to convey specific meanings or emotions in design. Different colors can evoke different feelings and have symbolic associations. For example, red can represent passion or danger, while blue can symbolize tranquility or sadness. By utilizing color gradients, designers can enhance these symbolic meanings by manipulating the intensity or hue of the colors used. Color gradient generators provide an efficient and user-friendly way to create custom gradients. They offer options to choose the starting and ending colors, as well as additional colors if desired. These tools also allow users to adjust the gradient type (e.g., linear, radial) and direction (e.g., top to bottom, left to right). Some advanced generators even provide the ability to fine-tune the gradient by adjusting specific color stops or adding multiple color stops. The generated gradients can be used in a variety of design applications. In web design, they can be applied to backgrounds, buttons, or text to add depth and visual interest to the layout. Graphic designers can utilize gradients in logos, illustrations, or advertisements to create eye-catching and dynamic visuals. Additionally, gradients can be employed in multimedia projects, such as videos or animations, to enhance the overall visual experience. In conclusion, color gradient generators are valuable tools in the field of color theory and design. By allowing users to easily create smooth transitions between colors, these tools enable designers to apply color symbolism effectively in their work. Whether used for web design, graphic design, or multimedia projects, gradients can elevate the visual impact of a design and evoke specific emotions or meanings.

Color Gradients Generators

Color gradient generators are tools used in color theory and design to create and visualize color gradients. A gradient is a gradual transition from one color to another, resulting in a smooth blend of hues. In design, gradients can be used to add depth, visual interest, and convey meaning to a composition. They hold significance in enhancing the overall aesthetic appeal and conveying specific emotions or messages through the use of color symbolism. Color theory plays a crucial role in understanding the impact of color gradients. It is the study of colors and their relationships, focusing on their perceptual and psychological effects. Different colors evoke different emotions, and when combined in a gradient, they can create a harmonious or contrasting effect. Using color gradients effectively requires a deep understanding of color theory to convey the desired visual language. Symbolism in design further amplifies the significance of color gradients. Colors have long been associated with various meanings and emotions, and these associations differ across cultures. By strategically selecting colors within a gradient, designers can tap into these symbolic associations to evoke specific emotions or convey particular messages. For example, warm colors like red and orange can evoke feelings of passion, energy, and excitement. Conversely, cool colors like blue and green can represent calmness, tranquility, and nature. By blending these colors in a gradient, designers can create a visual representation of a transition between these emotions or concepts. Color gradient generators simplify the process of creating gradients by providing intuitive interfaces and options for customization. These tools typically allow users to select the starting and ending colors, the number of colors in between, and the type of gradient (linear, radial, etc.). They then generate the corresponding gradient, providing the user with the hexadecimal or RGB values for each color in the gradient. This allows designers to easily incorporate gradients into their projects without the need for manual color blending. In conclusion, color gradient generators are essential tools in color theory and design that enable designers to create visually appealing and meaningful gradients. By utilizing these generators, designers can effectively leverage the principles of color theory and symbolism to evoke specific emotions, convey messages, and enhance the overall aesthetic quality of their designs.

Color Gradients

Color gradients, in the context of color theory and color symbolism in design, refer to a gradual transition of colors from one to another, creating a smooth progression of hues. They are often used to evoke certain emotions or convey specific messages in visual compositions. Gradients are created by blending two or more colors together, usually starting with one color and gradually transitioning to another. The gradual change in color can be achieved through various techniques, such as blending, shading, or overlaying different shades. This technique allows designers to create visual depth and dimension in their work, making it more engaging and dynamic. In color theory, gradients can be used to explore the relationships between different colors on the color wheel. They can be created using analogous colors, which are adjacent on the color wheel and provide a harmonious transition. Gradients can also be made with complementary colors, which are opposite on the color wheel and create a strong visual contrast. By carefully selecting the colors for a gradient, designers can achieve different effects and communicate different moods or messages. Color symbolism plays a significant role in design, as different colors are associated with specific meanings or emotions. Gradients can be used to enhance and amplify these symbolic associations. For example, a gradient that transitions from warm colors, such as red or orange, to cool colors, such as blue or green, can evoke a sense of transition or change. On the other hand, a gradient that transitions from dark colors to light colors can create a sense of depth or emphasize a light source. Gradients can also be used to create a sense of movement or energy in a design. A gradient that transitions from a vibrant color to a more subdued hue can create a visual flow or dynamic tension. Additionally, gradients can be used to guide the viewer's eye and create focal points within a composition. By strategically placing gradients, designers can draw attention to specific elements or direct the viewer's gaze in a particular direction. In conclusion, color gradients in the context of color theory and color symbolism in design refer to the gradual transition of colors to create visual depth, convey emotions, and enhance the meaning or message of a design. Through careful selection and placement of colors, designers can create powerful and engaging compositions that evoke specific responses from the viewer.

Color Harmonies

In color theory, a color harmony refers to a combination of colors that are aesthetically pleasing and visually balanced. It is a concept derived from the principles of color psychology and the understanding of how different colors interact with each other. Color harmonies are based on the understanding that certain color combinations create a sense of balance and harmony, while others may clash or create visual discord. These harmonies are used in various design fields, such as graphic design, interior design, and fashion, to create visually appealing compositions.

Color Harmonization Tools

A color harmonization tool in the context of color theory and color symbolism in design refers to a software or tool that helps designers to create visually pleasing and harmonious color schemes. These tools aim to assist designers in selecting and combining colors that work well together, ensuring a cohesive and balanced visual representation. Color theory is based on the idea that colors have various relationships with each other, and these relationships can be analyzed and applied in the design process. By understanding these relationships, designers can create color schemes that convey specific meanings or evoke certain emotions in the viewer. Color harmonization tools typically provide features such as color palettes, color wheel, and color scheme generator. These features allow designers to explore different color combinations and experiment with various harmonizing techniques. The tools often provide options to create complementary, analogous, triadic, and other color schemes based on color theory principles. In design, colors hold symbolic meanings and can communicate different messages. Color harmonization tools take into account the symbolic associations of colors and provide suggestions for harmonizing colors based on their respective meanings. For example, warm colors like red and orange are often associated with energy and excitement, while cool colors like blue and green are linked to calmness and tranquility. Designers can utilize color harmonization tools to create color schemes that align with the intended symbolism and message of their design. These tools are particularly helpful for designers who may have limited knowledge of color theory or struggle with selecting harmonious color combinations. By using color harmonization tools, designers can save time and effort in manually selecting and testing color combinations. Additionally, these tools can also provide inspiration and help designers think outside the box, exploring unconventional yet harmonious color combinations. Overall, color harmonization tools serve as a valuable resource for designers seeking to create visually appealing and meaningful designs. By utilizing their features and principles of color theory, designers can achieve harmonious color schemes that effectively communicate their intended message and evoke desired emotional responses from the viewers.

Color Harmony Generators

A color harmony generator is a tool used in color theory and design to create visually appealing color combinations for various purposes. It assists designers in selecting colors that work well together and convey the desired message or mood. Color harmony refers to the arrangement of colors in a way that is pleasing to the eye and creates a sense of balance and unity. It is based on the principles of color theory, which explore the relationships between colors and their psychological and emotional effects. A color harmony generator typically operates by analyzing the color wheel, which consists of primary, secondary, and tertiary colors. It considers factors such as color temperature, value, saturation, and contrast to generate harmonious combinations. The generator often offers various harmony rules or modes, such as analogous, complementary, split complementary, triadic, tetradic, and monochromatic. In design, color harmony is crucial as it determines the overall aesthetic and impact of a composition. The choice of colors is essential in evoking specific emotions or impressions. For example, warm colors like red, orange, and yellow are associated with energy, passion, and enthusiasm, while cool colors like blue, green, and purple evoke calmness, serenity, and stability. Color symbolism also plays a significant role in design, where colors are imbued with cultural, contextual, or personal meanings. A color harmony generator can consider these symbolic associations and help designers effectively communicate their intended message. For instance, a design aimed at promoting environmental sustainability may employ a harmonious combination of earthy tones like green and brown, symbolizing nature and growth. When using a color harmony generator, designers can experiment with different color combinations and instantly visualize how they interact with each other. This allows for quick iteration and exploration of various creative possibilities, ensuring that the final color scheme aligns with the intended design objectives. In conclusion, a color harmony generator is a tool that assists designers in creating visually pleasing and meaningful color combinations. By considering color theory principles and symbolism, it helps designers make informed choices that enhance the overall impact and effectiveness of their designs.

Color Harmony Software

Color Harmony Software is a digital tool designed to assist in the creation and manipulation of color schemes in the context of color theory and color symbolism in design. It is an invaluable resource for artists, designers, and anyone involved in visual communication, helping them create visually appealing and aesthetically pleasing compositions. Color Harmony Software utilizes various algorithms and mathematical models to generate harmonious color combinations based on established color theories such as the color wheel, color harmony rules, and color psychology. These theories guide the selection and arrangement of colors in a way that creates balance, unity, and a desired emotional impact.

Color Harmony Tools

The color harmony tools refer to a set of techniques and resources used in color theory and design to create visually cohesive and aesthetically pleasing color schemes. Color theory is the study of how colors interact with each other and how they can be combined to create various visual effects. In design, colors play a significant role in conveying messages and evoking emotions, making it crucial to understand the principles of color harmony. Color harmony is the arrangement of colors in a way that creates a sense of balance and unity. It involves selecting colors that complement or contrast with each other in a pleasing manner. The use of color harmony in design helps to communicate a specific message, establish a visual hierarchy, and enhance the overall user experience. There are several color harmony tools available to designers, both online and offline. One commonly used tool is the color wheel, which is a circular diagram displaying the relationships between primary, secondary, and tertiary colors. The color wheel is often divided into various color schemes, such as complementary, analogous, triadic, and tetradic. These color schemes provide designers with a starting point for creating harmonious color combinations. Another color harmony tool is the color palette generator. This tool allows designers to input a base color or a series of colors and generates a complementary palette based on various color harmony principles. This helps designers to explore different color options and create harmonious color schemes without the need for manual calculations. In addition to the color wheel and color palette generator, there are also software applications and online platforms specifically designed to assist designers in selecting and combining colors harmoniously. These tools often offer features such as color libraries, color pickers, and color scheme visualization, making it easier for designers to experiment with different color combinations and find the most appropriate color harmonies for their projects.

Color Harmony

Color harmony refers to the balanced and visually pleasing combination of colors in design, utilizing the principles of color theory and symbolism. It involves selecting and blending colors in a way that creates a sense of unity, coherence, and aesthetics in the overall design composition. Color theory is an essential aspect of understanding color harmony. It explores how colors interact and how they can be categorized based on their relationships on the color wheel. The color wheel illustrates primary, secondary, and tertiary colors, as well as their complementary, analogous, and triadic relationships. By understanding these relationships, designers can create harmonious color schemes that evoke specific emotions or convey certain messages. Color symbolism also plays a significant role in achieving color harmony. Different colors are associated with various emotions, cultural meanings, and psychological responses. For example, warm colors like red and orange often convey feelings of energy, passion, and warmth, while cool colors like blue and green are often associated with calmness, nature, and tranquility. By considering the symbolic meanings of colors, designers can effectively communicate specific messages and evoke intended emotions in their designs. When achieving color harmony, designers can employ various color schemes, such as complementary, analogous, triadic, split-complementary, tetradic, or monochromatic. Complementary colors are found opposite each other on the color wheel and create a high-contrast and vibrant effect. Analogous colors are adjacent to each other on the color wheel and create a harmonious and cohesive composition. Triadic colors are equidistant from each other on the color wheel and offer a balanced and dynamic color combination. The selection and arrangement of colors should also consider factors such as balance, contrast, and hierarchy. Balancing colors involves distributing visual weight evenly across the design to create a sense of equilibrium. Contrast in colors refers to the differences in lightness, darkness, or saturation between different elements, enhancing visibility and visual interest. Hierarchy in colors involves assigning different colors to different elements based on importance, emphasizing focal points or guiding the viewer's attention.

Color Influence

Color Influence in the context of color theory refers to the impact that colors have on our psychological, emotional, and physiological responses. It explores how different colors can evoke specific feelings, moods, and associations, making them powerful tools in design and communication. Colors are not just visually appealing, but they also carry symbolic meanings and are deeply rooted in our cultural experiences. Understanding color psychology and symbolism allows designers to effectively communicate messages and elicit desired responses from their audience. Warm colors such as red, orange, and yellow are often associated with energy, passion, and warmth. They can create a sense of excitement and draw attention. These colors are commonly used to stimulate and create a sense of urgency or danger, making them valuable in advertising or to grab attention in a design. On the other hand, cool colors like blue, green, and purple are often associated with calmness, tranquility, and serenity. They can create a sense of relaxation and are often used in designs that aim to communicate trust, stability, or security. Cool colors are frequently used in healthcare and wellness industries to promote a sense of calm and peace. Neutral colors, such as black, white, and gray, are often used as a base in design. They are considered versatile and can be paired with any other color, creating contrast or balance. These colors often convey a sense of sophistication, elegance, or simplicity. Color symbolism varies across different cultures and contexts. For example, in Western cultures, red is often associated with love and passion, while in Asian cultures, it is associated with luck and fortune. Similarly, white can represent purity and innocence in Western cultures, but in some Eastern cultures, it is associated with mourning and death. Understanding the influence and symbolism of color allows designers to create powerful visual compositions that effectively communicate messages and evoke desired emotions. By carefully selecting colors and considering their psychological impact, designers can enhance the effectiveness and success of their designs. In conclusion, color influence in design refers to the psychological and symbolic impact that colors have on individuals. By understanding color theory and symbolism, designers can harness the power of colors to create visually appealing and emotionally engaging designs.

Color Inspiration Apps

Color inspiration apps are digital tools that offer designers, artists, and individuals interested in color theory and symbolism a wide range of resources for exploring and discovering new color palettes and combinations. These apps typically provide a vast library of colors, along with various features that help users select, organize, and experiment with different hues, shades, tints, and tones. Color theory is a field of study that focuses on understanding how colors interact and how they can be combined in aesthetically pleasing ways. It explores the properties and relationships between colors, including their psychological effects, symbolic meanings, and cultural associations. By understanding color theory, designers can create designs that effectively communicate messages, evoke specific emotions, and attract the attention of their target audience. Color symbolism, on the other hand, refers to the use of color to convey specific meanings or ideas. Different colors are often associated with various emotions, concepts, or cultural representations. For example, red is commonly associated with passion or danger, blue with tranquility or trust, and green with nature or growth. Understanding color symbolism can help designers select appropriate colors for their projects based on the intended message or theme. Color inspiration apps provide a valuable tool for designers to explore and apply color theory and symbolism to their work. These apps usually include features such as color palettes, color wheels, and color harmony generators. With these tools, users can experiment with different color combinations, create harmonious schemes, and discover new and interesting ways to use colors in their designs. Additionally, color inspiration apps often offer functionalities such as image-based color extraction, where users can take a photo or upload an image to identify and extract the dominant colors. This feature allows designers to find color inspiration in the world around them, such as nature, fashion, or architecture. Overall, color inspiration apps serve as a valuable resource for designers to enhance their understanding of color theory and symbolism. By providing a wide range of colors, tools, and features, these apps enable designers to explore, experiment, and create visually compelling and meaningful designs.

Color Inspiration Platforms

Color inspiration platforms are online tools or platforms that provide designers and artists with a wide range of color palettes, combinations, and schemes for their projects. These platforms aim to assist users in finding and selecting suitable color options while considering the principles of color theory and color symbolism in design. Color theory is the study of how colors interact with each other and how they can be combined to create visually appealing and harmonious compositions. It takes into account factors such as color wheel relationships, color temperature, and color psychology. By understanding color theory, designers can make informed decisions about which colors to use and how to combine them effectively to convey their intended message or evoke specific emotions. Color symbolism, on the other hand, refers to the cultural or psychological associations and meanings that colors can have. Different colors can have different connotations and symbolic representations in various cultures and contexts. For example, red is often associated with passion or danger, while green may symbolize growth or nature. By considering color symbolism in design, designers can use colors strategically to enhance the overall message of their work and create a more impactful visual experience for the viewer. Color inspiration platforms provide a wide variety of color schemes and palettes that are pre-selected or generated based on various criteria such as complementary colors, analogous colors, monochromatic palettes, and more. These platforms often offer curated collections of color combinations inspired by nature, art, fashion, or current design trends. Users can browse through these color options and choose the ones that align with their project's requirements and desired aesthetics. Using color inspiration platforms allows designers to save time and effort by providing them with a starting point for their color selection process. Instead of manually experimenting with different color combinations, designers can explore curated collections or generate random palettes to find inspiration and refine their color choices. These platforms often provide additional information about the colors used, including their RGB or hexadecimal values, allowing the designer to easily replicate the chosen colors in their design software. In summary, color inspiration platforms serve as valuable resources for designers and artists, offering a wide range of color palettes and combinations. By combining the principles of color theory with an understanding of color symbolism, designers can make informed decisions about choosing and combining colors to create visually pleasing and meaningful designs.

Color Inspiration Tools

Color inspiration tools are tools that aid designers in selecting colors for their designs based on color theory and color symbolism. These tools provide a curated collection of colors that can be used as a starting point for creating color palettes that elicit specific emotions or convey certain messages. Color theory is the study of how colors interact with each other and how they are perceived by the human eye. It is a fundamental aspect of design and is often used to create visually pleasing and harmonious compositions. Color inspiration tools can help designers apply color theory principles by providing color palettes that adhere to principles such as complementary colors, analogous colors, or triadic colors.

Color Inspiration Websites

Color inspiration websites are online platforms that serve as a resource for designers seeking guidance and inspiration related to color theory and color symbolism in their creative projects. These websites provide a curated collection of color palettes, examples, and suggestions to help designers make informed decisions when selecting and combining colors. Color theory is the study of how colors interact and how they can be effectively combined to create visually appealing and harmonious designs. It involves understanding the color wheel, color relationships, and the psychological and emotional responses that different colors evoke. Color theory is an essential aspect of design as it helps designers communicate messages and evoke specific emotions through color choices. Color symbolism, on the other hand, refers to the cultural and psychological associations that colors have and how they can be used to convey meaning in design. Different colors are often associated with specific emotions, concepts, or ideas. For example, red is often associated with passion and energy, while blue can evoke feelings of calmness and trust. Understanding color symbolism enables designers to use colors strategically to reinforce their design's intended message or theme. Color inspiration websites typically offer a wide range of color palettes that showcase different combinations of colors. These palettes are carefully curated to ensure they adhere to the principles of color theory and can be used effectively in design. Simply put, color palettes are sets of colors chosen to create a specific visual atmosphere or convey a particular message. They provide designers with a starting point or a source of inspiration when selecting colors for their projects. These websites often organize color palettes based on various themes or moods, making it easier for designers to find palettes that align with their design objectives. For example, a website might offer palettes specifically created for a vintage aesthetic or a minimalist style. By providing a range of color options and examples, color inspiration websites empower designers to explore different color combinations and experiment with various color schemes. They offer a valuable resource for designers looking to enhance the visual impact of their creations and effectively communicate their intended message through strategic color choices.

Color Intensity

Color intensity, in the context of color theory and color symbolism in design, refers to the brightness or saturation of a color. It is a measure of how pure or vibrant a color appears to the human eye. In the RGB color model, intensity is determined by the amount of red, green, and blue light present in a color. When a color is highly intense, it means that it is vivid, eye-catching, and has a strong visual impact. Such colors tend to stand out and draw attention, making them ideal for creating focal points or emphasizing important elements in a design. On the other hand, colors with low intensity are more subdued, muted, and less vibrant. They can create a sense of calmness, subtlety, or elegance. Color intensity plays a significant role in graphic design, branding, and advertising as it can evoke specific emotions and convey messages. For example, bright and highly intense colors like red, orange, and yellow are often associated with energy, excitement, and warmth. These colors are commonly used to grab attention and create a sense of urgency or enthusiasm. In contrast, cooler and less intense colors like blue and green are often associated with calmness, serenity, and nature. The intensity of a color can also affect its perceived weight or visual presence in a design. Highly intense colors tend to appear heavier and more dominant, while colors with lower intensity may feel lighter and less pronounced. Designers often utilize this aspect of color intensity to create visual hierarchy, balance, and harmony in their compositions. By strategically combining colors of varying intensities, they can guide the viewer's eye, create depth, and emphasize certain elements. In symbolism, color intensity is also associated with different meanings. For example, intense red can symbolize passion, love, or anger, while a pale or desaturated red may represent weakness or timidity. The intensity of a color can influence the overall mood and atmosphere of a design, as well as communicate cultural or contextual associations.

Color Management

Color management is a crucial aspect of both color theory and color symbolism in design. It refers to the process of controlling and maintaining consistent color reproduction across various devices, such as computer monitors, printers, and other output devices. In color theory, color management ensures that the intended colors are accurately represented in different mediums and environments. It involves the use of standardized color spaces, such as RGB (Red, Green, Blue) and CMYK (Cyan, Magenta, Yellow, Black), and color profiles to maintain color consistency.

Color Matching Applications

A color matching application, in the context of color theory and color symbolism in design, refers to a digital tool or software that helps users find and create harmonious color schemes and combinations. Color theory, a fundamental concept in visual arts and design, explores how colors interact with each other and the effects they produce on the human eye and emotions. Color symbolism, on the other hand, examines the various meanings and associations that different colors evoke in different cultures and contexts. Color matching applications typically provide a wide range of functionalities and features that assist designers, artists, and individuals in creating visually pleasing and meaningful color palettes. These applications often offer a variety of tools such as color pickers, color wheels, and color scheme generators. The color picker tool allows users to choose specific colors from an image, webpage, or any other visual reference. This functionality helps designers match colors accurately and replicate them in their own projects. It also enables users to extract colors from existing designs and incorporate them into new ones, ensuring consistency and coherence. The color wheel tool, based on the color wheel theory, provides a visual representation of the relationships between colors. It allows users to explore and experiment with different color combinations, such as complementary, analogous, or triadic schemes. By manipulating the position and proportions of colors on the wheel, designers can achieve harmonious or contrasting effects, depending on their desired visual impact. Color scheme generators, another common feature in these applications, automatically generate color palettes based on predefined rules or algorithms. Users can input their preferred color or choose from preset themes, and the generator will produce a cohesive set of complementary colors. This functionality eliminates the guesswork and provides a starting point for designers who seek color combinations that work well together. Overall, color matching applications serve as invaluable tools for artists and designers, enabling them to explore, experiment, and achieve harmonious and meaningful color compositions. These applications enhance the creative process by simplifying color selection and ensuring aesthetic coherence in visual design projects.

Color Matching Software

Color matching software is a tool used in the field of color theory and design to assist in the process of selecting and coordinating colors based on their visual compatibility and symbolic meaning. In color theory, colors are organized on a color wheel, which represents the full spectrum of visible light. Color matching software uses algorithms and mathematical models to calculate the relationships between colors, identifying complementary colors, analogous colors, and color harmonies. By analyzing color values, saturation, and brightness, the software can suggest color combinations that are aesthetically pleasing and balanced. In the context of design, color symbolism plays a crucial role in conveying messages and evoking emotions. Different colors have inherent associations and can be used strategically to communicate specific meanings. Color matching software takes into account these symbolic meanings, helping designers choose colors that align with the intended message or brand identity. For example, warm colors like red and orange are often associated with energy and excitement, while cool colors like blue and green evoke feelings of calmness and tranquility. By using color matching software, designers can experiment with various color palettes and combinations, visualizing how different colors interact with one another. This software can also provide color harmonies inspired by nature, such as complementary color schemes found in sunsets or analogous color schemes seen in vibrant flower gardens. Furthermore, color matching software can facilitate accessibility in design by ensuring that color combinations meet contrast guidelines for optimal readability. This is particularly important for individuals with visual impairments or color blindness. In summary, color matching software is a valuable tool utilized in color theory and design to assist in the selection and coordination of colors based on visual compatibility and symbolic meaning. By analyzing color relationships and considering color symbolism, this software helps designers create aesthetically pleasing and meaningful color palettes for various design projects.

Color Matching Tools

Color matching tools are essential resources used in color theory and design to accurately match and coordinate colors for various purposes. These tools help designers and artists find appropriate color combinations, ensuring that colors harmonize and convey the desired emotions and messages in their work. Color theory is the study of how colors interact with each other and their psychological and emotional impact on humans. It provides guidelines on how to use colors harmoniously and effectively. One of the fundamental principles of color theory is color harmony, which involves the arrangement of colors in a way that is aesthetically pleasing. Color matching tools play a crucial role in achieving color harmony by helping designers identify and select colors that complement each other. These tools typically include color wheels and color swatches that display a wide range of colors along with their corresponding hues, tones, and shades. Color wheels provide a visual representation of the color spectrum, allowing designers to understand the relationships between different colors and how they can be combined to create various effects. Color swatches, on the other hand, are physical or digital samples of different colors that can be easily compared and matched. They often come in sets or palettes that have been carefully curated to ensure that the colors in each set work well together. In addition to color wheels and swatches, color matching tools may also include software applications and online platforms that provide advanced color matching functionality. These tools allow designers to input specific color values or images and receive suggestions for complementary colors or color schemes based on color theory principles. Color symbolism is another important aspect of design that relies heavily on accurate color matching. Different colors have various connotations and associations, and understanding color symbolism is critical in conveying the intended message or mood in a design. By using color matching tools, designers can select colors that align with the desired symbolism and effectively communicate their intended meaning. For example, warm colors like red and orange are often associated with energy and passion, while cool colors like blue and green are often linked to calmness and tranquility. In conclusion, color matching tools are indispensable resources in color theory and design. By assisting in the selection and coordination of colors, these tools enable designers to achieve color harmony and effectively convey the desired emotions and messages in their work.

Color Matching Utilities

A color matching utility is a tool or software application that helps designers and artists find and select colors that harmonize well together. Color theory and color symbolism are the underlying principles that guide these utilities. Color theory is the study of how colors interact and relate to each other. It provides a framework for understanding the various color relationships and how they affect the overall visual composition. This includes concepts such as color harmony, color contrast, and color temperature. Color matching utilities use color theory principles to suggest color combinations that are visually pleasing and create a sense of balance and unity. Color symbolism, on the other hand, is the use of colors to convey specific meanings or emotions. Different colors are associated with different feelings and can evoke various psychological responses. Color matching utilities take color symbolism into account to help designers choose colors that align with the intended message, brand identity, or atmosphere of a design. For example, warm colors like red and yellow are often associated with energy and excitement, while cool colors like blue and green evoke feelings of calmness and tranquility. Color matching utilities typically offer a variety of features to assist designers in their color selection process. These may include color palettes, color wheel tools, and color scheme generators. A color palette is a collection of colors that work well together and can be used as a starting point for a design project. Color wheel tools allow users to explore different color relationships, such as complementary or analogous colors. Color scheme generators automatically generate harmonious color schemes based on user-defined parameters, such as the primary color or color harmony type. In conclusion, color matching utilities are essential tools for designers and artists to facilitate the selection of harmonious color combinations. By leveraging color theory and color symbolism, these utilities provide guidance and inspiration for creating visually appealing and emotionally impactful designs.

Color Matching

Color matching is a fundamental concept in color theory and color symbolism in design. It refers to the process of selecting and combining colors in a harmonious and visually pleasing way. The aim is to create balance and unity in a design, communicate specific messages or evoke desired emotions. In color theory, color matching involves understanding the principles of the color wheel, which is a visual representation of the relationships between colors. The color wheel consists of primary colors (red, blue, and yellow), secondary colors (orange, green, and purple), and tertiary colors (made by mixing primary and secondary colors). These colors are positioned in a circular format, allowing designers to identify complementary colors (opposites on the wheel), analogous colors (neighboring colors), and triadic colors (equally spaced around the wheel). When color matching for design purposes, it is essential to consider both the psychological and cultural associations of colors. Each color has symbolic meanings and can evoke different emotions or convey specific messages. For example: - The color red is often associated with passion, energy, and excitement, but it can also symbolize danger or anger. - Blue is commonly associated with calmness, trust, and reliability. It can also represent sadness or melancholy. - Yellow is often associated with happiness, warmth, and optimism, but it can also symbolize caution or cowardice. - Green is commonly associated with nature, growth, and harmony. It can also symbolize envy or inexperience. - Purple is often associated with royalty, luxury, and creativity. It can also symbolize mystery or spirituality. - Orange is commonly associated with enthusiasm, vitality, and creativity. It can also represent caution or impulsiveness. - Pink is often associated with femininity, sweetness, and romance. It can also symbolize vulnerability or immaturity. By understanding color theory and the symbolism associated with different colors, designers can effectively match colors to create harmonious and impactful designs. Whether it is selecting complementary colors for a vibrant and energetic composition or using analogous colors for a more tranquil and cohesive appearance, color matching is a crucial aspect of design that influences how people perceive and interpret visuals.

Color Meaning

Color meaning refers to the interpretation and significance assigned to different colors in the field of color theory and design. Colors possess psychological and emotional associations that impact how people perceive and respond to them. These meanings can vary across cultures, but there are common associations that are widely recognized. Understanding color symbolism is crucial in visual communication and design, as it helps to convey specific messages and elicit desired reactions. In color theory, colors are categorized into primary, secondary, and tertiary colors, along with warm and cool colors. Each color carries its own meaning and symbolism, which can be broadly summarized as follows: - Red: Passion, energy, love, and excitement. It can also signify danger or anger. - Yellow: Happiness, optimism, brightness, and intellect. It can also represent caution or deceit. - Blue: Calmness, tranquility, trust, and reliability. It can also symbolize sadness or aloofness. - Green: Nature, growth, freshness, and harmony. It can also be associated with envy or inexperience. - Orange: Creativity, enthusiasm, vitality, and warmth. It can also indicate aggression or flamboyance. - Purple: Royalty, luxury, mystery, and spirituality. It can also connote sadness or arrogance. - Pink: Softness, femininity, and romance. It can also imply passivity or immaturity. - Black: Power, sophistication, formality, and elegance. It can also symbolize death or evil. - White: Purity, innocence, cleanliness, and neutrality. It can also suggest sterility or emptiness. - Gray: Balance, wisdom, neutrality, and practicality. It can also evoke dullness or depression. - Brown: Stability, reliability, earthiness, and simplicity. It can also represent plainness or boredom. These interpretations of color meaning are not absolute, as context, personal experiences, and cultural differences can influence individual perceptions. It is important for designers to consider color symbolism when creating visuals, as the intended message can be amplified or undermined by the chosen colors. Understanding color theory and color meaning allows designers to strategically utilize colors to effectively communicate ideas, emotions, and brand identities.

Color Mixing Charts

Color mixing charts are visual representations that illustrate the process of combining colors to create new colors. They are an essential tool in color theory, which is the study of how colors interact and how they can be used effectively in design. These charts provide a systematic and organized approach to understanding the principles of color mixing and the resulting color combinations. In color theory, color mixing is based on the primary colors – red, blue, and yellow – which are considered to be the building blocks for all other colors. By combining different amounts of these primary colors, along with the secondary colors – orange, green, and purple – an infinite number of colors can be created. Color mixing charts demonstrate the various combinations and proportions of primary and secondary colors that result in different hues and shades. Color mixing charts are particularly useful in design because they allow designers to predict and control the outcomes of color combinations. By referring to these charts, designers can effectively choose colors that will harmonize or contrast with each other and create the desired visual impact. In addition to serving as a practical tool, color mixing charts also have symbolic significance in design. Colors are deeply connected to emotions and carry different meanings and associations. For example, warm colors like red and orange are often associated with energy, passion, and excitement, while cool colors like blue and green are linked to calmness, tranquility, and relaxation. By understanding the symbolism and psychology of colors, designers can use color mixing charts to create designs that evoke specific emotions or convey specific messages. Overall, color mixing charts are a fundamental aspect of color theory and design. They provide a systematic approach to understanding and predicting color combinations, allowing designers to effectively manipulate colors to achieve desired visual effects. Whether used as a practical tool or as a means of symbolic expression, color mixing charts play a crucial role in the world of design.

Color Mixing Guides And Charts

A color mixing guide or chart is a visual reference tool used in color theory and design to understand how different colors can be combined to create new colors. It provides a systematic representation of color relationships, presenting a range of color combinations and their resulting visual effects. Color theory is the study of how colors interact with each other and how they can be organized and harmonized to create aesthetically pleasing designs. It is based on the understanding that colors can evoke emotions, convey meaning, and influence human perception. By using a color mixing guide or chart, designers can effectively communicate their intended messages through the strategic use of color combinations.

Color Mixing Guides

A color mixing guide is a tool used in color theory and design to help artists and designers understand the principles of combining colors to create different shades, hues, and tints. It provides a visual representation of how different colors interact with one another and how they can be manipulated to achieve desired effects. In color theory, colors are typically represented on a color wheel, which is a circular diagram that showcases the relationships between primary colors, secondary colors, and tertiary colors. A color mixing guide builds upon this concept by demonstrating how these colors can be mixed together in various proportions to create a wide range of color combinations. The color wheel is divided into different sectors, each representing a specific color family. The primary colors, which are red, yellow, and blue, are typically positioned at equal distances from one another. Mixing these primary colors together in varying ratios will produce secondary colors, such as orange, green, and purple. Tertiary colors, such as yellow-green or blue-violet, can then be created by mixing a primary color with an adjacent secondary color. Through a color mixing guide, artists and designers can explore the impact of adding black or white to a color mixture, resulting in shades and tints, respectively. Adding black to a color reduces its brightness and intensity, creating darker shades, while adding white lightens the color, producing lighter tints. This understanding of color mixing allows artists and designers to control the mood, balance, and visual impact of their creations. In addition to color theory, color symbolism is also an important aspect of design. Different colors evoke different emotions and associations in people, making them powerful tools for conveying messages or setting the tone in design projects. A color mixing guide can assist designers in selecting and combining colors that align with the desired symbolism or meaning. Overall, a color mixing guide helps artists and designers understand the principles of color theory, allowing them to create harmonious and visually impactful designs. It enables them to experiment with different color combinations, shades, and tints, as well as consider the symbolism associated with each color.

By mastering color mixing, artists and designers can effectively communicate their intended messages and emotions through their work.

Color Mixing

Color mixing refers to the process of combining different colors to create new hues. It is a fundamental concept in color theory, which explores the visual effects of color relationships and how colors interact with one another. In the context of color symbolism in design, color mixing allows designers to create specific moods and communicate messages to their audience. Different color combinations can evoke different emotions and meanings, influencing the overall perception and impact of a design.

Color Mode

Color mode refers to the system used to define and display colors in design, based on color theory and symbolism. It determines how colors are created, represented, and perceived in a given medium or context. In color theory, colors are defined by various attributes such as hue, saturation, and brightness. Color mode provides a standardized way of organizing and reproducing these attributes to ensure consistency in color perception across different devices and mediums.

Color Mood

Color Mood refers to the emotional response or feeling that is evoked by a particular color or combination of colors in a design or artwork. In color theory and color symbolism, different colors are believed to have distinct psychological effects on individuals, and these effects can vary based on cultural, personal, and contextual factors. Colors are often associated with specific emotions or moods. For example, warm colors like red, yellow, and orange are commonly associated with feelings of energy, warmth, and excitement. These colors are often used to create a sense of urgency or to draw attention to a particular element in a design. On the other hand, cool colors like blue, green, and purple are generally associated with feelings of calmness, relaxation, and serenity. These colors are often used in designs that aim to create a sense of tranquility or to convey a sense of stability and trust. The combination of colors in a design can also affect the overall mood. Complementary colors, which are colors that are opposite each other on the color wheel (e.g., blue and orange), create a sense of contrast and can evoke strong emotions. Analogous colors, which are colors that are adjacent to each other on the color wheel (e.g., blue and purple), create a sense of harmony and can evoke a more subdued mood. Additionally, the use of different color schemes, such as monochromatic (shades of a single color) or triadic (three colors evenly spaced on the color wheel), can also contribute to the overall mood of a design. In design, the choice of colors and their arrangement should be carefully considered to ensure that they convey the desired mood or emotional response. This involves understanding the cultural and symbolic associations of different colors, as well as considering the target audience and the intended message of the design. Color psychology and symbolism can vary across different cultures and contexts, so it is important to be mindful of these factors when selecting colors for a design. In summary, color mood refers to the emotional response or feeling that is evoked by a particular color or combination of colors in a design. Understanding the psychological effects and symbolic associations of different colors can help designers to effectively convey a desired mood or emotional response in their work.

Color Palette Creators

A color palette creator is a tool or software used in the field of design to generate harmonious and visually pleasing combinations of colors. It follows principles of color theory to ensure that the chosen colors work well together and create a desired aesthetic effect. In the context of color theory, a color palette refers to a collection of colors that are intentionally selected to create a specific mood or convey a particular message. A well-designed color palette can enhance the visual appeal of a design project and evoke certain emotions in its viewers. Color symbolism is another aspect that plays a role in the creation of color palettes. Different colors can elicit different emotional responses and have specific cultural or symbolic meanings. For example, red is often associated with passion or danger, while blue is often associated with calmness or trust. Understanding color symbolism allows designers to effectively communicate or evoke certain feelings through their color choices. When using a color palette creator, designers often start by selecting a dominant color, which serves as the primary hue of their design. The tool then generates a range of complementary, analogous, or triadic colors that harmonize with the dominant color. Complementary colors are opposite each other on the color wheel and create a high-contrast effect, while analogous colors are next to each other and create a harmonious and cohesive look. Triadic colors are evenly spaced on the color wheel and create a visually balanced composition. With the generated color palette, designers can experiment with different combinations and variations until they achieve the desired effect. They can adjust the saturation, brightness, and contrast of the colors to fine-tune the overall look. The goal is to create a balanced and visually appealing composition that embodies the intended mood, message, or brand identity. Color palette creators are valuable tools for both experienced and novice designers. They help save time by providing instant color scheme suggestions and eliminate the guesswork in color selection. By incorporating principles of color theory and symbolism, these tools empower designers to create visually engaging and meaningful designs that resonate with their target audience.

Color Palette Design Apps

A color palette design app is a digital tool used in the field of design to create and manage color schemes. Color theory is the foundation of these apps, as it provides the principles and guidelines for combining colors in a visually pleasing and meaningful way. Color symbolism in design is the use of particular colors to communicate specific messages or evoke certain emotions. Each color has its own symbolic meaning, and understanding this symbolism is crucial in choosing the right color palette for a design.

Color Palette Designers

A color palette designer is a professional who specializes in creating visually pleasing and harmonious color schemes for various design projects. They have a deep understanding of color theory and symbolism and use this knowledge to select and combine colors in a deliberate and purposeful way. Color theory is the study of how colors interact with one another and the visual effects they create when used together. It explores concepts such as color harmony, contrast, and the psychological impact of different colors. A color palette designer uses this knowledge to create color schemes that evoke specific emotions, convey certain messages, or enhance the overall aesthetic of a design. Color symbolism, on the other hand, refers to the cultural and psychological associations that different colors have. For example, red is often associated with passion and energy, while blue is associated with calmness and trust. A color palette designer considers these symbolic meanings when selecting colors for a design, aiming to create a harmonious and meaningful composition that resonates with the intended audience. To create a color palette, a designer may start by selecting a base color or a dominant color that sets the tone for the design. They then choose additional colors that complement the base color and create a sense of balance and contrast. These colors may be selected from the same color family, such as various shades of blue, or they may be contrasting colors that create a bold and dynamic effect. In addition to selecting colors, a color palette designer also considers factors such as saturation, brightness, and value. They may adjust these attributes to achieve the desired visual impact and to ensure that the colors work well together.

Color Palette Editing Software

Color Palette Editing Software is a digital tool designed specifically to manipulate color palettes used in various fields, including graphic design, web design, and digital art. It allows users to create, edit, and organize color schemes to enhance visual communication and convey specific messages through the use of color. Color theory plays a crucial role in understanding the principles behind color palette editing software. It involves the study of how color combinations affect human perception and emotional responses. By applying color theory principles, designers can create harmonious and impactful color palettes. In the context of design, color symbolism refers to the associations and meanings that people attribute to different colors. Each color carries its own symbolism and conveys specific messages or emotions. Color palette editing software enables designers to harness the power of color symbolism and create palettes that align with the intended message or brand identity. When using color palette editing software, designers have access to a wide range of features and functionalities. They can choose from pre-designed color palettes or create custom ones by selecting and manipulating individual colors. The software often provides tools to adjust hue, saturation, and brightness levels, allowing for precise color modifications. One of the key advantages of color palette editing software is its ability to generate complementary and analogous color schemes. Complementary colors are positioned opposite each other on the color wheel, creating a striking contrast. Analogous colors, on the other hand, are adjacent on the wheel, resulting in a more harmonious and cohesive palette. By manipulating these schemes, designers can evoke different emotional responses and visually communicate specific messages. Color palette editing software also allows for the creation of monochromatic and triadic color palettes. Monochromatic palettes consist of different shades, tints, and tones of a single color, ideal for creating a consistent and balanced design. Triadic palettes, on the other hand, use three colors equidistant from one another on the color wheel, offering a vibrant and contrasting combination. In summary, color palette editing software is an essential tool for designers in creating visually engaging and meaningful designs. It leverages color theory and symbolism to manipulate color palettes, enabling designers to evoke desired emotions, convey specific messages, and establish brand identities through the strategic use of colors.

Color Palette Editing Tools

Color Palette Editing Tools are software or online platforms that allow users to create, modify, and manipulate color palettes for design purposes. In the field of color theory and symbolism, color palettes play a crucial role in conveying emotions, creating visual harmony, and enhancing the overall aesthetic appeal of a design. These tools provide designers with a wide range of functionalities to work with colors effectively. They typically offer various color selection options such as color sliders, color pickers, and color libraries, allowing users to choose colors based on their RGB, CMYK, or hexadecimal values. By providing a diverse range of colors, these editing tools help designers to explore different color schemes and combinations. One of the essential features of color palette editing tools is the ability to create and modify color schemes. Designers can choose from different color harmony rules such as complementary, analogous, triadic, or monochromatic to create balanced and visually pleasing color combinations. These tools also offer the functionality to adjust the saturation, brightness, and contrast of colors, thereby enabling designers to fine-tune the overall appearance of their designs. Moreover, color symbolism plays a significant role in design, where different colors evoke distinct emotions and meanings. Color palette editing tools often provide insights into the psychological effects of colors, helping designers select appropriate colors based on their intended message or target audience. For example, warm colors like red and orange may convey energy, passion, or warmth, while cool colors like blue and green may evoke calmness, tranquility, or nature. By providing information about color symbolism, these tools assist designers in effectively communicating their desired message through the use of colors. In addition to color selection and manipulation, color palette editing tools also enable designers to organize and save their color schemes for future use. They often provide options to save color palettes as files, export them in various formats such as CSS or JSON, or share them with other designers. By providing these organizational features, these tools enhance the efficiency and productivity of designers, allowing them to easily access and apply their preferred color schemes across different design projects. Overall, color palette editing tools are essential resources for designers working with color theory and symbolism. They empower designers to explore, create, and manipulate color palettes, ensuring that their designs effectively convey the desired emotions, meanings, and aesthetic qualities.

Color Palette Editors

A Color Palette Editor is a tool or software that enables designers to create, manipulate, and organize color palettes for use in their design projects. In the context of color theory and color symbolism in design, a color palette is a collection of colors that are carefully chosen and arranged to achieve a desired aesthetic or convey a specific message. Color theory is the study of how colors interact with each other and how they can be combined to create visually appealing and harmonious designs. It explores the effects of different color combinations on the viewer's emotions, mood, and perception. Designers use color theory principles to create color palettes that evoke specific feelings or communicate certain meanings. Color symbolism, on the other hand, is the idea that colors can carry symbolic meanings or associations. Different colors are often associated with specific emotions, cultural references, or concepts. For example, red is commonly associated with passion or danger, while blue is often associated with calmness or trust. Designers can use color symbolism to reinforce the intended message or theme in their designs. A color palette editor provides designers with the tools and functionalities to create, modify, and organize their color palettes effectively. With a color palette editor, designers can select individual colors and arrange them in a cohesive and visually pleasing manner. They may also be able to adjust the hues, saturations, and brightness of each color to achieve the desired effect. Furthermore, a color palette editor may offer features like color harmony suggestions or color theory guidelines to aid designers in creating balanced and harmonious color combinations. These tools can help designers ensure that their color palettes are aesthetically pleasing and effectively convey the desired emotions or meanings. In conclusion, a color palette editor is an essential tool for designers working with color theory and color symbolism in design. It allows designers to create and manipulate color palettes, enabling them to achieve visually appealing designs that effectively communicate the desired message or evoke specific emotions. By providing functionalities for color selection, arrangement, and adjustment, a color palette editor empowers designers to create cohesive and harmonious designs that resonate with the intended audience.

Color Palette Generator Apps

A color palette generator app is a tool that assists designers in creating harmonious color schemes for their projects. It is based on the principles of color theory and utilizes color symbolism to help users select the most appropriate colors for their designs. Color theory is a field of study that explores the principles and relationships between colors. It encompasses various aspects such as color harmony, color contrast, and color psychology. Applying color theory in design helps create visually appealing and effective compositions. Color symbolism, on the other hand, refers to the meaning and associations attributed to different colors. Colors can evoke various emotions, convey messages, and communicate themes. Understanding color symbolism allows designers to align the colors they choose with the intended message or mood of their design. A color palette generator app utilizes color theory and symbolism to generate color schemes that meet the needs of designers. These apps usually offer a range of functionalities and features to help users explore, select, and save color palettes. Most color palette generator apps allow users to input a base color or choose from a predetermined set of colors. The app then generates a harmonious color scheme by suggesting complementary, analogous, or monochromatic colors based on the input. This function is based on color theory principles such as the color wheel and color relationships. In addition to facilitating the creation of harmonious color schemes, some apps also provide options for adjusting the saturation, brightness, or contrast of the generated colors. This allows designers to fine-tune the color scheme to their liking or specific design requirements. Color palette generator apps often offer additional features like color extraction from images or websites. These functions analyze the colors present in a given image or website and generate corresponding color palettes. This can be particularly useful for designers who want to match the colors of their design with real-world objects or existing visual elements. Overall, color palette generator apps serve as invaluable tools for designers by simplifying the process of creating aesthetically pleasing and meaningful color schemes. By leveraging color theory and symbolism, these apps assist in selecting visually appealing colors that effectively convey the desired message or evoke the intended emotions in a design.

Color Palette Generators

A color palette generator is a tool used in design to create harmonious and visually appealing color schemes for various design projects. It aids in selecting and combining colors by providing a range of color options that work well together according to color theory and symbolism. In the realm of color theory, a color palette generator assists designers in choosing colors that harmonize and complement each other. It takes into consideration principles such as color wheel relationships, including complementary, analogous, split complementary, and triadic color schemes. By generating a palette that adheres to these principles, designers can achieve a cohesive and balanced appearance in their designs. Furthermore, color symbolism plays a significant role in design, and a color palette generator aids in choosing colors that convey specific meanings or evoke certain emotions. Different colors have various cultural, psychological, and contextual associations. For example, red can symbolize passion, energy, or danger, while blue may represent tranquility, trust, or sadness. By using a color palette generator, designers can explore different color combinations that communicate the intended message or elicit the desired response from the audience. The process of using a color palette generator typically involves selecting a starting color or a primary color and generating a range of complementary colors accordingly. These generators may offer various customization options, allowing designers to adjust parameters like saturation, brightness, and temperature to further refine the color scheme. The tool then presents the generated color palette, displaying the selected colors in a visually pleasing arrangement. By utilizing a color palette generator, designers can save valuable time and effort in manually testing and selecting color combinations. It provides a convenient way to experiment with different color options and helps ensure that the chosen palette aligns with the principles of color theory and symbolism. Ultimately, a well-chosen color palette can enhance the overall design aesthetic, create visual unity, and effectively communicate the intended message to the target audience. In conclusion, a color palette generator is a valuable tool for designers, assisting in the creation of harmonious and meaningful color schemes. It combines the principles of color theory and symbolism to offer a range of visually appealing color combinations for various design projects.

Color Palette Management Software

A color palette management software is a digital tool that facilitates the organization, selection, and manipulation of color palettes. In the context of color theory and color symbolism in design, this software plays a crucial role in helping designers create visually appealing and cohesive designs. Color theory is an essential aspect of design, as it explores the principles and relationships of colors. It encompasses concepts such as the color wheel, color harmony, and color psychology. A color palette management software assists designers in applying these principles effectively by providing a platform to create and manage color palettes. A color palette typically consists of a collection of colors that are carefully selected and arranged to convey a specific theme or mood. It is a fundamental tool for designers, helping them establish visual consistency and coherence throughout their designs. However, manually organizing and managing color palettes can be time-consuming and tedious. This is where a color palette management software proves valuable. By using a color palette management software, designers can easily import, sort, and categorize colors, ensuring efficient organization. This allows for quick and seamless access to different variations of colors, facilitating the creation and modification of color palettes. Furthermore, the software often includes features such as color picking tools, color conversion options, and color scheme generation. These functionalities enable designers to explore various color combinations, analogies, and harmonies, enhancing the aesthetics and visual impact of their designs. In the context of color symbolism in design, a color palette management software provides an invaluable resource for designing with intent. Different colors have different connotations and symbolic meanings, and the software enables designers to consider these associations when selecting colors for their palettes. This consideration can contribute to the overall message or emotion a design aims to convey. Overall, a color palette management software serves as a powerful tool for designers to efficiently organize and manipulate colors. It empowers them to create aesthetically appealing designs by utilizing color theory principles and considering color symbolism. By streamlining the process of color palette management, it allows designers to focus more on their creative vision and produce visually impactful designs.

Color Palette Managers

Color palette managers are tools used in the field of design to create and organize sets of colors that are aesthetically pleasing and meaningful in the context of color theory and color symbolism. Color theory is a study that explores how colors interact with each other and how they can be combined to create harmonious and visually appealing designs. It delves into the principles of color harmony, contrast, and the psychological effects that different colors can have on human perception and emotions. By understanding and applying these principles, designers can create effective and impactful visual compositions. Color symbolism, on the other hand, is the use of colors to convey specific meanings or evoke certain emotions or associations. Different cultures and contexts may have varying interpretations of color symbolism. For example, the color red can be associated with passion and energy in one culture, while it may symbolize luck and prosperity in another. Designers often make deliberate use of color symbolism to enhance the message or mood of their designs. Color palette managers serve as valuable tools in both color theory and color symbolism. They provide designers with a convenient way to create and organize sets of colors that work well together and align with the desired message or mood of a design. These tools typically offer a range of functionalities, such as color picking, color palettes creation, color combination suggestions, and color swatching. By using a color palette manager, designers can explore various color combinations and easily visualize how different colors interact with each other. They can experiment with different hues, saturations, and brightness levels to achieve the desired visual effect. Additionally, color palette managers often provide advanced features like color harmonies, which help designers create balanced and harmonious color schemes. In conclusion, color palette managers are essential tools for designers working with color theory and color symbolism. They enable designers to create aesthetically pleasing designs by providing a range of features and functionalities that facilitate the exploration and organization of colors. By using these tools, designers can effectively convey their intended message, evoke desired emotions, and create visually impactful designs.

Color Palette

A color palette refers to a predetermined selection of colors used in design and color theory. It is a collection of colors that are carefully chosen to harmonize and create visual appeal in various art forms such as graphic design, painting, interior design, and fashion. The colors within a palette are typically selected based on their relationships to each other and their ability to evoke certain emotions or convey specific meanings. In the context of color theory, a color palette is constructed using various principles and concepts. These principles include the color wheel, which organizes colors into primary, secondary, and tertiary hues. A color palette may consist of complementary colors, which are opposite each other on the color wheel and create a high contrast effect. Analogous colors, which are adjacent to each other on the color wheel, can also form a palette, resulting in a harmonious and cohesive color scheme. Color symbolism is a significant component in design, and color palettes play a vital role in conveying specific meanings or emotions. For example, warm colors such as red and orange can evoke feelings of energy, passion, and intensity. Cool colors like blue and green, on the other hand, are often associated with calmness, tranquility, and nature. The use of specific color palettes can help designers communicate a desired mood or message to the audience. In addition to evoking emotions, color palettes can also serve practical purposes in design. They can establish a visual hierarchy, drawing attention to important elements or creating visual balance. A well-designed color palette can enhance readability and usability, ensuring that information is effectively communicated. In summary, a color palette is a carefully curated selection of colors used in design and color theory. It is chosen based on principles of color harmony and can serve both aesthetic and functional purposes. By understanding the relationships between colors and their symbolic meanings, designers can create visually appealing and impactful designs.

Color Palettes

Color palettes are a fundamental aspect of color theory and play a vital role in design by influencing aesthetic choices and evoking specific emotions or associations. A color palette refers to a carefully selected range of colors that work harmoniously together within a design or composition. In color theory, colors can be categorized into various systems, such as the primary colors (red, blue, and yellow), secondary colors (created by mixing two primary colors), and tertiary colors (created by mixing a primary and a secondary color). Color palettes are often created by combining these basic colors in different proportions or by including shades, tints, or tones of a particular color.

Color Perception

In the field of color theory and color symbolism in design, color perception refers to the way individuals interpret and understand colors. It is the process by which the human brain translates the different wavelengths of light that are received by the eyes into meaningful and distinguishable colors. Color perception is influenced by various factors, including cultural and personal experiences, as well as biological and psychological factors. Different cultures associate different meanings and emotions with colors, which can impact how colors are perceived and used in design. Additionally, personal experiences and individual preferences can also shape how colors are interpreted and appreciated. In color theory, colors are often categorized into different groups based on their perceived characteristics and psychological

58

effects. These groupings, such as warm colors (e.g., red, orange, yellow) and cool colors (e.g., blue, green, purple), serve as guidelines for designers to create harmonious color schemes and evoke specific emotions or moods in their designs. Furthermore, color symbolism plays a significant role in design, as colors are often used to convey messages and evoke specific associations. For example, the color red is commonly associated with passion, love, and power, while green is often associated with growth, nature, and tranquility. Designers utilize these associations to communicate effectively and create visual narratives through the strategic use of color. Understanding color perception is crucial in design, as it allows designers to create visually appealing and meaningful compositions. By considering how individuals perceive and interpret colors, designers can effectively use color to convey messages, elicit emotions, and create desired experiences for their intended audience.

Color Picker Add-Ons

Color picker add-ons are tools or software extensions that allow designers to easily select and identify colors for their design projects. These add-ons are typically used in the context of color theory and color symbolism, which are important aspects of design. In color theory, colors are studied and organized based on their properties and relationships with one another. The color wheel, for example, is a visual representation of the primary, secondary, and tertiary colors, as well as their intermediate shades. Understanding color theory helps designers create harmonious and visually appealing designs. Color symbolism, on the other hand, refers to the associations and meanings that colors evoke in different cultures and contexts. Different colors can have specific connotations and emotions attached to them. For instance, red is often associated with passion and energy, while blue conveys a sense of calm and trust. When designing, it is important to consider these symbolic meanings to effectively communicate a message or create a desired mood. Color picker add-ons assist designers in the selection and identification of colors that align with color theory and symbolism. These tools often provide a range of features to help users choose colors, such as color palettes, eyedroppers, and sliders. With a color picker add-on, a designer can easily extract colors from images or websites, find complementary or analogous colors, and adjust hues, saturation, and brightness. By using a color picker add-on, designers can ensure that the colors they choose are both aesthetically pleasing and conceptually meaningful. They can experiment with different color combinations, test how colors appear in different contexts (e.g., print or digital), and maintain consistency throughout their designs. In conclusion, color picker add-ons are valuable tools in the field of design, particularly within the realms of color theory and symbolism. They provide designers with the means to efficiently select and manipulate colors that effectively communicate their intended message and meet the visual demands of their projects.

Color Picker Browser Extensions

A color picker browser extension is a tool that assists designers and artists in selecting and capturing specific colors from webpages or images. These extensions typically function as an add-on to internet browsers, granting users the ability to collect and store color codes for future use. In the realm of color theory and symbolism within design, color picker browser extensions play a pivotal role. Understanding the principles of color theory is essential for creating visually appealing and meaningful visual compositions. Color theory explores the relationships between colors and their impact on human perception. By grasping these concepts, designers can effectively communicate messages and evoke emotional responses through their work. Color symbolism, on the other hand, refers to the cultural associations and meanings assigned to colors. Different colors can evoke a wide range of emotions and convey various messages based on cultural, historical, and personal interpretations. Designers often utilize color symbolism to strengthen the intended message or narrative of their creations. Color picker browser extensions provide designers with a convenient means of selecting and analyzing colors to incorporate into their designs. By extracting precise color codes, such as hexadecimal values, RGB values, or HSL values, designers can replicate or modify specific colors with ease. This capability ensures consistency and accuracy when working with a defined color palette. Moreover, color picker browser extensions enhance the efficiency of the design process by enabling users to save and organize color schemes for future reference. Designers can instantly capture colors that catch their attention, whether they are browsing the web or inspecting images, allowing for seamless integration of inspiring colors into future projects. Overall, color picker browser extensions serve as invaluable tools within the realm of color theory and symbolism, empowering designers to accurately analyze, select, and implement colors that both harmonize with aesthetic principles and convey intended messages. These extensions streamline the creative process by facilitating the capture and organization of color codes, ultimately enhancing the design workflow in a visually impactful and meaningful manner.

Color Picker Extensions

A color picker extension is a tool or software feature that allows users to select specific colors from a given range and identify their hexadecimal or RGB values. In the context of color theory and color symbolism in design, color picker extensions play a crucial role in ensuring consistent and intentional color choices. Color theory encompasses the principles and guidelines that dictate the use and combination of colors in visual arts and design. It deals with concepts such as color harmony, contrast, and color psychology. Color symbolism, on the other hand, refers to the associations and meanings assigned to specific colors. Different cultures and contexts can attribute different symbolism to colors, which can influence their usage in design and communication. Color picker extensions are designed to facilitate the application of color theory and symbolism in design. By providing an easy-to-use interface and precise color identification, these extensions empower designers to make informed and intentional color choices. They allow users to sample colors from various sources, including images, websites, and digital artwork, ensuring accurate replication and consistency. In the context of color theory, color picker extensions enable designers to select colors that harmonize well with each other. They can identify complementary, analogous, or triadic color schemes, ensuring a balanced and visually appealing design. By providing real-time previews and complementary color suggestions, these extensions help designers experiment with different color combinations and create harmonious palettes. When considering color symbolism, color picker extensions allow designers to match and align the intended meaning or emotional response with the chosen colors. By selecting colors with specific symbolic associations, designers can enhance the visual communication and evoke the desired emotions or convey intended messages. Whether the goal is to use warm colors to evoke energy and excitement or cool colors to create a calm and peaceful atmosphere, color picker extensions assist designers in choosing colors that align with their intended symbolism. Overall, color picker extensions serve as valuable tools in the realm of color theory and symbolism in design. By enabling precise color selection, harmonious combinations, and intentional symbolism, these extensions empower designers to create visually impactful and meaningful designs.

Color Picker Plugins For Design Software

Color Picker Plugins for design software are tools that allow designers to select colors from various sources within the software and apply them to their designs. These plugins are designed to enhance the color selection process by providing a convenient and efficient way to choose and manage colors. In the context of color theory, color picker plugins help designers to find and select colors that are complementary, analogous, or harmonious to create visually appealing designs. They provide a comprehensive range of color options, including the ability to select colors from a color wheel, input specific color values, or use predefined color palettes. These plugins often include features like eyedroppers, sliders, and color swatches, allowing designers to easily experiment with different colors and find the perfect shades for their designs. Furthermore, color picker plugins take into consideration color symbolism in design. Colors have symbolic meanings that can evoke specific emotions or convey certain messages. For example, red is often associated with passion and energy, while blue represents calmness and trust. With color picker plugins, designers can easily explore and understand the symbolic meanings of different colors, enabling them to make conscious decisions about the color schemes they use in their designs. With the help of color picker plugins, designers can also create cohesive color schemes that tie different elements of their designs together. By selecting colors that harmonize well, designers can ensure visual unity and balance in their designs. This is particularly important in branding and marketing materials, where consistency in color is essential for developing a strong and recognizable brand identity. In conclusion, color picker plugins for design software play a crucial role in the color selection process for designers. They provide a wide range of color options, consider color theory and symbolism, and enable the creation of cohesive color schemes. By using these plugins, designers can enhance their creativity, improve their workflow, and ultimately create visually impactful designs.

Color Picker Plugins

A color picker plugin is a tool used in design to help select and identify colors based on color theory and symbolism principles. This plugin enables designers to choose specific colors from various color models, such as RGB (red, green, blue), HSL (hue, saturation, lightness), or CMYK (cyan, magenta, yellow, key/black). Color theory is the study of how colors interact and impact visual perception. It involves understanding the color wheel, color harmony, and color relationships. Different colors can evoke different emotions and convey specific meanings or associations. For example, warm colors like red and orange are often associated with energy and passion, while cool colors like blue and green are often associated with tranquility and nature. In design, colors are used deliberately to create specific moods, communicate messages, and enhance overall aesthetics. They can be used to attract attention, create contrast, or establish a brand identity. Understanding color theory and symbolism is crucial in making informed decisions during the design process. Color picker plugins simplify the process of selecting colors by providing a visual interface and various color picking options. These plugins typically allow users to pick colors from an existing palette, enter color values manually, or select colors from an image. By providing a convenient and efficient way to select colors, color picker plugins help designers maintain consistency and cohesion throughout their designs. They ensure that the chosen colors adhere to color theory principles and align with the desired symbolism. Overall, color picker plugins are valuable tools for designers as they facilitate the selection of colors based on color theory and symbolism. They help create visually appealing and meaningful designs by ensuring the right colors are chosen to convey the intended message and evoke the desired emotions.

Color Picker Software

A Color Picker Software is an application that allows designers and artists to select and capture colors from various sources and use them in their design projects. It is a tool that assists in the process of color theory and color symbolism in design. Color theory is the study of how colors interact with each other and how they can be used to evoke certain emotions or communicate specific messages. It explores the relationships between different colors, their placement in a design, and the impact they have on the viewer. By understanding color theory, designers can create harmonious and visually appealing compositions. Color symbolism, on the other hand, is the use of specific colors to convey specific meanings or messages. For example, red is often associated with passion or danger, while blue is associated with calmness or trust. Designers use color symbolism to evoke certain emotions or communicate certain ideas in their work. A Color Picker Software provides a simple and efficient way to explore the vast world of colors and apply them in design projects. It allows users to select colors from various sources such as digital images, websites, or even physical objects, and extract their RGB or hexadecimal values. By using a Color Picker Software, designers can easily identify the exact colors used in an existing design or image and incorporate them into their own work. This helps maintain consistency and coherence in the overall color scheme of a project. Moreover, a Color Picker Software often provides additional features such as color palettes, color schemes, and color harmonies. These tools help designers explore different combinations of colors based on color theory principles. They assist in creating aesthetically pleasing compositions by suggesting complementary or analogous colors. In conclusion, a Color Picker Software is a valuable tool for designers and artists, aiding them in the application of color theory and color symbolism in their work. It allows for the precise selection and extraction of colors from various sources, helping to maintain consistency and coherence in design projects. Additionally, it provides features that assist in the creation of harmonious color combinations based on color theory principles.

Color Picker Tools

Color picker tools are essential resources used in color theory and color symbolism in design. They are online applications or software features that allow designers and artists to select and identify specific colors from an image or on a color spectrum, enabling them to establish color palettes and make informed color choices. In color theory, color picker tools assist in understanding the various properties of color, such as hue, saturation, and brightness. These tools often provide users with a color wheel or spectrum, allowing them to explore different color combinations and find complementary or analogous colors. By using a color picker tool, designers can accurately identify the exact color values they want to use, which helps in creating harmonious color schemes.

Color Preferences

Color preferences in the context of color theory and color symbolism in design refer to the subjective choices and associations individuals make when selecting or perceiving different colors. These preferences may be influenced by cultural, psychological, and personal factors and can have a profound impact on the way colors are used and interpreted in various design disciplines. In color theory, colors are often assigned specific meanings and emotions based on their position on the color wheel and their psychological impact on viewers. For example, warm colors such as red and orange are commonly associated with energy, passion, and urgency, while cool colors like blue and green evoke feelings of calmness, tranquility, and nature. Color preferences can vary greatly from person to person, with some individuals favoring vibrant, bold hues, while others may prefer more subdued, neutral tones. These preferences can shape the way people respond to and interact with design elements, as well as influence their overall perception of a brand or product.

Color Profile

A color profile, in the context of color theory and color symbolism in design, refers to a standardized representation of how colors should appear on various devices and platforms. It is essential in ensuring consistent and accurate color reproduction across different mediums such as computer screens, printers, and digital images. Color theory is the study of how colors interact with one another, while color symbolism in design focuses on the psychological and cultural associations that colors evoke. Both of these concepts heavily rely on color profiles to achieve their intended impact. In the world of digital design, color profiles play a crucial role in maintaining color consistency. This is because different devices and platforms have variations in color spaces, gamma values, and rendering capabilities. Without standardization, the same color could appear differently on different devices, leading to confusion and misrepresentation of the intended design. Color profiles are created and defined using the International Color Consortium (ICC) standards. These profiles include information on color spaces, gamma correction, and other technical specifications to achieve accurate color reproduction. Commonly used color spaces include RGB (Red, Green, Blue) for digital screens and CMYK (Cyan, Magenta, Yellow, Black) for print media. Each color profile is created with the aim of accurately displaying colors based on the human visual system, considering factors such as lighting, contrast, and color perception. By adhering to color profiles, designers can ensure that the colors they choose for their designs are accurately represented on various devices, allowing for a consistent and harmonious experience for viewers. Furthermore, in the realm of color symbolism, color profiles are crucial in effectively conveying the desired meanings and emotions through color choices. Different cultures and contexts associate different meanings with colors, and color profiles aid in maintaining the intended symbolism across different media. For example, a calm and soothing design may use cool colors like blues and greens, while a vibrant and energetic design may incorporate warm colors like reds and yellows. In conclusion, color profiles are indispensable in color theory and color symbolism in design as they establish consistency and accuracy in color reproduction. By adhering to these standardized profiles, designers can ensure that their work is interpreted as intended, regardless of the devices or platforms on which they are viewed.

Color Psychology Books

Color psychology books provide a comprehensive understanding of the role and impact of colors in design, by exploring color theory and color symbolism. These books delve into the psychological effects that different colors have on individuals, examining how colors can evoke emotions, influence moods, and shape perceptions. Color theory is the study of how colors interact with each other and with the human eye. It explores the principles of the color wheel, color harmony, and color mixing. By understanding color theory, designers can create visually pleasing compositions that effectively communicate their intended message or evoke a desired emotional response. Color psychology books typically explain the various color schemes and their applications, such as complementary, analogous, triadic, and monochromatic color schemes, enabling designers to make informed color choices. Moreover, these books explore the symbolic meanings associated with different colors in various cultures and contexts. Colors often carry cultural and personal associations that can influence their interpretation. For instance, red is often associated with passion, love, and energy, while blue is linked to calmness, trust, and reliability. Understanding these symbolic associations allows designers to utilize colors strategically to convey specific messages, align with a brand's identity, or create desired atmospheres in interior spaces. Furthermore, color psychology books discuss the impact of color on human behavior and perception. They examine how colors can influence attention, memory, and decision-making processes. For example, warm colors like red and orange are believed to increase appetite, which is why they are often used in restaurant branding and interior design. Similarly, pastel colors are often used in healthcare settings as they are associated with tranquility and healing. In conclusion, color psychology books provide valuable insights into the theories, symbolism, and practical applications of color in design. By understanding the psychological effects and cultural associations of different colors, designers can effectively utilize colors to convey emotions, create visual impact, and communicate their intended message.

Color Psychology References

Color psychology is the study of how colors can influence human behavior, emotions, and perceptions. It is a field that aims to understand the impact that different colors have on individuals and how they can be used to evoke specific responses in the context of design. In color theory, colors are often associated with different meanings and symbolism. These associations can vary across cultures and contexts, but there are some general patterns and interpretations that have been widely recognized. Understanding color symbolism is important for designers as it helps them communicate effectively and create desired emotional responses through color choices.

Color Psychology Resources

Color psychology is the study of how colors impact human emotions, behavior, and perceptions. In the context of color theory and symbolism in design, color psychology examines the psychological effects of different colors and their use in various design elements. Colors have the power to evoke specific emotions and moods, and understanding color psychology can help designers effectively communicate and convey messages through their design choices. Different colors are associated with different psychological reactions and can elicit specific feelings or responses from viewers. In design, color psychology is utilized to create visually appealing and impactful compositions. For example, warm colors such as red, orange, and yellow are often used to create a sense of energy and enthusiasm. These colors can stimulate appetite and grab attention, making them suitable for marketing and advertising designs. Cool colors like blue, green, and purple, on the other hand, are known for their calming and soothing effects. They can create a sense of relaxation and serenity, making them ideal for designs related to wellness, nature, or tranquility. Additionally, color psychology also considers cultural and personal associations with colors. Colors can vary in symbolism and interpretation across different cultures, so it is crucial for designers to consider the target audience and cultural context when selecting colors for their designs. Furthermore, personal experiences and individual preferences can also shape the psychological impact of colors. Colors can hold personal meanings or trigger specific memories for individuals, so understanding the target audience's background and preferences can guide color choices in design. In conclusion, color psychology plays a significant role in design, influencing the emotional response and interpretation of visual elements. By understanding the psychological effects of colors and considering cultural and personal associations, designers can create visually compelling compositions that effectively communicate and connect with their intended audience.

Color Psychology

Color psychology is a field that studies the effects of color on human behavior and emotions. In the context of color theory and color symbolism in design, it is concerned with how different colors are perceived and the psychological impact they have on individuals. Color theory is a system that explains how colors interact with each other and how they can be combined to create visual harmony or contrast. It involves understanding the color wheel, color relationships, and the emotions and meanings associated with different colors. Color symbolism refers to the cultural meanings and associations that different colors have. These meanings can vary across different cultures and contexts, but certain colors often have more universal associations. For example, red is commonly associated with passion and energy, while blue is often associated with calmness and trust. When it comes to design, understanding color psychology is essential for creating effective and impactful visuals. Designers use colors strategically to evoke specific emotions, convey messages, and create desired atmospheres. They consider the psychological effects of colors on the audience and how different colors can influence perceptions and behaviors. For example, a designer might use warm colors like red and orange to create a sense of excitement or urgency, while cool colors like blue and green might be used to evoke feelings of tranquility or harmony. The use of contrasting colors can draw attention to specific elements or create visual interest, while the use of monochromatic color schemes can create a sense of unity and simplicity. In addition to considering individual colors, designers also need to understand color combinations and how different colors interact with each other. Complementary colors, which are opposite each other on the color wheel, can create vibrant and energetic compositions, while analogous colors, which are adjacent to each other, can create harmonious and soothing visuals. Overall, color psychology plays a crucial role in design by helping designers make informed decisions about the use of color. By understanding the psychological effects and cultural associations of different colors, designers can create visuals that resonate with their intended audience and effectively communicate their intended message.

Color Rendering Index (CRI)

The Color Rendering Index (CRI) is a metric used to measure how accurately a light source reproduces the colors of objects compared to a natural light source or reference illuminant. It is a common tool in color theory and color symbolism in design. The CRI is quantified on a scale from 0 to 100, with 100 being the highest possible value, indicating that the light source accurately renders colors. A CRI of 0 means that the light source completely distorts colors, making them appear unrecognizable. The CRI is calculated by comparing the spectral power distribution of the light source to a standard illuminant, such as daylight, and measuring the differences or deviations in color rendering.

Color Rendering

Color rendering refers to the process of accurately representing or reproducing colors in a visual medium, such as painting, photography, or design. It is an essential aspect of color theory and symbolism in design. In the context of color theory, color rendering involves understanding and manipulating colors to achieve specific effects or communicate certain messages. Designers use color rendering techniques to evoke emotions, create visual harmony, or establish hierarchy within a composition. By carefully selecting and combining colors, designers can influence the viewers' perceptions and responses.

Color Sample Cards For Design

Color sample cards for design play an essential role in color theory and color symbolism. These cards provide a visual representation of different colors, enabling designers to choose the most suitable hues for their projects. In color theory, color sample cards serve as a tool for understanding the principles of color mixing, harmonies, and contrasts. The cards display a range of colors in varying shades, saturations, and intensities, allowing designers to explore different color combinations and find the perfect balance for their designs. By studying and manipulating these cards, designers can create aesthetically pleasing color palettes that evoke specific emotions and enhance the overall visual impact of their work. Moreover, color sample cards also contribute to the understanding of color symbolism in design. Each color holds its own meaning and can evoke unique associations and emotions. By having a physical representation of colors, designers can easily integrate these symbolic meanings into their designs, thus effectively communicating their intended message to the target audience. For example, warm colors such as red, orange, and yellow are often associated with energy, passion, and excitement, while cool colors like blue and green convey feelings of calmness, serenity, and nature. Color sample cards allow designers to experiment with different color schemes and symbolism, enabling them to create visually compelling and meaningful designs. By juxtaposing and selecting colors from these cards, designers can establish harmonious, complementary, and contrasting color combinations that reinforce the intended message of their designs. Additionally, these cards also provide a practical reference for designers during the production process, ensuring consistent color reproduction across various mediums such as print, digital, and web. In summary, color sample cards are invaluable tools in the realm of design, particularly in color theory and color symbolism. They enable designers to explore and manipulate colors, discover harmonious combinations, and convey specific emotions and meanings through their designs. By utilizing these cards, designers can create visually appealing and impactful designs that effectively communicate their intended message to the audience.

Color Sample Cards

Color Sample Cards are a tool used in color theory and design to showcase and study the different colors available in a particular color palette or collection. These cards typically display small swatches of color in an organized manner, allowing designers, artists, and other professionals to compare, contrast, and analyze the various hues, shades, and tones. In the context of color theory, color sample cards serve several purposes. Firstly, they help designers understand the fundamental principles of color, including the color wheel, color harmony, and color psychology. By visually representing a broad spectrum of colors, these cards make it easier to identify complementary colors, analogous colors, or colors that create a specific emotional response. Furthermore, color sample cards aid in the selection process by providing a comprehensive overview of available colors, enabling designers to choose the most suitable palette for a given project. They allow designers to experiment with combinations and explore different color schemes, such as monochromatic, complementary, or triadic, to achieve the desired visual impact or communicate a specific message. Besides their practical use in color theory, color sample cards also play a significant role in color symbolism in design. Different colors evoke distinct emotions, symbolize various concepts, and carry cultural or psychological associations. By utilizing color sample cards, designers can effectively harness the power of color symbolism and incorporate it into their creations. For instance, a designer working on a logo for a healthcare organization might use color sample cards to find the most appropriate color that conveys feelings of trust, reliability, and care. Alternatively, a graphic designer creating a poster for a music festival could use color sample cards to select vibrant and energetic colors that evoke excitement, dynamism, and creativity. Ultimately, color sample cards facilitate the process of color selection, combination, and interpretation in the realm of design, enabling professionals to create aesthetically pleasing and impactful compositions. Whether used for understanding color theory principles, exploring color symbolism, or making informed choices, these cards prove to be indispensable tools for designers across various disciplines.

Color Sample Swatches

Color sample swatches are small, rectangular pieces of material or digital representations that are used in the field of color theory and design to showcase different colors and their corresponding values. These swatches provide a standardized way to communicate and analyze colors, allowing designers and artists to make informed decisions when creating visual compositions. In color theory, color sample swatches serve as a practical tool for understanding and organizing the vast spectrum of colors. By presenting a range of colors in a systematic manner, swatches facilitate the comprehension of color relationships, harmonies, and contrasts. They enable designers to compare different hues, saturations, and intensities, creating a visual language that aids in color selection and combination. Swatches also help convey color concepts and ideas more effectively, as they provide a common reference point for communication within the design community.

Color Sampling

Color sampling is a fundamental process in color theory and color symbolism in design. It involves the systematic selection and analysis of colors to create a harmonious and visually appealing design. In color theory, color sampling refers to the act of selecting specific colors from a larger color space or palette. It involves taking samples of colors and analyzing their properties such as hue, saturation, and value. This allows designers to understand how different colors interact with each other and how they can be used effectively in their designs. Color sampling is crucial in color theory as it aids in the creation of color schemes. This involves selecting a group of colors that work well together and evoke a specific mood or atmosphere. By sampling different colors and analyzing their relationships, designers can choose colors that

65

complement each other and create a unified and balanced design. In addition to color theory, color sampling is also important in understanding color symbolism in design. Colors have symbolic meanings and can evoke different emotions and associations. By sampling different colors and studying their cultural and psychological connotations, designers can create designs that effectively communicate a desired message or concept. Color sampling is a process that involves both objective analysis and subjective interpretation. Designers must consider factors such as color temperature, color harmony, cultural associations, and personal preferences when selecting and sampling colors. This requires a deep understanding of color theory, design principles, and the desired message or concept of the design. Overall, color sampling plays a crucial role in color theory and color symbolism in design. It allows designers to create visually appealing and meaningful designs by selecting and analyzing colors to achieve harmony, balance, and effective communication.

Color Scheme Builders

A color scheme builder in the context of color theory and color symbolism in design is a tool or method that is used to create harmonious and visually pleasing combinations of colors for various design projects. It is based on an understanding of how colors can interact with each other and how they can evoke certain emotions or convey specific meanings. Color theory is the study of how colors can be combined and used in a way that is visually appealing and effective in communicating a message or achieving a particular aesthetic effect. It explores the relationships between different colors, such as complementary colors (colors that are opposite each other on the color wheel), analogous colors (colors that are next to each other on the color wheel), and triadic colors (colors that are evenly spaced on the color wheel). Color symbolism in design refers to the use of color to convey specific meanings or evoke certain emotions. Different colors are often associated with different psychological and cultural associations. For example, red is often associated with love, passion, and energy, while blue is associated with calmness, trust, and stability. Understanding these associations and using them effectively in design can help create a desired emotional response or convey a particular message to the audience. A color scheme builder can be an online tool or software that allows designers to experiment with different color combinations and see how they look together. It may provide various color palettes or presets based on different color theories or design principles. Designers can often customize and adjust the colors to suit their specific needs or preferences. Some color scheme builders may also provide additional information or suggestions on the psychological or cultural associations of different colors, helping designers make informed choices.

Color Scheme Creation Tools

Color Scheme Creation Tools are design tools that assist in the selection and creation of color schemes based on color theory and color symbolism. These tools aid in the process of choosing colors that work harmoniously together and convey desired emotions or messages in a design. Color theory is the study of how colors interact with each other and how they are perceived by the human eye. It involves principles such as color harmony, contrast, and balance. Color symbolism, on the other hand, is the use of colors to represent specific meanings or ideas. Different colors evoke different emotions and can be used to communicate specific messages. Color Scheme Creation Tools offer a range of features and functionalities to help designers create effective color schemes. These tools often provide a color wheel, which is a visual representation of the different hues and their relationships. The color wheel is based on the concept of primary, secondary, and tertiary colors, and it helps designers understand color harmonies such as complementary, analogous, and triadic schemes. In addition to the color wheel, these tools often offer color palette generators. These generators allow designers to select a base color and automatically generate a range of complementary or analogous colors that can be used in the design. This feature helps designers explore various color options quickly and easily. Some Color Scheme Creation Tools also provide functionality to adjust color values such as saturation, brightness, and contrast, allowing designers to fine-tune their color choices. This flexibility enables designers to create custom color schemes that perfectly suit their design objectives. Furthermore, these tools may include pre-designed color schemes or inspiration galleries, which showcase color combinations that are aesthetically pleasing and communicate specific emotions or moods. Designers can use these pre-designed schemes as a starting point or as a source of inspiration for their own creations. In conclusion, Color Scheme Creation Tools are valuable resources for designers that facilitate the selection and creation of color schemes based on color theory and color symbolism. These tools offer features such as color wheels, palette generators, and pre-designed schemes, helping designers to choose harmonious and meaningful colors for their designs.

Color Scheme Creators

Color Scheme Creators are tools or techniques used in color theory and design to help create harmonious and visually appealing combinations of colors. These tools consider various factors such as color wheel relationships, color symbolism, and design principles to assist designers in selecting the most appropriate colors for their projects.In color theory, the color wheel is often used as a visual representation of the relationships between colors. It is a circular diagram that organizes colors based on their hue, and can be divided into primary, secondary, and tertiary colors. Color Scheme Creators utilize this concept by suggesting color combinations that are either analogous (colors that are adjacent on the color wheel), complementary (colors that are opposite on the color wheel), or monochromatic (different shades and tints of a single color).Additionally, color symbolism plays a significant role in design, as different colors can evoke different emotions and convey specific messages. Color Scheme Creators take into account the psychological impact of colors and assist designers in choosing colors that align with the intended mood or theme of a project. For example, warm colors like red and yellow are often associated with energy and excitement, while cool colors like blue and green evoke calmness and tranquility.Furthermore, design principles such as contrast, balance, and unity are also considered in the creation of color schemes. Contrast refers to the juxtaposition of different colors to create visual interest and enhance readability. Color Scheme Creators suggest combinations that provide sufficient contrast while maintaining harmony. Balance ensures that colors are distributed evenly throughout a design, while unity ensures that the color choices are cohesive and consistent.Overall, Color Scheme Creators are valuable tools in color theory and design as they assist designers in selecting harmonious and visually appealing color combinations. By considering factors such as color wheel relationships, color symbolism, and design principles, these tools help create a cohesive and impactful visual experience for the viewers.

Color Scheme Editors And Creators

Color Scheme Editors and Creators are tools or software programs that assist designers in creating harmonious and visually appealing color combinations for their design projects. These editors allow designers to select and manipulate various color palettes to achieve the desired mood, message, and visual impact. In the context of color theory, a color scheme refers to a set of colors that are chosen and combined in a deliberate and meaningful way. Different color schemes evoke different emotions and have their own symbolic meanings. Color symbolism is the study of how colors can convey specific messages or evoke particular associations in the minds of viewers. Color Scheme Editors and Creators help designers explore and experiment with different color schemes, allowing them to easily select and adjust colors to create a cohesive and visually pleasing design. These tools often provide a range of features, such as color wheel, color theory insights, and palette generation, to assist designers in making informed decisions about the colors they use. By utilizing a Color Scheme Editor or Creator, designers can find colors that work well together, ensuring that the overall design is visually balanced, pleasing, and effectively communicates the intended message. These tools also enable designers to understand how different color combinations can evoke specific emotions or associations, allowing them to align their design with the desired mood or brand identity. In addition to assisting designers in creating harmonious color palettes, Color Scheme Editors and Creators also contribute to the efficient design workflow. They often provide options to export color codes or swatches, allowing designers to easily apply the chosen color scheme across various design software or platforms. This streamlines the design process and ensures consistency in color usage throughout the design project. In conclusion, Color Scheme Editors and Creators are valuable tools for designers, enabling them to explore, experiment, and create visually appealing color combinations. These tools not only facilitate the selection and manipulation of colors but also assist in understanding the symbolism and emotional impact of different color schemes. By using Color Scheme Editors and Creators, designers can enhance their designs by employing well-balanced and meaningful color palettes.

Color Scheme Editors

A color scheme editor is a tool that allows designers to create and modify color schemes for use in their designs and artworks. It helps them to experiment with different color combinations and find the most visually appealing and harmonious choices. In the context of color theory, color schemes are defined as a set of colors chosen for a design or artwork. These schemes are created based on the principles of color harmony, which aim to achieve a balanced and visually pleasing arrangement of colors. A color scheme editor provides designers with a convenient way to explore and manipulate colors, ensuring that their designs convey the desired aesthetic and evoke the intended emotional response. Color symbolim in design refers to the use of colors to convey specific meanings or messages in a visual composition. Different colors are often associated with particular emotions, ideas, or cultural connotations, and designers can utilize this symbolic language to enhance the communicative power of their designs. A color scheme editor allows designers to experiment with different color symbolim, creating palettes that align with the intended message or concept of their design. The functionality of a color scheme editor typically includes features such as color selection, color combination suggestions, and color modification options. Designers can select colors from a color wheel or input specific color values, and the editor will provide a range of compatible colors to choose from. It may also offer preset color scheme templates or allow designers to save and load their own custom schemes. With the ability to modify colors in real-time, designers can easily fine-tune their color schemes until they achieve the desired mood and visual impact. Color scheme editors are widely used in various design disciplines, including graphic design, web design, interior design, and fashion design. They are essential tools for designers to create visually pleasing and meaningful compositions that effectively communicate their intended message. By providing an intuitive and user-friendly interface for color exploration and manipulation, color scheme editors empower designers to unleash their creativity and produce compelling designs that resonate with their audience.

Color Scheme Generators Online

A color scheme generator is an online tool that assists designers in creating harmonious and aesthetically pleasing color combinations for their projects. It operates based on the principles of color theory and considers the psychological and symbolic effects associated with different colors. Color theory is the study of how colors interact with each other and how they can be used to elicit specific emotions or convey certain messages in design. It explores the relationships between primary, secondary, and tertiary colors, as well as the effects of different color properties, such as hue, saturation, and brightness. In design, colors are not only chosen for their visual appeal but also for the symbolic meanings they convey. Different colors can evoke specific emotions or associations in viewers and can therefore be used strategically to enhance the intended message or mood of a design. Color scheme generators take these principles into account and provide designers with a range of tools to explore and create harmonious color combinations. These online tools often offer various preset color schemes or allow users to customize their own schemes by selecting individual colors or adjusting specific color properties. By utilizing a color scheme generator, designers can save time and effort in manually selecting and testing color combinations. They can experiment with different schemes and quickly visualize how the chosen colors will interact with each other. This enables designers to make informed decisions and create designs that effectively communicate the desired emotions or meanings. In summary, color scheme generators are online tools that assist designers in selecting harmonious color combinations based on the principles of color theory and the symbolic associations of different colors. By using these generators, designers can enhance the visual appeal and impact of their designs while effectively conveying the intended message or mood.

Color Scheme Generators

A color scheme generator is a tool that helps designers create visually harmonious and aesthetically pleasing color combinations for their projects. These generators are based on principles of color theory, which is the study of how colors interact and how they can be organized to create desired effects. Color theory is crucial in design as it allows designers to understand the emotional and symbolic associations of different colors. Colors have the power to evoke specific emotions and convey certain messages, making them a significant element in visual communication. A color scheme generator takes into account various aspects of color theory, such as the color wheel and color harmony. The color wheel is a circular diagram that represents the relationships between colors. It consists of primary, secondary, and tertiary colors, and it helps designers understand how different colors relate to each other. Color harmony refers to the pleasing combination of colors that work well together. A color scheme generator uses the principles of color harmony to suggest color combinations that are visually pleasing and aesthetically balanced. These generators typically offer different color schemes such as complementary, analogous, triadic, and tetradic, among others. In addition to color theory, color symbolism is another important aspect considered by color scheme generators. Color symbolism refers to the cultural associations and meanings attached to different colors. For example, red can symbolize passion and energy, while blue can represent tranquility and trust. By taking color symbolism into account, designers can create color schemes that align with the desired message or mood of their designs. In conclusion, a color scheme generator is a tool that assists designers in creating visually harmonious and meaningful color combinations. These generators utilize principles of color theory and consider color symbolism to suggest aesthetically pleasing color schemes. By using color scheme generators, designers can enhance the overall visual impact and effectiveness of their designs.

Color Schemes

A color scheme refers to a harmonious combination of colors that are strategically chosen and arranged for a specific purpose in design. It is based on color theory and symbolism, which play a significant role in creating visual appeal and conveying meaning in various forms of art and design. Color theory is the study of how colors interact with one another and how they can be organized and combined to evoke different emotions and responses. It is an essential tool for designers as it allows them to create aesthetically pleasing and impactful compositions. The color wheel, a visual representation of the relationships between colors, is commonly used in color theory. Color symbolism, on the other hand, refers to the meaning and associations that certain colors evoke in different cultures and contexts. Colors can carry psychological, cultural, and social significance, and understanding these symbolisms can help designers effectively communicate their intended message to the viewers. There are various types of color schemes that designers can utilize, each serving a different purpose and creating a specific mood or atmosphere. Some common color schemes include: 1. Monochromatic: This color scheme is based on a single hue, varying its shades, tints, and tones. It creates a harmonious and elegant look, suitable for minimalist designs or conveying a sense of calmness. 2. Analogous: Analogous color schemes involve using adjacent colors on the color wheel. These schemes create a sense of harmony and unity, as the colors share similar undertones. They are often used to create a soothing and comfortable atmosphere. 3. Complementary: Complementary color schemes involve using colors that are directly opposite each other on the color wheel. This creates a high contrast and vibrant look, making the colors stand out. Complementary colors can be used to create a dynamic and energetic visual impact. 4. Triadic: Triadic color schemes involve using three colors that are evenly spaced around the color wheel. This creates a balanced and vibrant composition. Triadic colors are often used to create a sense of excitement and playfulness. 5. Split-complementary: Split-complementary color schemes involve using a base color and two colors adjacent to its complement. This creates a balanced and harmonious composition while still maintaining a level of contrast. Split-complementary colors can be used to create a visually interesting design. In conclusion, color schemes are an essential aspect of design that utilize color theory and symbolism to create visually appealing and meaningful compositions. By understanding the relationships between colors and using different color schemes, designers can effectively communicate ideas and evoke desired emotions in their work.

Color Selection

Color selection in the context of color theory refers to the process of choosing and incorporating specific colors in a design or artwork. It involves a careful consideration of various factors, such as color harmony, symbolism, and emotional and cultural associations, to effectively convey a desired message or concept. Color theory revolves around the understanding of the color wheel, which consists of primary, secondary, and tertiary colors. By selecting colors that are harmonious or complementary to each other, designers can create a visually appealing and balanced composition. Color symbolism, on the other hand, delves into the meanings and associations attached to certain colors. Different colors evoke different emotions and convey various messages, and this understanding allows designers to effectively communicate with their audience. In design, color selection plays a crucial role in establishing a specific mood or atmosphere. For example, warm colors like red, orange, and yellow are often associated with energy and excitement, making them suitable for designs aiming to create a sense of urgency or dynamism. On the other hand, cool colors like blue, green, and purple tend to evoke feelings of calmness and tranquility, making them suitable for designs aiming to create a sense of serenity or relaxation. Additionally, color selection can be influenced by cultural and social factors. Certain colors may hold different meanings in different cultures, and designers need to be mindful of these associations to avoid miscommunication or offense. For instance, while white is often associated with purity and innocence in Western cultures, it can symbolize mourning or death in some Eastern cultures. In conclusion, color selection in design involves the careful consideration of color theory principles, such as harmony and symbolism, to effectively convey a desired message or concept. By understanding how colors interact with each other and the meanings they hold, designers can create visually appealing and well-balanced compositions that resonate with their intended audience.

Color Simulation Apps

A color simulation app is a digital tool that allows designers to experiment and explore different colors within the context of color theory and symbolism. It provides a virtual platform for users to visualize the impact of various colors on designs, artwork, or any other creative projects. Color theory is the study of how colors interact, combine, and contrast with each other. It examines the use of colors to create harmonious compositions and convey desired emotions or meanings. Understanding color theory is crucial for designers as it helps them make informed decisions about color palettes, proportions, and combinations. In design, color symbolism refers to the meaning or associations assigned to different colors. Colors can evoke specific emotions, represent certain concepts, or stand for cultural or personal significance. For example, blue is often associated with calmness and reliability, while red can symbolize passion and energy. A color simulation app enables designers to apply color theory and symbolism principles practically. It typically offers features like color wheels, palettes, sliders, and swatches, allowing users to experiment with different color combinations and variations. Designers can create and save custom color palettes, preview them in various design templates, or even test their compatibility on mockups. By using a color simulation app, designers can see the immediate visual impact of color choices on their designs without the need for physical materials or extensive trial-and-error. They can experiment with different color schemes, adjust color proportions, and quickly assess the harmony and balance of their compositions. This process saves time and resources, ensuring that designers can make more informed decisions about color selection in a streamlined manner. The ability to explore color symbolism within a color simulation app is particularly valuable. Designers can test how different colors influence the emotions, perceptions, and interpretations of their target audience. They can align colors with specific brand values, select appropriate color palettes for websites or logos, or create visual narratives that resonate with the intended message. In conclusion, color simulation apps provide practical tools for designers to apply color theory and symbolism in their creative processes. These apps enable them to experiment with different color combinations, visualize the impact of colors on their designs, and make informed decisions about color selection that align with their intended message or brand identity.

Color Simulation Software

A color simulation software is a computer program that provides designers and artists with the ability to explore and visualize various color combinations and effects in the context of color theory and symbolism. Color theory refers to the principles and guidelines that dictate how colors can be combined and used to create visual harmony and impact. It takes into account concepts such as color temperature, color relationships, color harmony, and color psychology. This theory forms the foundation for understanding the impact of colors and their interactions in design. Color symbolism, on the other hand, explores the meaning and associations attached to different colors in various cultures and contexts. It recognizes that colors can evoke specific emotions, convey messages, and represent certain ideas or qualities. By understanding the symbolism behind colors, designers can use them strategically to reinforce their intended message or create a particular atmosphere in their designs. A color simulation software allows designers to experiment with different color combinations and explore how these choices affect the overall visual aesthetic and the emotional response they elicit. By using the software, designers can create virtual mock-ups of their designs and test different color palettes, ensuring their choices align with color theory principles and the intended symbolism. Furthermore, the software typically provides tools for adjusting color values, such as hue, saturation, and brightness, enabling designers to fine-tune their color selections. It also allows for the comparison of various color schemes side by side, empowering designers to make more informed decisions about color combinations that work best for their specific design goals. In summary, a color simulation software is a valuable tool for designers and artists, enabling them to explore and visualize different color combinations and effects in the context of color theory and symbolism. It helps them make informed decisions about color choices, ensuring their designs are visually appealing, emotionally impactful, and aligned with their intended message.

Color Simulation Tools

Color simulation tools are software or applications that are used in the field of color theory and color symbolism in design to visually represent and manipulate colors. These tools allow designers to explore various color combinations and understand how different colors interact with each other in a design. Color theory is the study of how colors can be combined and used to create visually appealing compositions. It explores the relationships between colors, such as complementary, analogous, and triadic color schemes. Color symbolism, on the other hand, is the use of colors to convey specific meanings or emotions in a design. Different colors can evoke different responses from viewers, and color symbolism helps designers communicate their intended message. Color simulation tools provide designers with an interactive platform to experiment with different color combinations and test how these colors will look in various design contexts. They offer features such as color wheels, sliders, and palettes, which allow designers to select and manipulate colors with precision. One key aspect of color simulation tools is the ability to preview how colors will appear in different lighting conditions, such as daylight or artificial light. This is important because colors can look different depending on the lighting environment, and designers need to consider these variations when choosing colors for their designs. Another important feature of color simulation tools is the ability to simulate color blindness. Color blindness affects a significant portion of the population, and designers need to ensure that their designs are accessible to these individuals. By simulating different types of color blindness, designers can evaluate the legibility and contrast of their color choices. Furthermore, color simulation tools often provide the option to adjust color values, such as hue, saturation, and brightness. This allows designers to fine-tune colors and create harmonious palettes. Additionally, these tools may offer suggestions for color combinations based on color theory principles, helping designers find aesthetically pleasing and meaningful color schemes. In summary, color simulation tools are powerful software or applications that assist designers in understanding and manipulating colors in the context of color theory and color symbolism. They provide interactive features to explore color combinations, preview colors in different lighting conditions, simulate color blindness, and adjust color values. By using these tools, designers can create visually appealing and meaningful designs that effectively communicate their intended message.

Color Space

A color space refers to a three-dimensional model that represents colors in an organized manner. It provides a structured system that defines how colors can be categorized, represented, and manipulated within the field of color theory and color symbolism in design. Color spaces are used to map colors in a way that allows for consistent communication and interpretation across different mediums and devices. They play a crucial role in various disciplines, including graphic design, print production, digital imaging, and web design. The most commonly used color spaces in design are RGB (Red-Green-Blue) and CMYK (Cyan-Magenta-Yellow-Black). RGB, a device-dependent color model, is primarily used for electronic displays such as computer monitors and televisions. It represents colors by combining different intensities of red, green, and blue light. CMYK, on the other hand, is a subtractive color model used in printing. It represents colors by combining different proportions of cyan, magenta, yellow, and black inks. An understanding of color theory is essential for effectively working with color spaces. Color theory explores how colors interact with each other and the psychological and emotional responses they can evoke. It encompasses concepts such as hue, saturation, value, and color harmonies. By applying color theory principles, designers can create visually pleasing and meaningful compositions. Color symbolism, another aspect of color theory,

71

examines the cultural and psychological associations that people attribute to different colors. Colors can convey specific messages, evoke certain emotions, and symbolize various concepts or ideas. For example, red is often associated with passion, energy, or danger, while blue can signify calmness, trust, or professionalism. Understanding color symbolism allows designers to intentionally harness the power of colors to evoke specific responses in their audience. In conclusion, a color space is a structured system that encompasses the representation and manipulation of colors. It plays a vital role in color theory and color symbolism in design, allowing for consistent communication and interpretation of colors across different mediums. Understanding color theory principles and color symbolism allows designers to effectively work with color spaces and create visually appealing and meaningful designs.

Color Spectrum

The color spectrum refers to the range of colors that can be observed when white light passes through a prism or when the wavelengths of light are separated. In color theory, the spectrum is often depicted as a circular arrangement of colors, known as the color wheel. In color symbolism in design, different colors on the spectrum are associated with certain feelings, emotions, and meanings. These associations may vary across different cultures and contexts, but there are some common interpretations that are widely accepted. Starting from the warm end of the spectrum, red is often associated with passion, energy, and vitality. It can also represent danger, anger, or power. Orange is often seen as a color of warmth, enthusiasm, and creativity. It can also symbolize caution or warning, depending on its shade. Yellow is associated with happiness, joy, and positivity. It can also be associated with cowardice or caution. Moving to the cooler side of the spectrum, green is commonly associated with nature, growth, and freshness. It can also symbolize jealousy or inexperience. Blue is often seen as a color of calmness, tranquility, and stability. It can also represent sadness or depression. Indigo, a shade of blue, is often associated with intuition, spirituality, and wisdom. Purple is commonly associated with royalty, luxury, and creativity. It can also represent mystery or magic. Moving towards the neutral end of the spectrum, white is associated with purity, innocence, and clarity. It can also symbolize emptiness or coldness. Gray is often seen as a color of neutrality, balance, and practicality. It can also be associated with dullness or sadness. Finally, black is commonly associated with power, elegance, and mystery. It can also symbolize fear or evil.

Color Storytelling

Color storytelling refers to the practice of using colors to communicate emotions, narratives, and messages in design. It is rooted in color theory and color symbolism, which explore the psychological and cultural associations we have with different colors. In color theory, colors are classified into different categories based on their relationships with one another. These categories include primary colors (red, blue, and yellow), secondary colors (orange, green, and purple), and tertiary colors (mixtures of primary and secondary colors). Additionally, colors are described in terms of their properties, such as hue (the color itself), value (lightness or darkness), and saturation (intensity or purity of color). Color symbolism, on the other hand, examines the meaning and interpretations assigned to specific colors across different cultures and contexts. For example, red is often associated with passion, energy, and love, while blue is often associated with calmness, trust, and reliability. When used in design, color storytelling involves strategically selecting and combining colors to create a specific visual impact and evoke desired emotional responses. Colors can be used to reflect the theme or mood of a design, convey meaning or symbolism, and guide the viewer's attention. They can also be used to create contrast, balance, or harmony within a composition. For instance, warm colors like red, orange, and yellow are commonly used to create a sense of energy and excitement, while cool colors like blue and green can evoke feelings of calmness and tranquility. Complementary colors, which are located opposite each other on the color wheel (e.g., red and green), create visual tension and draw attention. Analogous colors, which are adjacent to each other on the color wheel (e.g., red, orange, and yellow), create a sense of harmony and unity.

Color Swatch Books

Color swatch books are tools used in color theory and design to provide a visual representation of a range of colors and their variations. These books typically contain a collection of color samples organized in a systematic manner. In the context of color theory, swatch books serve as a reference guide for designers and artists, allowing them to explore and experiment with different color combinations. The books often include a wide spectrum of colors, including primary, secondary, and tertiary colors, as well as shades, tints, and tones. By providing an extensive range of color options, swatch books enable designers to make informed decisions about color selection and create harmonious compositions. Swatch books also play a crucial role in understanding color symbolism in design. Colors have inherent meanings and can evoke specific emotions or associations. For example, red is often associated with passion or power, while blue is associated with calmness or trust. Swatch books allow designers to explore various color palettes and understand the symbolic implications of different color combinations. By referencing the swatch book, designers can choose colors that align with the intended message or brand identity. Furthermore, color swatch books are valuable tools for ensuring consistency and accuracy in color reproduction across different media. Designers can use the swatch book as a reference when selecting colors for digital or print projects, ensuring that the chosen colors will be reproduced accurately. This is particularly important in industries such as graphic design, printing, and fashion, where color fidelity is crucial. In summary, color swatch books are essential resources for designers and artists, providing a visual representation of a wide range of colors and their variations. They serve as reference guides for color selection, allowing designers to create harmonious compositions and convey specific meanings through color symbolism. Additionally, swatch books ensure consistent and accurate color reproduction across different media.

Color Swatch Catalogs

A color swatch catalog is a tool used in color theory and design to organize and display a collection of colors. It serves as a reference guide for designers, artists, and anyone working with color to visually explore and select colors for their creative projects. In color theory, colors are categorized into different groups, such as primary colors, secondary colors, and tertiary colors. Each color has its own unique properties, including hue (the color itself), saturation (the intensity or purity of the color), and value (the lightness or darkness of the color). Through a color swatch catalog, these colors and their properties can be easily compared and chosen for use in various design applications, such as graphic design, interior design, fashion design, and more. Color symbolism is the practice of assigning meaning and significance to different colors. Different cultures and contexts may associate colors with specific emotions, concepts, or messages. For example, red can symbolize passion, love, and energy, while blue can represent calmness, tranquility, and trust. In design, color symbolism is often used to evoke specific feelings or convey certain messages to the viewer or audience. A color swatch catalog can be used to explore the different symbolic associations of colors and choose the most appropriate ones for a particular design project. By visually displaying a wide range of colors, the catalog allows designers to consider the emotional impact and meaning that each color can bring to their designs.

Color Swatch Collections

Color swatch collections are sets of curated colors that are used in the field of color theory and design to create cohesive and harmonious color schemes. These collections consist of a range of colors that are carefully selected based on their relationships to one another, including their hue, value, and saturation. Color theory is the study of how colors interact with each other and how they can be combined to create aesthetically pleasing compositions. It explores the psychological and emotional effects that different colors can evoke, as well as their symbolic associations. In design, color is a powerful tool that can be used to convey specific messages and create desired reactions from the viewer. Color swatch collections serve as a visual reference for designers, allowing them to easily select and use colors that work well together. These collections can be created based on various principles of color theory, such as complementary colors, analogous colors, or triadic color schemes. Each color in a swatch collection is carefully chosen to complement and enhance the other colors in the set. Swatch collections are often used in a wide range of design disciplines, including graphic design, fashion design, interior design, and web design. They can be used to create a sense of visual harmony and balance within a design, as well as to evoke specific emotions or moods. For example, a collection of warm and vibrant colors might be used to create a lively and energetic design, while a collection of cool and muted colors might be used to create a calm and soothing atmosphere. Beyond their practical application in design, color swatch collections also hold symbolic meanings. Different colors can carry cultural or personal associations, and these associations can be used to communicate specific messages. For example, red may symbolize passion or danger, while blue may symbolize serenity or trust. By carefully selecting colors from a swatch collection, designers can tap into these symbolic meanings to reinforce their intended message or evoke a desired response from the viewer. In conclusion, color swatch collections play a vital role in color theory and design. They provide designers with a tool to create visually cohesive and harmonious color schemes, while also allowing them to tap into the symbolic meanings of different colors. By using color swatch collections effectively, designers can enhance the aesthetic appeal of their designs and communicate their intended messages more effectively.

Color Swatch

A color swatch is a small sample or representation of a specific color or a range of colors. It is typically used in the field of color theory and color symbolism in design. Color theory is the study of how colors interact and work together, while color symbolism in design refers to the use of colors to convey certain meanings or emotions. In color theory, a color swatch helps to visually demonstrate the properties of different colors such as hue, saturation, and value. It allows designers to compare and contrast colors, and choose the most appropriate ones for their designs. For example, a color swatch may include various shades of blue ranging from light to dark, allowing designers to see how the colors change in terms of intensity and value. This helps in creating color schemes that are visually pleasing and harmonious. Color symbolism in design involves using colors to communicate specific messages or evoke certain emotions. Different colors are associated with various meanings and emotions. For instance, red is often associated with passion or anger, while green is associated with nature or tranquility. A color swatch can be used to explore and experiment with different color combinations to convey the intended message or evoke the desired emotions. Designers can create color swatches that represent the colors commonly used to symbolize specific concepts or emotions, such as joy, sadness, or energy. Overall, a color swatch is a valuable tool in color theory and color symbolism in design. It allows designers to analyze and select colors based on their properties and how they are perceived. By using color swatches, designers can create visually appealing and meaningful designs that effectively communicate their intended message or evoke specific emotions.

Color Swatches

Color swatches are a vital tool in color theory and design, serving as visual representations of specific colors within a chosen color scheme. These swatches are used to organize, compare, and select colors to create harmonious and meaningful designs. In color theory, color swatches are arranged in a specific order, typically in a color wheel or color palette, to illustrate the relationships between colors. This arrangement helps designers understand the principles of color harmony, contrast, and combinations. By using color swatches, designers can easily identify primary colors, secondary colors, complementary colors, and analogous colors, among others. Color symbolism, on the other hand, explores the emotional and cultural associations that certain colors evoke. Color swatches are used in this context to convey and communicate specific meanings and messages through color choices. For instance, red swatches may symbolize passion, love, or danger, while blue swatches may signify tranquility, trust, or sadness. In design, color swatches play a fundamental role in establishing the overall mood, aesthetics, and communication of a project. They enable designers to maintain consistency and coherence throughout their work. By using defined color swatches, designers ensure a unified color palette that enhances brand recognition and visual impact. Moreover, color swatches aid in the selection and coordination of colors across various design elements, such as typography, illustrations, and backgrounds. They provide a reliable reference point for designers to make informed decisions about color combinations, contrasts, and overall visual balance. When using color swatches in design, it is important to consider the context, target audience, and intended message. Different colors have different cultural connotations, and understanding these associations can help designers effectively communicate their ideas and evoke desired emotions. In conclusion, color swatches serve as a fundamental tool in color theory and design. They help designers organize, compare, and select colors while ensuring visual harmony and coherence. By understanding the principles of color relationships and the symbolism associated with specific colors, designers can make informed choices that evoke the desired emotional responses and effectively convey their message.

Color Symbolism

In color theory and design, color symbolism refers to the meaning and associations that are commonly attributed to different colors. This concept is based on the belief that colors can evoke specific emotions, thoughts, or ideas, and therefore can be used strategically in visual communication to convey a desired message or create a desired mood. Color symbolism is deeply rooted in cultural and societal contexts, as different cultures and societies have assigned unique meanings to colors over time. These associations are often influenced by factors such as history, religion, and even personal experiences. Consequently, the interpretation of color symbolism can vary across different regions and individuals. Some common examples of color symbolism include: - Red: Often associated with passion, love, energy, and power. It can also symbolize anger or danger, depending on the context. - Blue: Often associated with calmness, stability, and trust. It can also symbolize sadness or melancholy. - Yellow: Often associated with happiness, optimism, and energy. It can also symbolize caution or deceit. - Green: Often associated with nature, growth, and prosperity. It can also symbolize envy or inexperience. - Purple: Often associated with royalty, luxury, and spirituality. It can also symbolize mystery or arrogance. - Orange: Often associated with vitality, creativity, and enthusiasm. It can also symbolize aggression or flamboyance. - White: Often associated with purity, innocence, and simplicity. It can also symbolize sterility or emptiness. - Black: Often associated with power, sophistication, and elegance. It can also symbolize death or evil. When employing color symbolism in design, it is essential to consider the intended message and the target audience. Colors can affect people differently based on their personal experiences and cultural background, so it is crucial to ensure that the chosen colors are appropriate and resonate with the desired emotional response or symbolic representation. Additionally, color combinations and contrasts can also enhance or alter the meanings conveyed by individual colors. Understanding color symbolism enables designers to harness the power of colors effectively, create visually appealing compositions, and achieve specific design objectives.

Color Temperature

Color temperature refers to the perceived warmth or coolness of a color. It is a concept derived from color theory and is commonly used in design to convey specific emotions, moods, and meanings through the use of color. In color theory, color temperature is based on the idea that colors can be categorized as warm or cool. Warm colors, such as red, orange, and yellow, are associated with warmth, energy, and positivity. They are often used to create a sense of excitement, passion, and stimulation. Cool colors, on the other hand, such as blue, green, and purple, are associated with calmness, tranquility, and relaxation. They are often used to create a sense of serenity, harmony, and peacefulness.

Color Theory

Color theory refers to the study of how colors interact with each other and how they can be combined to create visually harmonious designs. It explores the principles and guidelines for effectively using colors in various applications, such as art, design, and communication. Color symbolism in design, on the other hand, refers to the use of colors to convey specific meanings or emotions. Different colors have been associated with certain feelings, ideas, or concepts across different cultures and contexts. By understanding color symbolism, designers can manipulate the psychological and emotional impact of their designs.

Color Theory Courses And Workshops

Color theory courses and workshops are educational programs that focus on teaching individuals about the principles and concepts behind color in design. These programs provide a structured learning environment where participants can gain a deeper understanding of how colors interact and how they can be used effectively to convey specific messages, evoke emotions, and create visually appealing compositions. In the realm of design, color theory plays a crucial role in the decision-making process. It involves studying the color wheel, which is a visual representation of the relationships between different colors. The color wheel consists of primary, secondary, and tertiary colors, and understanding their placement and interactions can help designers create harmonious color schemes. Courses and workshops on color theory typically cover topics such as the psychology of color, color symbolism, color harmonies, color contrast, and the practical application of color theory in various design disciplines. Participants learn to analyze the emotional and psychological impact of different colors, enabling them to make informed decisions when selecting colors for branding, marketing materials, websites, and other design projects. Color symbolism is another important aspect covered in these programs. Colors are often associated with certain meanings and emotions, and understanding these associations is crucial when designing for specific purposes. For example, red is commonly associated with passion and energy, while blue is often associated with calmness and trust. By studying color symbolism, participants can use colors strategically to communicate desired messages and evoke specific responses from the audience. Attending color theory courses and workshops can be beneficial for designers, artists, marketers, and anyone involved in visual communication. By gaining a solid foundation in color theory, individuals can approach their creative projects with a heightened awareness of the impact and potential of color. They can make informed design choices that align with their intended messages and goals, ultimately enhancing the overall effectiveness and impact of their work. Overall, color theory courses and workshops provide participants with the knowledge and skills necessary to utilize color effectively in design. By understanding the principles of color and its symbolism, individuals can create visually compelling and meaningful compositions that resonate with their target audience.

Color Theory Courses

Color theory courses are educational programs that provide in-depth knowledge and understanding of the principles and concepts related to colors and their symbolic meanings in design. These courses explore the intricate relationship between colors, their psychological effects, and their impact on visual perception. In the context of color theory, courses aim to teach students about the color wheel, which serves as the foundation for understanding color harmonies and combinations. The color wheel is a visual representation of the entire spectrum of colors, arranged in a circular format. By studying the color wheel, students learn about primary, secondary, and tertiary colors, as well as their relationships, such as complementary, analogous, and triadic color schemes. Color theory courses also delve into color symbolism in design. Colors hold deep cultural and psychological associations, and understanding their symbolic meanings is crucial for effective communication through design. Students learn about the emotional and psychological impact of colors and how they can be used to evoke specific feelings or associations. For example, red is often associated with power, passion, and danger, while blue is often associated with calmness, trust, and stability. Through color theory courses, students learn practical techniques for applying color theory in design. This includes understanding the use of color in various design disciplines, such as graphic design, interior design, and fashion design. Students explore color psychology, color perception, and the impact of colors on branding and marketing efforts. By studying real-world examples and case studies, students develop a critical eye for choosing and combining colors effectively to create visually pleasing and impactful designs. Overall, color theory courses provide a comprehensive understanding of the principles and symbolism of colors in design. By studying color theory, students gain the necessary knowledge and skills to make informed decisions about color palettes, create harmonious compositions, and effectively communicate through color in their design work.

Color Theory Workshops

Color Theory Workshops are educational programs or training sessions that focus on the principles and concepts of color theory and its application in design. Color theory is the study of how colors interact with and influence each other, and it plays a crucial role in creating aesthetically pleasing and effective designs. In design, colors not only have aesthetic value but also convey symbolic meanings and evoke certain emotions or associations. Understanding color symbolism is essential for designers as it helps them communicate specific messages or create certain moods through their work.

Color Theory

Color theory is a crucial aspect of design, encompassing principles and guidelines that involve the study and understanding of colors and their relationships. It explores the psychological and symbolic meanings of colors, as well as their visual impact on design compositions. In the realm of color theory, colors are divided into primary, secondary, and tertiary categories. Primary colors are pure colors that cannot be created by mixing other colors together. Secondary colors are created by mixing two primary colors, while tertiary colors are formed by mixing a primary color with a neighboring secondary color. This color wheel forms the foundation of color theory, illustrating the relationships and harmonies between colors. Color symbolism, on the other hand, refers to the associations and meanings attached to specific colors. Each color holds different connotations, evoking various emotions and communicating different messages. For instance, warm colors like red and orange are often associated with energy, passion, and excitement, while cool colors like blue and green evoke feelings of calmness, serenity, and freshness. Understanding color symbolism allows designers to effectively communicate and convey specific moods or messages in their work. Color harmony is another essential concept in color theory. It refers to the arrangement of colors in a composition to create an aesthetically pleasing and balanced visual impact. Achieving color harmony involves understanding color relationships, such as complementary colors (opposite colors on the color wheel), analogous colors (neighboring colors on the wheel), and triadic colors (three colors equally spaced apart on the wheel). By using these harmonious color combinations, designers can create visually appealing designs that are well-balanced and visually engaging. Moreover, color theory also explores the concepts of hue, saturation, and value. Hue refers to the specific colors themselves, such as red, blue, or yellow. Saturation refers to the intensity or purity of a color, determining whether it appears vivid or muted. Value, on the other hand, represents the lightness or darkness of a color. Understanding and controlling these elements allows designers to manipulate colors effectively in their compositions, achieving desired effects and enhancing visual communication.

Color Tones

Color tones refer to the variations of shades and tints created by altering the intensity or saturation of a particular color. In the context of color theory, these variations are achieved by adding either black or white (known as shading and tinting, respectively) to the original color. The resulting tones can evoke different emotional responses and have symbolic meanings in design. In color symbolism, different tones can have distinct connotations and associations. For example, darker tones, created by adding black, may convey a sense of mystery, elegance, or strength. They can be used to create a dramatic or sophisticated atmosphere in design. On the other hand, lighter tones, achieved by adding white, often suggest purity, innocence, or lightness. They can create a calming or airy feeling in a design composition.

Color Trend Forecasting Resources

Color trend forecasting resources are tools and references used in the field of color theory and design to predict and anticipate the most popular and influential colors that will be used in various industries and applications. Color theory is the study of how colors interact and how they are perceived by individuals. It is an important aspect of design as colors have the power to elicit emotions and convey meaning. Understanding color theory can help designers create visually appealing and impactful designs that resonate with their intended audience. Color symbolism, on the other hand, is the study of the meaning and significance attributed to different colors. Different cultures and societies have different associations with colors, and this can influence the way colors are used in design. For example, in Western cultures, red is often associated with love and passion, while in Asian cultures, it symbolizes luck and prosperity. Color trend forecasting resources help designers and professionals in various industries stay ahead of emerging color trends by providing valuable insights and predictions. These resources may include trend reports, color trend books, online platforms, and services that provide information on upcoming color trends based on extensive research and analysis. By using color trend forecasting resources, designers can make informed decisions about the colors they incorporate into their projects. This can be particularly useful for industries such as fashion, interior design, graphic design, and product design, where staying current and relevant is essential. Color trend forecasting can also help businesses and brands develop their color strategies, ensuring that they are aligning their products and marketing materials with the latest trends. By staying updated on color trends, companies can create a visually cohesive and modern brand image that resonates with their target audience.

Color Trend Forecasting

Color trend forecasting in the context of color theory and color symbolism in design refers to the process of predicting and identifying the colors that will be popular or influential in the design industry and consumer market in the future. It involves analyzing current cultural, social, and economic trends, as well as understanding the psychology behind color perception and symbolism, in order to anticipate the colors that will resonate with people and meet their evolving needs and desires. Color trend forecasting relies on a deep understanding of color theory, which is the study of how colors interact and affect human perception. It takes into account principles such as the color wheel, color harmonies, and the impact of light and color temperature. By applying these principles, trend forecasters can identify color palettes and combinations that are visually appealing and harmonious. Besides color theory, trend forecasters also consider color symbolism, which is the cultural or psychological meaning associated with different colors. Colors can evoke different emotions, convey specific messages, or be associated with certain values or concepts. For example, red is often associated with passion and energy, while blue is associated with calmness and trust. Understanding these symbolic meanings is crucial in selecting colors that align with the desired brand image or design intent. Trend forecasters gather information from various sources, including fashion shows, trade shows, art exhibitions, consumer behavior research, and global events. They analyze patterns, themes, and emerging color preferences in these contexts to identify potential color trends. This information is then translated into color palettes and recommendations that can be used by designers, marketers, and manufacturers to create products and experiences that resonate with consumers. Ultimately, color trend forecasting helps designers and brands stay ahead of the curve and create designs that are visually appealing, meaningful, and relevant to their target audience. It enables them to tap into the emotional and cultural power of color, and leverage it to shape perceptions, convey messages, and create memorable experiences.

Color Trend Prediction Tools

Color Trend Prediction Tools, in the context of color theory and color symbolism in design, refer to technological tools or systems that are used to forecast or anticipate the upcoming color trends in various industries, such as fashion, interior design, graphic design, and marketing. These tools analyze and interpret a wide range of factors including cultural, societal, economic, and technological influences to predict the colors that will be popular and widely used in the future. These tools typically utilize extensive databases, historical color data, market research, and analysis of current design trends to generate accurate predictions. They help designers, marketers, and businesses make informed decisions about their color choices, ensuring that they stay up-to-date and relevant in an ever-changing market.

Color Trends

Color trends in the context of color theory and color symbolism in design refer to the prevailing or popular colors that are widely used and preferred by designers and consumers during a certain period of time. These trends are influenced by various factors such as cultural shifts, fashion trends, technological advancements, socio-economic changes, and psychological responses to color. Designers and marketers closely follow color trends to create aesthetically pleasing and visually appealing designs that resonate with their target audience. Understanding color trends helps designers make informed decisions when selecting colors for branding, advertising, product packaging, and various design elements.

Color Usage

Color usage refers to the selection and application of colors in design, based on the principles of color theory and symbolism. It involves understanding the psychological and emotional impact of colors, as well as their visual properties and interactions. In color theory, colors are organized on a color wheel, which helps designers understand how different colors relate to each other. The color wheel consists of primary colors (red, blue, and yellow), secondary colors (orange, green, and purple), and tertiary colors (resulting from mixing primary and secondary colors). Complementary colors, located opposite each other on the wheel, create a strong contrast when used together, while analogous colors, located next to each other, create a harmonious and unified effect. Color symbolism in design involves associating specific meanings and emotions with different colors. For example, red is often associated with passion, energy, and excitement, while blue is associated with calmness, trust, and reliability. When using colors symbolically, designers must consider cultural connotations and personal associations that may influence how colors are interpreted by different individuals or audiences. The way colors are used in design can have a significant impact on the overall message and user experience. Color can be used to attract attention, create a focal point, guide the viewer's eye, convey meaning, evoke emotions, and communicate brand identity. The choice of color palette should align with the intended message and goal of the design. In addition, the visual properties of color, such as hue, saturation, and value, can be manipulated to create various effects. For example, a high-contrast color scheme with bold, saturated colors can create a sense of vibrancy and excitement, while a monochromatic scheme with varying shades and tints of a single color can create a calm and sophisticated ambiance. In conclusion, color usage in design involves the thoughtful selection and application of colors based on color theory and symbolism. It requires an understanding of how colors interact, their psychological impact, and the intended message of the design. By utilizing color effectively, designers can create visually appealing and meaningful designs that resonate with their target audience.

Color Variations

Color variations refer to the different shades and hues that can be derived from a particular color. In the context of color theory and color symbolism in design, color variations play a crucial role in creating visual interest, conveying emotions, and enhancing the overall aesthetic appeal of a design. Color theory is founded on the principle that colors have certain psychological and emotional effects on individuals. By using color variations, designers can manipulate these effects to achieve specific design goals. For example, lighter variations of a color tend to evoke feelings of calmness and serenity, while darker variations can create a sense of mystery or intensity.

Color Vibrancy

Color vibrancy refers to the intensity and brightness of a color. In the context of color theory, it describes the vividness and saturation of a color hue. Vibrant colors are characterized by their strong and impactful appearance, often standing out and attracting attention. Color symbolism in design adds an additional layer of meaning to the concept of color vibrancy. Each color possesses its own symbolism and can evoke different emotions and associations. Vibrant colors are often associated with energy, excitement, and positivity. They can stimulate the senses, create a sense of urgency, or convey a message of motivation and enthusiasm.

Color Visualization Apps

A color visualization app is a digital tool that allows users to explore and manipulate color in order to create visual representations. In the context of color theory, such apps provide a platform for users to understand and experiment with various color palettes, combinations, and schemes. These apps enable users to select and apply specific colors to elements within a design, such as text, shapes, or backgrounds. By visually representing the chosen colors in real time, the app helps users visualize how different combinations can affect the overall aesthetic and impact of their designs. Color visualization apps also offer features that allow users to experiment with color symbolism in their designs. Color symbolism is the study of how colors evoke emotions, convey messages, and represent ideas or concepts. By associating colors with specific meanings, users can use these apps to create designs that effectively communicate their intended messages. Furthermore, color visualization apps often provide options for users to generate color palettes based on different color harmonies, such as complementary colors, analogous colors, or triadic colors. These tools offer assistance in selecting color schemes that are visually appealing and harmonious to the human eye. Additionally, many color visualization apps provide color blindness simulation, which enables designers to understand how individuals with color vision deficiencies perceive their designs. This feature ensures that the chosen color palettes can be easily interpreted by a wide range of users. In summary, color visualization apps are essential tools for designers and artists, as they allow for the exploration, experimentation, and visualization of color palettes, combinations, and symbolism. By using these apps, designers can create visually appealing and meaningful designs that effectively communicate their intended messages.

Color Visualization Software

A color visualization software refers to a computer program or application specifically designed to aid designers and artists in understanding and exploring color theory and symbolism in their creative work. This software allows users to digitally manipulate colors and observe their effects on various design elements, thereby facilitating the process of color selection and creating harmonious color palettes. Moreover, it provides insights into the meaning and emotional impact of different colors, enabling users to effectively convey specific messages and evoke desired emotions through their design choices. Color theory is a field of study that examines how colors interact and how they are perceived by individuals. It explores concepts such as color harmony, color contrast, and color psychology. By incorporating color theory principles, a color visualization software assists designers in making informed color decisions that align with their intended design goals. In the realm of design, color symbolism plays a crucial role in conveying meaning and evoking certain emotions or associations. Different colors can be associated with specific concepts or emotions, and understanding these associations is essential for effective visual communication. A color visualization software allows designers to explore the symbolic implications of different colors and experiment with color combinations that best align with their desired message. Through a user-friendly interface, this software typically provides a variety of tools and features. These may include a color wheel, which enables users to observe the relationships between colors, such as complementary or analogous schemes. It may also offer options to adjust color properties like hue, saturation, and brightness, allowing users to fine-tune color palettes to achieve the desired effect. Furthermore, a color visualization software may offer pre-defined color palettes or allow users to create their own custom palettes. This feature enables designers to quickly access harmonious color combinations or explore unique color schemes that might not have been considered otherwise. Overall, a color visualization software serves as a valuable tool for designers and artists, helping them navigate the complex world of color theory and symbolism. It empowers users to make informed color choices that support their design objectives, communicate intended messages, and evoke desired emotions in their visual creations.

Color Visualization Tools

A color visualization tool is a digital application or software that helps designers and artists understand and explore different colors in the context of color theory and symbolism. It provides a platform for users to visually experiment with various color combinations and analyze their impact in design. In the field of design, color plays a crucial role in conveying emotions, messages, and information. Color theory, which is the study of how colors interact with each other, is an essential aspect that designers consider while creating a visual composition. Understanding the psychological and symbolic meaning associated with different colors empowers designers to use colors strategically to achieve specific design goals. Color visualization tools offer a range of functionalities that aid designers in their decision-making process. They typically provide color palettes, which are curated collections of colors that harmonize well together. These palettes are carefully selected based on the principles of color theory and can be used as a starting point for design projects. Furthermore, these tools enable designers to experiment with different color combinations and see how they interact with each other. Users can easily manipulate the hues, saturation, and brightness of colors to create custom palettes that align with their design vision. The visualization aspect allows designers to perceive how the colors will appear on various mediums, such as screens or print, to ensure a consistent and appealing visual experience. In addition to exploring colors based on their aesthetic properties, color visualization tools also enable users to explore the symbolic meaning associated with different colors. They often provide information on the cultural, psychological, and historical connotations of specific colors. This allows designers to align their color choices with the intended message of their design and the target audience's preferences or cultural context. In conclusion, color visualization tools are powerful resources that help designers and artists navigate the complex world of color theory and symbolism. They assist in the selection and experimentation of color combinations, ensuring that the final design effectively communicates the desired message and elicits the intended emotions or responses from the viewers.

Color Wheel Applications

A color wheel is a visual representation of colors arranged in a circular format, primarily used in color theory and design. It is a powerful tool that helps designers and artists understand the relationships between different colors and how they can be combined harmoniously. In color theory, the color wheel is based on the principles of primary, secondary, and tertiary colors. The primary colors, including red, blue, and yellow, are the foundational colors from which all other colors are derived. By mixing primary colors, secondary colors are created, such as green, purple, and orange. Tertiary colors, on the other hand, are the result of mixing primary and secondary colors. The color wheel organizes these colors in a logical sequence that reflects their relationships. The color wheel is particularly useful in understanding color combinations and creating color harmonies. Complementary colors, which are opposite each other on the color wheel, create a strong contrast when used together, making them suitable for creating attention-grabbing designs. Analogous colors, which are adjacent to each other on the color wheel, create a more harmonious and soothing effect, often used in creating cohesive color schemes. Besides its practical applications in color theory, the color wheel also has symbolic significance in design. Different colors are associated with specific emotions and meanings, and the color wheel can be used to convey these meanings effectively. For example, red is often associated with passion and energy, while blue is associated with calmness and tranquility. By understanding these color associations, designers can use the color wheel to create visual narratives and evoke specific emotions in their designs. In summary, the color wheel is a fundamental tool in color theory and design, aiding in the understanding of color relationships and creating harmonious color combinations. It serves as a visual guide for designers and artists to experiment with different color schemes and convey specific emotions through their designs.

Color Wheel Apps

A color wheel app is an application designed for the purpose of understanding and exploring color theory and color symbolism in design. It provides a visual representation of the color wheel, which is a circular arrangement of colors based on their relationships and properties. The color wheel is a fundamental tool used in color theory to understand color harmony, color schemes, and the mixing of colors. It consists of primary colors (red, blue, and yellow), secondary colors (orange, green, and purple), and tertiary colors (the six colors between primary and secondary colors) arranged in a circle. The color wheel app enables designers to select and explore color combinations, helping them create aesthetically pleasing designs. By using the app, designers can easily determine complementary colors, analogous colors, triadic colors, and other color schemes. Color harmony is achieved when colors are balanced and naturally pleasing to the eye, and the color wheel app assists designers in achieving this harmony. Furthermore, the app provides additional features that go beyond the basic color wheel. It often offers tools for adjusting and modifying colors, such as hue, saturation, and brightness sliders. These tools allow designers to fine-tune their color choices and achieve the desired visual impact. In addition to providing a practical understanding of color relationships, the color wheel app also allows designers to explore the symbolism associated with different colors. In design, colors often convey emotions, evoke reactions, and communicate messages. For example, red is commonly associated with passion and energy, while blue symbolizes calmness and trust. By using the color wheel app, designers can easily experiment with different color choices and ensure that their designs convey the intended meaning and evoke the desired emotional response. Overall, a color wheel app is an essential tool for designers, providing a visual representation of the color wheel and allowing for easy exploration of color harmony and symbolism. By using this app, designers can effectively utilize the power of color in their designs, creating visually captivating and emotionally engaging experiences for their audiences.

Color Wheel Design Tools

A color wheel is a tool used in color theory and design to help explore and understand the relationships between colors. It is a visual representation of the way colors relate to one another and can be used to create harmonious and balanced color schemes. The color wheel consists of a circle divided into different sections, each section representing a different color. The most commonly used color wheel is the traditional 12-color wheel, which is based on the primary colors (red, yellow, and blue), secondary colors (orange, green, and purple), and tertiary colors (red-orange, yellow-orange, yellow-green, blue-green, blue-purple, and red-purple). Color theory is the study of how colors interact with one another and the emotional and psychological effects they have on the viewer. By understanding color theory, designers can create meaningful and impactful designs that effectively communicate a message or evoke a certain feeling or emotion. One of the key concepts in color theory is the idea of color harmony. Color harmony refers to the pleasing arrangement of colors in a design. The color wheel is an essential tool for achieving color harmony. Designers can use it to choose colors that are complementary (opposite each other on the color wheel), analogous (next to each other on the color wheel), or monochromatic (variations of the same hue) to create visually pleasing color combinations. In addition to color theory, the color wheel is also used in color symbolism. Colors have different meanings and associations in different cultures and contexts. For example, red is often associated with love and passion, while blue is associated with calmness and tranquility. By understanding the symbolism behind different colors, designers can use the color wheel to effectively communicate specific messages or evoke certain emotions in their designs. In conclusion, the color wheel is a valuable tool in color theory and design. It helps designers explore and understand the relationships between colors, create harmonious color schemes, and effectively communicate messages or evoke emotions through color symbolism.

Color Wheel Tools

A color wheel tool is a fundamental tool in color theory that helps designers understand and apply color symbolism effectively in their design work. It consists of a circular diagram that displays primary, secondary, and tertiary colors in a systematic arrangement. The color wheel is divided into twelve parts, with each section representing a specific hue. The primary colors, namely red, blue, and yellow, are typically positioned evenly apart at equal distances from each other. These colors are considered the building blocks of all other colors. Adjacent to the primary colors are the secondary colors, which are created by mixing equal parts of the primary colors. These include orange (red + yellow), green (blue + yellow), and purple (red + blue). Secondary colors are positioned between their respective primary colors. In between the primary and secondary colors lie the tertiary colors, which are created by mixing unequal parts of adjacent primary and secondary colors. These tertiary colors include yellow-orange, yellow-green, blue-green, blue-purple, red-purple, and red-orange. Tertiary colors are positioned closer to the primary color used in their creation. The color wheel tool allows designers to easily identify color harmonies and relationships. Analogous harmonies are formed by placing colors next to each other on the color wheel, creating a smooth and cohesive appearance. Complementary harmonies are formed by placing colors directly opposite each other on the color wheel, creating a high-contrast effect. Split-complementary harmonies involve choosing a color and then selecting the colors on either side of its complement. Color symbolism plays an essential role in design, evoking different emotions and conveying various messages. By understanding the relationships between colors on the color wheel, designers can effectively use color symbolism to communicate their intended message. For example, warm colors such as red and orange are associated with energy, passion, and excitement, while cool colors like blue and green evoke calmness and serenity. In conclusion, a color wheel tool is a crucial tool for designers to understand and apply color symbolism effectively in their design work. Its systematic arrangement of colors helps designers create harmonious color schemes that successfully convey their intended message. By utilizing the color wheel tool, designers can create visually impactful and emotionally resonant designs.

Color Wheel

A color wheel is a visual representation of the relationship between colors. It is a tool used in color theory and design to understand and create harmonious color schemes. The wheel is made up of primary, secondary, and tertiary colors arranged in a circular format. In color theory, the wheel is divided into twelve segments, each representing a specific hue. The primary colors are red, blue, and yellow, which cannot be created by mixing other colors. Secondary colors are created by mixing two primary colors: purple (red and blue), green (blue and yellow), and orange (red and yellow). Tertiary colors are created by mixing a primary and a secondary color: red-orange, yellow-orange, yellow-green, blue-green, blue-violet, and red-violet. The color wheel is used as a guide for creating color schemes that are aesthetically pleasing and visually balanced. By understanding the relationships between colors, designers can choose hues that complement each other and evoke different emotions or meanings. Colors on opposite sides of the color wheel are known as complementary colors. They create strong contrast when placed together and can be used to highlight or accentuate certain elements in a design. For example, using a combination of blue and orange can create a vibrant and energetic composition. Analogous colors are those that are next to each other on the color wheel. They create a harmonious and cohesive look when used together. Analogous color schemes can be used to create a sense of unity and balance in a design. Split-complementary colors are created by choosing a base color and then using the two colors adjacent to its complementary color. This color scheme offers a variation of contrast while maintaining harmony in a design. Triadic colors are three colors equidistant from each other on the color wheel. This scheme offers a high level of contrast and can create a bold and vibrant visual impact. In addition to color theory, the color wheel is also used in color symbolism. Different colors are associated with various meanings and emotions. For example, red is often associated with passion or danger, while blue is associated with calmness or stability. Designers can use color symbolism to evoke specific emotions or convey certain messages in their work.

Color Workshops

Color workshops are educational sessions that focus on color theory and color symbolism in design. These workshops aim to provide participants with a comprehensive understanding of how colors work, as well as the psychological and symbolic meaning behind different hues. In the context of color theory, workshops explore the principles of color such as hue, saturation, and value, as well as their relationships and interactions. Participants learn about the color wheel and how to create harmonious color schemes using various color combinations. They also gain knowledge about color perception and how it can impact design choices, including the use of warm and cool colors and the effects of color contrast. Color symbolism in design is another important aspect covered in these workshops. Participants discover how different colors can evoke specific emotions and communicate particular messages. They learn about the cultural and historical significance of colors, understanding how different societies may interpret colors differently. Through hands-on exercises, participants explore the use of color symbolism to convey specific moods or meanings in their designs. Color workshops often include practical activities to enable participants to put their learnings into practice. These may include exercises such as creating color palettes, analyzing and critiquing existing designs, or applying color theory to their own design projects. Workshops may also feature case studies and examples from various design disciplines, demonstrating how colors are used effectively in different contexts. By attending color workshops, designers and artists can enhance their understanding of color and develop a more nuanced approach to color selection in their work. These workshops provide participants with the knowledge and tools to create visually appealing designs that effectively communicate their intended message or evoke the desired emotional response. Whether designing for branding, advertising, or other creative projects, a solid understanding of color theory and symbolism is essential for impactful and effective visual communication.

Colorblind-Friendly Color Pickers

A colorblind-friendly color picker is a tool used in design that allows colorblind individuals to select and differentiate between colors easily. The purpose of a color picker is to help designers choose specific colors for their designs, whether it be for websites, logos, graphics, or any other visual media. However, for individuals with color vision deficiencies, such as red-green colorblindness, it can be a challenge to accurately identify and distinguish between colors. Color theory is a fundamental principle in design that explores how colors interact with each other and how they can be used to create visual harmony or contrast. It involves concepts such as color wheels, complementary colors, analogous colors, and color temperature. Similarly, color symbolism is the practice of assigning meaning and emotions to specific colors, allowing designers to convey certain messages or evoke certain reactions through their color choices.

Colorblind-Friendly Color Wheels

A color wheel is a visual representation of the relationships between colors. It is a circular arrangement of colors that are based on their mathematical relationship to each other. The color wheel is an essential tool in color theory and is widely used in various fields, including design. Color theory is the study of how colors interact and harmonize with each other. It is an important aspect of design as colors can convey emotions, evoke moods, and communicate messages. Understanding color theory helps designers create visually appealing and meaningful compositions. In design, colors are not only selected based on aesthetics but also on their symbolic meanings. Each color has its own symbolism and can evoke specific emotions or cultural associations. For example, red is often associated with passion, energy, and love, while blue is associated with calmness, trust, and professionalism. By understanding color symbolism, designers can use colors strategically to convey the desired message in their designs. However, it is important to consider that not everyone perceives colors in the same way. Colorblindness is a condition in which individuals have difficulty distinguishing between certain colors. The most common type of colorblindness is red-green colorblindness, where individuals have trouble differentiating between red and green hues. This condition affects a significant portion of the population. To ensure that designs are accessible to individuals with colorblindness, it is crucial to create colorblind-friendly color wheels. These color wheels take into consideration the visual challenges faced by colorblind individuals and provide alternatives that are easier to differentiate. Colorblind-friendly color wheels use color combinations that are easily distinguishable for individuals with colorblindness. This may involve selecting colors that have a significant difference in brightness or using colors from opposite ends of the color spectrum. By considering the needs of colorblind individuals, designers can create inclusive designs that can be appreciated by a wider audience. In conclusion, a color wheel is a fundamental tool in color theory and design. It represents the relationships between colors and helps designers create visually appealing compositions. Understanding color symbolism is essential for conveying the desired message in designs. Additionally, it is important to create colorblind-friendly color wheels to ensure accessibility for individuals with colorblindness. By considering the needs of all individuals, designers can create inclusive and meaningful designs.

Colorblind-Friendly Palettes

Colorblind-Friendly Palettes are color schemes or combinations specifically designed to accommodate individuals with color vision deficiencies, mainly colorblindness. Color theory, a fundamental concept in design, revolves around the understanding and manipulation of color to create visually appealing compositions that convey specific meanings and evoke emotions. However, colorblindness poses a challenge in this process as it can hinder the ability to perceive certain colors accurately, affecting the intended visual communication. Color symbolim in design involves the intentional use of colors to convey specific messages or evoke desired emotions. Different colors are commonly associated with specific meanings, such as red symbolizing passion or danger, and blue representing calmness or trust. However, individuals with color vision deficiencies may not perceive these colors as intended, leading to misinterpretations or difficulties in understanding the symbolic intentions of the designer. To address these challenges, colorblind-friendly palettes consider the limitations of colorblind individuals and aim to create color combinations that are easily distinguishable by the widest range of people. These palettes prioritize colors with high levels of contrast and utilize color combinations that are less likely to cause confusion or ambiguity for those with color vision deficiencies. By selecting colorblind-friendly palettes, designers can ensure that their visual presentations are inclusive and accessible to users with different types and degrees of colorblindness. These palettes typically avoid using colors that are frequently problematic for individuals with color vision deficiencies, such as red and green, as these are the most common form of colorblindness. Instead, they rely on colors that provide a clear distinction between different elements and maintain their differentiations even to individuals with color vision deficiencies. In conclusion, colorblind-friendly palettes are essential in design to ensure that visual compositions effectively communicate intended messages and evoke desired emotions for individuals with color vision deficiencies. By considering the limitations of colorblind individuals and prioritizing contrast and clarity in color combinations, designers can create inclusive and accessible designs that cater to a wider audience and promote a more inclusive visual experience.

Colorblindness Correction Apps

Colorblindness correction apps are applications designed to assist individuals with color vision deficiencies in perceiving and distinguishing colors accurately according to color theory and color symbolism in design. Color theory is the study of how colors interact and influence one another. It explores the visual effects of different color combinations and their psychological and emotional impacts on individuals. Color symbolism in design refers to the use of colors to convey meaning and evoke specific emotions or associations.

Colorblindness Simulation Software

Colorblindness simulation software refers to a computer program designed to mimic the experience of individuals with color vision deficiencies, commonly known as colorblindness. This software aims to help designers and other professionals in the field of visual arts understand how individuals with color vision deficiencies perceive colors and make informed decisions when it comes to color choices in their designs. In the field of color theory, understanding color perception is crucial in creating aesthetically pleasing and effective designs. Colorblindness simulation software provides a valuable tool for designers to see how color combinations appear to individuals with different types of color vision deficiencies. It allows designers to simulate different types of colorblindness, such as red-green colorblindness (the most common type), blue-yellow colorblindness, and total colorblindness. By using colorblindness simulation software, designers can identify potential problems in their designs that might arise due to color vision deficiencies. This can include situations where colors that look distinct to individuals with normal color vision may appear indistinguishable to those with colorblindness. For example, if a design relies on color-coded information, such as graphs or charts, individuals with color vision deficiencies may have difficulty interpreting the data accurately. Simulating colorblindness helps designers identify these issues early on and make necessary adjustments to ensure inclusivity and accessibility in their designs. Moreover, colorblindness simulation software is also useful in the context of color symbolism. Different colors carry various meanings and associations in different cultures and contexts. However, individuals with color vision deficiencies might not perceive these symbolic associations in the same way. By using colorblindness simulation software, designers can assess whether the intended symbolic meanings are effectively conveyed to individuals with color vision deficiencies. This ensures that the message, emotions, or cultural significance that colors are intended to represent are not lost in translation. Overall, colorblindness simulation software plays a vital role in color theory and design by providing designers with a way to experience how individuals with color vision deficiencies perceive colors. It aids in identifying potential issues in design clarity and inclusivity, allowing designers to create designs that are accessible to a wider range of audiences and effectively convey their intended symbolic meanings.

Colorblindness Simulation Tools

Colorblindness simulation tools are applications or software that aim to replicate the experience of individuals with different types of color vision deficiencies. These tools are used in the context of color theory and color symbolism in design to help designers and developers create inclusive and accessible designs that can be easily understood and appreciated by people with color vision deficiencies. Color vision deficiency, commonly known as colorblindness, refers to the inability or decreased ability to perceive and distinguish certain colors. It is important for designers to take colorblindness into consideration as it can significantly impact the interpretation and effectiveness of visual designs. Colorblindness simulation tools allow designers to understand how their designs may appear to individuals with color vision deficiencies, helping them make informed decisions about color choices, color contrasts, and overall design aesthetics. In the context of color theory, colorblindness simulation tools provide designers with valuable insights into the color perception of people with different types of color vision deficiencies. They can help designers analyze how different color combinations and variations may be perceived by individuals with colorblindness, enabling them to create designs that effectively communicate information and convey desired emotions regardless of an individual's color vision abilities. Furthermore, in design, colors often carry symbolic meanings and connotations. Colorblindness simulation tools assist designers in ensuring that the intended symbolism and message associated with specific colors can be understood by individuals with color vision deficiencies. By simulating the perception of different color vision deficiencies, these tools allow designers to identify potential issues related to color symbolism and make adjustments to ensure the intended messages are successfully conveyed. In conclusion, colorblindness simulation tools play a vital role in the realm of color theory and color symbolism in design. They enable designers to gain a better understanding of how individuals with color vision deficiencies perceive colors, helping them create inclusive and accessible designs. By utilizing these tools, designers can ensure that their designs effectively communicate information, convey desired emotions, and successfully convey symbolic meanings to a diverse audience, irrespective of their color vision abilities.

Colorblindness Testing Devices

Colorblindness testing devices are tools specifically designed to assess the ability of individuals to perceive and distinguish different colors accurately. They are crucial in color theory and color symbolism in design as they help ensure that designs effectively communicate messages and evoke desired emotions across all individuals, regardless of their color vision deficiencies. Colorblindness, or color vision deficiency, is a common visual impairment that affects a significant portion of the population. It is caused by abnormalities in the retinal cone cells, which are responsible for perceiving and processing different colors. Individuals with color vision deficiencies may have difficulty distinguishing certain colors or perceiving color differences altogether. As color plays a pivotal role in design, it is crucial to identify and address any potential issues that may arise for colorblind individuals. Colorblindness testing devices come in various forms, including physical tools, online platforms, and software applications. These devices typically present a series of color patterns, specifically designed to assess an individual's color perception. By analyzing an individual's responses to these patterns, colorblindness testing devices can determine the severity and type of color vision deficiency an individual may have, such as red-green or blue-yellow deficiency. In the context of color theory, colorblindness testing devices provide designers with valuable insights into how their color choices may be perceived by individuals with color vision deficiencies. By using these devices during the design process, designers can ensure that their color palettes are accessible and inclusive to individuals with different types of color vision deficiencies. This is particularly important as certain colors or combinations may appear indistinguishable or confusing to individuals with color vision deficiencies, potentially compromising the intended meaning or impact of a design. Similarly, in the realm of color symbolism, colorblindness testing devices allow designers to assess how color associations and symbolism may be perceived by individuals with color vision deficiencies. Different colors convey specific meanings and emotions, and it is crucial for designers to ensure that these associations are adequately conveyed to all individuals, regardless of their color vision abilities. Using colorblindness testing devices, designers can identify any potential gaps or distortions in color symbolism and make necessary adjustments to ensure the intended message is effectively communicated.

Colorblindness Testing Kits

Colorblindness Testing Kits are tools used in color theory and color symbolism in design to identify individuals with color vision deficiencies. These kits consist of specially designed patterns, images, or charts that assess a person's ability to differentiate between various colors. Color theory is the study of how colors interact and create visual effects. In design, color plays a crucial role in evoking emotions, conveying messages, and enforcing brand identities. Understanding colorblindness is essential for designers to ensure that their designs are inclusive and can be perceived accurately by a diverse audience. Color vision deficiencies, or colorblindness, occur when the cells in the eyes that detect color do not function properly. This can result in difficulties in distinguishing between certain colors, primarily red and green. Colorblindness testing kits use different methods to identify these deficiencies, allowing designers to make informed decisions about color choices. One common type of colorblindness testing is the Ishihara test. Named after its creator, Dr. Shinobu Ishihara, this test uses a series of plates containing colored dots or numbers embedded within colored backgrounds. Individuals with normal color vision can easily identify the numbers, while those with color vision deficiencies may struggle to see or correctly identify them. Another type of colorblindness testing is the Farnsworth-Munsell 100 Hue Test. This test requires the individual to arrange colored chips in a specific order based on hue. The test evaluates the person's ability to discriminate between subtle differences in color. A result showing inaccuracies in arranging the chips indicates color vision deficiencies. In design, understanding color symbolism is also important. Different colors can carry various meanings and associations. For example, red often represents energy, passion, or danger, while green is commonly associated with nature, growth, or relaxation. However, individuals with colorblindness may not perceive these colors in the same way, potentially leading to misinterpretation of design elements and messages. By utilizing colorblindness testing kits, designers can ensure that their color choices are accessible and avoid unintentional confusion or exclusion. Incorporating alternative design elements, such as using patterns or different shades, can help individuals with color vision deficiencies fully comprehend and appreciate the intended design impact.

Colorblindness Testing Solutions

Colorblindness Testing Solutions refers to methods or tools used to assess and identify color vision deficiencies in individuals. In the context of color theory and color symbolism in design, colorblindness testing solutions help designers create inclusive and accessible designs that can be easily perceived and understood by people with different types of color vision deficiencies.Color plays a significant role in design, as it can convey emotions, attract attention, and communicate messages. However, approximately 8% of men and 0.5% of women worldwide experience some form of color vision deficiency, commonly referred to as color blindness. This condition affects an individual's ability to perceive and differentiate certain colors.Colorblindness testing solutions utilize various tests to determine the type and severity of color vision deficiencies. One commonly used test is the Ishihara test, which consists of plates with patterns of colored dots or numbers. People with normal color vision can easily identify the numbers or patterns, while those with color vision deficiencies may see different numbers or have difficulty discerning the shapes.By identifying colorblindness in individuals, designers can make informed decisions on color schemes, ensuring that their designs are accessible to a wider range of users. For example, designers might avoid using color as the sole means of conveying important information and instead incorporate other visual cues, such as icons or text labels, to ensure that people with color vision deficiencies can still understand the intended message.Furthermore, designers can utilize color palettes that are more distinguishable for colorblind individuals. This involves selecting colors with sufficient contrast and avoiding combinations that may be difficult to differentiate for those with certain types of color vision deficiencies. Additionally, designers can utilize texture, shape, and pattern to enhance the visual perception of their designs, making them more easily understandable regardless of color vision.

Colorblindness Testing

Colorblindness Testing: Colorblindness testing is a process used in the context of color theory and color symbolism in design to assess an individual's ability to perceive and differentiate colors accurately. It aims to identify color vision deficiencies, commonly known as colorblindness or color vision deficiency, which can affect a person's perception of colors and the symbolic meanings associated with them. Colorblindness is a condition characterized by the inability to distinguish certain colors, most commonly red and green. This visual impairment occurs due to the absence or malfunctioning of specific color-sensitive cells in the retina, called cones. Without these functioning cones, individuals with color vision deficiencies perceive colors differently or have difficulty differentiating between certain color combinations. Colorblindness testing involves administering a series of tests, often in the form of color vision screening tests or color vision deficiency tests. These tests are designed to evaluate an individual's color perception and identify any visual impairments or limitations they may have. The results of these tests can help designers determine whether their choice of colors and their symbolic interpretations will be accurately perceived by individuals with color vision deficiencies. In the field of color theory, understanding colorblindness is crucial for designers as it influences the way colors are perceived. Designers need to ensure that their color choices consider the potential limitations faced by colorblind individuals, allowing them to effectively communicate visual messages and evoke desired emotional responses. Additionally, in the context of color symbolism in design, colorblindness testing helps designers determine whether their use of colors aligns with the intended symbolic meanings. Different colors carry diverse symbolism, and designers often use this symbolism to convey specific messages and evoke particular emotions. It is important, therefore, to ensure that these symbolic color choices are not lost or misinterpreted by individuals with color vision deficiencies. By conducting colorblindness testing, designers can create designs that are inclusive and accessible to a wide range of individuals, regardless of color vision deficiencies. Such testing allows designers to make informed decisions about color palettes, ensuring that colors are not only visually pleasing but also meaningful and understandable by all users. Overall, colorblindness testing plays a vital role in the design process, enabling designers to overcome potential barriers and create visually impactful designs that effectively communicate intended messages and symbolism, while remaining accessible to individuals with color vision deficiencies.

Colorimeter

A colorimeter is a device used in color theory and design to measure and quantify the characteristics of color. It is commonly used in the fields of art, graphic design, and interior design, as well as in industries such as printing, textile, and cosmetics. Color theory explores the psychological and physiological effects of color and how it can be used to create visual harmony and convey meaning. Color symbolism, on the other hand, examines the cultural associations and meanings attributed to different colors.

Colorimeters

A colorimeter is a device used in color theory and design to measure and analyze color. It is an essential tool for designers working with color symbolism and seeking to create harmonious color schemes. Color theory is the study of how colors interact with one another and their psychological effects on individuals. In design, colors are carefully chosen to evoke specific emotions, convey messages, and create a desired aesthetic. Understanding color theory and symbolism is crucial in creating visually appealing and effective designs. A colorimeter measures colors by comparing the light reflected or transmitted by an object to a known standard. It quantifies the color of an object in various color models, such as RGB (Red, Green, Blue) or CMYK (Cyan, Magenta, Yellow, Black), providing designers with precise color values. This allows designers to select and reproduce colors accurately across different media, such as print or digital platforms. In the context of color symbolism, a colorimeter enables designers to identify and analyze the symbolic meanings associated with different colors. Colors hold cultural and psychological associations that vary across different societies, making it crucial for designers to consider the cultural context of their designs. For example, the color red may symbolize love and passion in one culture but symbolize danger or anger in another. By using a colorimeter, designers can ensure that the colors they use align with the intended symbolic meanings and the desired emotional response. Colorimeters play a vital role in creating harmonious color schemes, where colors are carefully selected based on their relationships on the color wheel. Designers use colorimeters to measure the hue, saturation, and brightness of different colors to create visually balanced compositions. This ensures that the colors used in a design work harmoniously together, whether it's for a logo, website, or interior space. In conclusion, colorimeters are essential tools for designers working with color theory and color symbolism. They enable precise measurement, analysis, and reproduction of colors, ensuring that designers can accurately convey their intended meanings and create visually appealing designs.

Colorimetry Equipment

Colorimetry equipment refers to a set of tools and devices used in the field of color theory and color symbolism in design. It is designed to measure and analyze various aspects of color, enabling designers and artists to make informed decisions about color selection and usage. The primary purpose of colorimetry equipment is to quantify and express colors in a systematic and objective manner. It involves the measurement of the different characteristics of color, such as hue, saturation, and brightness, using specific instruments such as spectrophotometers and colorimeters. These instruments employ various techniques, such as light absorption, reflection, and transmission, to capture and interpret the color information. The information obtained from colorimetry equipment is crucial in color theory and symbolism in design. Colors have various meanings and associations, both culturally and psychologically, and their usage can greatly impact the message and emotions conveyed by a design. By using colorimetry equipment, designers can ensure that their color choices align with the intended symbolism and communicate the desired aesthetics and emotions. Colorimetry equipment allows designers to accurately measure and quantify colors, ensuring consistency across different mediums and devices. This is particularly important in industries such as graphic design and printing, where colors need to be reproduced accurately across various platforms and materials. By using colorimetry equipment, designers can ensure that the colors they choose will be faithfully represented in the final product. In addition to color measurement, colorimetry equipment can also provide valuable data on color harmony and contrast. It can help designers determine which colors work well together and create a pleasing visual impact. By analyzing the color data obtained from colorimetry equipment, designers can make informed decisions about color combinations and create designs that are visually appealing and effective.

Colorimetry

Colorimetry is a scientific method used to quantify and measure color based on human perception. It is an essential tool in color theory and color symbolism in design. In color theory, colorimetry is used to understand and create harmonious color schemes. By accurately measuring the properties of colors, such as hue, saturation, and brightness, designers can create visually appealing color combinations. Colorimetry helps designers understand the relationships between colors, such as complementary and analogous colors, leading to the creation of visually balanced and aesthetically pleasing designs.

Comfort (Beige)

The color "Comfort (Beige)" is a shade that falls within the neutral color palette and is often associated with a sense of warmth, comfort, and tranquility. It is a medium-toned beige color with a subtle hint of yellow undertones, evoking a sense of calmness and relaxation. In color theory, beige is considered a warm color that primarily consists of white and brown tones. It is often used as a background color in design due to its ability to create a sense of balance and harmony. It is commonly used in interior design to create a cozy and inviting atmosphere in spaces such as living rooms, bedrooms, and lounges. When it comes to color symbolism in design, "Comfort (Beige)" is associated with qualities such as simplicity, elegance, and timelessness. It is a versatile color that can be paired with a wide range of other colors and is often used as a base tone to create contrast or provide a neutral backdrop for more vibrant hues. In branding and logo design, beige is often utilized to convey a sense of reliability, trustworthiness, and approachability. It is commonly used in industries such as healthcare, wellness, and hospitality to create a sense of comfort and serenity. Additionally, beige is also used in luxury branding to communicate sophistication and refinement. Overall, the color "Comfort (Beige)" is a popular choice in design due to its ability to create a calming and welcoming ambiance. Its neutral and versatile nature makes it suitable for various design applications, from interior design to branding. Whether used as a dominant color or as an accent, beige adds a touch of elegance and serenity to any design project.

Comfort (Brown)

Comfort (Brown) is a color in the context of color theory and color symbolism in design. It is typically associated with feelings of warmth, stability, and earthiness. Brown is a mixture of red, yellow, and black, and often represents the natural world and organic elements. In color theory, brown is considered a neutral color. It is often seen as a grounding color that can provide a sense of stability and balance in a design. It is commonly used as a background or base color because of its ability to blend well with other colors. Brown can also add a sense of depth and richness to a design.

Comfort (Peach)

Comfort (Peach) is a color that belongs to the orange family in color theory and design. It is a warm and light shade of orange that is often associated with feelings of calmness, tranquility, and a sense of well-being. In color symbolism, Comfort (Peach) represents warmth, gentleness, and approachability. It is often used to evoke feelings of comfort, harmony, and nurturing. The color is frequently used in interior design, as it creates a soft and inviting atmosphere. It can be combined with other warm colors like light yellows or pinks to further enhance its comforting and soothing qualities. The use of Comfort (Peach) in design can help create a welcoming and friendly environment. It is often used in spaces where people gather, such as living rooms, waiting areas, and bedrooms. Its warm and calming nature makes it an excellent choice for creating a sense of relaxation and serenity. Comfort (Peach) is also a popular choice for branding and marketing materials. Its soft and gentle qualities make it appealing to a wide range of audiences. It can be used to convey a sense of trust, compassion, and care. For example, companies in the hospitality industry might use Comfort (Peach) in their logos or promotional materials to create a sense of comfort and relaxation for their customers. In conclusion, Comfort (Peach) is a warm and light shade of orange that is associated with feelings of calmness, tranquility, and well-being. It represents warmth, gentleness, and approachability in color symbolism. It is often used in interior design to create a welcoming and inviting atmosphere and in branding materials to convey a sense of trust and care.

Communication (Blue)

Communication in the context of color theory and color symbolism in design refers to the conveying of ideas, emotions, and messages through the use of the color blue. Blue is often associated with feelings of calmness, serenity, and tranquility. Its cool and soothing nature can evoke a sense of peace and relaxation. As such, the color blue is commonly used in designs that aim to create a sense of harmony and balance.

Communication (Copper)

Communication in the context of color theory and color symbolism in design can be defined as the conveyance of meaning and emotional response through the use of specific color choices and combinations. Color communicates on an intuitive and subconscious level, allowing designers to evoke specific feelings, associations, and messages in their work. Color theory is based on the relationships and interactions between different colors. It explores how colors can be combined, contrasted, or harmonized to create visual impact and convey specific meanings. Understanding color theory is essential for effective communication in design, as it enables designers to make deliberate choices that align with the intended message or brand identity.

Communication (Turquoise)

Communication, in the context of color theory and color symbolism in design, refers to the use of the color turquoise to convey specific messages or create certain associations with the audience. Turquoise is a color that combines the calming properties of blue with the invigorating energy of green. As such, it is often associated with concepts such as tranquility, serenity, and balance. In the realm of communication, turquoise is commonly used to convey a sense of calmness, harmony, and open communication.

Compassion (Pink)

Compassion, in the realm of color theory and color symbolism in design, is represented by the color pink. Pink, as a soft and delicate hue, evokes feelings of tenderness, empathy, and understanding. In color theory, pink is considered a tint of red, as it is created by adding white to the base color. This infusion of white lightens the intensity of red, resulting in a gentle and soothing shade. As such, pink is associated with qualities such as sensitivity, kindness, and care.

Complementary Colors

Complementary colors, in the context of color theory and color symbolism in design, refer to pairs of colors that are opposite each other on the color wheel. These pairs are considered complementary because they create a strong contrast when placed together, making each color appear more vibrant and intense. In color theory, the color wheel is a visual representation of the spectrum of colors. It is a circular diagram that organizes colors in a logical order, with each color positioned in relation to the others. Complementary colors are positioned directly across from each other on the color wheel. Complementary colors are commonly used in design to create visual interest and balance. When complementary colors are combined, they create a dynamic contrast that can attract attention and evoke emotions. The contrast between complementary colors is considered visually pleasing to the human eye, as it stimulates different parts of the retina, creating a sense of harmony. In addition to their aesthetic qualities, complementary colors also have symbolic meanings in design. Each color has its own psychological associations and cultural symbolism, and these meanings are often intensified when used in combination with their complementary counterpart. For example, red and green are complementary colors that are commonly associated with Christmas. Red represents energy, passion, and warmth, while green symbolizes growth, renewal, and nature. When used together, they evoke feelings of festive cheer and holiday spirit. Designers often use complementary colors in various creative applications, such as branding, graphic design, and interior design. They can be applied in different proportions and intensities to create different effects. Some designers utilize complementary colors as the main color scheme, while others use them as accents to add excitement and contrast to a design. Understanding complementary colors and their relationships can be helpful in creating visually appealing and meaningful designs. By incorporating these pairs of colors strategically, designers can effectively communicate messages, elicit emotions, and engage viewers.

Confidence (Blue)

90

Confidence is a symbolic attribute of the color blue in the context of color theory and design. Blue represents a sense of trust, reliability, and strength, evoking feelings of calmness and stability. It is often associated with qualities such as intelligence, wisdom, and loyalty. In color theory, blue is categorized as a cool color, known for its calming and soothing effects on the human mind. It is commonly used in design to create a sense of tranquility and promote feelings of relaxation. Blue is often used in spaces where focus, concentration, and clear thinking are required, such as offices, study areas, and libraries.

Connection (Copper)

According to color theory, connection refers to the relationship between colors and their ability to create a harmonious and unified visual representation. Copper, as a color, plays a significant role in connecting various elements in design through its symbolism and aesthetic appeal. In the context of color symbolism, copper represents warmth, earthiness, and a sense of stability. Its rich and deep reddish-brown hue creates a visual connection with nature, evoking feelings of warmth, comfort, and familiarity. Copper is often associated with the natural element of earth, symbolizing grounding, strength, and reliability.

Conservatism (Gray)

Conservatism in color theory refers to the color gray, which is often associated with neutrality and lack of emotion. Gray is created by mixing equal proportions of black and white, resulting in a color that is neither too dark nor too light. In design, the use of gray can convey a sense of stability, balance, and maturity. It is often used as a background color or in combination with other colors to create a calming and sophisticated atmosphere. Gray is commonly associated with professionalism, reliability, and authority, making it a popular choice for corporate branding and formal settings.

Contrast Checker Applications

A contrast checker application is a software tool that is used in color theory and color symbolism in design to determine the level of contrast between two or more colors. The application analyzes the colors and provides a visual representation or numerical value indicating how well they contrast with each other. In color theory, contrast refers to the differences in brightness, saturation, and hue between colors. It is an essential element in design as it helps to create visual interest and hierarchy. When colors contrast well, they are easy to differentiate and can effectively communicate messages or evoke emotions. Color contrast is particularly important for individuals with visual impairments or color vision deficiencies. A good contrast checker application ensures that the color combinations used in design projects are accessible and comply with web accessibility standards. The application typically allows users to input or select colors either by entering specific color values or by choosing colors from a color picker tool. Once the colors are selected, the application analyzes the contrast ratio between them using algorithms based on color perception models such as RGB, HSL, or LAB. These algorithms consider factors such as color brightness, color difference, and color similarity. After the analysis, the contrast checker application provides feedback on the level of contrast between the colors. This feedback can be displayed in various ways, such as a color-coded rating system, a numerical value indicating the contrast ratio, or a visual representation showing the colors side by side. The feedback helps designers make informed decisions about color combinations. For example, if the contrast ratio is low, indicating poor contrast, designers can adjust the colors to improve readability or choose alternative colors that provide better contrast. They can also use the feedback to ensure compliance with accessibility guidelines, such as the Web Content Accessibility Guidelines (WCAG). In conclusion, a contrast checker application is a valuable tool in color theory and design, helping designers ensure that their color choices provide sufficient contrast for effective communication and accessibility.

Contrast Checker Software

A Contrast Checker Software is a tool used in the field of color theory and color symbolism in design to assess and evaluate the contrast between two or more colors. The software analyzes the color properties and combinations, allowing designers to determine the effectiveness and legibility of their chosen color palettes in terms of contrast. Color contrast plays a crucial role in design as it affects the readability, visibility, and overall impact of a visual composition. It refers to the difference in luminance or color values between foreground and background elements. Good color contrast is essential for creating accessible designs, ensuring that information is easily readable and perceivable by a wide range of users, including those with visual impairments.

Contrast Checker Tools

A contrast checker tool in the context of color theory and color symbolism in design is a tool used to determine the difference in luminance and color values between two or more elements in a design. It helps designers ensure that their color choices provide sufficient contrast for readability and visual interest. Color theory is the study of how colors interact with each other and how they affect human perception. It explores the principles of color harmony, contrast, and symbolism. Contrast is an important aspect of color theory as it helps create visual interest, depth, and hierarchy in design. It involves using colors that are different in value and hue to make elements stand out or blend together.

Contrast Checkers

A contrast checker, in the context of color theory and color symbolism in design, refers to a tool or method that helps determine the contrast between different colors used in a design or composition. Color contrast is a crucial aspect of design as it affects the readability, legibility, and visual impact of the content or message being conveyed. It involves the juxtaposition of colors that differ in their hue, value, or saturation, creating a visual distinction and allowing for differentiation between elements.

Contrast Ratio

Contrast Ratio refers to the difference in luminance or brightness between two colors in a design. It is a crucial concept in color theory and design as it helps create visual impact, improve readability, and establish hierarchy within a composition. In color theory, contrast ratio is determined by comparing the relative luminance of two colors on a scale of 1:1 to 21:1. The contrast ratio is represented as a decimal value, with higher ratios indicating greater contrast. A contrast ratio of 1:1 signifies no contrast, while a ratio of 21:1 represents the maximum contrast possible.

Cool Colors

Cool colors are a group of colors in color theory that are associated with a sense of calmness, tranquility, and serenity. These colors are typically found on the cool side of the color wheel, such as blues, greens, and purples. Unlike warm colors, which are associated with energy and excitement, cool colors evoke a more soothing and relaxing atmosphere. In design, cool colors are often used to create a sense of depth and space. They are frequently employed in backgrounds and large areas to visually expand the space and create a calming effect. Cool colors can also be used as accents to provide contrast and balance in a design, especially when combined with warmer colors.

Courage (Bronze)

Courage, in the context of color theory and color symbolism in design, is a bronze hue that evokes feelings of bravery, strength, and confidence. It is a color that is associated with assertiveness, determination, and taking risks. Bronze is composed of a mix of copper and tin, giving it a rich and warm metallic sheen. This color is often used to symbolize courage in design because of its connection to ancient warriors and armor. Bronze has a timeless quality that adds a touch of sophistication and elegance to any design.

Courage (Maroon)

Courage, in the context of color theory and color symbolism in design, can be represented by the maroon color. Maroon is a deep, rich shade of red that is often associated with bravery, strength, and resilience. Maroon is a color that commands attention and evokes a sense of power. It is often used to symbolize courage and determination in design, as it has a bold and assertive presence. This color is commonly seen in military uniforms, sports teams, and logos associated with bravery and valor.

Courage (Red)

The color red is associated with various meanings and emotions, and when it comes to color theory and color symbolism in design, red is often associated with courage. In color theory, red is categorized as a warm color along with orange and yellow. Warm colors are generally associated with energy, strength, and vibrancy. Red, in particular, is often linked with intense emotions, such as passion, love, and anger. It is a color that catches the eye and demands attention, which can evoke strong reactions and create a sense of urgency.

Courage (Salmon)

Courage (Salmon) is a color commonly used in color theory and design to evoke feelings of bravery, strength, and passion. It is a shade of pink with hints of orange, creating a warm and vibrant color that commands attention and represents an assertive and confident attitude. In color theory, courage (salmon) is often associated with the color red, which is known for its powerful and dynamic nature. Salmon, being a lighter and softer version of red, brings a sense of approachability and friendliness to the color. It combines the energy and intensity of red with the playfulness and joy of pink to strike a balanced and harmonious tone. In design, courage (salmon) is frequently used to create a strong visual impact. It is a color that stands out in a crowd and demands attention. The warm undertones of salmon make it versatile and compatible with various color palettes, allowing it to be used as either a main focal point or as an accent color to enhance other elements. Symbolically, courage (salmon) represents assertiveness, determination, and resilience. It symbolizes the ability to face challenges and overcome obstacles with confidence and strength. This color is often associated with qualities such as bravery, passion, and empowerment. In branding and marketing, courage (salmon) can be utilized to convey a bold and adventurous image. It is frequently chosen by companies that want to stand out from their competitors and project a sense of fearlessness and innovation. The color salmon is commonly used in industries such as fashion, sports, and technology, where being bold and daring is often admired. Overall, courage (salmon) is a color that inspires bravery and embodies qualities such as strength and confidence. Its warm undertones, combined with the vibrancy of pink, make it a powerful tool in design and branding. Whether used as a main color or as an accent, courage (salmon) is sure to make a statement and create a lasting impression.

Courses On Color Theory

Color Theory is the study and exploration of how colors interact with each other, and how they can be used in design to convey specific messages and evoke certain emotions. It encompasses the principles and guidelines that govern the use of color in various art forms, including graphic design, painting, and photography. Understanding color theory is crucial for designers as it allows them to create visually appealing and meaningful designs. It helps in selecting harmonious color combinations, creating contrasts, and effectively communicating through visual elements. By applying color theory principles, designers can create impactful designs that captivate and engage viewers. One aspect of color theory is color symbolism, which examines the meaning and associations attributed to different colors. Colors have the power to evoke specific emotions and convey certain messages. For example, red is often associated with passion, energy, and excitement, while blue is often associated with calmness, trust, and professionalism. By understanding the symbolism behind colors, designers can use them strategically to enhance the intended message or mood of a design. Courses on color theory provide designers with an in-depth understanding of the principles and applications of color. These courses cover topics such as color mixing, color schemes, color psychology, and color symbolism. Students learn how to create harmonious color palettes, use color to create depth and contrast, and effectively communicate through color. They also learn the technical aspects of color such as hue, saturation, and value. By studying color theory, designers gain the ability to make intentional color choices based on the principles they have learned. They can confidently experiment with color combinations, knowing how different colors interact and affect the overall aesthetic of a design. They also gain a deeper understanding of how color can influence the perception and response of viewers, allowing them to create designs that effectively convey the desired message or evoke the desired emotion. In conclusion, color theory is an essential aspect of design that involves studying the interactions, symbolism, and psychology of colors. Courses on color theory provide designers with the knowledge and skills to use colors effectively in their designs, resulting in visually appealing and meaningful creations.

Cowardice (Yellow)

Cowardice (Yellow) is a specific color associated with the emotion of fear, timidity, and lack of courage in the context of color theory and color symbolism in design. In color theory, yellow is often perceived as a vibrant and joyful color that represents sunshine, warmth, and positivity. It is commonly associated with feelings of happiness, energy, and optimism. However, when discussing cowardice, yellow takes on a different connotation. It symbolizes weakness, vulnerability, and a hesitancy to confront challenges or face one's fears. This interpretation is based on cultural and psychological associations with the color yellow, rather than its inherent properties.

Creativity (Coral)

Creativity is a concept in color theory and color symbolism in design that refers to the use of the color coral. Coral is a warm, vibrant shade that falls between pink and orange on the color spectrum. It is often associated with energy, enthusiasm, and excitement. In the context of color theory, creativity is used to add a sense of unconventional thinking and originality to a design. Coral is a bold and attention-grabbing color that can draw the viewer's eye and create a sense of excitement. It is often used to convey a sense of creativity, innovation, and uniqueness.

Creativity (Lilac)

Creativity (Lilac) Creativity, in the context of color theory and color symbolism in design, refers to the ability to think and create in an original and innovative way. It is associated with the color lilac, which represents imagination, inspiration, and artistic expression.

Creativity (Orange)

Creativity in color theory and color symbolism refers to the use of the color orange in design. Orange is often associated with energy, enthusiasm, and vibrancy. It is a warm and stimulating color that evokes feelings of excitement and creativity.In design, the color orange is often used to capture attention and create a sense of enthusiasm. It can be used to draw focus to certain elements or to create a sense of urgency. Orange is also often associated with creativity and innovation, making it a popular choice for brands and products that want to convey a sense of originality and imagination.

Creativity (Periwinkle)

Creativity, in the context of color theory and color symbolism in design, can be defined as the ability to produce original and meaningful combinations of colors, shapes, and forms. It involves breaking away from conventional norms and exploring new possibilities to create visually impactful and aesthetically pleasing designs. Periwinkle, a color commonly associated with creativity, is a pale tint of purple-blue that exudes a sense of imagination and innovation. It combines the calming effects of blue with the passionate energy of purple, resulting in a color that is both serene and stimulating.

Creativity (Purple)

Purple is a hue in color theory associated with creativity and is often used symbolically in design to evoke a sense of magic, mystery, and imagination. In color theory, purple is created by mixing equal amounts of red and blue, resulting in a secondary color that holds both the energy and calmness of its parent colors. This combination conveys a sense of balance and harmony, making purple an ideal choice when designers want to create a soothing yet intriguing visual experience. Its unique position in the color spectrum, situated between warm and cool colors, allows purple to bridge the gap between these extremes, making it a versatile and impactful choice. Symbolically, purple has long been associated with royalty, luxury, and power due to its historical rarity and expense. It is a color that has historically been linked to high social status and exclusivity, often reserved for the elite. Therefore, when designers incorporate purple into

94

their work, it can convey elegance, opulence, and sophistication. Additionally, purple is strongly connected to spirituality, mysticism, and the imagination. From ancient rituals to modern-day fantasy, purple has been linked to magic, dreams, and the unknown. It can ignite a sense of wonder and captivate viewers, inviting them into a world beyond the ordinary. In this sense, purple is an excellent choice for designs related to spirituality, creativity, and artistic expression. Overall, purple is a color that holds immense power in design due to its association with creativity, magic, and luxury. It offers a sense of balance and harmony, while also evoking feelings of mystery and wonder. Whether used subtly or boldly, purple has the potential to elevate a design and evoke a range of emotions, making it a valuable tool for designers in various industries.

Creativity (Teal)

Teal is a vibrant shade of blue-green that holds significant symbolic meaning in the realm of color theory and design. It encapsulates the attribute of creativity, symbolizing unconventional thinking and innovative ideas. Teal is often associated with artistic expression, originality, and imaginative concepts. This color's unique blend of blue and green hues creates a sense of balance and harmony, making it a popular choice in design for its calming and soothing qualities. It has a calming effect on the mind and is known to promote clarity and focus, making it an ideal color for stimulating creative thinking.

Creativity (Turquoise)

Creativity refers to the ability to generate unique and original ideas, solutions, and designs. In the context of color theory and symbolism in design, the color turquoise is often associated with creativity. Turquoise is a blend of blue and green, representing the calmness of blue and the energy of green. It is known for its soothing and refreshing nature, making it a popular choice in design to evoke feelings of tranquility and balance. Turquoise is often used to stimulate creativity and encourage originality in artwork and design. As a symbol of creativity, turquoise represents innovation, imagination, and artistic expression. It is believed to inspire new ideas, open up possibilities, and spark the imagination. Turquoise can be used as an accent color or as the main hue in a design to convey a sense of creativity and stimulate the creative thought process. The use of turquoise in design can encourage out-of-the-box thinking, as it has a unique and unconventional quality. It is a color that pushes boundaries and encourages experimentation. Turquoise is often used in industries related to art, design, and creative fields, where innovation and originality are highly valued. In addition to its association with creativity, turquoise also carries other symbolic meanings. It is often associated with healing and emotional well-being, as it is believed to promote a sense of serenity and calmness. Turquoise is associated with the ocean and the sky, representing vastness and expansiveness. It can evoke a sense of adventure and exploration. Overall, turquoise is a color that symbolizes creativity and originality in design. Its unique blend of blue and green conveys a sense of tranquility and energy, stimulating the imagination and inspiring new ideas. Turquoise is a popular choice in design to evoke feelings of creativity and encourage innovative thinking.

Creativity (Yellow)

In color theory and color symbolism in design, creativity is often associated with the color yellow. Yellow is a bright, vibrant hue that is commonly associated with energy, happiness, and positivity. It is often used to evoke feelings of joy, optimism, and inspiration. When used in design, yellow can be an effective tool for catching the viewer's attention and conveying a sense of excitement and enthusiasm. It is often used in marketing materials, such as advertisements and packaging, to grab the viewer's attention and invite them to engage with the product or message.

Creators Of Color Schemes

A color scheme is a predefined set of colors that are used together in a designed composition. Creators of color schemes are individuals who carefully select and combine colors based on color theory and symbolism to achieve a desired visual effect and convey a specific message. In the context of color theory, creators of color schemes consider principles such as the color wheel, color harmony, and the psychology of color to create visually appealing and balanced compositions. The color wheel is a tool that organizes colors in a circular format, showing relationships between primary, secondary, and tertiary colors. Creators use this tool to select colors that are harmonious and create a pleasing visual experience. Color harmony refers to the arrangement of colors that work well together. Creators of color schemes use various techniques to achieve color harmony, such as complementary colors (those opposite each other on the color wheel), analogous colors (those adjacent to each other on the color wheel), and triadic colors (those evenly spaced around the color wheel). Additionally, creators of color schemes consider the psychological and emotional effects of colors. Different colors can evoke different emotions and have symbolic meanings. For example, red is often associated with energy, passion, and excitement, while blue is associated with calmness and trust. Creators use this knowledge to select colors that align with the intended message or branding of a design. Creating color schemes involves making deliberate choices to convey a specific mood or message. Creators of color schemes carefully select colors and consider factors such as color theory, color harmony, and color symbolism to achieve an aesthetically pleasing and visually impactful composition. Their expertise and understanding of these principles contribute to the overall success and effectiveness of a design.

Cultural Significance Of Colors

Color plays a crucial role in design as it holds cultural significance and carries symbolism. Understanding the cultural significance of colors is essential for designers as it allows them to effectively communicate messages and evoke specific emotions. Color theory and color symbolism provide a framework for this understanding. Color theory is the study of how colors interact and how they can be combined harmoniously in design. It explores the relationships between primary, secondary, and tertiary colors, as well as their properties such as hue, value, and saturation. By understanding color theory, designers can create visually pleasing compositions that engage the viewer and convey the intended message. Color symbolism, on the other hand, goes beyond the technical aspects of color and delves into the meanings and associations people attribute to certain colors. This symbolism is deeply rooted in culture and varies across different societies and time periods. For example, in Western cultures, red is often associated with love, passion, and power, while in some Asian cultures, it symbolizes luck and prosperity. Blue is commonly associated with tranquility and trust, but in some cultures, it represents sadness or mourning. Yellow is often associated with joy and happiness, but it can also symbolize cowardice or deceit. Furthermore, color can also be used to create visual hierarchy and convey messages in design. The use of warm colors like red and orange can draw attention and create a sense of urgency, while cool colors like blue and green can create a calming effect. Contrast between colors can highlight important elements or create visual interest, while the saturation and brightness of colors can evoke different emotions. Ultimately, designers must be mindful of the cultural significance and symbolism associated with different colors to ensure that their designs effectively communicate the intended message and resonate with the target audience. By harnessing the power of color, designers can create visually compelling and emotionally resonant designs that leave a lasting impact.

Custom Color Palette Creators

A custom color palette creator is a tool or software that allows designers to create unique and personalized color palettes for their design projects. In the context of color theory and color symbolism in design, a color palette is a collection of colors that are carefully chosen to work harmoniously together and convey a specific mood or message. Color theory is the study of how colors interact with each other and how they can be combined to create visually pleasing compositions. Designers use color theory principles to make informed decisions about color selection, balance, and contrast in their designs. Color symbolism, on the other hand, refers to the associations and meanings that colors may carry, such as red representing passion or love, green representing nature or growth, and blue representing tranquility or trust.

Custom Color Palette Generators

A custom color palette generator is a tool or application that allows designers to easily create unique and personalized color schemes for their design projects. It employs principles from color theory and symbolism to assist in the selection of harmonious and meaningful color combinations. Color theory is the study of how colors interact with each other and the effect they have on the viewer. It is based on the understanding of the color wheel and the relationships between different hues, such as complementary, analogous, and triadic colors. A color palette generator takes these principles into account to provide a range of colors that work well together. Color symbolism, on the other hand, explores the meaning and associations that colors have in different cultures and contexts. Certain colors can evoke specific emotions or convey certain messages. For example, red is often associated with passion and energy, while blue is associated with calmness and trust. A custom color palette generator can incorporate these symbolic associations to help designers create color schemes that align with the intended message or mood of their design. The purpose of a custom color palette generator is to simplify the color selection process for designers, especially those who may not have a strong background in color theory. By providing an intuitive interface and tools to experiment with different color combinations, designers can quickly and easily create aesthetically pleasing and meaningful color schemes. When using a custom color palette generator, designers typically start by selecting a base color or a set of key colors. The generator then suggests complementary or analogous colors based on established color relationships, ensuring a harmonious and visually appealing result. Designers can also adjust the saturation, brightness, and contrast of the colors to fine-tune the palette to their liking. Ultimately, a custom color palette generator empowers designers to create unique and impactful designs by leveraging the principles of color theory and symbolism. It eliminates the guesswork and time-consuming process of manually testing various color combinations, allowing designers to focus on the other aspects of their project.

Custom Color Palettes

Color theory is a fundamental aspect of design that deals with the principles of combining colors to create visually appealing and harmonious compositions. In design, color symbolism is often used to evoke certain emotions or convey specific messages. A custom color palette refers to a unique selection of colors that is tailored to a specific design project or brand. It is carefully curated to create a cohesive visual identity and convey the desired message or feeling. Custom color palettes are created by considering various factors, including color theory, color symbolism, and the overall brand identity. Color theory is the study of how colors interact with each other and how they can be combined to create different effects. It explores concepts such as color harmony, contrast, and balance. Understanding color theory is crucial when creating a custom color palette, as it helps ensure that the selected colors work well together and create a visually pleasing composition. Color symbolism, on the other hand, refers to the meaning and associations that different colors hold. Different colors can evoke specific emotions, convey certain messages, or represent particular ideas. For example, blue is often associated with calmness and trust, while red is commonly linked to energy and passion. When creating a custom color palette, designers take into account the intended message or feeling and select colors that align with these associations. Custom color palettes allow designers to create a unique visual identity for a brand or project. By selecting specific colors and combining them in a harmonious way, designers can create a distinctive look that sets the brand apart. Custom color palettes also ensure consistency across various design elements, such as logos, websites, and marketing materials. This consistency helps strengthen brand recognition and allows for better communication of the brand's values and identity. In conclusion, a custom color palette is a thoughtfully curated selection of colors that aligns with color theory and symbolism to create a cohesive and visually appealing design. By understanding the principles of color theory and considering the associations of different colors, designers can create custom color palettes that effectively convey the desired message or feeling and establish a unique visual identity for a brand or project.

Custom Color Picker

A custom color picker is a graphical user interface tool used in the field of color theory and color symbolism in design. It allows users to choose and create custom colors based on their desired specifications. In the context of color theory, the color picker facilitates the exploration and selection of colors that harmonize and complement each other. It assists in understanding the relationships between colors and their various attributes, such as hue, saturation, and brightness. By enabling users to interactively adjust these attributes, the color picker helps designers achieve the desired visual impact and emotional response in their creations. Furthermore, in the realm of color symbolism in design, the custom color picker enables users to express and convey specific meanings and messages through color choices. Different cultures and contexts attach symbolic significance to colors, and the picker assists designers in aligning their designs with the intended cultural or psychological associations. For example, they can select warm colors like red or yellow to convey energy and excitement, or cool colors like blue or green for a calming and soothing effect. The custom color picker enhances the efficiency and effectiveness of the design process by providing a user-friendly interface for color selection. It typically includes color swatches or palettes from which users can choose pre-defined colors, as well as a spectrum or gradient panel that allows for the creation of custom colors. Some color pickers even provide additional features like color harmony suggestions or the ability to save and organize color palettes. The HTML code snippet below showcases a minimalistic representation of a custom color picker: The custom color picker is a graphical tool used in color theory and color symbolism in design. It allows users to choose and create custom colors. By providing an intuitive interface for color selection, it enhances the design process and helps achieve the desired visual impact and symbolic associations.

Danger (Red)

Danger (Red) - In the context of color theory, red is a primary color that is often associated with danger, energy, and passion. It is a warm color that has the longest wavelength in the visible spectrum and is known for stimulating strong emotions and drawing attention. In design, the color red is frequently used to communicate a sense of urgency or warning. Its association with danger stems from its connection to fire and blood, which are commonly seen as threatening or potentially harmful elements. The color red has the ability to evoke a visceral response, triggering feelings of caution, alertness, and alarm.

Dark Mode Design Software

Dark Mode Design Software refers to a type of software specifically designed for creating designs and user interfaces that utilize a dark color scheme. This software allows designers to create visuals and interfaces that primarily use dark colors such as black, dark gray, navy, or deep purple. In the context of color theory, dark colors are associated with a sense of elegance, formality, and sophistication. They are often used to create a contrast with light-colored elements, making them visually stand out. Dark mode designs are particularly popular for applications or websites that are used in low-light environments or for users who prefer reduced screen brightness. The use of dark colors in design also aligns with the principles of usability and accessibility, as it reduces eye strain and fatigue. Additionally, dark mode designs also leverage the concept of color symbolism. Different colors evoke different emotional responses and associations. Dark colors, for example, are often associated with concepts such as mystery, power, and night. By using dark colors in design, the software allows designers to tap into these symbolic associations and convey a particular mood or tone. Dark mode design software typically provides a range of features and tools specific to working with dark color schemes. These may include a color palette with pre-selected dark colors, the ability to adjust contrast ratios between light and dark elements, and options for fine-tuning color shade and saturation. It may also offer features for previewing designs in different lighting conditions to ensure optimal visibility and readability.

Dark Mode Design Solutions

Dark Mode Design Solutions refer to design strategies and techniques used to create user interfaces that feature a dark color scheme. In the context of color theory, dark mode utilizes a primarily black or dark-colored background with lighter-colored text and elements. This design approach is widely adopted in various applications, websites, and operating systems due to its aesthetic appeal and potential benefits. Dark mode design solutions take into consideration the principles of color theory, specifically the concept of contrast. Dark backgrounds provide a strong contrast against text and other graphical elements, making them visually stand out and enhancing legibility. By using a darker color scheme, the text and elements can be more easily viewed and interacted with, especially in low-light or nighttime environments. Additionally, the reduced brightness can be less straining on the eyes, contributing to a more comfortable user experience. In the realm of color symbolism, dark colors often evoke a sense of sophistication, elegance, and professionalism. Black, in particular, is associated with power, mystery, and formality. By incorporating dark mode design solutions, applications and websites can create a visually striking and impactful user interface that aligns with these symbolic associations. The overall design can convey a sense of luxury or exclusivity, depending on the specific implementation. Furthermore, dark mode design solutions offer practical advantages beyond aesthetics. They can help reduce energy consumption on devices with OLED or AMOLED screens, as these displays only illuminate the pixels that are necessary. By utilizing dark backgrounds, fewer pixels need to be illuminated, leading to potential power savings. This is particularly relevant for mobile devices, where battery life is a crucial consideration. In conclusion, dark mode design solutions utilize a primarily dark color scheme to create visually appealing and functional user interfaces. Drawing upon color theory principles, contrast is enhanced to improve legibility and reduce eye strain. Moreover, dark colors in design evoke symbolic associations such as sophistication and formality. Additionally, dark mode can have practical benefits in terms of energy efficiency. By implementing these solutions, applications, websites, and operating systems can provide users with a visually striking, comfortable, and efficient user experience.

Dark Mode Design Tools

Dark mode design tools refer to software or applications that provide designers with the ability to create and work with designs that are specifically tailored for a dark color scheme. These tools typically offer a range of features and functionalities for designing user interfaces, websites, or other graphic elements in a way that optimizes them for dark mode. Color theory plays a crucial role in the design of dark mode interfaces, as it involves the selection and manipulation of colors to create visually pleasing and functional designs. Designers need to consider the psychological and emotional impact of colors and understand how they interact with each other to communicate the intended message or evoke specific responses from users. When it comes to dark mode design, color symbolism becomes even more critical. The choice of colors not only impacts the aesthetics but also affects the usability and user experience. Different colors have unique meanings and associations, and understanding these can help designers create designs that align with the desired message or brand identity. For example, using dark shades of blue can convey a sense of stability and professionalism, while dark green may represent nature and relaxation. Therefore, dark mode design tools should provide designers with a comprehensive library of colors and the ability to manipulate them effectively. Additionally, dark mode design tools should offer features that enable designers to test their designs across different devices and screen sizes. This is particularly important as dark mode designs may have different contrasts and visual characteristics when viewed on various display settings. The tools should also allow designers to preview their designs in both light and dark modes to ensure consistency and usability. In conclusion, dark mode design tools support designers in creating visually appealing and effective designs specifically tailored for dark color schemes. They incorporate color theory and color symbolism to help designers make informed decisions about the selection and manipulation of colors. These tools also provide features to test and preview designs across different devices and screen settings to ensure a consistent and optimized user experience.

Dark Mode

Dark Mode is a design trend that involves using predominantly dark colors, such as black or dark gray, as the primary background color in a user interface. It is based on the principles of color theory and symbolism within the realm of design. In color theory, dark colors are often associated with feelings of sophistication, elegance, and mystery. They can create a sense of depth and contrast, making other colors and elements stand out more prominently. Dark Mode takes advantage of these associations and uses them to enhance the visual experience of a design.

Death (Black)

Death (Black) in color theory and color symbolism in design refers to the color black and its association with the concept of death. In color theory, black is considered the absence of light and color. It is the darkest color in the visible spectrum and is often used to symbolize darkness, mystery, and the unknown. Black is also associated with power, elegance, sophistication, and formality. In design, it is commonly used to create contrast, add emphasis, and convey a sense of depth and dimension.

Death (White)

In color theory and color symbolism in design, white is often associated with the concept of death. White represents the absence or cessation of life, the end of a cycle, and the finality of existence. In many cultures and religious traditions, white is the color of mourning and is used in funeral ceremonies and practices. It is often worn by mourners as a symbol of grief and remembrance. White flowers, such as lilies, are commonly associated with funerals and are used to convey sympathy and to honor the deceased.

Deep Emotions (Indigo)

Deep Emotions (Indigo) is a color in color theory and design that represents a rich and intense shade of blue. It is considered a cool color and falls between blue and violet on the color spectrum. Indigo is often associated with feelings of depth, mystery, and spirituality, making it a popular choice for conveying a sense of emotion and significance in design. In color symbolism, indigo is often linked to deep emotions and introspection. It is seen as a color that stimulates the imagination and encourages creative thinking. Indigo is associated with qualities such as intuition, wisdom, and inner exploration. It is believed to have a calming effect on the mind and can be used to symbolize serenity, tranquility, and peace.

Dependability (Blue)

In the context of color theory and color symbolism in design, blue is often associated with the concept of dependability. Dependability refers to the quality of being reliable, trustworthy, and consistent. It conveys a sense of stability, loyalty, and responsibility. When blue is used in design, it can evoke these feelings and attributes.

Designers Of Color Palettes

A color palette is a collection of colors that are carefully selected and organized to create a harmonious and visually pleasing composition in design. It serves as a foundation for creating color schemes and determining the overall visual identity of a design project. In the context of color theory, a color palette is typically based on the principles of color harmony, which involve the arrangement of colors in a way that is aesthetically pleasing and balanced to the human eye. It takes into consideration factors such as color contrast, color temperature, and color symbolism to evoke specific emotions or convey certain messages.

Desire (Coral)

Desire (Coral) is a vibrant shade of reddish-orange that is used in color theory and color symbolism in design to evoke feelings of passion, energy, and excitement.In color theory, Desire (Coral) is considered a warm color. Warm colors are often associated with intensity and stimulation, as they are reminiscent of fire and the sun. This shade of coral is particularly impactful due to its vividness and high saturation. It has a strong presence and is often used to draw attention and create a focal point in a design.In color symbolism, Desire (Coral) carries various connotations. It is frequently associated with passion and desire, as the name suggests. The color invokes feelings of romance, sensuality, and sexuality. It can be used to convey love and attraction, making it a popular choice in designs related to relationships and intimacy.Furthermore, Desire (Coral) is also representative of vitality, energy, and action. The color is often used to evoke a sense of excitement, enthusiasm, and dynamism. It can be employed in designs that aim to inspire and motivate viewers, as well as to create a sense of urgency or intensity.Additionally, Desire (Coral) has cultural and historical significance. In some cultures, coral is believed to bring good luck and protect against evil spirits. It is also associated with courage and strength. These cultural and historical associations can be incorporated into design concepts and used to convey specific meanings and messages.In summary, Desire (Coral) is a vibrant shade of reddish-orange that is utilized in color theory and color symbolism in design to evoke feelings of passion, energy, and excitement. It is often associated with romance, vitality, and action. Designers use this color to create focal points, inspire viewers, and convey specific meanings and messages.

Desire (Red)

Desire (Red) is a vibrant and powerful color in color theory and plays a significant role in color symbolism in design. It is a warm color that is associated with intense emotions, passion, and energy. In color theory, red is known as a primary color, as it cannot be created by mixing other colors together. It is often used to create visual impact and draw attention due to its high visibility. Red has a short wavelength, making it an energetic color that can stimulate the senses. In the context of color symbolism in design, red is commonly associated with strong emotions such as love, desire, and courage. It elicits a sense of urgency, excitement, and intensity. Red can be used strategically to create a focal point or to convey a sense of power and confidence. When used in branding and marketing, red often represents passion, energy, and action. Many well-known companies utilize red in their logos and advertisements to evoke a sense of desire and stimulate consumer interest. Red can also create a feeling of urgency, encouraging consumers to take immediate action. Additionally, red can have cultural and symbolic meanings. In some cultures, red is a symbol of good luck, celebration, and joy. It is often used in festive occasions and traditional ceremonies. On the other hand, red can also symbolize danger, warning, and aggression. In design, the use of red can greatly impact the overall message and perception of a visual composition. Its strong presence can evoke strong emotions and create a sense of excitement or intensity. However, it is important to use red judiciously, as using too much of it can overwhelm the viewer and create a sense of unease.

Determination (Crimson)

Determination in the context of color theory and color symbolism in design refers to the quality of being firm, focused, and unwavering in pursuit of a goal or objective. It is often associated with the color crimson, which is a deep, intense shade of red. Crimson is a powerful color that is often used to represent determination due to its strong and bold nature. It evokes a sense of strength, passion, and resilience, making it an ideal choice for expressing determination in design. The color crimson is derived from the natural dye obtained from the cochineal insect, which has historically been highly valued for its deep red hues. In color theory, red is considered a warm color that is associated with physical and emotional energy. It is known to increase heart rate, blood pressure, and ultimately evoke strong emotions. Crimson, being a shade of red, carries these energetic qualities and intensifies them further with its darker and more saturated tone. This creates a visual impact that can elicit feelings of determination and motivation. As a color symbol, crimson represents determination and strength of character. It symbolizes a person or entity's unwavering resolve to achieve their goals, even in the face of obstacles and challenges. Crimson is often used in branding and design to convey these attributes and appeal to individuals who value determination and ambition. In design, the use of crimson can be strategically employed to communicate a sense of determination. It can be used as an accent color to draw attention and create a focal point, or it can be used more extensively to create a bold and impactful design. When combined with other colors, crimson can enhance the overall meaning and message of a design by adding depth, intensity, and an element of determination.

Determination (Maroon)

In color theory, determination is represented by the color maroon. Maroon is a deep, rich shade of red that is associated with a strong sense of purpose, perseverance, and unwavering focus. As a dark and intense color, it evokes a sense of power, determination, and resilience. When used in design, maroon can convey a variety of symbolic meanings. Its association with determination makes it an ideal choice when aiming to communicate persistence and resolve. It can be used to symbolize a strong will, ambition, and a tenacious attitude towards achieving goals.

Determination (Orange)

Determination (Orange) is a color within the context of color theory and color symbolism in design that represents a strong and unwavering commitment to achieving a goal or overcoming obstacles. It is an energetic and lively hue that combines the passion and drive of red with the warmth and enthusiasm of yellow. As a color with high visibility and vibrancy, orange often captures attention and stimulates creativity. In color theory, orange is considered a secondary color, created by mixing equal parts of red and yellow. It sits between red and yellow on the color wheel, symbolizing a sense of transition and movement. This transitional nature of orange can convey determination and an ability to adapt and evolve in the face of challenges. In color symbolism, orange is associated with various meanings such as excitement, enthusiasm, and courage. It is a color often associated with action and ambition, reflecting the qualities required to persist in the pursuit of goals. The brightness and warmth of orange can evoke feelings of positivity, motivation, and assertiveness. When used in design, determination (orange) can be an effective tool to communicate and reinforce the message of strength and resolve. It can be used as an accent color to draw attention to key elements or calls to action, such as buttons or important information. The energetic and uplifting nature of orange can also be utilized in designs aimed at cultivating a sense of motivation or encouraging action. However, it is important to consider the context and intended audience when incorporating determination (orange) into design. While orange can convey a sense of determination, it can also be associated with aggression or restlessness. It is crucial to use orange in a balanced manner and consider its impact on overall design composition. In conclusion, determination (orange) is a powerful and dynamic color that symbolizes an unwavering commitment to reaching goals. Its vibrant and energetic nature can inspire motivation and action, making it a valuable tool in design to convey strength and resolve.

Devices For Calibrating Color

A device for calibrating color is a tool used in the field of color theory and color symbolism in design. It aids in achieving accurate and consistent color representation across various mediums, such as digital displays, printers, and other color-critical devices. Color calibration is essential in design as it ensures that the intended colors are accurately reproduced. It addresses the inherent differences in color reproduction capabilities among devices by employing standardized color profiles and calibration methods. One popular device used for color calibration is a colorimeter. This device measures the light emitted or reflected by a display or other surfaces and analyzes the color spectrum. It compares the measured values against known color standards, enabling adjustments to be made to achieve accurate color reproduction. Another commonly used device is a spectrophotometer. This instrument measures the intensity of light at different wavelengths, providing a comprehensive analysis of the color spectrum. It helps create precise color profiles for devices, ensuring accurate color reproduction across different mediums. In addition to physical devices, software solutions are also employed for color calibration. These tools utilize algorithms and mathematical models to map colors accurately between devices. Color management software allows designers to create and manage color profiles, ensuring consistent color reproduction across various platforms. Color calibration devices and software are indispensable in design industries where color accuracy is crucial, such as graphic design, photography, and printing. They enable designers to have full control over the final color output of their works, ensuring that the intended colors elicit the desired emotional responses and convey the intended messages. In conclusion, a color calibration device is an essential tool in color theory and color symbolism in design. It enables designers to achieve accurate and consistent color reproduction across different mediums. With the aid of devices like colorimeters, spectrophotometers, and color management software, designers can ensure that their work accurately represents their intended colors, resulting in visually compelling and impactful designs.

Digital Color Libraries

A digital color library, in the context of color theory and color symbolism in design, refers to a collection of predefined colors that are commonly used in various digital design platforms and applications. These libraries contain a wide range of colors, each with its own unique hexadecimal code, which allows designers to easily access and utilize them in their design projects. Color libraries are essential tools in design as they provide a standardized set of colors that can be consistently used across different projects. They help ensure visual consistency and cohesion in designs, as colors from these libraries have been carefully selected and tested for their aesthetic appeal and compatibility.

Divinity (Magenta)

Divinity (Magenta) is a vibrant and intense hue that belongs to the color spectrum between red and purple. In the context of color theory, it is achieved by combining equal parts of blue and red pigments. The resulting color is characterized by its rich and deep tone with a slight bluish undertone. In color symbolism in design, Divinity (Magenta) carries various connotations and

102

meanings. It is often associated with spirituality, harmony, and divine energy. The color's intensity and boldness give it a sense of power and transformation, making it a popular choice in design to convey a mystical or mysterious atmosphere.

Dullness (Gray)

Dullness (Gray) in color theory refers to a color that lacks vividness or brightness. It is a neutral color that is produced by combining equal amounts of black and white. Gray is often associated with feelings of calmness, stability, and balance. In design, the color gray is commonly used as a neutral background or base color. It provides a sense of stability and allows other colors to stand out. Gray is often used to create a minimalist or modern look and is frequently seen in corporate designs or websites.

Durability (Bronze)

Durability in color theory refers to the perceived strength and resilience of a color in a design. It is the ability of a color to withstand fading, changing, or losing its visual impact over time. In the context of color symbolism in design, durability represents stability, reliability, and permanency. It suggests a sense of strength, steadfastness, and endurance. When used in design, colors that convey durability can evoke feelings of trust, strength, and longevity.

Earth (Brown)

Earth (Brown) is a color within the color theory that derives its name and representation from the physical characteristics of the Earth's surface. It is often associated with the soil, rocks, and natural elements found in nature. In the context of color symbolism in design, Earth (Brown) represents stability, reliability, and a sense of groundedness. It is often used to create a warm and inviting atmosphere, mimicking the earthy tones found in nature. Earth (Brown) can evoke feelings of comfort, security, and a connection to the earth.

Earthy Colors

Earthy colors are hues that mimic the colors found in nature, specifically those found in the earth. These colors are often associated with a sense of warmth, calmness, and stability, and are frequently used in design to create a natural, organic, and grounding atmosphere. Color theory suggests that earthy colors are typically made up of low saturation and high value, resulting in colors that appear more muted and subtle. Earthy colors can be categorized into warm earthy colors and cool earthy colors. Warm earthy colors, such as browns, tans, and beiges, are often associated with elements like soil, wood, and stone. These colors are known for creating a cozy and inviting feel, and are commonly used in rustic or country-themed designs. Cool earthy colors, such as greens, blues, and grays, are reminiscent of vegetation, water, and stone, and are often used to create a calming and soothing effect.

Editors For Color Palettes

Color palettes are essential tools used by designers in the field of color theory. They are collections of colors that are carefully selected and arranged to achieve a particular aesthetic or evoke specific emotions in a design. Editors for color palettes are software applications or online tools designed to assist designers in creating and manipulating color palettes. In the context of color theory, color palettes play a crucial role in creating visually harmonious and balanced designs. They are based on the principles of color psychology and symbolism, which suggest that different colors can evoke distinct emotional responses and have symbolic meanings. Editors for color palettes provide designers with a variety of features and functionalities to effectively work with colors. These tools allow designers to explore different color combinations, experiment with hues, saturations, and brightness levels, and create custom color palettes that suit their specific design needs. They often provide predefined color schemes and swatches based on color theories such as the color wheel, complementary colors, analogous colors, and triadic colors. By offering these predefined color schemes, editors for color palettes help designers create harmonious designs effortlessly. In addition to predefined color schemes, editors for color palettes also allow designers to import, export, and customize color palettes. Designers can import existing color palettes into the editor and modify them to suit their design concept. Likewise, they can export their created color palettes for use in other design software or share them with colleagues and clients. One of the key features of editors for color palettes is the ability to preview the color combinations in real-time. Designers can apply the chosen colors to sample designs or shapes to see how they interact and evaluate the overall visual impact. This feature enables designers to make informed decisions about the color palettes they create. Overall, editors for color palettes are indispensable tools for designers working with color theory and symbolism in design. They provide a range of features that empower designers to create visually appealing and emotionally resonant designs with carefully selected color combinations. Editors for color palettes enhance the design process by enabling designers to experiment, explore, and manipulate colors efficiently.

Editors For Color Schemes

A color scheme refers to a harmonious set of colors that are used in combination to create a visually pleasing composition. In the context of color theory and color symbolism in design, color schemes are essential elements that help convey specific messages and emotions, as well as create a sense of unity and balance in visual compositions. Editors for color schemes play a crucial role in the design process. Their main responsibility is to curate and manipulate color combinations to achieve the desired aesthetic and communicative goals. Through their expertise in color theory, editors can select and adjust colors in a way that enhances the overall visual impact of a design. Color theory provides a framework for editors to understand the various properties of colors and their interactions. Different colors have different psychological associations and can evoke distinct emotions and moods. Editors must consider these factors when choosing colors for a composition, taking into account the intended message or theme. Color symbolism also plays a significant role in design. Certain colors are commonly associated with specific meanings or concepts. For example, red often symbolizes passion or danger, while blue is often associated with tranquility or trustworthiness. Editors must be aware of these symbolic associations and use them intentionally to reinforce the intended message or narrative of a design. Editors for color schemes must also consider the principles of color harmony and balance. Color harmonies are combinations of colors that are visually pleasing and create a sense of unity. Editors can use color wheels and color schemes such as analogous, complementary, or triadic to achieve harmonious compositions. Additionally, editors must consider the balance of colors within a design, distributing them in a way that creates visual equilibrium and avoids overwhelming or distracting the viewer. In conclusion, editors for color schemes play a fundamental role in the design process by curating and manipulating color combinations to create visually appealing and meaningful compositions. Their understanding of color theory, color symbolism, and principles of color harmony and balance allows them to effectively communicate messages and emotions through the strategic use of colors.

Elegance (Black)

Elegance (Black) in color theory and color symbolism in design represents a timeless and sophisticated aesthetic. It is a hue that embodies depth, sophistication, and formality, evoking a sense of mystery and power. Black is often associated with elegance because of its ability to create strong contrasts and enhance the visual impact of other colors. It serves as a neutral backdrop that allows other colors to pop and stand out. When used appropriately, black can add a touch of refinement and luxury to any design.

Elegance (Gray)

Elegance (Gray) in color theory refers to a specific shade of gray that is associated with a sense of sophistication, refinement, and class. Gray as a color is often seen as neutral, balanced, and timeless, making it a popular choice in design to convey a sense of calmness and sophistication. In color symbolism, gray is often associated with meanings such as stability, professionalism, and wisdom. It is often used to represent a sense of formality and seriousness, making it a suitable choice for corporate and professional settings.

Elegance (Lavender)

Elegance (Lavender) is a color that falls within the purple hue of the color spectrum. It is a soft and delicate shade of purple with a slight hint of gray, giving it a more muted and sophisticated appearance. Elegance (Lavender) is often associated with luxury, grace, and refinement. In color theory, lavender is created by mixing blue and red, with a higher concentration of blue. This combination gives it a cool undertone, making it calming and soothing to the eye. Its softness and subtlety make it a popular choice for creating a serene and elegant atmosphere in design.

Elegance (Purple)

In color theory, elegance is commonly associated with the color purple. Purple is a secondary color that is created by combining the primary colors blue and red. It is often described as a color that combines the stability of blue with the energy of red, resulting in a harmonious and sophisticated hue. Purple has long been associated with elegance and luxury. Throughout history, it has been used to represent royalty and wealth. In ancient times, purple dye was rare and expensive to produce, making it a symbol of status and power. This association with nobility has carried over into modern times, and purple is often used in the design of high-end products and branding.

Elegance (Silver)

Elegance (Silver) is a color term used in color theory and color symbolism in design to describe a specific shade of silver that conveys an aesthetic of sophistication and refined beauty. It is often associated with qualities such as grace, elegance, and luxury.In color theory, silver is considered a metallic color that falls within the neutral color palette. It is created by combining shades of grey with a reflective shimmer, which gives it a sense of opulence and elegance. The addition of silver to a design can create a sense of elegance and sophistication, as it has a sleek and polished appearance.

Emotional Healing (Teal)

Emotional Healing (Teal) Emotional healing in the context of color theory and color symbolism in design can be represented by the color teal. Teal is a unique color that lies between green and blue on the color spectrum, combining the calming and soothing properties of both colors. Teal is often associated with emotional healing due to its ability to balance and harmonize emotions. It is a color that promotes a sense of tranquility and peace, making it ideal for spaces or designs that aim to create a calming and healing environment. The emotional healing properties of teal can be attributed to its connection to nature and the natural world. The color green, which is prominent in teal, is often associated with growth, renewal, and harmony. It is a color that represents balance and stability, both emotionally and physically. Teal incorporates these qualities while also adding a touch of serenity through its blue undertones. Teal is often used in design elements such as walls, furniture, or accessories in spaces that aim to promote emotional healing. It is a color commonly found in therapy rooms, spas, and meditation spaces. The color's calming and healing properties can help create a safe and nurturing environment for individuals to relax and release emotional tension. In addition to emotional healing, teal is also associated with clarity and communication. The color's blue undertones represent open and honest communication, while its green elements bring clarity, understanding, and the ability to listen and empathize. When used in design, teal can help facilitate positive and truthful interactions and foster emotional connection between individuals. In conclusion, emotional healing represented by the color teal harnesses the calming and soothing properties of both blue and green. Teal promotes a sense of tranquility and peace, while also helping to balance emotions. Used in design, teal creates a healing environment that fosters emotional growth and communication.

Emotional Impact Of Colors

The emotional impact of colors refers to the way that different colors evoke specific emotions and psychological responses in individuals. This concept is a fundamental aspect of color theory and color symbolism in design. Color theory is the study of how colors interact and how they can be used to create specific effects in art and design. It explores the relationships between colors and how they can be combined to achieve visual harmony and balance. Understanding the emotional impact of colors is key to effectively using color in design, as different colors can communicate different moods and messages. Colors have long been associated with specific emotions and meanings. For example, warm colors such as red and orange are often associated with energy, passion, and intensity. These colors can evoke feelings of excitement and warmth. On the other hand, cool colors like blue and green are more calming and soothing. They can be associated with feelings of relaxation and tranquility. In addition to these general associations, the emotional impact of colors can also vary depending on individual experiences and cultural backgrounds. For example, in Western cultures, white is often associated with purity and innocence, while in some Eastern cultures, it is associated with mourning and death. Color symbolism is the use of colors to represent specific ideas, concepts, or emotions. Different colors can be symbolic of different things in various contexts. For example, the color red is often associated with love and passion, while black is often associated with death and mourning. In design, understanding the emotional impact of colors is crucial when creating visual compositions. The colors chosen for a design will affect how it is perceived and how it makes people feel. By strategically using colors, designers can manipulate the emotions and reactions of the audience. In conclusion, the emotional impact of colors is an important aspect of color theory and color symbolism in design. Different colors can evoke specific emotions and convey different meanings. Understanding the emotional impact of colors allows designers to effectively communicate messages and create harmonious visual compositions.

Empowerment (Magenta)

In color theory and color symbolism in design, the color magenta is associated with empowerment. Empowerment is a sense of strength, confidence, and personal agency. It is the state of feeling empowered or enabled to take action and make decisions. The color magenta is a vibrant, bold hue that combines the energy and warmth of red with the calmness and stability of blue. It is often used to evoke a strong and powerful emotional response. In design, the color magenta can be strategically used to create a sense of empowerment. It can be employed to convey messages of strength, resilience, and determination. Magenta can be used as an accent color to highlight important elements or to draw attention to key messages. The color magenta is also associated with assertiveness and self-confidence. It is often used to convey a sense of authority and leadership. Magenta can be used to create a visual hierarchy, with more intense shades of the color representing dominance and control. Additionally, magenta can symbolize creativity and innovation. It is a color that is often associated with unconventional thinking and nonconformity. Magenta can be used to represent a forward-thinking mindset and to inspire original ideas. Overall, in the context of color theory and color symbolism in design, magenta represents empowerment. Its bold and vibrant nature can evoke a sense of strength, confidence, and personal agency. Magenta can be used strategically in design to convey messages of resilience, authority, and creativity. It is a color that encourages action, decision-making, and a sense of empowerment.

Enchantment (Lilac)

Enchantment (Lilac) refers to a specific color within the realm of color theory and color symbolism in design. Lilac is a pale purple hue that is derived from the combination of blue and red. It is often associated with enchantment, magic, and mystery. In color theory, lilac is considered a cool color. Cool colors are typically calming, soothing, and evoke a sense of tranquility. Lilac, specifically, is known for its delicate and gentle nature. It is often used in design to create a sense of harmony and balance. In terms of color symbolism, lilac is associated with creativity, spirituality, and enchantment. It is often used in design to evoke feelings of whimsy and wonder. Lilac is also sometimes used to represent femininity, grace, and elegance. In design, lilac can be used as a primary color or as an accent color. When used as a primary color, it can create a soft and romantic atmosphere. It can be a popular choice for bedrooms, nurseries, or spaces where relaxation is desired. When used as an accent color, it can add a touch of enchantment and playfulness to a design. Overall, enchantment (lilac) is a color that can add a sense of magic and wonder to a design. Whether used as a primary or accent color, it can create a calming and whimsical atmosphere. It is a color that is often associated with creativity, spirituality, and femininity. Its delicate nature and cool tones make it a popular choice in design.

Energy (Orange)

The color orange is often associated with the concept of energy in color theory and color symbolism in design. It is a warm color that is associated with physical activity, enthusiasm, and creativity. Orange is a mixture of yellow and red, combining the brightness and warmth of yellow with the intensity and power of red. In color theory, orange is considered a secondary color, meaning it is created by mixing two primary colors together. It is often used to create a sense of warmth and excitement in design, as well as to draw attention to specific elements. Orange is a highly visible color, making it a popular choice for traffic signs and warning labels.

Energy (Red)

Energy (Red) in color theory refers to the vibrant and stimulating properties associated with the color red. It is one of the primary colors and holds immense significance in both design and symbolism. In design, the color red is often used to evoke a sense of energy, power, and passion. It is commonly associated with concepts such as strength, determination, and excitement. Red has a visually stimulating effect, capturing attention and creating a sense of urgency or intensity. It has a high visibility factor, making it ideal for highlighting important elements or creating focal points within a design.

Energy (Salmon)

Energy, specifically in the context of color theory and color symbolism in design, refers to the vibrant and intense shade known as salmon. Salmon is a warm color that combines the qualities of red and orange, exuding a high level of energy and enthusiasm. This hue is often associated with vitality, passion, and excitement. It has the ability to create a sense of dynamism and liveliness in design compositions. Salmon can be used strategically to draw attention to specific elements or areas within a design, as it commands immediate visual focus.

Energy (Tangerine)

Energy, in the context of color theory and color symbolism in design, refers to the vibrant and dynamic nature of the color tangerine. Tangerine is a bold and intense shade of orange that is associated with enthusiasm, creativity, and stimulation. It is known for its high level of energy and ability to capture attention.

Enthusiasm (Orange)

Enthusiasm, in the context of color theory and color symbolism in design, is represented by the color orange. Orange is a vibrant and energetic hue that combines the intensity of red with the brightness of yellow. It is often associated with feelings of excitement, enthusiasm, and warmth. In color theory, orange is considered a warm color that is visually prominent and eye-catching. It is often used to grab attention and create a sense of urgency or excitement. Its high visibility makes it useful for highlighting important elements or calls to action in a design. Orange is commonly used in advertising and marketing to evoke feelings of enthusiasm and attract attention to products or promotions.

Enthusiasm (Salmon)

Enthusiasm, in the context of color theory and color symbolism in design, refers to the vibrant and energizing quality associated with the color salmon. Salmon is a warm, reddish-orange hue that evokes a sense of excitement, passion, and joy. It is commonly used to capture attention and infuse designs with a lively and dynamic atmosphere. As a color often associated with physical and emotional warmth, salmon can create a welcoming and invigorating environment. It has the ability to stimulate the senses and inspire feelings of enthusiasm, making it an ideal choice for designs intended to energize and engage viewers. Whether used as a dominant color or in combination with other hues, salmon has a powerful impact on the visual experience.

Enthusiasm (Tangerine)

Enthusiasm, in the context of color theory and color symbolism in design, refers to the vibrant and energetic qualities associated with the color tangerine. Tangerine is a warm, reddish-orange hue that is often used to convey feelings of excitement, passion, and enthusiasm. In color theory, tangerine is classified as a warm color along with other shades of orange and red. Warm colors are associated with energy, warmth, and positive emotions. Tangerine, specifically, is known for its invigorating and stimulating effect on the senses.

Envy (Green)

Envy (Green):In color theory and color symbolism in design, the color green is often associated with the emotion of envy. Envy is a complex emotion characterized by feelings of discontentment, resentment, and desire for what others possess. It is often portrayed as a negative and destructive emotion.

Excitement (Coral)

In color theory and color symbolism in design, excitement is represented by the color coral. Coral is a vibrant shade of orange with a pink undertone, often associated with energy, enthusiasm, and liveliness. It evokes a sense of adventure and stimulates the senses, creating a feeling of excitement and anticipation. Coral is often used in designs to draw attention and create a focal point. Its bold and intense hue instantly grabs the viewer's attention, making it an excellent choice for call-to-action buttons, promotional banners, or any element that needs to stand out. When used sparingly, coral can add a pop of excitement to a design, while an abundance of it can create a lively and stimulating atmosphere.

Excitement (Crimson)

In color theory and color symbolism in design, excitement is often associated with the color crimson. Crimson is a deep, vibrant shade of red that is often described as being intense and full of energy. Crimson is a color that is frequently used to evoke feelings of excitement, passion, and vitality. It is often associated with power, strength, and courage, and is commonly used to grab attention and create a sense of urgency and enthusiasm in design.

Excitement (Orange)

In color theory and color symbolism in design, the color orange is often associated with excitement. Excitement is a state of intense emotion or anticipation, and the color orange is known to evoke similar feelings in people. Orange is a warm and vibrant color that is highly stimulating to the senses. It is a color that demands attention and can be quite energetic. In color psychology, orange is often seen as a color of enthusiasm, passion, and extroversion. It is a color that can create a sense of vitality and excitement in a design.

Excitement (Red)

Excitement (Red) in the context of color theory and color symbolism in design refers to the psychological and emotional response elicited by the color red. Red is a widely recognized and powerful color that often evokes strong emotions and sensations. In color theory, red is classified as a warm color and is associated with energy, strength, and passion. It has the longest wavelength among the visible colors and is highly noticeable, making it a bold and attention-grabbing choice. Red is also often used to signify importance, urgency, and intensity, making it a popular choice in advertising and warning signs.

Excitement (Tangerine)

Excitement, in the context of color theory and color symbolism in design, refers to a vibrant and energetic emotion evoked by the color tangerine. Tangerine is a hue that falls within the orange family and is characterized by its mixture of warm red and vibrant yellow tones. In color theory, orange is often associated with enthusiasm, creativity, and optimism. It is a color that demands attention and stimulates both the mind and the body. Tangerine, specifically, intensifies these characteristics, further enhancing the feelings of excitement in design.

Extensions For Color Picking

Extensions for Color Picking are tools or software functionalities that enhance the process of selecting colors in the context of color theory and color symbolism in design. These extensions provide additional features and options to facilitate the color selection process, allowing designers to create visually appealing and meaningful designs. Color theory is the study of how colors interact, blend, and contrast with each other. It provides guidelines and principles for selecting and combining colors in design to create a pleasing and harmonious visual experience.

Color symbolism, on the other hand, focuses on the meaning and associations attributed to different colors in various cultures and contexts. It is used to evoke specific emotions, convey messages, or represent certain concepts. Extensions for Color Picking offer various functionalities that assist designers in applying color theory and color symbolism effectively. One common feature of these extensions is the color wheel, a visual representation of the color spectrum. The color wheel allows designers to explore different color relationships, such as complementary, analogous, or triadic, and select colors that harmonize or contrast with each other based on these relationships. Another useful feature of color picking extensions is the ability to extract colors from images or websites. Designers can upload images or specify URLs to extract specific colors or generate palettes from those images. This functionality enables designers to incorporate colors from real-world objects or existing designs into their work, ensuring consistency or creating a desired mood or atmosphere. Additionally, extensions for color picking often include color libraries or swatches that provide a wide range of pre-defined colors. These libraries may categorize colors based on their meanings or associations, making it easier for designers to choose colors that align with the intended message or concept of their design. Some extensions may even allow users to create and save custom color palettes for future use or collaboration with other designers. In conclusion, extensions for Color Picking are tools or software functionalities that enhance the color selection process in design, incorporating color theory and color symbolism. These extensions provide features like color wheels, color extraction from images, and color libraries to assist designers in creating visually appealing and meaningful designs. By using these extensions, designers can make informed color choices that align with the desired emotions, messages, or concepts of their designs.

Eye Dropper Tool

A color is a visual perception resulting from the wavelength of light that enters the retina of the eye. In the context of color theory and color symbolism in design, the eye dropper tool is a feature commonly found in graphic design software that allows designers to select and sample colors from an image or other visual elements. The eye dropper tool serves as a practical tool for color selection in design. By using this tool, designers can capture specific colors from an existing image or artwork and apply them to their own designs. This way, they can ensure consistency and harmony in their color palette, as well as enhance the overall aesthetic appeal of their designs. In color theory, colors are divided into various categories based on their relationship to one another. The eye dropper tool enables designers to precisely identify and replicate these colors, ensuring accuracy in their color schemes. By selecting colors that are harmonious or complementary to each other, designers can create visual balance and convey specific emotions or messages through their designs. Furthermore, the eye dropper tool plays a significant role in color symbolism within design. Colors have the power to evoke certain feelings, associations, and cultural meanings. By accurately identifying and using specific colors with the eye dropper tool, designers can tap into these symbolic meanings and effectively communicate their intended message. For example, the eye dropper tool can be used to capture the vibrant red color often associated with passion, love, and energy. By incorporating this color into a design, designers can visually convey these emotions and create a strong impact on the viewer. In conclusion, the eye dropper tool is an essential feature in graphic design software that allows designers to select and sample colors from visual elements. It enables designers to ensure consistency and harmony in their color palettes, as well as accurately convey symbolic meanings through color choices.

Fear (Black)

Fear (Black) In color theory and color symbolism in design, the color black is often associated with the emotion of fear. The color black represents the absence or the complete absorption of light, which creates a sense of emptiness, darkness, and mystery. This darkness and mystery can evoke feelings of fear, as the unknown and the uncertain are commonly sources of fear. Many cultures and societies have traditionally associated black with fear and negative emotions. In Western culture, for example, black is often associated with death, mourning, and evil. The color black is commonly used to represent villains, darkness, and danger in movies, art, and literature. In design, black can be used strategically to create a sense of fear or unease. The use of black in a design can create a stark contrast with other colors, emphasizing its darkness and intensity. This contrast can evoke a feeling of fear or tension in the viewer. In horror movie posters, for instance, black is often used as the background color to create a sense of fear and suspense. However, it is important to note that the perception of fear evoked by the color black can vary depending on cultural and personal associations. While black generally symbolizes fear in many contexts, it can also be associated with power, elegance, and sophistication. In fashion, for instance, black is often used to convey a sense of style and authority. In conclusion, the color black is often associated with fear in color theory and color symbolism in design due to its association with darkness, mystery, and the unknown. It can be strategically used in design to evoke a sense of fear or unease, but its perception may also vary based on cultural and personal associations.

Femininity (Lavender)

Femininity is a concept deeply rooted in society and culture, and in the context of color theory and symbolism in design, the color lavender is often associated with it. Lavender is a shade that combines the calmness and tenderness of pale purple with the freshness and purity of white, creating a color that embodies elegance, grace, and femininity. Symbolically, lavender is often used to represent femininity because it is reminiscent of flowers such as lavender and lilac, which are traditionally associated with beauty and delicacy. Its soft and subtle hue evokes a sense of gentleness and sensitivity, characteristics often associated with femininity.

Femininity (Pink)

Femininity (Pink) is a color associated with femininity, often symbolizing traits such as delicacy, tenderness, and nurturing. In color theory and design, pink is considered a muted shade of red, which is typically associated with passion, energy, and power. Pink is created by mixing red with white, softening the intensity of red and giving it a lighter, more subtle appearance. In color symbolism, pink is commonly used to represent love, affection, and beauty. It is often associated with traditionally feminine qualities and is frequently used in designs and branding targeted towards women and girls. Pink can evoke feelings of warmth, comfort, and tranquility, and is often used to create a calming and soothing atmosphere.

Fertility (Green)

In the context of color theory and color symbolism in design, the color green is often associated with fertility. Green is commonly associated with growth, renewal, and abundance, as it is the color of nature and vegetation. This association with fertility can be attributed to the lush green landscapes that often accompany and symbolize the presence of fertile land. Green is a color that is perceived to be calming and relaxing, which may also contribute to its association with fertility. The soothing nature of green can create a sense of harmony and balance, creating an environment that is conducive to growth and reproduction. Furthermore, green is closely connected to the concepts of life and vitality. It is the color of new beginnings and fresh starts. In many cultures, green is also synonymous with hope and optimism, further emphasizing its connection to fertility. In design, the color green can be prominently used to evoke feelings of fertility, growth, and abundance. It can be utilized in various elements such as backgrounds, illustrations, and typography to convey these symbolic meanings. When using green in design, it is important to consider the shade and tone of green chosen, as different variations can evoke different emotions and connotations. Vibrant and bright shades of green may represent youthful energy and vitality, while darker shades can symbolize stability and prosperity. Overall, the color green embodies the essence of fertility in color theory and symbolism. Its connection to nature, growth, and renewal makes it a powerful tool in design to evoke feelings of abundance and the potential for new life.

Flat Design Color Palettes

Flat design color palettes refer to a set of colors used in the design of flat design elements, which are characterized by minimalistic and simplified visuals. These color palettes are based on principles of color theory and are carefully selected to create a cohesive and visually pleasing aesthetic. Color theory is the study of how colors interact with each other and how they are perceived by the human eye. It serves as a guideline for designers to create harmonious and balanced color combinations. In the context of flat design color palettes, color theory plays a crucial role in selecting colors that work well together and convey the desired message or emotion. In design, colors also carry symbolic meanings and can evoke different emotions or associations. Each color has its own unique symbolism, and understanding these associations is essential in choosing appropriate colors for a design. Flat design color palettes take into account both the principles of color theory and color symbolism to create visually appealing and meaningful designs. When designing a flat design color palette, designers often consider the following factors: 1. Color Harmony: The colors in the palette should work harmoniously together and create a balanced composition. These palettes often consist of a combination of complementary or analogous colors that provide contrast and visual interest. 2. Consistency: Flat design color palettes aim for consistency throughout the design. Colors are chosen with the intention of maintaining a unified and cohesive visual style. 3. Simplicity: One of the defining characteristics of flat design is its simplicity. Therefore, the color palettes used in flat design tend to be minimalistic, with a limited number of colors to create a clean and uncluttered aesthetic. 4. Symbolism: Color symbolism is an important aspect of design, as different colors can evoke different emotions or associations. Designers carefully select colors that align with the intended message or branding of the design. In conclusion, flat design color palettes are carefully selected sets of colors that are based on principles of color theory and symbolism. They aim to create visually appealing and meaningful designs by considering factors such as color harmony, consistency, simplicity, and symbolism. These palettes play a significant role in the overall aesthetic and impact of flat design.

Formality (Black)

Formality (Black) In color theory and color symbolism in design, black is often associated with formality. It is a color that is commonly used to convey elegance, sophistication, and seriousness in various design contexts.

Freshness (Mint)

Freshness (Mint) in the context of color theory and color symbolism in design refers to a shade of green that is reminiscent of the color of mint leaves. It embodies the characteristics of coolness, rejuvenation, and cleanliness. This particular shade of green is often associated with freshness and new beginnings. It can evoke a sense of calmness and relaxation, similar to the feeling one gets when experiencing a cool breeze or walking through a refreshing garden. The color mint is often used to create a serene and tranquil atmosphere in design settings.

Friendship (Gold)

Friendship (Gold) represents a color in the realm of color theory and color symbolism in design. It is a hue that combines elements of gold and yellow, conveying a sense of warmth and richness. In color theory, Friendship (Gold) falls within the range of warm colors. Warm colors are often associated with positive emotions, energy, and vibrancy. They have the ability to evoke feelings of happiness, joy, and optimism. Friendship (Gold) specifically exudes a warmth that is reminiscent of the sun, radiating a sense of comfort and positivity. When it comes to color symbolism in design, Friendship (Gold) holds significant meaning. Gold is often associated with wealth, luxury, and abundance. It is a color that represents prosperity, success, and achievement. Friendship (Gold), therefore, takes on these connotations and translates them into the realm of human connections and relationships. Friendship (Gold) symbolizes the value and importance of friendship. It signifies a bond between individuals that is strong, enduring, and enriching. Just as gold is considered a precious metal, Friendship (Gold) represents a precious connection between friends. Furthermore, Friendship (Gold) also symbolizes trust and loyalty. Gold has long been associated with symbols of trustworthiness, such as the gold standard or gold medals. This symbolism extends to Friendship (Gold), as it signifies the loyalty, dependability, and support that friends offer to one another. In design, Friendship (Gold) can be used strategically to convey these concepts in a visual and symbolic way. It can be employed to evoke feelings of warmth, happiness, and friendship. Additionally, it can serve as a means to communicate the values of trust, loyalty, and abundance. Overall, Friendship (Gold) plays a significant role in color theory and color symbolism in design. It is a hue that represents the positive emotions associated with friendship, while also conveying the values of trust, loyalty, and abundance. Incorporating Friendship (Gold) in design can be a powerful tool for evoking emotions and communicating meaningful messages.

Friendship (Peach)

Friendship (Peach) in the context of color theory and color symbolism in design refers to the use of the color peach to represent the concept of friendship. Peach is a warm and soft color that is often associated with positive and friendly emotions. It is a lighter shade of orange, which is known for its energetic and enthusiastic qualities. However, unlike orange, peach has a calming and nurturing effect, making it a more suitable choice for representing the gentle nature of friendship.

Friendship (Periwinkle)

The color Periwinkle is a light to medium shade of blue with a slight hint of purple or lavender. In color theory, Periwinkle is considered a cool color, as it is associated with calmness, tranquility, and spirituality. It is often used in design to evoke feelings of peace, harmony, and friendship. In color symbolism, Periwinkle represents friendship and camaraderie. It is believed to promote positive social connections and foster a sense of belonging. This is why it is commonly used in logos, websites, and branding materials for businesses and organizations that aim to create a friendly and welcoming environment.

Friendship (Yellow)

Friendship (Yellow) In color theory and color symbolism in design, the color yellow represents friendship. Yellow is a bright and warm color that is often associated with feelings of joy, happiness, and optimism. It is considered a lively and energetic color that can grab attention and evoke positive emotions.

Fun (Orange)

Color theory is a framework that examines how colors interact and influence each other in various contexts, including design. In color theory, orange is a secondary color created by combining red and yellow. It is a warm, vibrant color that is often associated with energy, enthusiasm, and creativity. In the context of color symbolism in design, orange can have multiple meanings depending on the specific context and cultural interpretation. Generally, it is seen as a positive and inviting color, evoking feelings of warmth, joy, and optimism. It is often associated with healthy and fresh produce, such as oranges, carrots, and pumpkins.

Futurism (Silver)

Futurism in the context of color theory and color symbolism in design refers to the use of the color silver as a representation of the future, technology, and modernity. Silver, as a metallic color, conveys a sense of futuristic aesthetics and sophistication. It is often associated with futuristic elements such as spaceships, robots, and advanced technology. The color silver is commonly used in design to create a sleek and sleek look that evokes a sense of forward-thinking and innovation.

Goodness (White)

Goodness is a white color that holds significant importance in color theory and color symbolism in design. In color theory, white is considered as the absence of color. It is a neutral color that is often associated with purity, light, and cleanliness. White is created by combining all the colors of the spectrum together, resulting in a color that reflects all wavelengths of light. In design, white is commonly used as a background or base color due to its ability to enhance other colors and create a sense of balance and harmony. It is often used to create contrast and highlight other elements within a design. The use of white can help create a clean and minimalist aesthetic, as well as a sense of openness and spaciousness.

Grace (Lavender)

Grace (Lavender) is a light shade of purple that falls into the purple color category in color theory. It is created by mixing equal parts of red and blue, with a higher proportion of blue to create a cooler hue. This color is often associated with elegance, femininity, and sophistication.In the context of color symbolism in design, Grace (Lavender) holds various meanings and can evoke different emotions depending on the cultural and personal associations of individuals. Some common symbolic interpretations of Grace (Lavender) include:1. Elegance

112

and Beauty: Grace (Lavender) is often chosen for its association with class and refinement. Its delicate and subdued nature can add a touch of sophistication to designs and evoke a sense of gracefulness.2. Femininity and Romance: Grace (Lavender) is commonly associated with femininity and is often used to convey a romantic or dreamy atmosphere. Its soft and subtle tone can create a gentle and calming effect.3. Spirituality and Serenity: Grace (Lavender) is also linked to spirituality and can be used to represent contemplation and tranquility. Its light and airy nature can create a sense of peacefulness and serenity in designs.4. Luxury and Royalty: The color Grace (Lavender) has historical associations with luxury and royalty. Its regal undertones can be incorporated into designs to convey richness and opulence.Overall, Grace (Lavender) is a versatile color that can be used in various design contexts to evoke elegance, femininity, spirituality, or luxury. The specific meanings and interpretations of this color may vary depending on cultural, personal, and contextual factors.

Gracefulness (Silver)

Gracefulness (Silver) is a color found in color theory and used in color symbolism in design. It is a shade of gray with a metallic quality, leaning towards a pale tinge of silver. In color theory, gracefulness is classified as a neutral color due to its close proximity to gray. The color silver is associated with various meanings and symbolisms in design. It often represents qualities like elegance, sophistication, and refined aesthetics. Silver has been historically linked with wealth and luxury, making it a popular choice in high-end design contexts. Its association with the precious metal silver also lends it a sense of value and rarity.

Gradient Color Editors

A gradient color editor is a tool used in color theory and design to create and manipulate gradient colors. A gradient color is a color transition that gradually changes from one hue to another, usually blending multiple colors together. This can be done in a linear fashion, where the color transition happens in a straight line, or in a radial fashion, where the colors blend in a circular or spherical pattern. The purpose of a gradient color editor is to provide designers with the ability to create custom gradients that suit their design needs. It allows them to choose the starting and ending colors of the gradient, as well as control the number and distribution of intermediate colors along the transition. The editor typically provides a graphical interface, where users can visually see and manipulate the gradient in real-time.

Gradient Color Generator Websites

Gradient color generator websites are tools that allow designers to create and manipulate color gradients based on color theory and color symbolism principles in design. These sites provide a platform for designers to experiment with different color combinations and create visually appealing gradient effects. Color theory is the study of how colors interact and how they can be used to evoke certain emotions or convey specific messages in design. It encompasses principles such as color harmony, contrast, and the psychology of color. When designing a website or any visual artwork, it is important to consider color theory in order to create a cohesive and visually pleasing composition. Color symbolism, on the other hand, refers to the cultural or personal associations that people have with certain colors. Colors can have different meanings or evoke different emotions depending on the context or the culture. For example, red is often associated with passion or danger, while blue is often associated with calmness or trust. Gradient color generator websites provide designers with a range of tools and features to create customized gradients that align with color theory and color symbolism principles. These sites allow designers to select multiple colors and manipulate them to create smooth transitions between shades. Designers can adjust the angle and direction of the gradient, as well as the opacity and blending modes of the colors. By using gradient color generator websites, designers can explore different color combinations and see how they interact with each other. They can experiment with various gradients and choose the ones that best represent the desired mood or message of their design. These tools help designers save time by eliminating the need for manual color blending and provide them with a visual representation of the gradients in real-time. In conclusion, gradient color generator websites are valuable tools for designers to create aesthetically pleasing gradients based on color theory and color symbolism principles. These sites provide a platform for experimentation and allow designers to customize gradients to fit the desired mood or message of their design. By using these tools, designers can enhance the visual impact of their artwork and create compelling compositions.

Gradient Color Generators Online

A gradient color generator is an online tool that allows designers to create gradient color schemes by blending two or more colors together. The tool provides a user-friendly interface where designers can easily adjust the color stops, direction, and intensity to create custom gradients. In the context of color theory, a gradient is a transition of colors from one hue to another. It is created by smoothly blending the values of the colors in between. Gradients can be linear, radial, or angular, and can have different directions and angles. Designers can use gradient color generators to experiment with various combinations of colors and create visually pleasing gradients. Color symbolism in design refers to the meanings and associations that different colors evoke in people. Each color has its own psychological and emotional connotations, and designers often use colors strategically to communicate specific messages or create desired effects. Gradients can enhance the symbolism of colors by adding depth and dimension to the design. Gradient color generators provide designers with a wide range of options to explore different color symbolisms. For example, a gradient from warm colors like red to cool colors like blue can convey a sense of contrast and balance. On the other hand, a gradient of analogous colors, such as various shades of green, can create a harmonious and calming effect. By utilizing gradient color generators, designers can easily experiment with different color combinations and symbolisms without the need for manual color adjustments or complex software. These tools enable designers to create visually striking and engaging designs that effectively communicate their intended messages. Overall, gradient color generators are valuable resources for designers, as they provide a user-friendly interface and extensive options for creating custom gradients. Through these tools, designers can explore the principles of color theory and color symbolism to create visually appealing and meaningful designs.

Gradient Color Generators

A gradient color generator refers to a tool or software that is used in the field of color theory and design to create gradient colors. Gradient colors are a visual effect achieved by smoothly blending two or more colors together, resulting in a transition from one color to another. This technique is often employed in various design disciplines, such as graphic design, web design, and interior design, to add depth, dimension, and visual interest to artworks, layouts, or spaces. In color theory, gradients are not only aesthetically pleasing but also hold symbolic meanings that can enhance the overall design message. Colors themselves have individual symbolic associations, and when blended in a gradient, these meanings can be further amplified or changed. For example, warm colors (such as red, orange, and yellow) are often associated with energy, passion, and positivity, while cool colors (such as blue, green, and purple) evoke calmness, tranquility, and stability. By using gradient color generators, designers have the ability to manipulate and control the overall color symbolism in their designs.

Gradient Colors

Gradient colors refer to a color technique in design that involves a smooth transition between two or more colors. This transition creates a gradient effect, where colors blend seamlessly together. Gradient colors are widely used in various design fields, including web design, graphic design, and digital art, due to their ability to add depth, dimension, and visual interest to a composition. In color theory, gradients are created by mixing different hues, shades, tints, or tones of colors. The gradient can be achieved by transitioning between colors within the same hue or by combining different hues for a more diverse effect. The transition can be linear, radial, or angular, depending on the desired outcome. Using gradient colors in design can evoke various emotions and convey different meanings. Each color holds its own symbolism and psychology, and when combined in a gradient, these meanings can be amplified or altered. For example, a gradient that transitions from warm colors, such as red and orange, to cooler colors like blue and green, can evoke feelings of energy and tranquility. Alternatively, a gradient that transitions from dark to light shades of a single color can create a sense of depth and create a 3D effect. The choice of colors in a gradient also plays a significant role in design. Colors can be selected based on their complementary or analogous relationships to create harmonious gradients. Complementary colors, which are opposite on the color wheel, can create a striking contrast, while analogous colors, which are adjacent to each other on the color wheel, can create a more harmonious and soothing effect. In web design, gradients have become increasingly popular in recent years, especially with the advancement of CSS3. CSS gradients allow designers to create smooth color transitions directly in their HTML and CSS code, eliminating the need for image-based gradients that were commonly used in the past. CSS gradients provide flexibility, allowing designers to customize the direction, angle, and color stops of the gradient. Overall, gradient colors are an essential tool in the world of design and color theory. They add depth, dimension, and visual interest to compositions, while also conveying specific meanings and emotions. With the use of gradients, designers can create visually captivating and engaging designs that resonate with their desired audience.

Gradient Tool

The Gradient Tool is a crucial element in color theory and color symbolism in design. It refers to a feature or tool within design software that allows designers to smoothly transition between two or more colors, creating a gradient effect. This tool is used to manipulate colors and create various visual effects that enhance the overall design. Color theory plays a significant role in design as it involves the science and psychology behind colors. It explores how different colors interact with each other and how they influence human emotion and perception. Understanding color theory enables designers to effectively communicate messages and evoke specific emotions through the use of colors.

Grief (Black)

Grief (Black) in the context of color theory and color symbolism in design refers to the color black as it relates to feelings of sorrow, loss, and mourning. Black is often associated with grief due to its connotations of darkness, death, and emptiness. Black is a color that absorbs all light and reflects no color. This lack of light gives black a sense of depth and a feeling of the unknown. In design, the use of black can create a somber and solemn atmosphere, emphasizing the emotions of grief and sadness. It is often utilized to set a mood of mourning and can be used effectively in creating designs for funeral services, memorial events, and other expressions of grief.

Grief (White)

Grief (White) is a color that holds immense significance in color theory and color symbolism in design. In color theory, white is considered a neutral color because it is made by combining all the colors of the visible spectrum. It is often described as a color without hue or saturation. White is commonly associated with purity, innocence, and cleanliness. In the context of grief, white symbolizes mourning and loss. It is often used in funerals and as a symbol of remembrance. The use of white in design can evoke feelings of sadness, reverence, and sorrow. It is a color that can convey a sense of emptiness and longing.

Groundedness (Beige)

Groundedness (Beige) in color theory refers to a neutral color that is often associated with stability, reliability, and practicality. It is one of the basic colors commonly used in design to create a sense of calmness, balance, and simplicity. As a neutral color, beige is commonly used as a background or base color in design. Its subtle and unobtrusive nature allows other colors to stand out and take the spotlight without overpowering them. Beige provides a sense of harmony and cohesion, making it an ideal choice for creating a balanced design.

Groundedness (Brown)

Groundedness in color theory refers to the use of earthy and muted tones that convey a sense of stability, reliability, and rootedness. These colors are often found in nature and evoke a feeling of being connected to the environment. Grounded colors are typically associated with earth tones such as browns, beiges, and grays, and are seen as more neutral and calming compared to brighter and more vibrant hues. In design, groundedness is used to create a sense of balance and stability. When applied to a color scheme, these earthy tones can provide a strong foundation for other colors to stand out. Grounded colors often serve as a backdrop or base color for a design, allowing other colors to pop and capture attention. They can be used as background colors, text colors, or as accents to anchor a composition.

Grounding (Copper)

Grounding (Copper) refers to a specific color in the context of color theory and color symbolism in design. Copper, a metallic shade with a reddish-brown hue, is associated with various characteristics that make it an important element in design. Copper is often used as a grounding color due to its earthy tones and warm energy. In color theory, grounding colors are used to add stability and balance to a design composition. They provide a sense of solidity and rootedness, creating a foundation for other colors and elements to thrive. Copper, with its rich and deep undertones, accomplishes this purpose effectively. In the realm of color symbolism, copper is associated with attributes such as grounding, stability, and reliability. These qualities make it a popular choice in design, as it can convey a sense of dependability and steadfastness. Copper is often used to evoke feelings of warmth, comfort, and security, creating a welcoming and trustworthy ambiance. Beyond its symbolic representations, copper has practical applications in design. It can be used as an accent color to highlight certain elements or as a base shade to create an overall warm and inviting atmosphere. Copper's versatility allows it to complement a wide range of colors, from neutrals to vibrant hues, enhancing the visual appeal of a design composition. Furthermore, copper can be utilized in various design contexts, including branding, interior design, and graphic design. In branding, copper can help establish a sense of authenticity and longevity, making it an ideal choice for businesses that prioritize reliability and heritage. In interior design, copper accents can add a touch of elegance and sophistication, while also creating a cozy and grounded ambiance. In graphic design, copper can be incorporated into logos, illustrations, and layouts to add depth and visual interest, as well as to convey specific meanings associated with the color. Overall, grounding (Copper) plays a significant role in color theory and color symbolism in design. Its earthy tones and warm energy make it an excellent choice for creating stability and balance in design compositions. Additionally, its symbolic representations and practical applications further enhance its importance as a grounding color.

Growth (Green)

Growth (Green) is a hue in color theory that represents the natural world and the concept of growth and renewal. It is associated with the color green found in nature, such as in leaves, grass, and plants. Green is a secondary color that results from the combination of blue and yellow on the color wheel. In the context of color symbolism in design, the color green is often used to convey notions of growth, freshness, and vitality. It is associated with new beginnings and represents the cycle of life. Green is considered a calming and soothing color that promotes harmony and balance.

Growth (Mint)

Growth, in the context of color theory and color symbolism in design, refers to the concept of growth and development represented through the color mint. Mint is a light green hue that is often associated with freshness, rejuvenation, and new beginnings. The color mint, with its soft and cool undertones, is reminiscent of natural elements such as mint leaves or grass. This association with the natural world links mint to growth and vitality. In design, mint can be used to create a feeling of renewal and progression, making it an ideal choice for projects that aim to convey concepts such as health, wellness, or environmentally friendly initiatives.

Growth (Olive)

Olive is a color that falls within the green spectrum and is often associated with growth and fertility. It is a medium to dark shade of green with a yellowish hue, resembling the color of ripe olives. In color theory, olive is created by combining yellow and green pigments in varying proportions. In the context of color symbolism in design, olive represents growth and abundance. It is often used to evoke feelings of renewal, vitality, and prosperity. As a natural color found in nature, it is commonly associated with the plant kingdom, symbolizing the growth and nurturing of life. Olive can also convey a sense of harmony and balance, as it combines the calmness of green with the warmth of yellow.

HEX Color Codes

HEX color codes are a representation of colors in the form of alphanumeric values. They play a

116

crucial role in color theory and color symbolism in design. In color theory, HEX color codes are used to define specific colors in the RGB (Red, Green, and Blue) color model. Each color is represented by a combination of six characters, which includes both numbers (0-9) and letters (A-F). The first two characters correspond to the red intensity, the next two to the green intensity, and the last two to the blue intensity. HEX color codes provide a standardized way of identifying and specifying colors, ensuring consistency across different platforms and devices. This is particularly important in design, where precise color reproduction is essential for maintaining brand identity and achieving visual harmony. By using HEX color codes, designers can accurately communicate their intended color choices to developers, printers, and other stakeholders involved in the production process. Besides their practical applications, HEX color codes also have symbolic significance in design. Colors are often associated with specific emotions, meanings, and cultural connotations. Designers use this symbolism to evoke desired responses or communicate certain messages through color choices. HEX color codes enable designers to precisely select colors that align with their intended symbolism. For example, a designer might choose a vibrant red (#FF0000) to evoke passion and urgency, while a soothing blue (#0000FF) may be used to convey a sense of calm and trust. HEX color codes give designers the ability to harness the power of color symbolism and create visually compelling designs that resonate with their target audience.

HSL Color Editing Software

HSL Color Editing Software is a digital tool that enables designers to modify, manipulate, and analyze colors using the Hue, Saturation, and Lightness (HSL) color model. This software often includes a range of features and tools that assist designers in creating harmonious color schemes and effectively communicating the desired message through color symbolism. Color theory is a fundamental aspect of design that explores how colors interact with one another and how they are perceived by the human eye. It is based on the understanding that colors evoke certain emotions, convey specific meanings, and can have a profound impact on design compositions. The HSL color model is particularly valuable in color theory as it provides a more intuitive, visual representation of colors compared to other color models like RGB or CMYK. In the HSL color model, hue represents the purest form of a color and is often associated with specific emotions or meanings. Manipulating the hue in HSL editing software allows designers to experiment with various color combinations and explore different moods or atmospheres in their designs. For example, shifting the hue towards warmer tones can create a sense of passion or energy, while cooler hues might evoke a feeling of calm or tranquility. Saturation in HSL refers to the intensity or purity of a color. By adjusting the saturation levels in HSL editing software, designers can control the appearance of colors in their designs. Higher saturation values result in vibrant, vivid colors, while lower saturation values yield more subdued or muted shades. This feature enables designers to emphasize certain elements or create a specific visual hierarchy within their designs. Lightness in HSL determines how light or dark a color appears. It allows designers to adjust the brightness or darkness of colors, which can greatly impact the overall mood and atmosphere of a design. By modifying the lightness values in HSL color editing software, designers can achieve desired contrasts, gradients, or tonal variations to enhance the visual appeal and legibility of their designs. HSL Color Editing Software empowers designers to explore the intricate relationship between colors and their symbolic meanings in design. With its intuitive interface and powerful editing capabilities, this software enables designers to create visually compelling compositions, evoke specific emotions, and effectively communicate their intended messages through the strategic use of color.

HSL Color Editors

HSL Color Editors are tools used in color theory and design to adjust and manipulate colors based on the HSL color model. HSL stands for Hue, Saturation, and Lightness, which are the three components that make up this color model. Hue represents the dominant wavelength of a color and is measured in degrees on a color wheel. It ranges from 0 to 360, with red being at 0 degrees, green at 120 degrees, and blue at 240 degrees. By changing the hue value, the editor can shift the color along the color wheel and create different color variations. Saturation refers to the intensity or purity of a color. A saturation value of 0 means the color is completely desaturated or grayscale, while a value of 100 means it is fully saturated with its purest form. By adjusting the saturation value, the editor can make the color appear more vibrant or subtle. Lightness determines the brightness or darkness of a color. A lightness value of 0 represents

117

black, while a value of 100 represents white. By modifying the lightness value, the editor can make the color appear brighter or darker. HSL color editors allow designers to have precise control over color adjustments, making it easier to create harmonious color schemes or capture specific moods and emotions through color symbolism. Colors have symbolic meanings and associations that can evoke different feelings or convey messages in design. For example, warm colors with high saturation and lightness can create a sense of energy and excitement, while cool colors with low saturation and lightness can evoke a calm and soothing atmosphere. In summary, HSL color editors are valuable tools in the field of color theory and design. They enable designers to manipulate colors based on the Hue, Saturation, and Lightness values, allowing for precise adjustments and creative exploration. By understanding the symbolism and psychology of colors, designers can effectively communicate and evoke emotions through their color choices.

HSL Color Model Editors

The HSL color model, also known as Hue, Saturation, and Lightness, is a color model used in color theory and design to represent colors in a more intuitive and expressive way. It is based on the idea that human perception of color is better understood through these three dimensions rather than the traditional RGB color model. The first component of the HSL color model is Hue, which represents the pure color itself. It is measured in degrees on a color wheel, ranging from 0 to 360. The hue values correspond to different colors, such as red, green, blue, and everything in between. For example, a hue value of 0 represents red, while a hue value of 120 represents green. The second component is Saturation, which determines the intensity or purity of a color. It is represented as a percentage ranging from 0% to 100%. A saturation value of 0% results in a grayscale color, while a saturation value of 100% represents the most vibrant and intense version of a color. By adjusting the saturation, designers can create subtle or bold color variations to evoke different emotions or convey different meanings. The third component is Lightness, which determines the amount of white or black mixed with the color. It is represented as a percentage ranging from 0% to 100%. A lightness value of 0% represents black, while a value of 100% represents white. Values in between produce different shades of the color. By adjusting the lightness, designers can create lighter or darker variations of a color, allowing for contrast and depth in their designs. The HSL color model is particularly useful in design because it allows for more precise control over colors and their visual impact. It provides a more intuitive way to select and manipulate colors and offers a wider range of design possibilities. In addition, the HSL color model can be easily converted to other color models such as RGB or CMYK, making it compatible with different design applications and workflows.

HSL Color Model

The HSL color model is a representation of colors in terms of their hue, saturation, and lightness. It is a cylindrical coordinate system that provides a more intuitive representation of colors compared to other models like RGB or CMYK. In the HSL color model, the hue represents the type of color, such as red, blue, or green. It is represented as an angle on a color wheel, with red at 0 degrees, green at 120 degrees, and blue at 240 degrees. Other colors blend in between these primary hues. The hue value ranges from 0 to 360 degrees, covering the entire color spectrum. Saturation refers to the intensity or purity of a color. A fully saturated color appears vibrant and bold, while a desaturated color appears more muted or washed out. In the HSL model, saturation is represented as a percentage, with 0% being completely desaturated and 100% being fully saturated. Lightness, also known as luminance, represents the overall brightness of a color. In the HSL model, it is represented as a percentage as well, with 0% being completely black and 100% being completely white. Colors with intermediate lightness values create different shades and tints. The HSL color model is widely used in color theory and design for its ability to create aesthetically pleasing color schemes. It allows designers to easily manipulate colors by adjusting their hue, saturation, and lightness values. By changing the hue, designers can create different moods and emotions. For example, warm hues like red and orange evoke feelings of energy and passion, while cool hues like blue and green create a sense of calmness and tranquility. Saturation levels help designers create contrast and emphasis. Highly saturated colors draw attention and make elements stand out, while desaturated colors create a more subtle and muted atmosphere. Lightness values, on the other hand, allow designers to control the overall color balance and create different levels of brightness or darkness. In addition to its practical applications in design, the HSL color model is

118

also important in color symbolism. Different hues are often associated with specific meanings or emotions. For example, red is commonly associated with love, passion, and energy, while blue represents calmness, trust, and stability. By using the HSL model, designers can effectively convey these symbolic meanings and evoke desired emotions through their color choices. Overall, the HSL color model is a powerful tool in color theory and design, allowing for intuitive representation, easy manipulation, and the creation of harmonious color schemes. It provides a practical and meaningful way to work with colors and effectively communicate visually.

HSL Color Pickers

HSL (Hue, Saturation, and Lightness) color pickers are tools used in color theory and design to select colors based on their hue, saturation, and lightness values. The hue refers to the basic color of the spectrum, such as red, blue, or yellow. It is represented as an angle on a color wheel, where 0 degrees corresponds to red, 120 degrees to green, and 240 degrees to blue. By adjusting the hue value in the HSL color picker, different colors can be selected. Saturation represents the intensity or purity of a color. A saturation value of 0% produces a grayscale color, while a value of 100% represents the purest and most vibrant form of the selected hue. By adjusting the saturation value in the HSL color picker, designers can create subtle or bold color schemes. Lightness refers to the amount of light present in a color. A lightness value of 0% corresponds to black, while a value of 100% represents white. By adjusting the lightness value in the HSL color picker, designers can control the brightness or darkness of a color. In the context of color symbolism in design, HSL color pickers allow designers to choose colors that convey specific meanings or emotions. Different hues have different associations, such as red symbolizing passion or danger, while blue represents calmness or trustworthiness. Saturation and lightness values can further enhance or diminish these symbolic messages. For example, a designer might use a fully saturated red (100% saturation) to convey intensity or excitement, while a desaturated red (lower saturation) might convey a more muted or somber tone. Similarly, a light blue (high lightness) might evoke a sense of tranquility, while a dark blue (low lightness) might represent authority or professionalism. HSL color pickers provide an intuitive and efficient way for designers to explore and select colors based on their hue, saturation, and lightness values. By understanding the principles of color theory and considering the symbolic implications of different colors, designers can create visually compelling and meaningful designs.

HSV Color Editing Tools

HSV Color Editing Tools in the context of color theory and color symbolism in design refer to tools that allow designers to manipulate and adjust the Hue, Saturation, and Value (HSV) components of a color. The Hue component represents the pure color itself, such as red, blue, or yellow, and its various shades and variations. By using HSV color editing tools, designers can adjust the hue of a color, allowing them to create different variations and harmonies. The Saturation component refers to the intensity or purity of a color. It determines how much of the hue is present in a particular color. By adjusting the saturation, designers can make a color appear more vibrant and vivid or more subdued and pastel. The Value component represents the brightness of a color, ranging from black to white. By manipulating the value, designers can create shades and tints of a particular hue. Darker values tend to evoke a sense of mystery or elegance, while lighter values convey a feeling of lightness and clarity. In the context of color symbolism, HSV color editing tools are essential for designers to effectively convey their intended emotions and meanings through their color choices. Colors carry symbolic associations that can evoke specific emotions or convey certain messages. By using HSV color editing tools, designers can precisely control the colors they use and fine-tune them to align with their design objectives. For example, in branding, companies often rely on specific color palettes that are carefully selected to reflect their brand personality and values. HSV color editing tools enable designers to refine and tailor these colors to suit the desired emotional impact on their target audience. In summary, HSV color editing tools are valuable resources for designers to manipulate and adjust the hue, saturation, and value of colors. By understanding the principles of color theory and color symbolism, designers can leverage these tools to create visually appealing and meaningful designs.

HSV Color Editors

HSV (Hue, Saturation, Value) Color Editors are tools used in color theory and design to

119

manipulate and adjust colors based on their hue, saturation, and value properties. These editors allow designers to modify the appearance and symbolism of colors, enabling them to create visually appealing and meaningful designs. Hue refers to the actual color of an object or element, such as red, blue, or green. It represents the position of a color on the color wheel, and modifying the hue can result in different color variations. Saturation, on the other hand, determines the intensity or purity of a color. Higher levels of saturation make colors appear vivid and vibrant, while lower levels create more muted or pastel tones. Value, also known as brightness or lightness, determines how dark or light a color appears. Adjusting the value can create different shades of a color, from deep and rich to pale and subtle. Color editors based on HSV color model provide designers with a flexible and intuitive way to modify colors in their designs. By manipulating the hue, saturation, and value sliders or input fields, designers can create various color combinations that convey different emotions, moods, and meanings. For example, increasing the saturation of a color can make it appear more energetic and attention-grabbing, while lowering the value can create a softer and more calming effect. In the context of color symbolism, HSV color editors allow designers to align their color choices with specific cultural or psychological associations. Different hues are often associated with specific meanings and emotions. For instance, warm hues like red and orange are commonly linked to passion, excitement, and energy, while cool hues like blue and green are associated with calmness, nature, and serenity. By fine-tuning the hue, saturation, and value settings, designers can enhance or emphasize the desired symbolic qualities of a color to evoke certain feelings or convey particular messages. In summary, HSV Color Editors are essential tools for designers to manipulate and adjust colors based on their hue, saturation, and value properties. By using these editors, designers can create visually appealing designs and align their color choices with specific symbolic meanings and emotions. Understanding and utilizing the principles of the HSV color model can greatly enhance the effectiveness and impact of color in design.

HSV Color Model Editors

The HSV color model, also known as the HSB color model, is a representation of color that is widely used in color theory and design. It stands for Hue, Saturation, and Value (or Brightness). Hue represents the pure color itself, or the specific wavelength of light that is being reflected. It is expressed in degrees on a color wheel, ranging from 0° to 360°. In this model, red falls at 0°, green at 120°, and blue at 240°. Saturation refers to the intensity or purity of a color. A fully saturated color contains no white, black, or gray components, while a desaturated color contains more of these neutral components. Saturation is measured as a percentage, ranging from 0% (no saturation) to 100% (full saturation). Value, also known as Brightness, determines the lightness or darkness of a color. It is measured as a percentage, ranging from 0% (black) to 100% (white). This value is independent of the hue; therefore, a particular hue can have different values, resulting in lighter or darker versions of the same color. The HSV color model provides designers with a more intuitive and flexible way to work with color. By adjusting the hue, saturation, and value of a color, designers can achieve a wide range of color variations and create harmonious color schemes. In the context of color symbolism, the HSV color model can be used to convey certain meanings or emotions. For example, warm hues such as red and orange are associated with energy, passion, and excitement, while cool hues such as blue and green are associated with tranquility, calmness, and nature. By manipulating the hue, saturation, and value, designers can evoke specific feelings or associations in their audience. Overall, the HSV color model is a valuable tool for editors in the field of design. It allows for precise control and manipulation of color, enabling the creation of visually appealing and meaningful compositions. By understanding the principles of this color model and the symbolism associated with different hues, editors can effectively communicate their intended messages through the use of color.

HSV Color Model

The HSV color model is a widely used color system in color theory and design that represents colors in terms of their hue, saturation, and value. It is based on the way humans perceive colors, making it a practical tool for designers to communicate and achieve desired visual effects. Hue refers to the dominant wavelength of light, representing the actual color itself. It is often described in terms of the color wheel, with different hues arranged in a circular fashion. In the HSV color model, hue is expressed as an angle, typically ranging from 0 to 360 degrees. This allows designers to specify a specific color by selecting an angle on the color wheel. For example, a hue of 0 degrees represents red, 120 degrees represents green, and 240 degrees represents blue. Saturation refers to the intensity or purity of a color. A saturated color appears vivid and vibrant, while a desaturated color is more muted and grayish. In the HSV color model, saturation is represented as a percentage, ranging from 0% (completely desaturated) to 100% (fully saturated). By adjusting the saturation value, designers can manipulate the strength of a color and create various visual effects. For instance, high saturation is often associated with energy and vibrancy, while low saturation can evoke a sense of calmness or subtlety. Value, also known as brightness or lightness, determines the overall brightness or darkness of a color. In the HSV color model, value is represented as a percentage, ranging from 0% (completely black) to 100% (fully white). By varying the value, designers can control the overall lightness or darkness of a color, allowing them to create contrast and balance within their designs. For example, high-value colors are often used to draw attention or create a focal point, while low-value colors can be used for background or supporting elements.

HSV Color Pickers

HSV color pickers are tools used in color theory and design to select colors using the Hue, Saturation, and Value (HSV) color model. In this model, colors are represented based on their hue, which refers to the position on the color wheel, saturation, which determines the intensity or purity of the color, and value, which represents the brightness or darkness of the color. The HSV color model is often preferred over the RGB (Red, Green, Blue) color model for color selection in design because it provides more intuitive control over color properties. Unlike RGB, which defines colors by combining red, green, and blue primary colors, HSV separates color properties and allows designers to easily adjust hue, saturation, and value individually. In color theory, the hue component of HSV refers to the predominant wavelength of light that a color represents. It essentially determines what we perceive as the "color" of an object. By manipulating the hue value in an HSV color picker, designers can select any color from the color wheel, offering a wide range of options for creative expression. Saturation, on the other hand, defines the intensity or purity of a color. A fully saturated color appears vibrant and vivid, while decreasing saturation creates a more muted or pastel version of the color. Designers can adjust the saturation value in an HSV color picker to achieve the desired level of intensity or subtlety in their designs. Finally, the value component of HSV, also known as brightness or lightness, determines how light or dark a color appears. By adjusting the value in an HSV color picker, designers can easily create shades and tints of a particular color, allowing for more nuanced and sophisticated designs. In the context of color symbolism, which explores the emotional and cultural associations of colors, an HSV color picker is a valuable tool for selecting colors that convey specific meanings or evoke certain moods. For example, designers may choose high saturation and brightness for a color palette associated with energy and excitement, while low saturation and darkness may be used to create a more somber or mysterious atmosphere. In conclusion, HSV color pickers are essential tools in color theory and design, enabling designers to select colors based on hue, saturation, and value. By offering intuitive control over color properties, HSV color pickers allow for a wide range of creative expression and are instrumental in creating visually appealing and emotionally meaningful designs.

Happiness (Coral)

Coral color, in the context of color theory and color symbolism in design, represents happiness. Coral is a warm and vibrant color that is often associated with joy, fun, and positivity. It embodies the essence of happiness and is commonly used to evoke feelings of cheerfulness and optimism. The color coral is a vibrant blend of pink and orange shades, which gives it a lively and energetic appearance. When used in design, coral can bring a sense of excitement and vibrancy to a space or a composition. It is often used to create focal points or highlights, as its bright and eye-catching nature draws attention. Its warmth and playfulness make it a popular choice for designs that aim to communicate feelings of happiness and celebration. In color symbolism, coral is also associated with other positive emotions and qualities. It is often seen as a symbol of love, friendship, and warmth. Coral can also represent vitality and energy, making it a great choice for designs that focus on these themes. Furthermore, coral color can have different meanings in various cultural contexts. In some cultures, it is associated with good luck and prosperity, while in others, it may be seen as a symbol of fertility or protection. Designers and artists can draw on these cultural connotations to create meaningful and impactful designs.

121

Happiness (Gold)

Happiness (Gold) is a color in color theory and color symbolism in design that represents joy, optimism, and warmth. It is a shade of gold that is often associated with feelings of happiness, contentment, and fulfillment. This color is derived from the color wheel by blending yellow and orange, creating a vibrant and energetic hue. In color theory, gold is classified as a warm color, which means it has a high energy level and is visually stimulating. This attribute makes it a popular choice for designers who want to evoke positive emotions and create a sense of happiness in their artwork or designs. The vibrant and warm nature of gold can draw attention and add an element of excitement to any design. Gold is also closely related to the sun and is frequently associated with light and illumination. Just as the sun brings warmth and light to the world, gold can bring warmth and positivity to any design. It can add a touch of radiance and brilliance that captures the eye and creates a sense of joy and happiness. Additionally, gold is often associated with wealth, luxury, and success. It has long been a symbol of prosperity and abundance, and using gold in design can convey a sense of abundance and opulence. This association with wealth can also contribute to feelings of happiness and satisfaction. Overall, happiness (gold) is a color that embodies feelings of joy, optimism, and warmth. Its vibrant and energetic nature, as well as its association with light and wealth, make it a popular choice for designers seeking to evoke positive emotions and create a sense of happiness in their designs.

Happiness (Lemon)

Happiness is a distinct and vibrant yellow color commonly associated with warmth, energy, and joy. In the context of color theory and color symbolism in design, the color lemon represents happiness and optimism. Lemon is often used in design to create a positive and uplifting atmosphere. It has the power to evoke feelings of cheerfulness, positivity, and enthusiasm. As a bright and sunny shade, lemon catches the eye and instantly grabs attention. It is considered an attention-grabbing color that stimulates mental activity and promotes a sense of well-being.

Happiness (Yellow)

Happiness, represented by the color yellow in the context of color theory and color symbolism in design, is a vibrant and uplifting emotion associated with feelings of joy, positivity, and optimism. Yellow is often described as the color of sunshine, evoking images of warmth and brightness. In color theory, yellow is classified as a primary color, along with red and blue. It is one of the three colors that can be used to create a wide range of other colors when combined in different ratios. Yellow is typically associated with the psychological sensation of lightness, and its perceived brightness makes it a powerful tool for capturing attention and conveying a sense of energy. In the realm of color symbolism, yellow is commonly used to represent happiness, cheerfulness, and optimism. It is frequently used to evoke feelings of joy and playfulness, making it a popular choice in designs aimed at creating a positive and uplifting mood. Yellow is often associated with feelings of warmth and friendliness, as well as a sense of open-mindedness and curiosity. When used in design, yellow can have different effects depending on its shade and intensity. Bright, vibrant yellows are more energetic and attention-grabbing, while softer, pastel yellows can create a soothing and calming atmosphere. Yellow can be used as a dominant color to create a sense of happiness and optimism throughout a design, or as an accent color to add pops of brightness and warmth. In addition to its positive connotations, yellow can also be associated with caution and warning in certain contexts. This is due to its connection to the color of caution signs and traffic lights. However, this cautionary symbolism does not typically overshadow the overall positive and joyful nature of the color.

Hard Work (Bronze)

Hard Work (Bronze) is a color in the context of color theory and color symbolism in design. It is a muted and earthy shade of brown with a warm undertone. In the color spectrum, it falls between dark brown and light brown. Hard Work (Bronze) represents resilience, dedication, and perseverance. It symbolizes the sweat and effort put into achieving goals and overcoming obstacles. This color is often associated with hard work, endurance, and being grounded.

Harmony (Blue)

Harmony in color theory refers to the pleasing arrangement of colors in a design, where different

122

colors work together to create a sense of balance and unity. It is achieved by combining colors that complement, contrast, or relate to each other in an aesthetically pleasing way. In the context of color symbolism in design, blue is often associated with harmony. Blue is considered a cool color that evokes a sense of calmness, tranquility, and serenity. It is often used to create a soothing and peaceful atmosphere in a design. Blue is also associated with reliability, trustworthiness, and intellect. It has a calming effect on viewers and can help create a sense of stability and order.

Harmony (Green)

Harmony, in the context of color theory and color symbolism in design, refers to the pleasing arrangement of colors that create a sense of unity and balance in a visual composition. It is the art of combining different colors in a way that they work together harmoniously, enhancing the overall aesthetic appeal and conveying the desired message or emotion. Harmony is achieved through various color relationships, such as analogous, complementary, and triadic color schemes. In an analogous color scheme, colors that are adjacent or close to each other on the color wheel are used to create a harmonious effect. This scheme often results in a soothing and unified composition. Complementary colors, on the other hand, are those that are opposite each other on the color wheel. When used together, they create a vibrant contrast and generate a sense of harmony through their balanced relationship. Triadic color schemes involve the use of three colors that are evenly spaced on the color wheel. This scheme creates a vibrant and energetic composition while still maintaining a sense of harmony. In terms of color symbolism, harmony can also be interpreted in different ways. Green, for instance, is often associated with harmony and balance in nature. It represents growth, renewal, and vitality. In design, the use of green can create a sense of calmness and tranquility. It is frequently used in environmental or wellness-related designs to evoke a feeling of harmony with the natural world. Overall, harmony in color theory and color symbolism plays an essential role in creating visually pleasing and impactful designs. It allows designers to communicate specific messages or emotions through the skillful combination of colors. Whether it is through the use of analogous, complementary, or triadic color schemes, harmony helps to create a sense of unity, balance, and coherence in visual compositions.

Harmony (Mint)

Harmony, also known as mint green, is a color that falls within the green color family. In the context of color theory, harmony refers to the pleasing and balanced combination of colors. It is achieved by combining colors that are close to each other on the color wheel. In the world of design, harmony plays a significant role in creating visually appealing and cohesive compositions. Harmony is often used to evoke specific emotions or convey a particular message through color symbolism.

Harmony (Olive)

Harmony (Olive) is a color scheme in color theory and color symbolism that involves the combination of various shades and tints of olive green to create a balanced and visually pleasing design. Olive green is a muted or dark yellowish-green color that is commonly associated with the natural world, particularly with olive trees and their fruit. It is often perceived as a calming and earthy tone that represents growth, harmony, and balance. In design, harmony (olive) is achieved by using different variations of olive green in a strategic and controlled manner to create a sense of unity and coherence. This color scheme typically includes a range of shades and tints of olive green, such as dark olive, olive drab, pale olive, and yellow-green. These colors can be combined in different proportions and used as dominant, secondary, or accent colors to create a harmonious and aesthetically pleasing composition. The use of harmony (olive) in design can evoke various emotional and psychological responses. Olive green is often associated with nature, tranquility, and healing, as it resembles the color of leaves and plants. It is also linked to qualities such as stability, peace, and fertility. When used in appropriate combinations and proportions, the color scheme can convey a sense of balance, growth, and natural beauty. Harmony (olive) is commonly used in designs related to nature, environment, and organic products. It can be applied in various design elements such as backgrounds, typography, illustrations, and graphics. The muted and earthy nature of olive green makes it a versatile color that can work well with other complementary and contrasting colors. It can be paired with warm tones such as yellows and oranges for a vibrant and energetic look, or with cool tones like blues and purples for a soothing and serene atmosphere. In summary, harmony (olive) is a color scheme in color theory and color symbolism that involves the use of various shades and tints of olive green. It is associated with nature, balance, and tranquility. When used effectively in design, it can create a harmonious and visually appealing composition that evokes emotions of stability, growth, and natural beauty.

Healing (Blue)

In color theory and color symbolism in design, the color blue is often associated with healing. Blue is a cool color that is often associated with calmness, serenity, and relaxation. It is often seen as a color that can help to soothe and heal both the mind and the body. In a psychological context, blue is known to have a calming effect on the mind. It is often used in spaces such as bedrooms, spas, and hospitals to create a sense of peacefulness and tranquility. The color blue has been found to lower blood pressure, reduce respiration rates, and slow down heart rates, all of which contribute to a sense of healing and well-being. Blue is also associated with water and the ocean. Water is often seen as a symbol of healing and purification, and the color blue can evoke these feelings. The color blue is often used in designs for products and spaces related to health and wellness, such as skincare products, hospitals, and therapy spaces. In terms of color symbolism, blue is often associated with trust, stability, and reliability. These qualities can contribute to a sense of healing and security. Blue is often used in logos and branding for businesses that want to convey a sense of trustworthiness and dependability. Overall, the color blue is often used in design to evoke feelings of healing, calmness, and relaxation. It is a color that is associated with a sense of peace and tranquility, making it a popular choice for spaces and products related to health and wellness. Whether it is used in a spa, hospital, or logo, the color blue can contribute to a sense of healing and well-being.

Healing (Copper)

Healing (Copper) in the context of color theory and color symbolism in design refers to the emotional and psychological effects associated with the color copper. Copper, a metallic shade with warm orange undertones, is often linked to healing due to its calming and soothing qualities. The color copper is believed to have the ability to promote balance and harmony in design. It has a grounding effect that helps to create a sense of stability and security. This makes it an ideal choice for spaces intended to promote relaxation, such as bedrooms, meditation rooms, or spa environments. Furthermore, copper is associated with the concept of physical and emotional healing. It is believed to have properties that can restore energy and vitality, making it suitable for spaces dedicated to wellness and rejuvenation. Copper is also considered to be a color that encourages self-acceptance and self-love, fostering a positive attitude and enhancing overall well-being. In color symbolism, copper is often associated with warmth, comfort, and nurturing. It evokes a feeling of coziness and contentment, making it a popular choice for interior design elements such as furniture, textiles, and accessories. Copper can create a welcoming and inviting atmosphere, particularly in spaces where social interactions and connections are encouraged, such as living rooms or dining areas. Moreover, copper is a versatile color that can be used in various design styles. It can add a touch of elegance and sophistication when paired with rich jewel tones or metallic accents. When combined with earthy tones such as brown or beige, copper can contribute to a rustic or organic aesthetic. Its warm undertones also make it an excellent complement to other warm colors like red or orange. In summary, healing (copper) within color theory and color symbolism in design refers to the use of the color copper to create a sense of balance, harmony, and emotional well-being. It is associated with healing, nurturing, and comfort, making it suitable for spaces intended for relaxation, rejuvenation, and social connection. Copper's versatility allows it to be used in various design styles, adding warmth and sophistication to any environment.

Healing (Turquoise)

Turquoise is a color that is associated with healing in color theory and color symbolism in design. It is a shade of blue-green that lies on the color spectrum between blue and green. Turquoise takes its name from the gemstone of the same name, which has been prized for its healing properties for centuries. In color theory, turquoise is considered a color of calmness and tranquility. It is soothing to the eye and can evoke a sense of relaxation and healing. Turquoise has a cool and refreshing quality that can help to create a sense of balance and harmony in design. It is often used in environments where healing and rejuvenation are desired, such as spas, hospitals, and wellness centers.

Health (Green)

Health (Green) - In color theory and color symbolism in design, the color green represents health and vitality. It is often associated with nature, growth, and renewal. Green is a color commonly associated with balance and harmony, as it sits in the middle of the visible light spectrum. The color green is often used in healthcare and wellness settings to create a calming and soothing atmosphere. It is believed to have a positive effect on both the physical and mental well-being of individuals. Green is known to have a calming and relaxing effect on the nervous system, making it an ideal color choice for environments aimed at promoting health and healing.

Heat (Red)

Heat (Red) is a fundamental color used in color theory and design to convey various meanings and evoke different emotional responses. In color theory, heat (red) is considered a warm color and is often associated with feelings of energy, passion, and intensity. It is located on one end of the color wheel and is known as one of the primary colors. In design, the color red is widely used for its powerful impact and ability to attract attention. It is frequently employed to create focal points or draw the viewer's eye to specific elements in a composition. Red can symbolize strength, courage, and determination, making it a popular choice for branding and advertising campaigns aimed at promoting products or services that embody these qualities.

Hex Color Code

A hex color code is a numerical representation used in color theory and design to depict specific colors. It consists of six alphanumeric characters which are divided into three pairs, each representing the intensity of red, green, and blue in a particular color. Color theory is the study of how colors interact with each other and with the human eye. It is an essential aspect of design as colors evoke emotions, convey messages, and enhance visual appeal. The hex color code provides a standardized method for specifying colors in web design and other digital applications. In design, colors are not merely aesthetic but hold significant symbolic meaning. Each color evokes different emotions and associations, and designers strategically use this symbolism to convey messages through their work. Understanding the symbolism behind colors allows designers to create visually appealing and meaningful compositions. The hex color code facilitates precise color specification, making it a valuable tool for designers. It allows for a vast range of colors to be represented, with 16,777,216 possibilities in total. By manipulating the intensity of red, green, and blue, designers can create an extensive palette and achieve the exact hues desired. Hex color codes are widely used in various areas of design, including graphic design, web design, branding, and advertising. They provide consistency across different platforms and ensure that colors remain consistent across different devices and browsers. This is particularly important in web design, where the same hex color code will result in the same color appearance regardless of the viewing environment. By understanding and utilizing hex color codes effectively, designers can enhance their compositions by incorporating colors that align with their desired messages and symbolism. Whether it's using warm tones to evoke passion or cool tones to convey tranquility, the hex color code enables designers to bring their creative vision to life while maintaining color accuracy and consistency across different mediums.

Hexadecimal Color Code Converters

Hexadecimal color code converters are tools used in color theory and design to convert color values from one format to another. In the context of color theory, the hexadecimal color system is widely used in digital design and web development to represent colors. The hexadecimal color system uses a combination of numbers and letters to represent colors. It consists of a hashtag (#) followed by six characters, which can be any number from 0 to 9 and any letter from A to F. Each pair of characters represents the intensity of the primary colors red, green, and blue (RGB) in the color. Color theory is an important aspect of design as colors convey emotions, messages, and meanings. Different colors have cultural and symbolic associations that can affect the mood, perception, and communication of a design. Understanding the hexadecimal color system is crucial for designers to accurately reproduce colors and achieve the desired visual effects. Hexadecimal color code converters provide a convenient way to convert color values from one format to another. They allow users to input a color value in a different format, such as RGB or CMYK, and convert it into the corresponding hexadecimal value. This is especially useful when working with different design software or when transferring designs between different platforms. By using a hexadecimal color code converter, designers can ensure consistency in color representation across various devices and applications. It allows them to easily communicate and share color values with clients, colleagues, and other stakeholders in a standardized format. Furthermore, these converters also facilitate the exploration and experimentation of color palettes. Designers can enter different values and see the corresponding colors in real-time, helping them choose the most appropriate colors for their projects. It streamlines the color selection process and enables designers to make informed decisions about color combinations and contrasts. In conclusion, hexadecimal color code converters are valuable tools in color theory and design. They enable the conversion of color values between different formats, ensuring accuracy and consistency in color representation. These converters enhance the efficiency of design processes and promote effective communication and collaboration among stakeholders.

Hexadecimal Color Codes

Hexadecimal color codes, often referred to as hex codes, are a crucial aspect of color theory and play an integral role in color symbolism in design. These codes are a way to represent colors in a digital format using a combination of letters and numbers. In color theory, colors are typically represented using the RGB (Red, Green, Blue) color model. Each of these three primary colors can have a value ranging from 0 to 255, indicating the intensity of each primary color. However, when it comes to digital design, specifying colors using hexadecimal codes offers greater precision and flexibility. Hex codes are composed of a hashtag (#) followed by six characters that represent the intensity of the red, green, and blue channels of the color. These characters can be any combination of numbers from 0 to 9 and letters from A to F. For example, #FF0000 represents pure red, #00FF00 represents pure green, and #0000FF represents pure blue. The hexadecimal system is based on the concept of base 16, where additional symbols (A to F) are used to represent numerical values greater than 9. This system allows for a total of 16 possible values for each channel, providing a wider range of colors compared to the decimal system used in RGB. In design, the choice of color can greatly influence the message and emotions conveyed by a project. Hex codes enable designers to precisely select and reproduce specific colors, maintaining consistency across different platforms and devices. These codes can be used in HTML, CSS, and digital design software to accurately define colors for elements such as backgrounds, text, buttons, and more. Moreover, color symbolism in design is another important aspect. Different colors can evoke various emotions and convey particular meanings. For instance, red can represent passion or danger, while blue may symbolize calmness or trust. By understanding color symbolism and using hex codes, designers have the ability to intentionally evoke specific emotions or align their design with a particular message. In conclusion, hexadecimal color codes are integral to color theory and symbolism in design. They provide a precise and flexible way to represent colors in a digital format. By utilizing these codes, designers can ensure consistency across platforms and devices, as well as leverage the emotional impact of color symbolism to enhance their design projects.

Hexadecimal Color Converters

A hexadecimal color converter is a tool used in color theory and design to convert colors from the hexadecimal format to other color formats, or vice versa. In design, colors are often represented using codes, and the hexadecimal system is commonly used because it allows for millions of different colors to be specified. In color theory, colors are represented using a combination of three primary colors: red, green, and blue. The hexadecimal color system uses a combination of numbers and letters, ranging from 0 to 9 and A to F, to represent these primary colors. Each primary color has a two-digit hexadecimal code, resulting in a six-digit code that represents a specific color. The hexadecimal color converter allows designers to easily convert colors between the hexadecimal format and other color formats, such as RGB (Red, Green, Blue) or CMYK (Cyan, Magenta, Yellow, Black). This is particularly useful when working with different software or devices that use different color systems, as it ensures consistency and accuracy in color representation. Additionally, the hexadecimal color converter enables designers to explore different color harmonies and combinations based on color symbolism. Colors have symbolic meanings and can evoke various emotions and moods, making them an essential element in design. By experimenting with different color codes, designers can create visually appealing and meaningful designs that effectively communicate the desired message or concept. For example, in web design, the hexadecimal color converter allows designers to ensure that the colors used in the design are accurately represented in different browsers and devices. This is because different browsers may interpret colors differently, and the hexadecimal format provides a universal representation that is widely supported. In conclusion, a hexadecimal color converter is a valuable tool in color theory and design that allows for the conversion of colors between the hexadecimal format and other color formats. It helps ensure consistency and accuracy in color representation, while also enabling designers to explore different color harmonies and combinations based on color symbolism.

Hexadecimal Color Editors

A hexadecimal color editor is a tool used in color theory and design to create and manipulate colors using hexadecimal color codes. Hexadecimal color codes are six-digit alphanumeric codes that represent specific colors. Each digit in the code corresponds to a combination of red, green, and blue (RGB) values. The first two digits represent the red component, the middle two digits represent the green component, and the final two digits represent the blue component. The editor allows designers to adjust these RGB values by directly manipulating the hexadecimal code, providing a precise and efficient method for selecting colors. By changing the values, designers can create a wide variety of colors, ranging from light pastels to bold and vibrant hues. In color theory and symbolism, different colors evoke different emotions and convey specific meanings. By using a hexadecimal color editor, designers can carefully select colors that align with the intended message or theme of a design. For example, red often represents power, passion, and energy, making it a popular choice for attention-grabbing elements. Blue, on the other hand, is associated with tranquility, trust, and professionalism, making it suitable for corporate branding or calming designs. Yellow is often used to convey warmth, happiness, and optimism. In addition to choosing individual colors, designers can also create color combinations using the hexadecimal color editor. Complementary colors, those that are opposite each other on the color wheel (e.g., red and green), create a visually striking contrast. Analogous colors, which are adjacent to each other on the color wheel (e.g., blue and green), create a harmonious and cohesive palette. Overall, a hexadecimal color editor is a powerful tool for designers to explore the world of colors and create visually appealing and meaningful designs. With its precise control over RGB values, it allows designers to bring their visions to life and effectively communicate through the language of color.

High Value (Gold)

High Value (Gold) is a color used in color theory and color symbolism in design to represent richness, wealth, and prosperity. It is a shade of yellow that exudes opulence and luxury. Gold is often associated with prestige and success. In color theory, it is considered a high value color because it is inherently bright and eye-catching. Its luminosity makes it an ideal choice for design elements that need to stand out and command attention. Gold has a high perceived value, both literally and symbolically, making it a popular choice in branding and marketing materials.

Hope (Pink)

Hope (Pink): In the context of color theory and color symbolism in design, hope (pink) represents a soft and delicate hue that carries positive connotations. Pink is commonly associated with hope as it embodies a sense of optimism, youthfulness, and possibility. It is often used to convey a warm and nurturing feeling, evoking sentiments of comfort and tranquility. Pink, as a pastel shade, falls under the red color family, but with a lighter and subtler tone. It is often described as a tint of red and is achieved by adding white to the base color. This gentle hue of pink is commonly associated with hope due to its ability to elicit feelings of tenderness and compassion. It is known to create a calming and soothing effect on the human mind, promoting a sense of serenity and overall well-being. In design, the use of hope (pink) can be strategic and intentional as it serves to create an inviting and uplifting atmosphere. The color is often employed to represent femininity and is associated with love, care, and nurturance. Its gentle nature embraces a nurturing spirit, making it suitable for designs related to health, healing, and emotional support. The color pink is often used in designs that aim to convey messages of positivity, encouragement, and optimism. It can be utilized to evoke a sense of comfort and compassion, providing a visual representation of hope and resilience. Whether used in branding, marketing, or visual communication, hope (pink) possesses the ability to evoke emotions and instill a hopeful mindset in individuals. It is important to note that the interpretation and perception of colors may vary across cultures and personal experiences. While pink is commonly associated with hope, its meaning can differ depending on the specific context and cultural background. Additionally, the combination of pink with other colors can influence its symbolic meaning, further adding depth and complexity to its representation. In summary, hope (pink) within color theory and color symbolism in design is a delicate and soft shade that represents a sense of optimism, youthfulness, and possibility. It is commonly utilized to convey tenderness, compassion, and a nurturing spirit. Hope (pink) holds the power to evoke positive emotions and create a hopeful atmosphere in various design contexts.

Hope (White)

The color white, in the context of color theory and color symbolism in design, represents hope. It is a versatile and essential color that signifies purity, innocence, and new beginnings. In color theory, white is known as an achromatic color, meaning it is devoid of hue. It is created by combining all the colors of the visible spectrum in equal amounts, resulting in a neutral and neutralizing effect. As such, white is often thought of as a color of light, illumination, and clarity. In design, white is commonly used to convey a sense of freshness, cleanliness, and simplicity. It has a calming and soothing effect, making it a popular choice in minimalist and modern designs. White backgrounds, in particular, provide a clean canvas that allows other colors and elements to stand out. Furthermore, white is frequently associated with purity and innocence. It evokes a sense of perfection and flawlessness, making it a suitable choice for bridal gowns, christening clothes, and other significant ceremonies. White also represents an absence of stain or impurity, symbolizing the start of something new and pure. White can also be used to create contrast and amplify the impact of other colors. When used alongside vibrant or contrasting colors, white helps to enhance their brightness and visual appeal. It acts as a luminous backdrop, giving a sense of energy and vitality to the overall design. Moreover, in many cultures and religions, white is associated with spirituality, divinity, and transcendence. It is often used to symbolize the divine or supernatural, and it is seen as a color that connects the earthly realm with the spiritual realm. In this way, white represents hope, enlightenment, and the possibility of transcendence. In conclusion, white is a color that embodies hope in color theory and color symbolism in design. It represents purity, freshness, simplicity, and new beginnings. It can be used to create contrast, enhance other colors, and convey a sense of spirituality. Whether used as a dominant color or as an accent, white is a versatile and powerful color that can evoke a feeling of hope in design.

Hue

Hue refers to one of the essential properties of color in color theory and holds significant importance in color symbolism in design. It is defined as the attribute that differentiates colors from one another, based on their perceived wavelength and position in the color spectrum. Hue is commonly associated with the concept of color itself and is often used interchangeably with the terms "color" or "primary color." In color theory, the color spectrum is divided into different hues, which can be described as the primary colors of a specific color model. These hues are typically categorized into twelve basic colors, including red, orange, yellow, green, blue, purple, and their variations. The specific hue of a color is determined by the dominant wavelength of light that is reflected or emitted by an object. In design, hue plays a vital role in conveying emotions, creating visual interest, and evoking specific meanings or associations. Different hues have the power to evoke various psychological and emotional responses from individuals. For example, warm hues like red and orange are often associated with passion, energy, and warmth, while cool hues like blue and green are associated with calmness, tranquility, and nature. Furthermore, hue is a fundamental element in color symbolism, where specific colors are assigned symbolic meanings or cultural connotations. Different cultures and contexts may attribute different symbolic meanings to specific hues. For instance, red can symbolize love and passion in Western societies, while it may symbolize luck or celebration in Eastern cultures. By understanding the characteristics and symbolism of different hues, designers can effectively utilize color in their creations to communicate messages, evoke emotions, and enhance the overall aesthetic appeal. Whether in graphic design, branding, or interior design, having a sound knowledge of hue and its role in color theory and symbolism is essential for creating visually compelling and meaningful designs.

Illumination (Gold)

Illumination refers to the brightness or lightness of a color in the context of color theory and color symbolism in design. It pertains to the amount of light that reflects or emits from a color, influencing its visual perception and emotional impact. Gold, in particular, is a color that exhibits a high level of illumination. It is associated with characteristics such as wealth, luxury, and abundance. In color theory, gold is often considered a warm color due to its resemblance to the hue of the sun and fire. Its bright and radiant nature signifies prestige and opulence.

Illumination (Yellow)

Illumination (Yellow) is a color within the context of color theory and color symbolism in design. Within color theory, illumination refers to the specific shade of yellow that embodies brightness, radiance, and lightness. It is often associated with the actual color of sunlight and is considered one of the primary colors in additive color mixing, along with red and blue. In terms of color symbolism in design, illumination (yellow) holds various meanings and connotations. Yellow is commonly associated with positivity, energy, joy, and happiness. It is a color that draws attention and creates a sense of optimism and excitement. In design, yellow is often used to create emphasis, attract the eye, and evoke feelings of warmth and cheerfulness.

Image Color Extractors

Image color extractors are tools or algorithms that analyze an image to determine the main colors present within it. In the context of color theory, these extractors help designers identify and work with specific colors present in an image, facilitating the creation of color palettes and schemes. In design, color is a powerful tool for expressing emotions, conveying messages, and establishing brand identities. Understanding the meanings and associations attached to different colors is essential for effective communication through design. Color theory provides a framework for understanding how colors work together and how they can be used to create specific visual effects. Color symbolism is the practice of assigning meaning to colors based on cultural, emotional, or psychological associations. Different cultures and contexts may attach varying meaning to colors, making it important for designers to consider these associations when choosing colors for their projects. Image color extractors play a crucial role in color theory and design by providing designers with a starting point for their color palettes. By analyzing the colors present in an image, these tools help designers identify the dominant colors, complementary colors, and other hues that can be used to create aesthetically pleasing and harmonious designs. Additionally, image color extractors can assist designers in aligning their visual choices with the intended symbolism behind the project. By understanding the meanings attached to different colors, designers can select colors that evoke the desired emotions or convey the intended messages. In conclusion, image color extractors are tools that aid designers in analyzing the colors present in an image, helping them create effective color schemes and align their design choices with the desired symbolism. By using these extractors, designers can harness the power of color theory and color symbolism to create visually appealing and meaningful designs.

Imagination (Indigo)

The color indigo is a deep, rich shade of blue that falls between blue and violet on the color spectrum. It is often associated with imagination and creativity, making it a popular choice in design and color theory. In color theory, indigo is considered a cool color, meaning that it has a calming and soothing effect on viewers. It is often used to create a sense of depth and mystery in designs, as well as to evoke a sense of spirituality and intuition. Its association with the imagination stems from its connection to the crown chakra, which is believed to be the center of higher consciousness and creativity.

Imagination (Lilac)

Imagination (Lilac) is a color associated with creativity, spirituality, and individuality. In color theory and color symbolism in design, imagination (lilac) represents the blending of blue and purple, resulting in a hue that evokes a sense of mystery and intrigue. The color lilac, with its soft and delicate appearance, is often used to symbolize imagination and inspire creative thinking. It represents the realm of dreams and imagination, encouraging people to let their minds wander and explore new ideas. As such, it is commonly employed in designs that aim to evoke a sense of wonder and imagination.

Imagination (Purple)

Imagination, in the context of color theory and color symbolism in design, is represented by the color purple. Purple is a hue that combines the stability of blue with the energy of red, resulting in a color that is associated with creativity, spirituality, and inspiration. Purple is often regarded as a symbol of imagination because of its association with intuition and the mind. It stimulates our creative thinking and encourages us to explore new ideas and possibilities. In design, the use of purple can evoke a sense of mystery and magic, as it is often associated with the mystical realm and the unknown.

Indecision (Gray)

Indecision (Gray) refers to the color gray and its representation in color theory and color symbolism in design. Gray is a neutral color that is created by mixing black and white. It is often associated with feelings of ambiguity, uncertainty, and indecisiveness. In color theory, gray is considered to be achromatic because it does not have any hue. It is created by decreasing the saturation of a color, effectively removing its chromatic properties. Gray is often used as a background color in design because of its ability to enhance other colors and allow them to stand out. It is a versatile color that can be used to create a sense of balance and harmony in a design.

Independence (Black)

Independence (Black) in color theory and color symbolism in design refers to the color black and its associated meanings and connotations. Black is often perceived as a color of strength, power, elegance, and formality. Black is a color that absorbs all light and reflects no color. It is often associated with darkness, mystery, and the unknown. In design, black is frequently used to convey a sense of sophistication, luxury, and authority.

Independence (Purple)

Independence (purple) is a color in the context of color theory and color symbolism in design. It is a hue that combines the stability and calming effect of blue with the energy and passion of red. This particular shade of purple, known as Independence, is a deeper and more saturated color that conveys a sense of luxury, creativity, and spirituality. In color theory, purple is considered a secondary color that is created by mixing blue and red together. It has a wavelength range between approximately 380 and 450 nanometers, placing it on the color spectrum between blue and violet. Independence, being a specific variation of purple, leans more towards the blue side of the spectrum, emphasizing qualities such as introspection, intuition, and serenity.

Innocence (Pink)

In the context of color theory and color symbolism in design, innocence is a color represented by the shade pink. Pink is a delicate hue that typically evokes feelings of innocence, sweetness, and femininity. In color theory, innocence is often associated with the lighter variations of pink. These shades are created by adding white to the pure red color. The resulting hues have a soft and gentle appearance, reminiscent of delicate flowers or newborn creatures. The lightness and subtlety of these pinks contribute to their representation of innocence.

Innocence (White)

In color theory and symbolism in design, the color white represents innocence. White is a shade that is often associated with purity, clarity, and untaintedness. It is considered the absence of color and therefore represents a blank canvas, untouched by any other pigment or influence. The symbolic meaning of white in design is closely related to its association with innocence. It is a color that evokes a sense of cleanliness, freshness, and simplicity. White is often used in design to create a feeling of spaciousness, as it reflects light and makes spaces appear larger. This is particularly beneficial in minimalist or contemporary designs, where the use of white can enhance the overall aesthetic and provide a sense of calmness and serenity.

Innovation (Periwinkle)

The color innovation, also known as periwinkle, is a shade that lies between blue and purple on the color spectrum. It is a unique and vibrant color that is often associated with creativity, imagination, and exploration. In the context of color theory, innovation is considered a tertiary color, created by mixing equal parts of blue and purple. It is often described as a light or pale shade, with a slight hint of gray. This gives it a sense of depth and sophistication, making it popular in various design fields. In design, periwinkle is often used to evoke a sense of innovation and originality. It is a color that symbolizes forward-thinking and pushing boundaries. Its cool undertones create a calming and soothing effect, making it a popular choice for designs that aim to promote relaxation and tranquility. Furthermore, periwinkle is also associated with communication and intuition. It is believed to stimulate the mind and enhance creativity, making it an ideal choice for designs that aim to inspire or motivate. Its soft and delicate nature also adds a touch of elegance and femininity, making it a favored color in fashion and beauty industries. When used in combination with other colors, periwinkle can create a harmonious and balanced palette. It pairs well with shades of white, gray, and silver, adding a touch of vibrancy without overpowering the overall design. It can also be paired with bolder colors, such as orange or yellow, to create a striking contrast and draw attention to specific elements. In summary, periwinkle or innovation is a unique and vibrant color that symbolizes creativity, originality, and exploration. It is a popular choice in design for its calming effect and its ability to stimulate the mind. Whether used as a primary or accent color, periwinkle adds a touch of sophistication and elegance to any design.

Innovation (Silver)

Innovation in color theory and color symbolism in design refers to the use of unique and original color combinations and applications to evoke creativity, novelty, and forward-thinking concepts. It involves the exploration and incorporation of unconventional color choices and arrangements to represent innovative ideas and to challenge traditional design norms. Innovation in color theory focuses on breaking away from established color schemes and explores new ways of using colors to create visual interest and impact. It encourages designers to experiment with contrasting hues, unexpected combinations, and unconventional palettes to evoke a sense of originality and innovation in their designs.

Inspiration (Aqua)

In color theory, aqua is a shade of blue-green that sits in between the colors teal and turquoise. It is commonly associated with water, specifically the clear, tropical waters of the ocean or a serene, tranquil swimming pool. Aqua is often used in design to create a sense of calmness, freshness, and relaxation. In terms of color symbolism, aqua is often associated with tranquility, purity, and clarity. Its close resemblance to water makes it a popular choice for designs that aim to evoke a sense of harmony and peacefulness. Aqua can also be seen as a symbol of healing, as water is often associated with renewal and rejuvenation.

Intellect (Yellow)

Color theory is a discipline that explores the interaction between colors and the visual effects they create. It provides designers with a framework to understand and manipulate colors in order to create aesthetically pleasing and effective designs. In color theory, each color carries specific meanings and emotions, making it a powerful tool in design. Intellect, also known as yellow, is one of the colors often associated with color theory and color symbolism. Yellow is a bright and vibrant hue that is often associated with energy, intellect, and optimism. It is typically perceived as a warm and inviting color that can grab attention and stimulate mental activity.

Intelligence (Blue)

131

Intelligence (Blue) is a color in the context of color theory and color symbolism in design that represents mental clarity, wisdom, and logic. It is often associated with qualities such as intellect, knowledge, and expertise. In color theory, blue is classified as a cool color. It is often described as calm and soothing, evoking a sense of tranquility and stability. Blue is known to have a calming effect on the mind and is considered to be mentally stimulating. It is commonly used in design to convey a sense of professionalism, reliability, and trustworthiness.

Intelligence (Silver)

Intelligence (Silver) In the context of color theory and color symbolism in design, intelligence is represented by the color silver. Silver is often associated with futuristic and innovative concepts, in addition to its perceived elegance and sophistication.

Intuition (Indigo)

Intuition is a dark, rich shade of blue known as indigo. In color theory, indigo is often classified as a tertiary color located between blue and violet on the color wheel. It is created by mixing blue and violet pigments in varying proportions, resulting in a deep, mysterious hue. In the context of color symbolism in design, indigo is associated with several meanings and emotions. It is often linked to spirituality, wisdom, and intuition. Indigo has a mystical quality, representing a deep understanding and connection to the divine or higher consciousness. It is a color that elicits introspection and inner reflection, inviting individuals to trust their instincts and tap into their inner wisdom.

Intuition (Magenta)

The color intuition, also known as magenta, is a combination of red and blue hues that creates a bright and vibrant shade. In the context of color theory, magenta is considered a secondary color, as it is derived from the primary colors of red and blue. In color symbolism in design, magenta is often associated with intuition, creativity, and spirituality. It is a color that represents a connection to the divine and the unknown. Magenta is often used in design to evoke feelings of inspiration and imagination.

Jealousy (Green)

Jealousy, in the context of color theory and color symbolism in design, is represented by the color green. Green is commonly associated with feelings of jealousy due to its historical and cultural associations. In color theory, green is classified as a cool color, positioned between blue and yellow on the color wheel. It is often described as a color that has a calming and refreshing effect, reminiscent of nature, growth, and renewal. However, when it comes to color symbolism, green can also evoke negative emotions, such as jealousy and envy.

Jealousy (Yellow)

"Jealousy (Yellow)" in the context of color theory and color symbolism in design refers to the psychological and emotional associations attributed to the color yellow. Yellow is commonly associated with feelings of jealousy, as it represents the intensity of envy and possessiveness. In color theory, yellow is classified as a warm color that stimulates mental activity and arouses emotions. It is often associated with energy, happiness, and optimism. However, yellow can also evoke negative associations, such as jealousy and deceit, due to its connection to the darker aspects of its symbolism.

Joy (Apricot)

Joy, when associated with the color apricot, is a concept rooted in color theory and symbolism in design. In color theory, apricot is a warm and vibrant hue that falls in the orange color family, derived from a mix of red and yellow. It is known for its vibrant and optimistic qualities, often evoking feelings of joy, enthusiasm, and happiness. Apricot is often used in design to create a sense of playfulness and energy. It is a color that can catch attention and create a positive emotional response. When used in branding or advertising, apricot can convey a sense of excitement and adventure, making it a popular choice for products or services targeting a younger and more energetic demographic.

132

Joy (Coral)

Joy (Coral) is a vibrant and energetic color often associated with feelings of excitement, enthusiasm, and happiness. It is a shade of orange that contains pink undertones, making it both warm and lively. In color theory, coral is created by mixing red and orange pigments, resulting in a captivating and attention-grabbing hue. In the context of color symbolism in design, joy (coral) is often used to convey a sense of youthful exuberance and playfulness. Its bright and cheerful nature makes it particularly suitable for designs aimed at capturing attention and evoking positive emotions. Joy (coral) can add a touch of spontaneity and creativity to any visual composition.

Joy (Gold)

Joy (Gold) is a color that holds great significance in color theory and color symbolism in design. It is a shade of the color yellow, which is known for its associations with happiness, positivity, and energy. Gold, specifically, is often associated with luxury, wealth, and abundance. In color theory, joy (gold) is considered a warm color. Warm colors are typically associated with emotions such as happiness, excitement, and enthusiasm. They are known to stimulate the senses and create a sense of warmth and vitality. Gold, in particular, exudes a sense of richness and opulence, creating a feeling of prestige and grandeur.

Joy (Lemon)

Joy (Lemon) is a bright and vibrant shade of yellow that falls within the color theory of warm colors. In color symbolism, yellow is often associated with happiness, cheerfulness, and positivity. When used in design, joy (lemon) can evoke a sense of energy and excitement. It is commonly used to create attention-grabbing designs and to symbolize joyous occasions or elements. Joy (lemon) can be employed to create a focal point in a design, drawing the viewer's eye and creating a sense of optimism and enthusiasm. It is often used in combination with other warm colors or contrasting shades to create dynamic and visually striking compositions.

Joy (Yellow)

Leadership (Bronze)

Leadership in the context of color theory and color symbolism in design refers to the prominent use of the color bronze. Bronze is often associated with qualities such as strength, durability, and power. As a color, it exudes a sense of confidence, authority, and leadership. When incorporated into design, bronze can serve as a visual representation of leadership and can be used to communicate a strong and authoritative message. Its warm and rich tones can evoke a sense of stability and reliability, making it an ideal choice for projects that require a strong and commanding presence.

Libraries Of Digital Colors

A library of digital colors refers to a collection or database of color swatches that can be used in various digital design applications. These libraries are often organized and categorized based on different color models, such as RGB (Red, Green, Blue) or CMYK (Cyan, Magenta, Yellow, Black), which are commonly used in digital design. These libraries serve as a valuable resource for designers, providing them with a wide range of pre-defined colors that they can choose from when creating digital designs. By having access to a library of digital colors, designers can easily experiment with different color combinations and find the most appropriate color scheme for their design projects. Color theory is a fundamental concept in design that explores the principles and effects of color. It delves into the psychological, emotional, and symbolic meanings associated with different colors. Color symbolism, on the other hand, refers to the specific meanings and associations assigned to colors in different cultures or contexts. In the context of color symbolism in design, libraries of digital colors can be used to enhance the intended meaning or message behind a design. Designers can strategically select colors from these libraries that align with the desired symbolism for their design. For example, they might choose warm colors like red or orange to evoke feelings of excitement or passion, or cool colors like blue or green to create a sense of calmness or freshness. Moreover, libraries of digital colors also enable designers to create harmonious color schemes based on the principles of color theory. They can easily access and compare colors with varying tones, shades, and tints to find the perfect balance and contrast in their designs. By understanding the principles of color theory, designers can create visually appealing compositions that effectively communicate their intended message. In summary, libraries of digital colors are valuable resources for designers, providing them with access to a wide range of pre-defined colors based on different color models. These libraries allow designers to experiment with color combinations and select colors that align with the intended symbolism or principles of color theory in their designs.

Life (Green)

The color green, in the context of color theory and color symbolism in design, represents life and nature. Green is often associated with growth, renewal, and freshness due to its connection with plants and foliage. Green is considered a secondary color, which means it is created by mixing blue and yellow pigments. In color theory, green is located in the middle of the color wheel, positioned between cool blue and warm yellow. This placement contributes to the feeling of balance and harmony associated with the color green.

Light Mode Design Applications

Light mode design applications refer to the use of bright, luminous colors in the design of digital interfaces, websites, and applications. This design approach is based on color theory and symbolism, which play a crucial role in creating visually appealing and effective designs. In color theory, light colors are associated with qualities such as vibrancy, positivity, and energy. By using light colors in design applications, designers can create a sense of optimism and evoke positive emotions in users. Light colors are particularly effective in capturing attention and drawing users' focus to important elements on a screen. These colors can create a sense of depth and dimension, making interfaces visually engaging and inviting for users. Furthermore, light mode design applications also make use of color symbolism to convey meaning and messages. Different colors have psychological associations and can elicit specific emotions and responses. For example, light blue is often associated with tranquility and trust, making it suitable for websites or applications related to healthcare or finance. Similarly, shades of green can symbolize growth, health, and environmental awareness, making them suitable for eco-friendly or wellness-related designs. This design approach also takes into consideration the principles of contrast and readability. Light colors are often paired with darker shades to create a pleasing contrast that enhances legibility. This ensures that the content is easily readable and the user can navigate the interface seamlessly. Additionally, the use of light mode design can contribute to a sense of clarity and cleanliness, making the interface appear modern and professional.

Light Mode Design Software

Light Mode Design Software refers to a type of software that is specifically designed to enable the creation and manipulation of designs using a light color palette. Color Theory plays a significant role in the development of design software as it helps in understanding the visual effects and emotions associated with different colors. When it comes to light mode design, the color theory principles focus on utilizing bright and light colors to create a visually appealing and positive user experience. In light mode design, the primary objective is to create a sense of lightness and clarity in the overall design. This is achieved by using colors that have high levels of brightness and contrast. Light colors are often associated with qualities such as purity, innocence, and positivity. The use of light colors in design can evoke a sense of calmness and can create a visually pleasing environment for users. Color symbolism is another important aspect of design, especially in light mode design. Different colors are associated with different meanings and emotions. For example, white is often used to symbolize purity, cleanliness, and simplicity. Yellow is associated with joy, energy, and friendliness, while blue is commonly associated with trust, stability, and professionalism. In light mode design software, the choice of colors and their symbolism should align with the intended message and purpose of the design. It is important to consider the psychological impact that colors can have on users and ensure that the chosen color palette effectively communicates the desired emotions and associations. To summarize, Light Mode Design Software refers to software specifically designed for creating designs using a light color palette. Color theory and color symbolism are essential aspects of such software, as they guide the choice and use of colors to create visually pleasing and

134

emotionally impactful designs.

Light Mode Design Solutions

Light mode design solutions refer to the use of lighter colors and a brighter overall design aesthetic in the context of color theory and color symbolism in design. In color theory, light colors are often associated with feelings of positivity, brightness, and warmth. Light mode design solutions utilize these colors to create a visually pleasing and inviting design that represents these positive emotions. Light mode designs typically feature a predominantly white or light-colored background, with additional lighter colors used for elements such as text, buttons, and icons. The use of lighter colors in a design can help create a sense of spaciousness and clarity, making it easier for users to navigate and understand the content. Color symbolism plays an important role in design, where different colors are associated with specific meanings and emotions. Light mode design solutions make use of colors that are commonly associated with positive emotions and symbolism. For example, white is often associated with purity, innocence, and clarity, while pastel colors are often associated with calmness and serenity. These colors can be used strategically to evoke specific emotions or to convey a particular message to the audience.

Light Mode Design Tools

Light Mode Design Tools refer to visually-oriented tools and software applications that utilize color theory and color symbolism to create design elements in a light or bright color scheme. In the context of web and graphic design, color theory is the study and application of color and its psychological effects on human beings. It involves understanding the color wheel, color harmony, and the different emotions and meanings associated with specific colors. Color symbolism, on the other hand, relates to the interpretation and meaning of different colors within a cultural or societal context. For example, red can symbolize passion or danger, while blue is often associated with calmness and trust. Design tools that cater to light mode primarily focus on using brighter shades and colors that are visually pleasing and often evoke positive emotions.

Light Mode

Light Mode refers to a color scheme or design choice where lighter tones and colors are predominantly used. It is based on the principles of color theory and symbolism in design. In color theory, light colors like white, pastels, and soft hues are associated with feelings of brightness, airiness, and positivity. Light Mode aims to create a visual experience that is vibrant, uplifting, and soothing to the viewer. By using lighter colors, Light Mode creates a sense of spaciousness and openness within a design, making it visually appealing and easy to navigate. In terms of color symbolism, Light Mode often evokes positive emotions and conveys a sense of purity, innocence, and simplicity. Lighter shades are commonly associated with attributes such as clarity, cleanliness, and tranquility. The use of light colors in design can create a sense of calmness and harmony, making it suitable for various applications and contexts. Light Mode is commonly used in user interface design, particularly in operating systems, applications, and websites. It provides a visually pleasing experience for users, reducing eye strain and enhancing readability. The contrast between light background colors and dark text or elements ensures legibility and accessibility. Light Mode can be further enhanced by incorporating subtle gradients, soft shadows, and delicate textures to add depth and dimension to the overall design. The combination of light colors with well-thought-out typography and proper spacing creates an engaging and inviting visual composition. Overall, Light Mode in color theory and design emphasizes the use of lighter colors to create a visually appealing and positive experience. It leverages the principles of color theory and symbolism to evoke emotions of brightness, simplicity, and tranquility. By focusing on lighter tones, Light Mode enhances readability, reduces eye strain, and creates a sense of openness and harmony within a design.

Love (Apricot)

Love (Apricot) is a color widely used in color theory and color symbolism in design. It is a warm, pale orange hue that conveys emotions of love, romance, and affection. In color theory, Love (Apricot) falls into the warm color category, alongside hues such as red, orange, and yellow. Warm colors generally evoke feelings of comfort, energy, and happiness. Love (Apricot) is specifically associated with warmth and tenderness, creating a soothing and inviting atmosphere when used in design.

Love (Aqua)

Love (Aqua) is a color commonly used in color theory and color symbolism in design. It is a light, cool shade of blue-green that is often associated with tranquility, harmony, and healing. In color theory, love (aqua) is classified as a tertiary color, created by combining equal parts of blue and green. Its name is derived from the Latin word "aqua," meaning water, which reflects its nature as a shade reminiscent of the ocean or tropical waters. In the context of color symbolism in design, love (aqua) can evoke a variety of emotions and meanings. It is commonly associated with calmness, serenity, and relaxation, making it a popular choice for designs promoting well-being, therapy, and meditation. Its soothing qualities also make it a suitable color for environments aimed at reducing stress, such as hospitals and spas. Furthermore, love (aqua) is often linked to harmony and balance. Its blend of blue and green represents the harmonious union of masculine and feminine energies, making it an appropriate choice for designs related to relationships, partnerships, and unity. Additionally, love (aqua) has connections to healing and renewal. Its association with water conveys a sense of fluidity and purification, making it a symbolic color for personal growth, transformation, and cleansing. It can be used in designs related to self-improvement, spiritual growth, and holistic healing. Overall, love (aqua) is a versatile color in color theory and color symbolism in design. Its calming, harmonious, and healing qualities make it a popular choice in various industries, including interior design, branding, and advertising, where the goal is to evoke positive emotions and create a sense of tranquility.

Love (Beige)

Love (Beige) is a color that holds great significance in color theory and symbolism, particularly in the realm of design. It is a gentle and subdued color, created by merging various shades of brown and white. Love (Beige) is often associated with warmth, comfort, and nostalgia, evoking a sense of tranquility and calmness. In color theory, Love (Beige) is classified as a neutral color, as it is a combination of warm and cool tones. It is generally considered to be a warm neutral, leaning towards the warmer side of the color spectrum. This makes it a versatile hue, as it can be used as a backdrop to enhance and balance other colors within a design. Love (Beige) symbolizes several qualities and emotions in design. The most prominent of these is love and affection. The color is reminiscent of natural elements such as sand and earth, invoking a feeling of grounding and nurturing. Love (Beige) is often associated with reliability, stability, and dependability, making it an ideal choice for creating a sense of trust and connection between the design and its audience. In addition to its emotional associations, Love (Beige) is also commonly used to convey elegance and sophistication. Due to its neutrality, it can be easily paired with other colors, helping to create a harmonious and balanced design. Love (Beige) also has the ability to create a sense of space and openness, especially when used in larger proportions or combined with lighter hues. When using Love (Beige) in design, it is important to consider the overall mood and message of the project. It can be used effectively in a variety of contexts, including branding, interior design, and fashion. The subtlety and versatility of Love (Beige) allows it to adapt to different design styles and aesthetics, whether it is used as the main color or in combination with other hues.

Love (Black)

In the context of color theory and color symbolism in design, black is the absence or complete absorption of light. It is often described as the darkest color, representing the absence of color itself. Black is typically associated with various emotions, concepts, and perceptions, making it an important element in visual communication. From a psychological standpoint, black evokes a sense of mystery, power, and authority. Its presence can convey elegance, sophistication, and formality. In many cultures, black is associated with mourning and sadness, representing grief and loss. However, it can also symbolize strength, resilience, and independence.

Love (Blue)

Love (Blue) Love, in the context of color theory and color symbolism in design, is represented by the color blue. Blue is often associated with feelings of calmness, tranquility, and serenity, which are qualities commonly associated with love.

Love (Bronze)

Love (Bronze) is a color that holds significant meaning in the realm of color theory and color symbolism in design. It is a warm, earthy hue that blends the intensity of red with the subtlety of brown. As a result, love bronze is often associated with emotions and qualities such as passion, strength, stability, and dependability. In color theory, love bronze falls under the category of warm colors. Warm colors are known to evoke feelings of comfort, energy, and excitement. Love bronze, in particular, has a rich and deep appearance that can create a sense of warmth and intimacy when used in design. Its reddish undertone gives it a lively and vibrant quality. When it comes to color symbolism, love bronze carries a range of connotations. It is often associated with the concept of love itself, as the warm and sensual nature of the color reflects the intensity and passion commonly associated with romantic love. Love bronze can be used in designs that aim to express feelings of desire, attraction, and affection. Additionally, love bronze also carries connotations of strength and stability. Its deep and solid appearance communicates a sense of reliability and dependability. This makes it a suitable choice for designs focusing on long-lasting relationships, endurance, and trust. Moreover, love bronze is often used in designs that aim to evoke a sense of sophistication and elegance. Its warm and earthy tones add a touch of luxury and refinement, making it a popular choice in interior design, fashion, and branding. Love bronze can be employed to convey a sense of timelessness, tradition, and classic beauty. In conclusion, love bronze is a color with a range of meanings within the realm of color theory and symbolism in design. With its warm, earthy tones and associations with passion, strength, stability, and sophistication, love bronze offers designers a versatile tool to communicate various emotions and qualities.

Love (Brown)

Love (Brown) is a color that holds significant meaning in the realm of color theory and color symbolism in design. It is a warm, earthy hue that combines red and yellow, evoking a sense of stability, warmth, and groundedness. In color theory, brown is often associated with the natural world, particularly with soil, wood, and other earthy elements. It represents durability, reliability, and a sense of security. Brown is often used as a grounding color in design, providing a solid foundation upon which other colors can be built. In the context of color symbolism, brown is often associated with feelings of comfort, warmth, and stability. It is seen as a nurturing color, reminding us of the warmth and safety of a cozy home. Brown can also evoke a sense of tradition, reliability, and dependability. It is often used to convey a sense of authenticity and timelessness, adding a touch of classic elegance to a design. When used in combination with other colors, brown can have different symbolic meanings. For example, when paired with warm colors such as red or orange, it can create a sense of energy and passion. On the other hand, when paired with cool colors such as blue or green, it can create a sense of balance and harmony. In design, brown is often used as a neutral color to create contrast and balance. It can be used as a background color to allow other colors to stand out, or as an accent color to add depth and richness to a design. Brown is also commonly used in the fields of fashion and interior design, where it is associated with sophistication, elegance, and a sense of timeless style. Overall, love (brown) holds a special place in color theory and color symbolism. It represents stability, warmth, and a sense of authenticity. Whether used as a grounding color or as an accent, brown adds depth and richness to a design, creating a sense of comfort and elegance.

Love (Copper)

Love (Copper) in the context of color theory refers to a specific shade of copper color that is associated with the concept of love and affection. Copper is a warm metallic color that is often perceived as a mixture of red and orange, with a hint of brown. Love (Copper) is a deeper, more intense shade of copper, which gives it a rich and luxurious appearance. In color symbolism, Love (Copper) is often associated with deep emotions, passion, and desire. It represents a strong and profound affection that goes beyond superficial feelings. Love (Copper) evokes warmth and intimacy, creating a sense of comfort and coziness. It is a color that can evoke strong emotional responses and is often used to convey a sense of love and connection in design.

Love (Coral)

Love (Coral) is a vibrant shade within the color theory and color symbolism in design. It is described as a warm and intense color that combines the energy of red with the brightness of orange. This hue is often associated with a sense of vitality, passion, and excitement. In color theory, Love (Coral) is categorized as a tertiary color, created by mixing equal parts of red and orange on the color wheel. It sits between pink and orange, making it a versatile color that can convey different emotions depending on its usage and context.

Love (Crimson)

Love (Crimson) in color theory refers to a specific shade of red that is associated with deep emotions, passion, and affection. It is a vibrant and intense hue that symbolizes love and romance in various cultural contexts. In design, the color love (crimson) is often used strategically to evoke strong emotional responses and create a sense of excitement or intensity in visual compositions. It can be employed as an accent color to draw attention and convey a powerful message. The vibrant nature of crimson makes it highly visible and captivating to the viewer's eye.

Love (Gold)

In color theory and color symbolism in design, gold is a warm, metallic hue that represents wealth, luxury, and extravagance. It is often associated with feelings of abundance, prosperity, and high value. Gold is a versatile color that can be used to evoke a variety of emotions and messages. In design, it is commonly used to create a sense of opulence and sophistication. The shimmering quality of gold adds a touch of elegance and glamour to any design, making it a popular choice for high-end products and branding.

Love (Green)

In color theory, green is one of the primary colors, along with red and blue, that can be used to create a wide range of other colors. It is considered a secondary color when mixed with primary colors. Green is often associated with nature and is commonly used to represent growth, freshness, and renewal. It is a soothing and calming color that is often used in designs to create a sense of harmony and balance. With its associations to nature, green is also used to represent environmental awareness and sustainability.

Love (Indigo)

Love (Indigo) is a color that holds significance in color theory and color symbolism in design. In color theory, indigo is considered a tertiary color, which is created by mixing blue and purple. It is often described as a dark purplish-blue hue. In terms of color symbolism, love (indigo) represents deep emotions, spirituality, introspection, and intuition. It is associated with the third eye chakra, which is located in the middle of the forehead and is believed to be connected to our intuition and ability to perceive higher truths. Love (indigo) is often associated with wisdom and enlightenment.

Love (Lavender)

Love (Lavender) is a hue in the purple color family that is commonly associated with deep emotions, spirituality, and tranquility. It is a lighter shade of purple that is created by mixing blue and red in equal proportions. In the context of color theory, Love (Lavender) is considered to be a cool color due to its proximity to blue on the color wheel. Cool colors are known to have a calming effect on individuals and are often associated with introspection and relaxation. When used in design, Love (Lavender) can create a sense of serenity and harmony.

Love (Lemon)

Love (Lemon) is a vibrant and energizing color in the context of color theory and color symbolism in design. It is a shade of yellow that incorporates elements of brightness, warmth, and positivity. In color theory, yellow is often associated with happiness, optimism, and creativity. It is a highly visible color that grabs attention and stimulates mental activity. Love

(Lemon) builds upon these traits by adding a hint of green, intensifying its vibrancy and adding a refreshing aspect to the color. Love (Lemon) is frequently used in design to evoke feelings of joy, enthusiasm, and warmth. It is especially popular in branding and marketing for products or services targeting a youthful and energetic audience. The color's brightness and liveliness make it stand out and grab attention, making it effective for creating a lasting impression. When used in combination with other colors, Love (Lemon) can represent various concepts and emotions. It pairs well with complementary shades, such as purple or blue, creating a visually striking contrast. This combination can convey a sense of harmony and balance. Additionally, Love (Lemon) can be used with analogous colors, such as orange or yellow-green, to create an energetic and cohesive design. In terms of color symbolism, Love (Lemon) is often associated with happiness, sunshine, and positivity. It can evoke feelings of warmth, joy, and optimism. The color also represents freshness and vitality, making it a perfect choice for designs related to nature, health, or natural products. Overall, Love (Lemon) is a color that energizes and brightens any design. Its vibrant and sunny nature makes it an excellent choice for creating a positive and uplifting visual experience, whether in branding, marketing, or other design applications.

Love (Lilac)

Lilac, in the context of color theory and color symbolism in design, is a pale purple color that lies between purple and white on the color spectrum. It is often associated with feelings of love, romance, and beauty. Lilac is created by mixing blue and red together with a higher proportion of blue than red. This combination results in a soft, delicate shade of purple that is lighter than lavender but darker than pink. Lilac is often seen as a more feminine color due to its association with flowers and its delicate, pastel hue. In color theory, lilac falls within the category of cool colors. Cool colors are typically calming and soothing, evoking a sense of tranquility and serenity. Lilac, in particular, is known for its calming effects on the mind and body. It can help create a relaxing and peaceful atmosphere, making it a popular choice for bedrooms and meditation spaces. From a color symbolism perspective, lilac is often associated with love and affection. It is commonly used in romantic settings or to represent feelings of tenderness and care. In design, lilac can be used to evoke a sense of elegance and sophistication. It is often used in weddings and other formal events to create a romantic atmosphere. Lilac is also associated with spring and new beginnings. It is a common color used in floral arrangements and can represent the arrival of warmer weather and blooming flowers. The soft and delicate nature of lilac can symbolize youth, purity, and innocence. Overall, lilac is a color that is often used for its calming and romantic qualities. Its association with love, romance, and beauty make it a popular choice in design, particularly in settings where a soft and elegant atmosphere is desired. Note: The requested answer cannot be provided in pure HTML format with only 2 tags as it exceeds the word limit.

Love (Magenta)

Love (Magenta) - a formal definition in the context of color theory & color symbolism in design: Love, represented by the color Magenta, is an intense and passionate emotion that holds significant significance in color theory and color symbolism in design. As a color that combines the qualities of red and blue, magenta is often associated with a harmonious combination of warmth and coolness, creating a unique and vibrant visual experience.

Love (Maroon)

The color maroon is a dark, reddish-brown shade that holds significant meaning in color theory and symbolism in design. Derived from the French word "marron," which means chestnut, it is often associated with warmth, richness, and depth. Maroon is created when red is combined with a small amount of black or blue, resulting in a color that exudes elegance and sophistication. In color theory, maroon falls within the red color family and is considered a "cool" color due to its association with the darker tones. It is often used to evoke feelings of strength, power, and stability, making it a popular choice in branding and logo design. Maroon can add a sense of seriousness and maturity to a design, creating a visually impactful and memorable experience for the viewer. In color symbolism, maroon is often associated with passion, vitality, and determination. It is seen as a color that represents ambition and can inspire action and motivation. Maroon can also convey a sense of tradition and heritage, making it a suitable choice for designs related to luxury, heritage brands, or high-end products. Furthermore, maroon can be used strategically to create contrast and highlight other elements in a design. Its dark and rich nature makes it an excellent choice for creating depth and adding visual interest to compositions. It can also be paired with other colors to create harmonious or contrasting color schemes, depending on the desired effect. When combined with warm colors, such as gold or orange, maroon can create a sense of opulence and luxury. On the other hand, when combined with cooler colors, such as blues or grays, it can bring a more subdued and calming effect to a design. The versatility of maroon lies in its ability to enhance and complement other colors, adding depth and complexity to any visual composition.

Love (Mint)

Mint is a color that falls within the green color family. It is a pale and light shade of green with a cool undertone. In color theory, mint is considered a tertiary color, created by mixing equal parts blue and yellow to create green, and then adding white to lighten the hue. In design, mint is often associated with freshness, cleanliness, and rejuvenation. It is a versatile color that can be both calming and invigorating, depending on its usage and context. Mint is commonly used in various design disciplines, such as graphic design, interior design, and fashion, due to its pleasing and harmonious nature. In color symbolism, mint is often associated with new beginnings, growth, and fertility. It can evoke a sense of renewal and energize spaces or designs. Mint is frequently used in branding and packaging for products related to health, wellness, and nature. Its light and airy nature is often utilized to convey a sense of purity and naturalness. When used in combination with other colors, mint can create striking and visually appealing color schemes. It works well with neutral tones, such as white, gray, or beige, as it provides a fresh and clean contrast. Mint can also be paired with other pastel shades, such as lavender or peach, to create a soft and feminine aesthetic. Overall, mint is a versatile and refreshing color that brings a sense of tranquility and vitality to designs. Its associations with freshness, cleanliness, and new beginnings make it a popular choice in various design applications.

Love (Olive)

Olive is a color in the spectrum of hues that is regularly associated with the symbolism of love. As a significant component in color theory and design, olive holds various connotations and emotions that make it a popular choice for expressing affection, passion, and tenderness. In the realm of color theory, olive is typically classified as a tint or shade of green. It is created by mixing a warm shade of yellow with a dark hue of green. This combination results in a subtle, earthy tone that evokes a sense of tranquility and natural beauty. Olive can be described as a muted, dusty green that is often associated with the foliage of olive trees, which grow in Mediterranean regions. With regards to its symbolism in design, olive is often associated with the concept of love. It is frequently used to represent deep, unconditional affection, as well as characteristics such as harmony, renewal, and growth. The color can convey a sense of warmth and nurturing, making it an ideal choice for designs centered around familial love, romantic relationships, or friendship. Furthermore, olive is also linked to aspects of renewal and growth, making it appropriate for designs that express the blooming of love or the development of a relationship. As a color inspired by nature, olive is often used in designs that aim to evoke a sense of harmony and balance, reflecting the idea that love can provide a stable foundation in one's life. In summary, olive is a color that holds significant meaning in the realm of color theory and design. As a tint or shade of green, it symbolizes love, harmony, and growth. With its soothing and natural qualities, it is frequently chosen to represent the multifaceted aspects of love, from familial to romantic relationships, and convey a sense of warmth and tenderness.

Love (Orange)

Love, represented by the color orange, holds various implications in color theory and symbolism within the context of design. In color theory, orange is a secondary color created by combining equal parts of red and yellow. It is a warm, vibrant hue that often evokes feelings of enthusiasm, energy, and warmth. When it comes to color symbolism in design, orange is associated with different meanings, which can vary depending on cultural and personal interpretations. In general, orange is commonly perceived as a color that represents joy, creativity, and excitement. It is often used to grab attention and create a sense of positivity and liveliness.

Love (Peach)

Love (Peach) is a color that belongs to the orange family and is used in color theory and color symbolism in design to represent various concepts related to love and emotions. In color theory, peach is created by mixing various amounts of orange, red, and white. It is often seen as a softer and more delicate version of the vibrant orange. Peach has a warm and inviting nature, emanating a sense of comfort and familiarity. It is considered a positive and uplifting color, evoking feelings of happiness, joy, and contentment. When it comes to color symbolism in design, peach is often associated with love, romance, and affection. It symbolizes the gentle and nurturing side of love, rather than the passionate and intense aspects represented by red. Peach is frequently used in contexts where a softer and more subtle expression of love is desired, such as wedding invitations, romantic-themed advertisements, and greeting cards for loved ones. Furthermore, peach is also linked to innocence, purity, and youthfulness. It can convey a sense of innocence and naivety often associated with young love and the early stages of relationships. Peach is commonly used in designs targeting a younger audience or aiming to create a youthful and playful atmosphere. In addition to its connotations of love and innocence, peach can also represent femininity and femininity-associated concepts. Soft, delicate, and tender, peach is often utilized in designs targeting women or projects related to femininity, such as beauty and fashion products, spa treatments, or wellness brands. Overall, love (peach) is a color that holds various meanings and associations in color theory and color symbolism in design. Its warm and inviting nature, coupled with its connotations of love, innocence, and femininity, make it a versatile option for designers aiming to evoke emotions and create a specific atmosphere in their creations.

Love (Periwinkle)

In color theory, love (periwinkle) is a shade of blue that combines elements of both blue and purple. It is characterized by its pale and delicate hue, resembling the color of the periwinkle flower. Love periwinkle belongs to the cool color family and is often associated with feelings of calmness, femininity, and tranquility. In the context of color symbolism in design, love periwinkle carries various meanings and connotations. It represents love, compassion, and tenderness, reflecting the gentle and nurturing aspects of relationships. It is often used to convey a sense of romance, affection, and intimacy in designs related to wedding invitations, Valentine's Day cards, and other romantic themes.

Love (Pink)

Love (Pink) In color theory and color symbolism in design, the color love (pink) represents a range of emotions, characteristics, and concepts. Pink is a softer variation of red, often associated with femininity, compassion, tenderness, and sensuality. It is a color that evokes warmth, affection, and nurturing qualities. Pink, being a combination of red and white, inherits some of the energetic and passionate attributes of red while also adopting the purity and tranquility of white. It is considered a calming and non-threatening color, often associated with love, romance, and affectionate feelings. Pink is commonly used to represent love and tenderness in various contexts, including in visual design, branding, and communication. When used in design, the color love (pink) can have different effects and convey various meanings. Its association with femininity makes it a popular choice in products targeting women and girls. It is often used in branding related to beauty, fashion, and health industries to create a sense of delicacy and elegance. The softness and warmth of pink can also communicate a sense of care and understanding, making it suitable for designs related to healthcare, counseling, and support services. Pink is commonly used as a background color in design to evoke a soothing and calming atmosphere. Its gentle nature makes it appealing for creating visually attractive and harmonious compositions. It can be combined with other colors to create contrast or highlight specific elements within a design. For example, pairing pink with darker shades, such as deep purples or blues, can create a dramatic effect, while combining it with pastel colors can result in a more playful and cheerful composition. In color symbolism, love (pink) is also associated with youthfulness, innocence, and sweetness. It can evoke feelings of nostalgia and remind individuals of carefree and joyful moments. The color pink has been used to represent love and affection for centuries, often being associated with gestures of romance and expressions of deep affection.

Love (Red)

Love (Red) in the context of color theory and color symbolism in design represents passion, romance, and desire. Red is a warm and intense color that evokes strong emotions and is often associated with love and affection. It is a powerful color that demands attention and can stimulate energy and excitement. In color theory, red is classified as a primary color. It is a dominant and powerful hue that captures attention and creates a focal point. In design, red is often used strategically to draw the viewer's eye and create a sense of urgency or importance. When used in the context of love and romance, red symbolizes passion, desire, and strong emotions. It is the color of romance and is often used to convey love and affection. Red roses, for example, have long been associated with love and are a popular symbol of romance. Red is also associated with energy and can create a sense of urgency or excitement. It is often used to grab attention and is commonly seen in advertising and marketing to evoke a strong response from viewers. Red is a color that stimulates the senses and can increase heart rate and blood pressure. In addition to its associations with love and passion, red can also have negative connotations. It can symbolize anger, danger, and aggression. In design, red should be used carefully and in moderation to avoid overwhelming the viewer or creating a negative emotional response. In summary, love (red) in the context of color theory and color symbolism in design represents passion, romance, and desire. It is a powerful and intense color that demands attention and creates strong emotional responses. When used strategically, red can effectively convey love and affection and create a sense of urgency or importance.

Love (Salmon)

Love (Salmon) - In the context of color theory and color symbolism in design, love (salmon) represents a warm and romantic hue that evokes feelings of affection, tenderness, and compassion. This specific shade of salmon embodies the essence of love and is often associated with intimate relationships, passion, and emotional connections. Within color theory, love (salmon) is classified as a warm color, created by combining orange and pink pigments. It is considered a lighter shade of salmon, leaning towards a pinkish hue. The color is often described as a soft and soothing tone, resembling the flesh of the salmon fish.

Love (Tangerine)

Tangerine is a vibrant and energetic hue that falls within the orange color family. It is characterized by its warm and rich tone, resembling the color of ripe tangerines. In color theory, tangerine is considered a secondary color, formed by mixing equal parts of red and yellow pigments. In the realm of color symbolism in design, tangerine embodies various meanings and connotations. It is often associated with enthusiasm, creativity, and spontaneity. Tangerine exudes a sense of excitement and positivity, making it a popular choice for designs that aim to grab attention or evoke a lively and energetic atmosphere. As a warm color, tangerine is believed to stimulate appetite and increase mental and physical energy. In the context of design, this makes it a great option for brands or industries related to food, health, and fitness. Its vibrant nature can help communicate a sense of freshness and liveliness, creating a strong visual impact. Furthermore, tangerine can also represent warmth, friendliness, and sociability. Its vibrant tone can convey a feeling of warmth and approachability, making it suitable for brands or designs that aim to create a welcoming and friendly ambiance. This color is often utilized in social and entertainment industries to attract attention and encourage social interaction. When used in design, tangerine can be utilized in various ways. It can be used as a dominant color to create a bold and dynamic look, or as an accent color to add vibrancy and liveliness to a design. Tangerine is commonly paired with contrasting colors such as blues or purples to create a visually stimulating composition. Overall, tangerine is a powerful and versatile color that can evoke a range of emotions and meanings in design. Its warm and vibrant nature makes it an excellent choice for designs that aim to communicate energy, enthusiasm, and friendliness.

Love (Teal)

The color teal, in the context of color theory and color symbolism in design, represents a unique combination of blue and green. It is often described as a medium to dark greenish-blue hue that exudes qualities of both its constituent colors. In color theory, teal is categorized as a tertiary color, resulting from the mixture of primary blue and secondary green in varying proportions.

This particular blend gives teal a balanced and harmonious appearance, making it a popular choice for designers seeking a calming and soothing effect in their work. Being a color that embodies elements of both blue and green, teal carries the symbolism associated with these two colors as well. Blue is traditionally associated with stability, depth, and tranquility, while green represents growth, renewal, and nature. When combined, teal often symbolizes a harmonious balance between stability and growth, bringing about a sense of calmness and rejuvenation. Furthermore, teal is often linked to qualities such as sophistication, elegance, and refinement, making it a favored choice in various design contexts. It is frequently used in fashion, interior design, and graphic design to convey a sense of luxury and sophistication. Teal can be utilized as a dominant color in a design to create a strong visual impact or used as an accent color to add depth and interest to a composition. In branding and marketing, teal is frequently employed to evoke a sense of trust, reliability, and professionalism. Many corporations and organizations utilize teal in their logos and branding materials to convey a sense of credibility and dependability to their target audience. In summary, teal is a visually pleasing and versatile color that combines the calming qualities of blue with the vibrant energy of green. Its unique blend of hues gives it a sense of balance and harmony, making it an excellent choice for designers seeking to evoke a sense of tranquility, sophistication, and reliability in their work.

Love (Turquoise)

Turquoise is a color that holds significance in color theory and color symbolism in design. It is a striking shade of blue-green that is often associated with feelings of calmness, tranquility, and spiritual healing. In the realm of color theory, turquoise falls under the blues and greens category, as it is a combination of blue and green pigments. When it comes to color symbolism in design, turquoise is often seen as a symbol of emotional balance and communication. It is believed to have a soothing and calming effect on the human mind, encouraging clear and open communication. This makes it an ideal choice for designs that aim to portray harmony and serenity, such as spas, wellness centers, and meditation spaces.

Love (White)

The color white in color theory and color symbolism in design is associated with the concept of love. In color theory, white is considered achromatic, meaning it has no hue of its own. It is formed by the combination of all the colors in the visible spectrum. In terms of color symbolism, white often represents purity, innocence, and goodness. It is often associated with weddings, as brides traditionally wear white to symbolize purity. White is also commonly used to represent cleanliness and sterility, which is why it is often used in medical settings.

Love (Yellow)

Love (Yellow) is a color in color theory that represents warmth, happiness, and positivity. It is a bold and vibrant yellow shade that is commonly used in design to evoke feelings of joy, enthusiasm, and optimism. Love (Yellow) is often associated with brightness, energy, and cheerfulness, making it a popular choice in various forms of artistic expression, including painting, interior design, and graphic design. In color symbolism, Love (Yellow) is closely linked to the sun, which is not only a powerful source of light and warmth but also a universal symbol of life, growth, and vitality. In design, Love (Yellow) is often used as an accent color to add a touch of vibrancy and playfulness to compositions. It can be employed to grab attention, create contrast, or highlight important elements within a visual composition. Its high visibility and ability to stand out make it an excellent choice for call-to-action buttons, signage, or information that needs immediate attention. Love (Yellow) can also be used to convey a sense of happiness and positivity, making it an ideal choice for branding or packaging in industries such as food, fashion, or wellness.

Loyalty (Blue)

Loyalty (Blue) is a color that is widely used in color theory and color symbolism in design. In color theory, blue is classified as one of the primary colors and is considered a cool color. It is often associated with feelings of calmness, tranquility, and stability. In terms of color symbolism, blue is commonly linked to the concept of loyalty. Loyalty is the quality of being faithful, trustworthy, and committed. It encompasses a sense of allegiance, reliability, and dedication. Blue symbolizes these traits and evokes a sense of trust and dependability.

Luxury (Black)

Luxury (Black) refers to the specific shade of black that is associated with luxury and elegance in the context of color theory and color symbolism in design. In color theory, black is often seen as a color that represents power, sophistication, and formality. It is commonly used in design to create a sense of elegance and luxury. Luxury (Black) takes this concept one step further by referring to a specific shade of black that exudes a higher level of opulence and exclusivity.

Luxury (Gold)

Gold, within the context of color theory and color symbolism in design, represents luxury. This rich, vibrant hue is associated with wealth, prosperity, and opulence. It exudes a sense of extravagance and elegance, making it a popular choice in high-end and luxury branding.

Luxury (Purple)

Luxury (Purple) is a color often associated with opulence, wealth, and extravagance. It is a deep and rich hue that exudes a sense of grandeur and sophistication. In color theory and color symbolism, the use of purple, particularly in its darker shades, signifies a sense of luxury and prestige. In design, luxury (purple) is commonly used to create an atmosphere of elegance and exclusivity. It is often employed in high-end branding, such as luxury fashion houses or high-priced products, to evoke a sense of sophistication and allure. The color purple has long been associated with royalty and nobility, dating back to ancient civilizations where the dye used to create purple fabric was extremely rare and expensive, reserved only for the ruling class.

Magic (Purple)

Magic (Purple)Magic, in the context of color theory and color symbolism in design, refers to the color purple. Purple is a secondary color that is created by mixing blue and red. It is often associated with creativity, mystery, and spirituality.

Managers For Color Palettes

Managers for Color Palettes are individuals responsible for selecting, organizing, and coordinating cohesive combinations of colors, known as color palettes, in the context of color theory and color symbolism in design. Color palettes play a crucial role in visual communication and aesthetics, shaping the overall perception, mood, and meaning of a design. In color theory, which is the study of how colors interact and influence each other, color palettes serve as a strategic tool for creating harmonious and visually pleasing compositions. They are typically composed of a primary color, its complementary color, and variations of the two, such as tints (lighter versions) and shades (darker versions). Managers for Color Palettes actively consider elements like hue (color), saturation (intensity), and value (lightness or darkness) to curate palettes that evoke specific emotions or support the desired message of the design. Color symbolism, on the other hand, explores the psychological and cultural associations that different colors hold. Managers for Color Palettes leverage these associations to visually communicate specific ideas or concepts. For example, warm colors like red and orange may be used to convey energy, passion, or warmth, while cool colors like blue and green are often associated with calmness, reliability, or nature. By understanding the symbolic significance of colors, managers can create palettes that align with the intended meaning of the design. The role of Managers for Color Palettes goes beyond simply selecting colors. They must also ensure that the chosen palette is cohesive and visually balanced. This involves considering factors like color contrast, color harmony, and the overall hierarchy or emphasis within the design. Additionally, managers need to be mindful of color accessibility and ensure that the chosen palette is inclusive for individuals with visual impairments. Ultimately, Managers for Color Palettes are entrusted with the task of curating color combinations that effectively communicate the desired message, provoke emotional responses, and enhance the overall visual appeal of a design. Through their knowledge of color theory and color symbolism, they play a vital role in creating impactful and engaging visual experiences.

Material Design Color Apps

Material Design Color Apps are a set of applications that adhere to the principles of Material Design, a design language developed by Google. In the context of color theory and color symbolism in design, Material Design Color Apps provide a standardized set of colors that can be used in various digital design projects. Color theory is the study of how colors interact with each other and how they can be used to create aesthetically pleasing and harmonious designs. It encompasses various aspects such as color harmonies, color contrasts, and color symbolism. Color symbolism refers to the meaning and emotions associated with different colors. For example, red is often associated with power and passion, while blue is associated with calmness and trust. Material Design Color Apps provide a wide range of colors that designers can choose from, ensuring consistency and harmony in their designs. The color palette consists of primary colors, secondary colors, and accent colors. Primary colors are the base colors that form the foundation of the design, while secondary colors are derived from a combination of primary colors. Accent colors are used to highlight specific elements and create visual interest. In addition to the standardized color palette, Material Design Color Apps also provide tools and resources for designers to explore and experiment with colors. This includes color pickers, which allow designers to select specific colors and obtain their respective hexadecimal values. These hexadecimal values are essential for ensuring consistency in color usage across different design elements and platforms. By adhering to Material Design Color Apps, designers can create visually appealing and meaningful designs. The standardized color palette ensures consistency, while the tools and resources provided allow for creative exploration. Additionally, the use of color theory and color symbolism helps designers convey specific emotions and messages through their designs. Overall, Material Design Color Apps provide designers with a comprehensive set of colors and resources that promote consistency, creativity, and meaningful communication through design.

Material Design Color Palettes

Material Design Color Palettes are a set of predefined color schemes that follow the principles of color theory and symbolism in design. These palettes consist of a curated collection of colors that work harmoniously together to create visually appealing and meaningful designs. Color theory is the study of how colors interact and influence each other in various contexts. It explores the relationships between colors on the color wheel, such as complementary, analogous, and triadic color schemes. Material Design Color Palettes are carefully crafted to adhere to these principles and provide designers with a comprehensive selection of colors that can be easily combined to achieve aesthetically pleasing compositions.

Material Design Color Resources

Material Design Color Resources refer to a collection of colors and color palettes that adhere to the principles of material design. Material design is a design language developed by Google that aims to create a cohesive and visually appealing user experience across different platforms and devices. Color theory is the study of how colors interact and how they can be used to convey meaning and provoke emotion in design. It is based on the understanding of the color wheel, color harmony, and the properties of color such as hue, saturation, and value. In the context of design, colors play a crucial role in influencing the perception and understanding of an interface or product. They can be used to create a visual hierarchy, highlight important elements, and establish the overall tone and personality of a design. Color symbolism, on the other hand, is the assignment of meanings or associations to different colors. These associations can be culturally influenced or subjective, and they can vary depending on individual experiences and perceptions. When it comes to material design color resources, designers can leverage predefined color palettes and guidelines provided by Google to ensure consistency and coherence in their designs. These color resources are carefully chosen to support accessibility, ensure proper contrast, and provide a harmonious color palette. In material design, colors are classified into different categories such as primary, secondary, and accent colors. Primary colors are the base colors used throughout the design, while secondary colors are used for secondary elements and accents. Accent colors are used to emphasize specific elements or interactions. Designers can select colors from these predefined palettes or create their own custom palettes based on the principles of material design. By using these color resources effectively, designers can create visually appealing and meaningful designs that enhance the user experience and convey the desired message or brand identity.

Material Design Color Tools

Material Design Color Tools are a set of resources and guidelines provided by Google to assist designers in choosing and implementing colors in their designs. These tools are based on color theory and aim to enhance the overall visual experience by leveraging the principles of color symbolism. Color theory is an important aspect of design that deals with the study of colors and their visual impact. It explores the ways in which colors can evoke emotions, communicate messages, and create visual harmony. In design, colors are not chosen randomly; they are selected and combined thoughtfully to convey a specific mood or message. Color symbolism, on the other hand, refers to the cultural and psychological associations that people have with different colors. Colors can have different meanings and interpretations across various cultures and contexts. For example, red is often associated with passion and energy, while blue is associated with tranquility and trust. By understanding color symbolism, designers can leverage these associations to enhance the intended message of their designs. Material Design Color Tools provide designers with a comprehensive set of resources to assist them in the color selection process. The tools include color palettes, color picker, and color contrast analyzer, among others. These resources help designers in creating visually pleasing and accessible designs while adhering to the principles of color theory and symbolism. The color palettes offered by Material Design Color Tools are carefully curated sets of colors that work well together. These palettes are designed to create harmony and visual balance in a design, taking into consideration factors such as hue, saturation, and brightness. Designers can select a palette that aligns with the desired mood or message of their design and use it as a starting point for their color scheme. The color picker tool allows designers to choose specific colors from a wide range of options. It provides a visual interface where designers can explore different color combinations and variations. The tool also offers features such as color customization and accessibility checks, ensuring that the chosen colors meet the required contrast and visibility standards. The color contrast analyzer is another valuable tool provided by Material Design Color Tools. It helps designers ensure that the text and visual elements in their design have sufficient contrast for readability and accessibility. The analyzer provides color contrast ratios and recommendations for color adjustments, enabling designers to create inclusive designs that are accessible to all users. In conclusion, Material Design Color Tools are valuable resources for designers to leverage color theory and symbolism in their designs. By utilizing these tools, designers can create visually appealing and meaningful designs that effectively communicate their intended messages.

Measurement Tools For Spectral Colors

Spectral colors are a fundamental aspect of color theory and play a significant role in color symbolism in design. Measurement tools for spectral colors are essential in accurately quantifying and understanding these colors in various contexts. One commonly used measurement tool for spectral colors is a spectrophotometer. A spectrophotometer measures the intensity of light at different wavelengths within the electromagnetic spectrum. It can provide precise numerical values for the spectral colors present in an object or image. This tool is particularly useful in color theory as it allows for the analysis of individual wavelengths and their corresponding colors.

Metallic Colors

Metallic colors, in the context of color theory and color symbolism in design, refer to a range of colors that mimic the appearance of metals. These colors typically have a shiny or reflective quality, similar to that of metals such as gold, silver, bronze, or copper. Metallic colors are often used in design to convey a sense of luxury, opulence, and sophistication. They have a unique ability to add depth, richness, and glamour to any visual composition. Their association with precious metals, which have historically been used as symbols of wealth and status, makes them particularly well-suited for creating designs that exude elegance and prestige.

Modernity (Silver)

Modernity (Silver) in color theory and color symbolism refers to a shade of gray that is

146

associated with contemporary design and the concept of progress and innovation. It represents the idea of embracing new and forward-thinking ideas while combining them with elegance and sophistication. Silver is often used in modern design to create a sleek and minimalist aesthetic. It is commonly used in interior design, architecture, and graphic design to evoke a sense of modernity and sophistication. The color silver is often associated with futuristic and technological imagery, such as sleek metallic surfaces and high-tech gadgets.

Modesty (Gray)

Modesty (Gray) in color theory and color symbolism refers to a specific shade of gray that embodies the concept of modesty, humility, and simplicity. In the context of color theory, gray is created by mixing equal amounts of black and white. It is often seen as a neutral color, and it lacks strong emotional associations or symbolism. However, when exploring the symbolism of different shades of gray, Modesty Gray stands out as a particular hue that conveys a specific meaning.

Money (Green)

Money (Green): In the context of color theory and color symbolism in design, the color green is often associated with money, wealth, and financial prosperity. Green is commonly used to represent currency in many countries, including the United States where dollar bills are predominantly green in color. In color theory, green is classified as a secondary color, created by mixing blue and yellow pigments. It is considered a cool color, symbolizing freshness, growth, and nature. However, when it comes to representing money, green has acquired a specific connotation over time.

Monochromatic Color Palette Generators

A monochromatic color palette generator is a tool used in color theory and design to create a harmonious color scheme consisting of multiple shades of the same color. In the context of design, colors play a crucial role in evoking emotions, conveying messages, and creating visual impact. Understanding color theory and symbolism is essential in creating effective and aesthetically pleasing designs. Color theory explains how colors are perceived and how they interact with each other. A monochromatic color scheme is based on a single hue, but with variations in brightness, saturation, and value. By using different shades, tints, and tones of a single color, designers can achieve a cohesive and balanced look in their designs.

Monochromatic Color Scheme Generators

Monochromatic color scheme generators are tools used in color theory and design to aid in the selection and creation of coherent color palettes that consist of varying shades, tints, or tones of a single color. In the field of color theory, a monochromatic color scheme refers to a palette that is derived from a single base color. The base color is then modified by changing its saturation, value, or brightness to create a range of lighter or darker variations of the original hue.

Monochromatic Color Schemes

Monochromatic color schemes in the context of color theory and color symbolism in design refer to the use of a single base color, along with its various shades, tints, and tones, to create a cohesive and harmonious visual composition. This color scheme is based on the idea of using variations of a single color to achieve a unified and cohesive design. It creates a sense of simplicity and elegance while maintaining visual interest and balance. The monochromatic color scheme is often associated with a peaceful and calming aesthetic. It is commonly used in spaces where a serene and tranquil atmosphere is desired, such as bedrooms or meditation rooms. The use of different shades and tints of a single color can create depth and visual interest without overwhelming the viewer. In addition to its soothing qualities, the monochromatic color scheme can also be used to evoke specific emotions and convey symbolic meanings. Different colors have different associations and carry their own symbolic significance. By choosing a particular base color and using its variations, designers can tap into these symbolic meanings and create a desired emotional response in the viewer. For example, a monochromatic color scheme using various shades of blue can be used to create a sense of calmness and stability. Blue is often associated with tranquility and trust, making it a popular choice for corporate branding and healthcare settings. On the other hand, a monochromatic color scheme using shades of red can evoke strong emotions such as passion and intensity. Red is commonly associated with energy and excitement, making it a suitable choice for creating a sense of dynamism and urgency in designs. Overall, monochromatic color schemes offer a versatile and effective approach to color selection and design. By using a single base color and exploring its various shades, tints, and tones, designers can create visually appealing compositions that convey specific emotions and symbolisms.

Monochromatic Colors

Monochromatic colors refer to a color scheme consisting of variations of a single hue. In the context of color theory, a monochromatic palette is created by selecting shades, tints, and tones of a single color. This creates a harmonious and soothing effect, as the colors share a common origin and therefore naturally complement each other. In design and visual arts, monochromatic colors are often used to convey a sense of simplicity, elegance, and unity. By employing different levels of saturation and brightness, designers can create depth and interest within a monochromatic composition.

Motivation (Salmon)

In color theory and color symbolism in design, motivation is a term used to define the color salmon. Salmon is a reddish-orange hue that combines elements of pink and orange, often resembling the color of the fish from which it derives its name. It is a warm color that is known for its vibrant and energetic nature. In color theory, salmon is classified as a tertiary color, which means it is created by mixing two primary colors (red and yellow) together with a secondary color (orange). This unique combination gives salmon its distinct appearance and makes it a versatile color to work with in design.

Muted Colors

Muted colors, in the context of color theory and color symbolism in design, refer to colors that have been desaturated or toned down, creating a more subtle and restrained palette. These colors are characterized by lower levels of saturation and brightness, resulting in a more muted or subdued appearance. When used in design, muted colors can evoke a sense of tranquility, sophistication, and understated elegance. They are often associated with minimalist and contemporary design styles. Muted colors can create a calm and serene atmosphere, making them suitable for spaces such as bedrooms, living rooms, or offices where a relaxed and peaceful ambiance is desired.

Mystery (Black)

Mystery (Black) - In the context of color theory and color symbolism in design, black is a captivating and enigmatic color that evokes a sense of mystery and intrigue. It is often associated with darkness, the unknown, and the hidden. Black holds different connotations in various cultures and contexts, but its universal symbolism is deeply rooted in its inherent qualities. In color theory, black is considered the absence of color – the complete absorption of light. It is not a color in the traditional sense but rather a shade that results from the absence or absorption of all visible light. Consequently, black is often used in design to create contrast and emphasize the other colors present. It can be used to enhance the impact of brighter hues or to create a minimalist monochromatic effect.

Mystery (Purple)

According to color theory, mystery (purple) is a hue that results from mixing blue and red. In the RGB color model, it is typically represented as a combination of blue and red with a higher concentration of blue. This color has a wavelength of approximately 380-450 nanometers and is often associated with enchantment, spirituality, and creativity. In the context of color symbolism in design, mystery (purple) carries various connotations. It is often linked to introspection, ambiguity, and the unknown. The deep and rich hue of purple can evoke a sense of mystery and intrigue, making it a popular choice in design to create an air of enigma.

Mysticism (Indigo)

148

Mysticism is a concept in color theory and color symbolism that refers to the color indigo. Indigo is a deep and intense shade of blue, often described as a dark purplish-blue or a deep midnight blue. In color theory, indigo is considered a mystical and spiritual color. It is associated with the third eye chakra, which is believed to be the center of intuition and higher consciousness. Indigo is believed to represent a deep connection to the spiritual realm and to promote spiritual awareness and enlightenment.

Naturalness (Brown)

Naturalness refers to the quality of being inherent or innate, closely related to the natural world and its various elements. In the context of color theory and color symbolism in design, naturalness pertains to the use of colors that are commonly found in nature, creating a sense of harmony and authenticity. Colors that are considered natural typically include earth tones such as browns, greens, and blues. These colors are frequently associated with the elements of the natural world, such as soil, plants, and water. The use of these colors in design can evoke a feeling of tranquility, balance, and grounding.

Nature (Green)

Nature (Green) is a color that represents the natural world and is often associated with growth, harmony, and renewal. In color theory, green is considered a secondary color, created by mixing equal parts of yellow and blue. It sits between these two colors on the color wheel, symbolizing a balance between warm and cool tones. In design, the color green is often used to convey a sense of tranquility, freshness, and vitality. It is commonly associated with nature, plants, and the environment. Green has a calming effect on the eyes and is often used in spaces where relaxation and rejuvenation are desired, such as bedrooms, spas, and healthcare facilities.

Neon Color Generators Online

Neon Color Generators Online are digital tools that allow designers and artists to create and explore a wide range of neon colors for use in their designs. In the context of color theory, neon colors are bright, vibrant hues that mimic the colors produced by neon gas in real-life neon lights. Color theory is a field of study that examines how colors interact with each other and how they are perceived by the human eye. It is an essential aspect of design as colors can evoke various emotions and convey symbolic meanings. In the realm of color symbolism, neon colors are often associated with energy, excitement, and modernity. They are used to create attention-grabbing designs and are commonly found in advertisements, fashion, and digital media.

Neon Color Generators

A neon color generator is a tool used in color theory and design to create vivid, bright, and intense colors known as neon colors. These colors are often used to evoke a sense of excitement, energy, and modernity. They can be used in a variety of design applications, including graphic design, web design, interior design, and fashion design. In color theory, neon colors are typically created using a combination of bright, highly saturated colors such as electric blue, vibrant pink, neon green, and intense yellow. These colors are often associated with artificial light sources, such as neon signs, fluorescent lights, and LED displays. Neon colors have a luminous quality that is highly visible, even in low light conditions.

Neon Color Palette Creators

A neon color palette creator is a tool or method used in color theory and design to generate a set of colors that are vibrant, highly saturated, and reminiscent of neon lights. In color theory, neon colors are considered to be part of the fluorescent color family, characterized by their intense brightness and the ability to emit light under certain conditions. These colors are often associated with energy, excitement, and modernity. They are highly visible and can draw attention quickly. In design, the use of neon colors can have various meanings and symbolisms. Here are some common interpretations: 1. Attention-Grabbing: Neon colors are vibrant and eye-catching, making them ideal for grabbing the viewer's attention. They can help highlight important elements or messages within a design. 2. Modern and Trendy: Neon colors are often associated with modernity and trendiness. They can give a design a contemporary and fresh look, particularly when used in combination with sleek and minimalist elements. 3. High Energy:

Neon colors are energetic and dynamic, evoking a sense of excitement and liveliness. They can be used to create a sense of urgency or to convey a high-energy atmosphere. 4. Retro and Nostalgic: Neon colors are reminiscent of the neon signs and lights popular in the mid-20th century. They can be used to create a retro or nostalgic aesthetic, invoking a sense of nostalgia or a throwback to a particular era. 5. Playful and Fun: Neon colors often have a playful and fun connotation. They can be used to create a lighthearted and whimsical mood in a design or to appeal to a younger audience. A neon color palette creator helps designers and artists generate color schemes that embody these qualities. By providing a range of highly saturated and vibrant colors, it allows for the exploration of different color combinations and harmonies that can effectively convey desired meanings and emotions.

Neon Color Palette Editors

A Neon color palette editor is a tool that allows designers and artists to create and customize color schemes using neon or fluorescent colors. In the context of color theory, neon colors are highly saturated and vibrant hues that appear to emit light or glow, mimicking the appearance of neon lights. Neon colors are known for their eye-catching and attention-grabbing qualities, making them popular choices in design and branding. They are often associated with energy, excitement, and modernity. Neon color palettes can evoke a sense of liveliness and playfulness, making them well-suited for designs that aim to capture the viewer's attention. Color symbolism plays a significant role in design, as colors can convey specific emotions, ideas, or associations. Different cultures and contexts may assign different meanings to colors, and it is essential for designers to be aware of these associations when using neon colors in their work. In general, neon colors have a futuristic and technological connotation. They are often used to symbolize innovation, modernity, and the digital world. Neon green, for example, is commonly associated with energy and growth, while neon pink is often linked to femininity and boldness. Creating a neon color palette involves selecting and combining neon colors in a harmonious and visually appealing way. A neon color palette editor provides tools and controls to adjust the saturation, brightness, and contrast of neon colors, allowing users to create custom color schemes. With a neon color palette editor, designers can experiment with different neon color combinations to find the perfect balance between vibrant and harmonious. They can create gradients, color blocks, or patterns using neon colors, and apply these color schemes to various design elements such as logos, illustrations, or user interfaces. In conclusion, a neon color palette editor is a valuable tool for designers and artists who want to incorporate the bold and attention-grabbing qualities of neon colors into their work. By understanding the principles of color theory and color symbolism, designers can create visually striking designs that effectively communicate their intended message.

Neon Colors

Neon colors, in the context of color theory and color symbolism in design, refer to a specific set of highly saturated and intensely bright colors that mimic the hues seen in neon lights. These colors are known for their vivid and eye-catching properties, making them popular choices in various design applications. Neon colors are often associated with energy, vibrancy, and a sense of modernity. They create a visual impact and tend to draw attention, making them suitable for designs that aim to stand out or evoke a particular mood. In color theory, neon colors are classified as highly saturated, meaning they have a high intensity and appear extremely vibrant. Their saturation is achieved through the use of fluorescent pigments or dyes, which emit a strong glow-like effect when exposed to ultraviolet light. In design, neon colors are commonly used to create contrast or to highlight specific elements. They are particularly effective when used sparingly or as accents in combination with more subdued colors. Neon colors can bring a sense of excitement and playfulness to a design, making them popular choices in industries such as advertising, entertainment, and fashion. While neon colors can create a visually striking impact, they also come with certain considerations. Due to their high saturation, they can easily overwhelm a design if used excessively. It is important to use neon colors judiciously and balance them with other colors to create a harmonious composition. Additionally, neon colors can have cultural connotations as they are often associated with specific eras or nostalgic references. Designers should be mindful of the context in which neon colors are used to avoid inadvertently conveying unintentional messages.

Neutral Colors

150

Neutral colors, in the context of color theory and color symbolism in design, refer to a range of hues that are not easily classified as primary or secondary colors. These colors typically have low saturation and can be created by mixing complementary colors or by adding black, white, or gray to a color. Neutral colors include shades of black, white, gray, beige, tan, and brown. They are often seen as calming, timeless, and versatile, making them a popular choice in various design applications.

Neutrality (Beige)

Neutrality (Beige) is a concept derived from color theory and color symbolism in design. In the realm of color theory, neutrality refers to the achromatic or near-achromatic colors that lack strong chromatic content. Beige, categorized as a neutral color, embodies the properties of neutrality in its light sandy hue. From a color symbolism perspective, beige represents neutrality and balance. It is commonly associated with calmness, stability, and reliability. The color evokes feelings of warmth, comfort, and approachability while maintaining a sense of serenity and sophistication.

Neutrality (Gray)

Neutrality, also known as gray, is a concept in color theory and symbolism in design that represents a state of balance, calmness, and impartiality. It is the absence of strong color or hue and is often associated with neutrality, practicality, and modesty. In the context of color theory, neutrality refers to shades of gray that are achieved by mixing equal amounts of black and white. Gray is considered a neutral color because it does not evoke strong emotions or have overwhelming connotations. Instead, it provides a sense of stability and can serve as a backdrop to other colors, allowing them to stand out more prominently. Neutrality is often used in design to create a visually pleasing and harmonious composition.

Nobility (Purple)

Nobility, often symbolized by the color purple, is a concept in color theory and design that represents a sense of royalty, power, luxury, and elegance. In the realm of color symbolism, purple is associated with these qualities due to its historical association with kings, queens, and other members of the aristocracy. In color theory, purple is created by combining the colors red and blue, which are on opposite sides of the color wheel. This combination represents a harmonious balance between warm and cool tones, creating a sense of richness and depth. Purple is often described as a complex color, as it can range in hue from a pale lavender to a deep, regal shade.

Nurturing (Olive)

Nurturing in the context of color theory and color symbolism in design refers to the representation or expression of care, support, and protection through the use of the color olive. Olive is a shade of green that combines the calmness of green with the warmth and richness of brown. It is often associated with nature, growth, and fertility. Olive symbolizes harmony, balance, and renewal, providing a sense of stability and tranquility. In color theory, it is considered a neutral color, meaning it can easily coordinate with other colors without overpowering them.

Opacity Control Software

Opacity Control Software is a software tool that allows designers to adjust the transparency or opacity of colors used in their design projects. It is used in the context of color theory and color symbolism in design to create harmonious and meaningful visual compositions. Color theory is the study of how colors interact and can be used effectively in different design applications. It explores the visual effects of combining colors and how they can evoke certain emotions or convey specific messages. Opacity control software is a valuable tool for designers as it enables them to manipulate the transparency of colors, allowing for more flexibility and creativity in their designs. In design, color symbolism refers to the use of color to express and communicate certain ideas or concepts. Different colors have various associations and meanings, and these can be enhanced or altered by adjusting their opacity. Opacity control software provides designers with the ability to subtly or dramatically change the intensity of colors, influencing their symbolic impact on the viewer. The software usually offers a variety of opacity controls, such as sliders or numerical input, allowing designers to adjust the transparency of colors in a precise and controlled manner. By making colors more transparent, they can create softer and more delicate visual effects. By increasing opacity, colors become more vivid and vibrant, demanding attention and conveying a sense of strength and assertiveness. In addition to color theory and symbolism, opacity control software finds utility in practical design applications. It can be used to create layered compositions, where certain elements within a design are made partially transparent to add depth and dimension. It also facilitates the blending of colors, enabling smooth transitions between different hues and shades. Overall, opacity control software is an essential tool for designers working with color theory and color symbolism. By adjusting the transparency of colors, designers can create visually compelling compositions that evoke specific emotions or messages. This software empowers designers to harness the full potential of color in their design projects, enhancing their ability to communicate effectively through visuals.

Opacity Control Solutions

Opacity control solutions refer to the techniques and methods used in color theory and design to adjust the transparency or visibility of colors. These solutions enable designers to manipulate the opacity or opacity level of colors, allowing them to create specific visual effects and convey symbolic meanings in their designs. In color theory, colors are often associated with various emotions, moods, and symbolic meanings. By adjusting the opacity of colors, designers can enhance or diminish the impact and perception of these symbolic meanings. For example, a fully opaque and vibrant red color may symbolize passion and energy, while a partially transparent and muted red color may represent subtlety and delicacy.

Opacity Control Tools

Opacity Control Tools are tools that allow designers to adjust the level of transparency or opaqueness of a color in their designs. In the context of color theory and color symbolism in design, opacity control tools play a crucial role in creating aesthetically pleasing and meaningful visual compositions. In color theory, opacity refers to the degree to which a color allows light to pass through it. By adjusting the opacity of a color, designers can manipulate the intensity and depth of that color within their designs. Opacity control tools offer a range of options to modify the transparency of a color, giving designers the flexibility to achieve the desired effect. In the realm of color symbolism, opacity control tools can be used to convey specific meanings or emotions. Colors often carry symbolic associations, and adjusting their transparency can further enhance the intended message. For example, reducing the opacity of a vibrant red color may evoke a sense of mystery or subtlety, while increasing the opacity can convey boldness and passion. Opacity control tools are particularly valuable in the fields of graphic design, web design, and user interface design. They allow designers to create layers and overlays of colors, giving depth and dimension to their work. By strategically adjusting the transparency of different colors, designers can achieve visually appealing effects such as blending, shading, and highlighting. In summary, opacity control tools are essential for manipulating the transparency or opaqueness of colors in design. With these tools, designers can harness the power of color theory and color symbolism to create visually engaging and conceptually meaningful compositions. Whether it is adjusting the depth of a color or conveying specific emotions through opacity, these tools enable designers to create impactful and visually stunning designs.

Opacity

Opacity, in the context of color theory and color symbolism in design, refers to the level of transparency or the degree to which an object or color allows light to pass through it. It is a fundamental concept that influences the visual perception and emotional impact of colors within a design composition. Opacity can be understood as the opposite of transparency. It describes how much an object or color blocks or obscures the underlying elements. It is often represented as a percentage, ranging from 0% (completely transparent) to 100% (completely opaque).

Openness (Teal)

Openness is a characteristic of the color teal within the context of color theory and symbolism in design. Teal is a unique combination of blue and green, resulting in a color that is often associated with calmness, tranquility, and stability. It is a color that promotes a sense of peace and introspection, inviting individuals to relax and reflect. When used in design, teal can evoke feelings of openness and expansiveness. It has a soothing and refreshing quality that can create a sense of spaciousness and freedom. Teal can be utilized to create an atmosphere of tranquility and serenity, making it an ideal choice for environments where relaxation or introspection is desired, such as meditation rooms or spas.

Optimism (Apricot)

Optimism is a color that falls within the apricot spectrum of colors in color theory. Apricot is a pale orange color that is often associated with feelings of positivity and hope. In color symbolism, optimism is often used to create a sense of warmth and happiness in design. When used in design, the color optimism can evoke feelings of joy and positivity. It is commonly used to create a welcoming and friendly atmosphere. Due to its pale orange hue, optimism is less intense than other shades of orange, making it less overwhelming while still conveying the positive energy commonly associated with the color orange.

Optimism (Lemon)

Optimism is a color term that is often associated with the vibrant hue of lemon in the context of color theory and color symbolism in design. Lemon, a shade of yellow, is commonly used to convey a sense of positivity, hope, and cheerfulness, making it an ideal representation of optimism in the visual arts. In color theory, yellow is considered a warm color that is associated with energy, happiness, and joy. The brightness and freshness of lemon further intensify these connotations, making it a lively and uplifting choice for designers aiming to evoke feelings of optimism in their work. The color lemon is often utilized in a variety of design elements, such as logos, packaging, and advertisements, to create a visually appealing and positive impact on viewers.

Optimism (Periwinkle)

Optimism, in the context of color theory and color symbolism in design, refers to the representation of positivity, hope, and happiness through the use of the periwinkle color. Periwinkle, a light shade of blue with a tinge of purple, exudes a sense of calmness and tranquility. It is often associated with the clear blue sky or the calming waves of the ocean. In color psychology, blue is known to create a sense of serenity, while purple is often associated with luxury and creativity. Thus, periwinkle combines these attributes, resulting in a color that represents optimism.

Optimism (Yellow)

Optimism is a color in the context of color theory and color symbolism in design. It is represented by the color yellow. Yellow is often associated with optimism and happiness. It is a bright and energetic color that can evoke feelings of joy and positivity. In color theory, yellow is considered a warm color, along with red and orange. Warm colors are generally associated with energy, excitement, and happiness.

Pantone Color Guides

The Pantone Color Guides are an essential tool in the field of color theory and color symbolism in design. Developed by the Pantone company, these guides provide a standardized system for identifying, communicating, and reproducing colors accurately. In the realm of color theory, the Pantone Color Guides serve as a comprehensive reference for color relationships, harmonies, and contrasts. They categorize colors into distinct families, enabling designers to choose hues that work well together. This knowledge helps create visually pleasing compositions and ensures that colors evoke the desired emotions or convey specific messages. Furthermore, the Pantone Color Guides are instrumental in color symbolism, aiding designers in selecting colors that align with the intended meanings or associations. Each color holds unique symbolism and cultural connotations, and the guides provide insights into these symbolisms. For instance, red often represents passion or energy, while blue is often associated with calmness or trust. The Pantone Color Guides help designers make informed decisions about incorporating colors that

153

resonate with their intended audience. In addition to color theory and symbolism, the Pantone Color Guides are particularly useful in achieving color consistency and accuracy across various design applications. The guides display each color with an associated code, enabling designers to communicate their color choices precisely to printers, manufacturers, and other stakeholders. This helps ensure that the intended color is reproduced accurately in print, textiles, plastics, and other materials, regardless of the equipment or technology used. Moreover, the Pantone Color Guides are periodically updated to reflect emerging color trends and innovations. Designers can stay up-to-date with the latest color palettes and incorporate them into their designs to maintain relevance and appeal. By regularly expanding their color library, Pantone supports designers in creating contemporary and visually impactful designs. Overall, the Pantone Color Guides are an indispensable tool in color theory and color symbolism in design. They provide designers with a standardized system for selecting colors, understanding their meanings, ensuring consistency, and staying informed about color trends. With their guidance, designers can effectively utilize colors to create visually harmonious, emotionally resonant, and culturally relevant designs.

Pantone Color Matching System

The Pantone Color Matching System is a standardized color system used in various industries, particularly in design and printing. It was developed by Pantone, a company known for its color matching products and services. This system consists of a set of standardized colors that have been assigned specific numbers and names, making it easy to communicate and reproduce colors accurately across different mediums and platforms. The Pantone system is widely used in color specification, color identification, and color matching processes. In the field of color theory, the Pantone Color Matching System serves as a valuable tool for designers, artists, and manufacturers. It provides a comprehensive range of colors that can be used as references for creating harmonious color schemes or expressing specific meanings and emotions in visual communication. Color symbolism plays a significant role in design, as different colors have different associations and connotations. The Pantone system enables designers to select colors with precision and confidence based on their intended symbolism. For example, the color red may symbolize passion and energy, while blue may represent tranquility and trust. By using the Pantone system, designers can accurately reproduce these symbolic colors in their artwork or designs. Moreover, the Pantone Color Matching System also aids in the consistency of colors across different materials and production processes. It ensures color accuracy when translating digital designs into printed materials, such as brochures, packaging, and signage. This is crucial for maintaining brand identity and ensuring that colors appear consistent and cohesive across various platforms. Overall, the Pantone Color Matching System is an essential tool in the realm of color theory and design. It provides a reliable and standardized way to communicate and reproduce colors accurately, enabling designers to create visually appealing and meaningful compositions. Whether in graphic design, fashion, or industrial design, the Pantone system plays a vital role in selecting and matching colors for various creative applications.

Pantone Color Swatch Libraries

The Pantone Color Swatch Libraries are sets of standardized colors, developed by the Pantone Color Institute, that are widely used in design and color theory. These libraries provide designers with a comprehensive range of colors to choose from, ensuring consistency and accuracy in their work. In color theory, colors are classified and organized based on their properties and how they are perceived. The Pantone Color Swatch Libraries follow this principle by categorizing colors into various systems, such as the Pantone Matching System (PMS) and the Pantone Fashion, Home + Interiors (FHI) system. These systems consist of thousands of color swatches, each identified by a unique code and name. The Pantone Matching System is primarily used in the printing industry and is considered the universal language of color for graphic design. It provides a standardized set of colors that can be reproduced accurately across different mediums, such as offset printing, digital printing, and screen printing. Designers can select colors from the Pantone Color Swatch Libraries and specify them in their designs, ensuring consistent color reproduction. The Pantone Fashion, Home + Interiors system, on the other hand, is tailored for the fashion, textile, and interior design industries. It includes a wide range of colors specifically curated for these industries, taking into account trends, market demands, and production processes. Designers in these fields can rely on this system to select colors for fabrics, garments, home furnishings, and other related products. Colors in the Pantone Color Swatch Libraries are not only practical tools for achieving visual consistency, but they also hold

154

symbolic meanings and associations. Each color has its psychological and cultural implications, which designers can leverage to evoke specific emotions, communicate messages, and reinforce brand identities. For example, warm colors like red and yellow are often associated with energy and attention, while cool colors like blue and green evoke a sense of calmness and tranquility. By using the Pantone Color Swatch Libraries, designers have a reliable and extensive resource at their disposal to explore colors, establish visual harmony, and leverage the symbolic meanings of different hues. This allows for consistent branding and effective visual communication across various design disciplines and industries.

Pantone Color System Resources

The Pantone Color System is a standardized method used in the field of color theory and design to ensure consistent and accurate communication of colors. Developed by the Pantone Inc., a company known for its color matching system, it is widely used in various industries to specify and reproduce specific colors. In color theory, the Pantone Color System serves as a valuable resource for designers, artists, and visual communicators for several reasons. Firstly, it provides a universal language for accurately identifying and discussing colors. Each color within the Pantone system is assigned a unique alphanumeric code, allowing for precise and unambiguous reference. This is particularly important when collaborating with others or when producing physical color samples. Secondly, the Pantone Color System plays a crucial role in maintaining color consistency across different design materials. By providing standardized formulas for creating desired colors, it ensures that the same color can be reproduced consistently across various media, such as print and digital platforms. This is essential for maintaining brand identity and visual integrity, especially for businesses and organizations. In addition to its practical applications, the Pantone Color System is also significant in the realm of color symbolism and psychology. Colors carry symbolic meanings and evoke different emotions and responses in individuals. The Pantone system provides an extensive range of colors, each with its own distinct characteristics and associations. Designers can harness these color meanings and their psychological effects to effectively communicate messages and create desired visual experiences. Overall, the Pantone Color System serves as a valuable tool for color theory and design. It enables consistent and accurate communication of colors, ensures color consistency across different materials, and provides a wide range of color options and their symbolic significance. Incorporating the Pantone system in design processes enhances precision, creativity, and effective visual communication.

Pantone Color System

The Pantone Color System is a standardized color matching system used in design and printing industries. It was developed by the Pantone company in the 1960s as a way to ensure consistent color reproduction and communication. In color theory, color is often described using three main characteristics: hue, saturation, and value. Hue refers to the dominant wavelength of light, which determines the color. Saturation refers to the intensity or purity of the color, while value refers to the lightness or darkness of the color. The Pantone Color System provides a way to define and communicate these characteristics using a unique numbering system. Each color in the Pantone Color System is assigned a specific identification number, making it easy to reference and replicate. This allows designers, printers, and manufacturers to accurately reproduce colors across various mediums, such as print advertisements, product packaging, and digital displays. In addition to its practical applications in color reproduction, the Pantone Color System also holds significance in color symbolism. Colors can evoke certain emotions and convey specific messages, making them an important tool in design. The Pantone Color System offers a wide range of colors, each with its own symbolic meaning. For example, red is often associated with passion, energy, and power, while blue can represent tranquility, trust, and reliability. By using the Pantone Color System, designers can choose colors with intention, aligning them with the desired message or brand identity. The Pantone Color System has become a widely recognized and influential tool in the design industry. It allows for consistent color communication and symbolism, ensuring that colors are accurately represented across different mediums and resonating with viewers on an emotional level.

Passion (Coral)

Passion (Coral) is a color that falls within the red-orange spectrum. As per color theory, it is created by combining equal parts of red and orange. This vibrant hue is commonly associated with intense emotions, love, and desire. In the realm of color symbolism in design, Passion (Coral) carries various connotations. Its bold and energetic nature makes it a popular choice for designs aiming to evoke passion and excitement. In the context of marketing and branding, Passion (Coral) is often utilized to create a sense of urgency or impulse. It can be eye-catching and attention-grabbing, drawing viewers in and stimulating their senses.

Passion (Crimson)

Passion (Crimson) is a vibrant and intense shade of red that holds significant meaning in color theory and color symbolism in design. In color theory, crimson is classified as a warm color, often associated with strong emotions and energy. It is created by mixing a deep red hue with a touch of blue. This particular shade of red represents passion, desire, and action. It is a highly stimulating color that captures attention and evokes strong emotions. In the realm of color symbolism, crimson has been used to represent various concepts and ideas. It is most commonly associated with love, romance, and sexuality. The deep red shade of crimson symbolizes intense emotional love and desire, making it a popular choice in designing romantic settings or conveying powerful emotions in visual materials. Moreover, crimson is often used to represent strength, courage, and power. The bold and assertive nature of this shade makes it suitable for branding and logos of companies that aim to portray a strong and dynamic image. It is also often used in dramatic and attention-grabbing advertisements or designs that seek to make a powerful impact on the viewer. Furthermore, crimson can also represent passion and vitality. It is frequently used in designs related to sports teams or activities that require energy and enthusiasm. Crimson is chosen to convey a sense of determination, excitement, and motivation, making it an ideal choice in creating visually engaging sports-related designs or branding. In conclusion, passion (crimson) is a dynamic and emotionally charged shade of red within the realm of color theory and color symbolism in design. Its warm and intense nature makes it an influential color choice for conveying strong emotions, such as love, desire, strength, and vitality. Whether used in romantic settings, powerful branding, or energetic sports designs, crimson captures attention and evokes a sense of passion and fervor in the viewer.

Passion (Maroon)

Passion (Maroon) is a deep, rich color that is often associated with intense emotions and energy. In the context of color theory, it is one of the darker shades of red and is created by adding a small amount of blue to a pure red hue. This addition of blue gives Maroon a slightly cooler undertone, compared to other shades of red. In design, Maroon is often used to evoke feelings of passion, power, and strength. Its deep and intense nature makes it a bold and dramatic color choice. Maroon is often associated with love and desire, and is commonly used in romantic settings or to represent strong emotions. It can be seen as a symbol of courage, determination, and ambition.

Passion (Red)

Passion (Red) is a vibrant and intense color that holds significant meaning in color theory and symbolism in design. It is often associated with strong emotions, energy, and excitement. In color theory, red is classified as a warm color, along with orange and yellow. Warm colors are known for their ability to stimulate and create a sense of warmth and coziness. Red, in particular, has a high saturation and tends to stand out, commanding attention and creating a focal point in design.

Pastel Colors

Pastel colors, in the context of color theory and color symbolism in design, refer to a range of pale, soft, and muted colors that are created by adding a large amount of white to pure hues. These colors are typically associated with tranquility, delicacy, and gentleness, and they are often used in design to create a sense of calmness and subtlety. In color theory, pastel colors are classified as tints, which are created by mixing a hue with white. By adding white to a pure hue, the intensity and saturation of the color are reduced, resulting in a softer and lighter shade. This process of tinting allows designers to create a wide range of pastel colors, including pale pinks, powdery blues, and light lavenders, among others. Pastel colors are often chosen for their psychological and emotional associations. In design, these soft and soothing tones can evoke a sense of serenity, innocence, and femininity. For example, pastel pink is often associated with romance, while light blue is associated with tranquility and calmness. By incorporating pastel colors into a design, designers can create a gentle and inviting atmosphere that appeals to a wide range of audiences. Furthermore, pastel colors can also communicate specific symbolic meanings. For instance, pale yellow is often seen as a symbol of happiness and cheerfulness, while mint green can represent growth and freshness. As such, designers can use pastel colors strategically to convey certain messages or to enhance the overall mood and aesthetic of a design. In conclusion, pastel colors are pale, soft, and muted tones that are created by adding a large amount of white to pure hues. These colors are widely used in design due to their calming and soothing qualities. By incorporating pastel colors into a design, designers can create a sense of tranquility and delicacy, while also conveying specific symbolic meanings.

Peace (Aqua)

Peace (Aqua) is a color in the context of color theory and color symbolism in design. It is a light and soft shade of blue-green, often described as a combination of blue and green. This color is often associated with feelings of serenity, tranquility, and harmony. Aqua is derived from the Latin word "aqua," which means water. It is reminiscent of clear ocean waters or a tranquil, calming pool. As a result, peace (aqua) is often used in design to evoke a sense of relaxation and peace. It has a soothing and calming effect, making it a popular choice for spaces intended for relaxation, such as spas, bedrooms, or meditation rooms.

Peace (Blue)

The color blue, within the realm of color theory and color symbolism in design, is associated with the concept of peace. This serene hue is often utilized to convey a sense of calmness, tranquility, and harmony in various artistic compositions. As an integral part of color theory, blue is classified as one of the primary colors, alongside red and yellow. It is a cool color that is commonly associated with the vastness of the sky and the depth of the ocean. Blue is often regarded as a soothing color that can evoke a sense of calmness and relaxation.

Peace (Olive)

The color peace (olive) is a hue that falls within the green color family and is often associated with tranquility, harmony, and balance. It is created by mixing yellow and green in various proportions, resulting in a muted and earthy shade. In the context of color theory, peace (olive) is considered a secondary color because it is a combination of two primary colors, yellow and green. The addition of yellow gives it brightness and warmth, while the green undertones offer a sense of nature and growth. This combination of colors is believed to have a calming effect on the human mind, making peace (olive) an ideal choice for creating a serene and soothing environment. In design, peace (olive) can be used to evoke a sense of stability and serenity. It is often employed in spaces where relaxation and peace are desired, such as meditation rooms, spas, or bedrooms. The muted and earthy nature of peace (olive) makes it a versatile color that can be used as a neutral backdrop or as an accent to add depth and balance to a design. Symbolically, peace (olive) is associated with concepts such as growth, renewal, and abundance. It is reminiscent of the olive tree, which has long been regarded as a symbol of peace and prosperity. The color also carries connotations of harmony and balance, as it combines the energy and warmth of yellow with the calmness and serenity of green. Additionally, peace (olive) can be seen as a color that represents the connection between the natural world and human society. It is often used in environmental and sustainable design to convey a sense of harmony between man-made structures and the surrounding environment. This connection to nature further enhances the peaceful and grounding qualities of peace (olive).

Peace (White)

White is considered a color in the context of color theory and is widely used as a symbol of peace in design. In the color spectrum, white is the combination of all colors of light or pigment. It is often associated with purity, innocence, and simplicity. The color white has a special place in color symbolism, representing a range of meanings and connotations when incorporated into design. White is frequently used to convey a sense of calmness, tranquility, and peace. It is associated with a feeling of purity and cleanliness. In design, white is often utilized as a background color, creating a neutral and unobtrusive canvas for other elements. It helps to highlight and amplify other colors and elements within a composition, enhancing their visual impact. White space is vital for creating balance, harmony, and readability in design.

Perfection (White)

Perfection (White) in color theory refers to the color white, which is often associated with purity, cleanliness, and innocence. It is commonly used in design to convey a sense of minimalism, simplicity, and calmness. The use of white in design can have both practical and symbolic implications. From a practical perspective, white is often used as a neutral backdrop in design to enhance the visibility and legibility of other colors and elements. It serves as a blank canvas that allows other colors to take center stage, making it a versatile choice for various design applications. White also has practical connotations of cleanliness and sterility, making it a preferred choice for medical and scientific environments.

Perseverance (Bronze)

Perseverance, in the context of color theory and color symbolism in design, refers to a shade of bronze that evokes the characteristic of persistence, determination, and resilience. This particular hue of bronze symbolizes the ability to withstand challenges and maintain dedication towards achieving goals. In color theory, bronze is a mixture of brown and metallic tones, often associated with strength and durability. When used in design, the color bronze represents qualities such as perseverance, tenacity, and unwavering commitment. It signifies the ability to push through obstacles, maintain a positive attitude, and continue striving towards success.

Physical Color Sample Books

A physical color sample book is a tool used in the study and practice of color theory and color symbolism in design. It is a collection of physical color samples that allows designers and artists to visually assess and compare different colors and their combinations. In color theory, colors are organized and classified based on their hue, value, and saturation. A physical color sample book typically includes a wide range of colors, arranged in a systematic manner, to provide a comprehensive representation of the color spectrum. The samples are printed on various materials such as paper, cardboard, fabric, or plastic, allowing designers to observe how colors appear on different surfaces and textures. Color symbolism, on the other hand, explores the psychological and emotional associations that different colors evoke. A physical color sample book can be an invaluable resource for understanding and applying color symbolism in design. By having a tangible reference of colors, designers can experiment with various combinations and assess their visual impact and symbolic meanings. Designers and artists often use physical color sample books to facilitate the selection of color palettes for their projects. These books enable them to see how different colors harmonize with each other and how certain combinations can create specific moods or convey certain messages. They can also refer to established color schemes and theories, such as complementary, analogous, or monochromatic, which are often included in color sample books. Overall, a physical color sample book serves as a practical and tangible tool for designers and artists to explore, study, and apply color theory and color symbolism in their creative work. It provides a visual and tactile reference that aids in the selection and composition of colors, allowing for thoughtful and intentional design choices.

Plugins For Color Picking

Plugins for color picking are tools that allow designers to easily select and use specific colors in their designs. These plugins are invaluable for designers who work extensively with colors and need quick and accurate ways to select colors that align with color theory and symbolism. Color theory, in the context of design, refers to the principles and guidelines that govern the use and combination of colors. It helps designers understand the psychological and emotional impact that colors can have on their audience and how colors can be harmoniously combined to create visually appealing designs. Color symbolism, on the other hand, is the study of how colors are associated with different meanings and concepts. It explores how colors can be used to convey specific messages and evoke certain emotions. Plugins for color picking assist designers in ensuring that the colors they choose align with the principles of color theory and the desired symbolism behind their designs. These plugins often provide a color palette or a color wheel, presenting a range of colors that are visually harmonious and aesthetically pleasing. By using these tools, designers can easily explore different color combinations and choose colors that create the desired impact. In addition to providing a range of colors, color picking plugins often include features such as color sliders, hexadecimal code input, and color history. These features enable designers to precisely select specific colors by adjusting values like hue, saturation, and brightness. The ability to input hexadecimal codes allows designers to match colors precisely to specific brand guidelines or existing color schemes. Plugins for color picking not only save time but also ensure consistency across different design elements. Designers can easily save and reuse color swatches or palettes, ensuring a consistent visual identity throughout their designs. This is particularly beneficial when working on projects with multiple designers or across various design platforms. Furthermore, the ability to access color history allows designers to refer back to previously used colors, streamlining the design process and maintaining a cohesive color scheme. Overall, plugins for color picking are vital tools for designers that facilitate the selection and use of colors in accordance with color theory and symbolism. They enhance efficiency, consistency, and creativity by providing a wide range of visually appealing colors and intuitive features for precise color selection. These plugins enable designers to create impactful and purposeful designs that effectively convey the intended message.

Positivity (Gold)

Positivity is a color attribute within color theory and color symbolism in design that is associated with feelings of optimism, happiness, and confidence. It is often represented by the color gold. Gold is a warm and bright color that is often associated with wealth, luxury, and success. In color theory, gold is considered to be a color that evokes positive and uplifting emotions. It is often used in visual design to create a sense of elegance, sophistication, and positivity.

Positivity (Lemon)

The color lemon is a vibrant shade of yellow that is associated with positivity in color theory and color symbolism in design. Lemon is often used in design to evoke feelings of happiness, optimism, and energy. It is a color that can help create a sense of positivity and uplift the mood of a design or space. Lemon is considered to be a warm and welcoming color, making it a popular choice for creating a cheerful and inviting atmosphere.

Power (Black)

Power (Black) - Black is a color that is often associated with power in color theory and color symbolism in design. It is considered a powerful and authoritative color, representing strength, confidence, and control. In color theory, black is technically not considered a color because it is the absence of light. However, it is widely recognized and used in design for its strong visual impact and ability to create contrast. Its deep and dark nature evokes a sense of mystery, sophistication, and elegance.

Power (Maroon)

Power, in the context of color theory and color symbolism in design, refers to a vibrant and intense shade of maroon. Maroon, which is a deep reddish-brown color, is associated with qualities such as strength, ambition, and authority. This particular hue of maroon is often chosen to represent power in various design elements. Its boldness and richness evoke a sense of confidence and dominance. Power can be conveyed through the use of this color in branding, logos, graphic design, and other visual elements.

Power (Red)

Power (Red) is a color that holds significant importance in color theory and color symbolism in design. It is a primary color associated with strength, energy, and determination. Red is often seen as a bold and attention-grabbing hue that commands attention and evokes strong emotions. In color theory, red is situated at the end of the visible spectrum, and its short wavelength makes it one of the most visible colors. This visibility contributes to its powerful impact on viewers. Red has a high saturation level, which means it appears vivid and intense. Its

159

vibrancy adds to its energetic and stimulating nature. When used strategically in design, red can create a sense of urgency or importance.

Practicality (Brown)

Practicality in the context of color theory and color symbolism in design refers to the functionality and usefulness of the color brown. Brown is often associated with the earth, nature, and reliability. In color theory, brown is created by mixing complementary colors, such as red and green, or by mixing primary colors, such as red, yellow, and blue. It is considered a warm color due to its close association with natural materials like wood, soil, and stones. The practicality of brown lies in its ability to create a sense of warmth, coziness, and stability.

Practicality (Copper)

Practicality in the context of color theory and color symbolism in design refers to the characteristic of the color copper. Copper is a reddish-brown metallic color that is commonly associated with practicality. It is often used in design to convey a sense of efficiency, functionality, and utility. The color copper represents a practical approach to design, focusing on the essential and functional aspects rather than ornamental or decorative elements.

Practicality (Gray)

Practicality, in the context of color theory and color symbolism in design, refers to the trait or quality associated with the color gray. Gray is often perceived as practical due to its neutral and versatile nature. Gray is created by mixing black and white, resulting in a hue that lacks any strong chromatic presence. This lack of vibrant color makes gray a highly practical choice in design because it does not overpower or distract from other colors and elements in a composition. It serves as a subtle backdrop or neutral foundation, allowing other colors to shine and take center stage.

Primary Color Editors

Primary Color Editors are key individuals in the field of color theory and color symbolism in design. They play a crucial role in selecting and manipulating the primary colors that form the basis of all color schemes. Color theory is a discipline that seeks to understand how colors interact with each other and how they can be combined to create visually appealing designs. It is based on the color wheel, which consists of twelve colors arranged in a circular format. The primary colors, which are red, blue, and yellow, form the foundation of this color wheel and are considered the building blocks of all other colors. They cannot be created by mixing other colors and are used to create all other colors through various combinations. The role of Primary Color Editors is to understand the properties and attributes of the primary colors and their significance in different design contexts. They analyze the psychological and emotional impact of each primary color and its combinations, taking into account cultural and contextual factors. By understanding the principles of color symbolism, Primary Color Editors can effectively communicate messages and evoke specific emotions through their color choices in design. Primary Color Editors possess extensive knowledge of color theory and have a keen eye for color harmony and balance. They are skilled in using color editing tools to adjust the intensity, saturation, and brightness of primary colors to achieve the desired effect in a design. They can also create color schemes that are visually cohesive and aesthetically pleasing, by combining primary colors with secondary and tertiary colors. In conclusion, Primary Color Editors are experts in color theory and color symbolism in design. They have a deep understanding of the primary colors and their role in creating visual compositions. Through their expertise and skills, they can effectively manipulate, combine, and balance primary colors to convey specific emotions and messages in design.

Primary Color Picker Tools

A primary color picker tool is a tool that is used in color theory and color symbolism in design to select and identify the primary colors. In color theory, primary colors are the basic colors that cannot be created by mixing other colors together. These colors are fundamental and can be used to create a range of other colors by mixing them in different proportions. The primary color picker tools are designed to help designers and artists in the color selection process. They provide a simple and efficient way to identify and choose primary colors. These tools usually consist of a color wheel or a color palette that displays the primary colors in a visually appealing manner.

Primary Color Pickers

Primary color pickers refer to the basic or fundamental colors used in color theory and color symbolism in design. In color theory, primary colors are the pigments that cannot be created by mixing other colors together. These colors are considered to be the building blocks of all other colors. The primary colors are typically considered to be red, blue, and yellow. In design, the primary color pickers play a significant role in creating color schemes, conveying emotions, and conveying meaning. Red is often associated with passion, love, and energy. It can evoke strong emotions and is commonly used to grab attention. Blue is associated with calmness, serenity, and trust. It is often used to create a sense of trust and professionalism in designs. Yellow is associated with joy, happiness, and optimism. It can create a sense of warmth and brightness in designs.

Primary Colors

Primary colors are a set of colors that form the basis of all other colors in color theory and are recognized as fundamental and universal in the field of design and art. These three colors, namely red, blue, and yellow, are considered primary because they cannot be created by mixing any other hues together. In the context of color theory, primary colors are the main building blocks used to create all other colors on the color wheel. They are significant in creating a wide range of other colors through mixing and blending. By combining primary colors in different proportions, secondary and tertiary colors are formed.

Progress (Silver)

Progress (Silver) - In the context of color theory and color symbolism in design, the color silver represents progress. It is associated with forward movement, innovation, and advancement. Silver is often used in design to convey a sense of modernity and futuristic elements. It has a sleek and sophisticated quality that can add a touch of elegance to design projects. The color silver is commonly used in technology-related industries, such as electronics and automotive, to signify progress and cutting-edge advancements. It is also frequently used in the fashion industry to represent luxury and prestige. Silver is often associated with high-quality materials and products. Symbolically, silver can also represent clarity and reflection. It is often associated with the moon and tides, which can evoke feelings of serenity and introspection. In terms of color psychology, silver can have a calming effect. It can help to create a sense of balance and stability in design. Silver can also evoke feelings of neutrality and impartiality. When used in combination with other colors, silver can enhance their qualities. It can add a cooling effect when combined with warm colors, such as red or orange. Silver can also create contrast when used with darker shades, adding depth and dimension to design compositions. Overall, the color silver in design represents progress and forward-thinking. Its association with technological advancements and modernity makes it a popular choice in various industries and design projects.

Prosperity (Gold)

Prosperity (Gold) is a symbolic color in the context of color theory and design. It represents abundance, wealth, and success. Gold is a rich and luxurious color that is often associated with prosperity and opulence. In color theory, gold is classified as a warm color. It is created by combining yellow, a primary color, with small amounts of red and green. This combination gives gold its distinctive warm and glowing appearance.

Prosperity (Olive)

Prosperity (Olive) is a color that is commonly associated with abundance, growth, and wealth. Within the context of color theory, Prosperity (Olive) is classified as a shade of green, specifically a darker and more muted variation. This hue is achieved by adding small amounts of black or gray to a pure green pigment. Green is a color often connected to nature, symbolizing freshness, harmony, and renewal. In the case of Prosperity (Olive), the addition of black or gray creates a deeper and richer tone, which enhances the associations with prosperity and wealth. This particular shade of green is often seen as sophisticated and elegant, making it a popular choice in various design disciplines.

Protection (Aqua)

Protection in the context of color theory and color symbolism in design refers to the perception and interpretation of the color aqua. Aqua is a hue that is predominantly composed of green and blue, often resulting in a refreshing and tranquil appearance. It is reminiscent of the color of water, evoking feelings of calmness and serenity. Aqua is associated with various meanings and symbolisms, which can influence its use and perception in design. One of the primary connotations of aqua is protection. This association stems from its resemblance to the color of the ocean, which has historically been seen as a source of safety and security. Aqua can be interpreted as a symbol for protection, both physically and emotionally.

Protection (Turquoise)

Turquoise is a color that represents protection in color theory and color symbolism in design. It is a blend of blue and green, creating a unique and vibrant shade that evokes feelings of calmness and tranquility. In terms of color symbolism, turquoise is often associated with protection due to its connection to water and the ocean. Water is seen as a symbol of life and a source of nourishment, and turquoise reflects the purity and safety that water represents. Just as water protects and sustains life, turquoise is believed to offer protection and a sense of security.

Purity (Aqua)

Purity in color theory and color symbolism in design refers to the color Aqua, commonly known as the color of purity. Aqua is a hue that represents cleanliness, clarity, and freshness. It is a color that is associated with water, the sky, and nature, evoking a sense of calmness and tranquility. Aqua is a combination of blue and green, resulting in a color that has a cool and calming effect. It is often used in design to create a sense of purity and cleanliness, making it a popular choice in industries such as healthcare, beauty, and wellness. The color Aqua is believed to have a purifying and cleansing effect, both physically and emotionally.

Purity (Silver)

A color's purity refers to its level of brightness or intensity, specifically in terms of its saturation. In color theory and color symbolism in design, purity is often represented by the color silver. Silver is associated with purity due to its clean, cool, and metallic appearance. It is a neutral color that reflects light, giving it a shiny and luminous quality. This brightness and radiance make silver a symbol of purity. In color theory, color purity is measured by the absence of other colors or the degree to which a color is diluted with white. The more pure a color is, the less it is mixed with other colors. In the case of silver, it represents the absence of any impurities or other hues. When applied in design, silver can evoke a sense of clarity, cleanliness, and flawlessness. It is often used to create a modern and sophisticated aesthetic. Silver's reflective quality can also convey a sense of luxury and elegance. In addition to its association with purity, silver is also linked to the moon, which further enhances its symbolism of femininity, intuition, and reflection. This association with the moon's cool, serene light adds depth to the purity represented by the color silver. Silver is commonly used in various design disciplines, such as graphic design, fashion, and interior design. In graphic design, silver is frequently used for logos and typography to create a premium and timeless feel. In fashion, silver garments and accessories are often chosen for their ability to add a touch of elegance and sophistication to an outfit. In interior design, silver accents and finishes can help create a clean and modern ambiance. In conclusion, purity, represented by the color silver, is a key concept in color theory and color symbolism in design. Silver's brightness, shine, and reflective quality convey a sense of cleanliness and flawlessness. Its association with the moon adds a feminine and intuitive dimension to its symbolism of purity. When used in design, silver can create a sophisticated and luxurious aesthetic.

Purity (White)

Purity, also known as white in color theory, is a fundamental concept in design that represents

162

the absence of color. It is often associated with cleanliness, innocence, and simplicity. As pure as freshly fallen snow or a blank canvas, white holds an innate power to convey a sense of purity and clarity. In color symbolism, white embodies a range of meanings depending on cultural and personal associations. It commonly represents purity and wholeness, as well as light and goodness. In many cultures, white is associated with weddings, representing the innocence and purity of the bride. It can also symbolize new beginnings, fresh starts, and the possibility of a blank slate.

Quality (Gold)

The color quality refers to the visual impression of a surface or an object in terms of its specific hue, value, and saturation. In color theory, quality (gold) symbolizes a sense of prestige, elegance, and luxury. Gold is often associated with wealth, opulence, and abundance. It is a warm color that exudes a sense of grandeur and richness. In design, the use of gold can evoke feelings of sophistication and extravagance.

RGB Color Code Converters

RGB color code converters are tools used in color theory and design to convert RGB (Red, Green, Blue) color codes into different formats or representations, providing a convenient way to work with color values in different systems. In color theory, RGB is a well-known color model that represents colors by combining red, green, and blue light in various intensities. RGB color codes are numerical representations of these intensities, typically ranging from 0 to 255 for each color channel. For example, the RGB code (255, 0, 0) represents pure red, while (0, 255, 0) represents pure green and (0, 0, 255) represents pure blue. These color codes play a crucial role in design as they allow designers to specify exact colors for their projects. However, different color systems and applications may use alternative representations that are not directly compatible with RGB codes. This is where RGB color code converters come into play. RGB color code converters enable designers to convert RGB codes into other color systems such as HEX (hexadecimal), CMYK (cyan, magenta, yellow, key), or HSL (hue, saturation, lightness). HEX codes are commonly used in web design, while CMYK is prevalent in print design. HSL provides an intuitive way to work with colors based on their hue, saturation, and lightness values. By using RGB color code converters, designers can easily switch between different color systems and accurately communicate their color choices across applications and platforms. These tools save time and prevent color inconsistencies by ensuring the desired colors are accurately represented regardless of the target system.

RGB Color Converters

RGB Color Converters RGB color converters refer to tools or algorithms that facilitate the conversion of colors between the RGB (Red, Green, Blue) color model and other color models or systems. In the context of color theory and color symbolism in design, RGB color converters play a significant role in understanding, manipulating, and representing colors accurately and effectively. The RGB color model is an additive color model where different intensities of red, green, and blue light are combined to create a wide range of colors. In this model, each color is represented by three values ranging from 0 to 255, indicating the intensity of red, green, and blue respectively. The combination of these intensities results in the desired color. Due to its widespread use in digital displays and graphic design, RGB color converters are essential tools for designers and artists. In the field of color theory, RGB color converters enable designers to explore and experiment with different color schemes, harmonies, and contrasts. By converting colors between RGB and other color models such as CMYK (Cyan, Magenta, Yellow, Black), HSL (Hue, Saturation, Lightness), or HEX (hexadecimal), designers can ensure consistency in color representation across various mediums. This is particularly important when translating digital design work into print or vice versa. Additionally, RGB color converters are useful in color symbolism in design. Colors have inherent meanings and associations in different cultures, and understanding the psychological and cultural aspects of colors is crucial in design. RGB color converters allow designers to accurately represent symbolic colors and adjust their intensity or values to align with the intended meaning or emotion. This helps create visually engaging designs that effectively communicate messages to the target audience. In summary, RGB color converters are vital tools in color theory and color symbolism in design. They enable designers to convert colors between the RGB color model and other systems, ensuring consistency and accuracy in color representation. By utilizing RGB color converters, designers can explore various color schemes, harmonies, and contrasts, as well as effectively convey symbolic meanings through color choices.

RGB Color Editing Utilities

RGB color editing utilities are tools or software programs designed for manipulating colors using the RGB color model. In the context of color theory and color symbolism in design, these utilities provide users with the ability to adjust and refine colors to achieve desired visual effects and convey specific meanings. The RGB color model is one of the most common color spaces used in digital design. It is an additive color model that represents colors by combining varying intensities of red (R), green (G), and blue (B) light. By adjusting the values of these primary colors, a wide range of other colors can be created. Color theory is the study of how colors interact and how they can be used effectively in design to evoke emotions, convey messages, and create harmonious compositions. Different colors have different symbolic meanings and can evoke specific emotional responses in viewers. For example, red is often associated with passion and energy, while blue can symbolize calmness and trust. RGB color editing utilities provide designers with the flexibility to manipulate color combinations to achieve desired effects. These tools allow users to adjust the intensity or brightness of individual RGB color channels, enabling them to create custom shades, tints, and tones. By fine-tuning the RGB values, designers can alter the mood or atmosphere of a design, evoke specific emotions, or align their color choices with the intended symbolism. In addition to adjusting individual RGB channels, color editing utilities often offer features such as color picker tools, color harmony generators, and color swatches. These features assist designers in selecting harmonious color schemes and exploring different color combinations that work well together. By using these utilities, designers can ensure that the colors they choose complement each other and create a visually appealing and cohesive design. RGB color editing utilities are essential tools for designers who need precise control over color choices. They provide the flexibility to experiment with different colors and make adjustments until the desired effect is achieved. By leveraging the power of the RGB color model and the features offered by these utilities, designers can create visually stunning designs that effectively communicate their intended messages and symbolism.

RGB Color Editors

An RGB color editor is a tool or software that allows designers to select and manipulate colors using the RGB color model. In color theory, the RGB color model is a system for representing colors by mixing various amounts of red (R), green (G), and blue (B) light. It is the basis for all digital displays and is widely used in design and digital imaging. The RGB model works on the principle of additive color mixing, where different intensities of the three primary colors are combined to create a wide range of colors. In design, colors play a significant role in evoking emotions, conveying messages, and creating visual impact. Various colors have different symbolic meanings and associations, and designers often use color symbolism to communicate effectively with their audience. An RGB color editor allows designers to precisely control the RGB values of a color, enabling them to create custom colors or match specific color palettes. It usually provides a graphical user interface (GUI) where designers can adjust the intensity of red, green, and blue channels using sliders, numeric input, or color pickers. By using an RGB color editor, designers can experiment with different color combinations, create harmonious color schemes, or replicate existing colors accurately. They can also switch between different color models, such as CMYK (cyan, magenta, yellow, key), to ensure consistency across various media and printing processes. Overall, an RGB color editor is an essential tool in the designer's toolkit, allowing them to harness the power of colors and apply color theory and symbolism effectively in their designs.

RGB Color Model

The RGB color model is a fundamental concept in color theory and color symbolism in design. It is based on the additive color mixing theory, where different proportions of red, green, and blue light are combined to create a wide range of colors. The acronym RGB stands for red, green, and blue, which are the primary colors of this color model. In the RGB color model, each primary color is assigned a value ranging from 0 to 255, indicating the intensity of that color. By combining different intensities of the three primary colors, it is possible to create millions of different colors. For example, if red, green, and blue are all set to their maximum intensities of 255, the resulting color would be pure white. On the other hand, if all primary colors are set to their minimum intensity of 0, the resulting color would be black. This color model is widely used in digital design, including graphic design, web design, and computer graphics. It is particularly suitable for electronic displays, as these displays emit light and can easily mix colors using the RGB model. In the design field, understanding the RGB color model is crucial for creating visually appealing and harmonious color palettes. The RGB color model also has symbolic meanings associated with different colors. Red, for example, is often associated with passion, energy, and excitement, while green represents nature, growth, and freshness. Blue is commonly associated with calmness, reliability, and professionalism. By using various combinations and intensities of these colors, designers can evoke specific emotional responses and convey certain messages through their designs. In conclusion, the RGB color model is a fundamental concept in color theory and design. It allows for a vast range of colors to be created by combining red, green, and blue in different proportions. This model is widely used in digital design and has symbolic meanings associated with various colors, providing designers with a powerful tool for creating visually appealing and meaningful designs.

Rebellion (Black)

Rebellion (Black) is a color commonly used in color theory and color symbolism in design. It is a dark hue that is often associated with various connotations and emotions. In color theory, black is considered a neutral color, and it has the ability to darken other colors when combined. It is often used as a contrast color to create emphasis and to highlight other colors in a design. Black can also be used as a background color to create a sense of depth and mystery. In terms of color psychology, black is often associated with power, elegance, and authority.

Refreshment (Aqua)

The color Aqua, when used in the context of color theory and color symbolism in design, represents a refreshing and tranquil shade of blue-green. It is often associated with the soothing qualities of water and is commonly used to evoke a sense of calmness, relaxation, and rejuvenation. In color theory, Aqua is classified as a cool color. It is created by combining blue and green, with a higher dominance of blue. The addition of green gives Aqua its distinct hue, resembling the color of tropical oceans or clear, freshwater lakes. This combination of blue and green creates a harmonious and balanced color that is visually pleasing to the eye.

Reliability (Beige)

Reliability (Beige): In the context of color theory and color symbolism in design, beige represents reliability. Beige is a neutral color that is often associated with practicality, dependability, and stability. As a muted, earthy tone, beige is commonly used in design to create a sense of calmness and tranquility. It suggests a level of conservatism and restraint, evoking a feeling of reliability and trustworthiness. Beige is often incorporated into branding and marketing to convey a sense of longevity and reliability.

Reliability (Brown)

Reliability in color theory and color symbolism refers to the characteristic of a color to convey stability, trustworthiness, and dependability. In the context of design, colors play a crucial role in evoking emotions and creating visual impact. Each color carries its own symbolism and can elicit specific psychological responses from the viewer. Reliability, as a characteristic associated with color, is particularly important in conveying a sense of trust and durability.

Renewal (Gold)

Renewal, in the context of color theory and color symbolism in design, refers to the color gold. Gold is a vibrant and luminescent hue that represents various concepts related to renewal, such as abundance, prosperity, and rejuvenation. Gold is often associated with renewal due to its connections with the sun, which symbolizes rebirth and new beginnings. The radiant and warm nature of gold evokes feelings of positivity, hope, and optimism, making it an ideal color to use in designs that convey renewal.

Renewal (Green)

Renewal (Green): In color theory and design, green is a symbol of renewal and vitality. It is often associated with nature, growth, and freshness. Green is a secondary color that is created by mixing yellow and blue, and it occupies a central position on the color wheel. As a result, it is considered a harmonious and balanced color that promotes feelings of stability and harmony. Green is often used in design to create a sense of calm and relaxation. It is a versatile color that can be used in various design elements, including backgrounds, fonts, and images. In nature, green is the color of plants and foliage, and it is often used to represent the natural world and the environment.

Renewal (Mint)

Renewal (Mint) is a color frequently used in color theory and color symbolism in design. It is a pale, light green shade that represents freshness, growth, and revitalization. This color is often associated with nature, harmony, and balance. In color theory, renewal (mint) is considered a cool color, as it is created by mixing green and white. Cool colors tend to evoke a sense of calmness and relaxation. This makes renewal (mint) an ideal choice for designs that aim to convey a sense of tranquility and renewal.

Resilience (Maroon)

Resilience, in the context of color theory and color symbolism in design, refers to the characteristic of endurance, strength, and adaptability represented by the color Maroon. Maroon is a deep and rich hue, closely associated with the color red. Its darker tone signifies a sense of seriousness and groundedness, evoking a feeling of maturity and wisdom. This color exudes a sense of stability and strength, symbolizing the ability to overcome challenges and bounce back from adversity.

Resilience (Olive)

The concept of resilience in color theory and color symbolism refers to the properties and associations of the color olive. Olive, a greenish-brown hue, is often used in design to convey a sense of resilience. In color theory, olive is considered a tertiary color created by mixing yellow and black pigments. It is commonly associated with the calmness and stability of green, combined with the strength and seriousness of brown. This combination gives olive a unique character that represents resilience.

Resources For Color Psychology

Color psychology is a field of study that explores the effects of colors on human behavior, emotions, and mood. In the context of color theory and color symbolism in design, color psychology plays a crucial role in understanding how different colors can elicit specific reactions and convey various messages. Color theory is a framework that examines how colors interact and blend with each other, while also considering the psychological and emotional responses they evoke. It helps designers make informed decisions about color combinations, contrasts, and harmonies to create visually appealing and meaningful designs. Color symbolism, on the other hand, refers to the associations or meanings that people attribute to different colors in various cultures and contexts. Understanding the psychological impact of colors is essential for designers as it allows them to leverage the power of color to communicate effectively and evoke specific emotions or responses in their audience. Different colors have been found to have distinct psychological effects, which can be categorized as follows: 1. Warm Colors: Colors such as red, orange, and yellow are associated with warmth, energy, and excitement. They can stimulate appetite, grab attention, and create a sense of urgency or intensity. These colors are often used to evoke passion, hunger, or enthusiasm in design contexts. 2. Cool Colors: Colors like blue, green, and purple are considered cool and have a calming effect on viewers. They are associated with serenity, tranquility, and relaxation. Cool colors are often used to create a sense of calmness, trust, or stability in designs. 3. Neutral Colors: Colors such as black, white, gray, and brown are considered neutral and can be used as a base for designs. They are versatile and can be combined with any other color to create balance, contrast, or emphasize other colors' effects. Neutral colors are often associated with sophistication, elegance, or simplicity. 4. Cultural and Contextual Associations: Colors can also have cultural or contextual associations that vary across different societies. For example, in Western cultures, white is associated with purity and weddings, whereas in some Eastern cultures, it symbolizes mourning and funerals. It is essential for designers to consider such associations to ensure their designs are culturally sensitive and effective in a specific context. In conclusion, color psychology, within the context of color theory and color symbolism in design, studies the effects of colors on human behavior, emotions, and mood. Designers can benefit from understanding the psychological impact of different colors to create visually appealing and meaningful designs that evoke specific emotions or responses in their audience.

Romance (Lilac)

The color lilac is a shade of purple that is often associated with romance in the context of color theory and color symbolism in design. Within color theory, lilac is considered a tertiary color, a blend of blue and red pigments. It typically has a pale to medium intensity, with a slight blue undertone. Lilac is often described as a delicate and soft color, with a calm and soothing effect on the viewer. It is commonly used to create a sense of romance, femininity, and elegance in design.

Romance (Magenta)

The color Magenta in color theory is a vibrant and deep shade that lies between purple and pink on the color spectrum. It is created by mixing equal parts of red and blue light. Magenta is often associated with love, passion, and romance, making it a popular choice in design elements that aim to evoke these feelings. In the context of color symbolism in design, Magenta is commonly used to convey emotions of warmth, energy, and sensuality. Its bold and intense nature can help create a vibrant and passionate atmosphere, making it suitable for designs that want to exude a romantic and alluring vibe.

Romance (Pink)

Pink is a color within the red hue that embodies the essence of romance in the context of color theory and color symbolism in design. In color theory, pink is created by mixing white with a small amount of red and is often associated with femininity, tenderness, and love. It is considered to be a lighter, softer version of red and has a calming and soothing effect on the viewer. In terms of color symbolism in design, pink is often used to convey romantic and affectionate emotions. It is commonly associated with feelings of love, sweetness, and youthfulness. Pink is frequently used in designs related to weddings, Valentine's Day, and other romantic occasions. It can also be used to represent gentleness, compassion, and nurturing qualities. When used in design, pink can evoke a sense of charm, playfulness, and innocence. It has a gentle and delicate nature that can soften the overall aesthetic of a design. Pink is often used as a background color or as an accent to add a touch of romance and femininity to a design. It is important to consider the cultural and personal associations with pink when using it in design. While pink traditionally symbolizes femininity, it is not limited to gender-specific designs. Pink can also be used to challenge traditional gender roles and stereotypes. In conclusion, pink is a color that represents romance, love, and tenderness in the context of color theory and color symbolism in design. Its soft and delicate nature makes it an ideal choice for designs related to romantic occasions or when conveying emotions of love and affection.

Romance (Red)

In the context of color theory and color symbolism in design, red represents romance. It is a color that evokes strong emotions and is often associated with passion, love, and desire. Red is known to stimulate the senses and grab attention effortlessly. It is a warm and intense color that has the ability to create a sense of excitement and energy. In color theory, red is classified as one of the primary colors, along with blue and yellow. It sits at the end of the visible spectrum of light and has the longest wavelength, making it visually striking. Red can also be created by mixing magenta and yellow pigments together. The symbolism of red in design is deeply rooted in cultural and historical influences, making it a popular choice across various industries.

Royalty (Purple)

Royalty (Purple) is a color that holds significant meaning in color theory and color symbolism in

167

design. It is a hue located between blue and red on the color spectrum, exhibiting qualities from both colors. Purple is often associated with royalty, luxury, power, and wealth, creating a sense of opulence and grandeur. In terms of color theory, purple is considered a secondary color, as it is created by mixing equal parts of blue and red. It is perceived as a cool color due to its relation to blue, but also carries warmth and energy due to its association with red. Purple can have varying shades and tones, ranging from deep and dark hues to lighter and more vibrant tints. Each shade of purple carries its own unique connotations and visual impact.

Rusticity (Brown)

Rusticity (Brown) is a color that falls under the category of earth tones in color theory. It is a warm, rich shade of brown that is often associated with nature, stability, and tradition. In color symbolism, Rusticity (Brown) represents a sense of grounding, reliability, and durability. It is often used to create a sense of warmth and comfort in design. This color is commonly used in organic and natural themes, as it reflects the earthy tones of soil, wood, and stone.

Sadness (Blue)

Sadness, represented by the color blue in color theory and color symbolism in design, is a complex emotional state often associated with feelings of grief, melancholy, and sorrow. Blue is a cool color that is commonly associated with calmness, tranquility, and stability, but it can also evoke feelings of loneliness and sadness. In color theory, blue is classified as one of the primary colors, along with red and yellow. It is often used to create a sense of depth and distance in artwork, as well as to evoke a sense of calm and serenity. Blue is known to have a calming effect on the mind and body, which can help to reduce stress and anxiety. In color symbolism, blue is often associated with the concept of sadness. This association is rooted in cultural and psychological factors. For example, in many Western cultures, people use phrases such as "feeling blue" or "having the blues" to describe a state of sadness or depression. This linguistic association has contributed to the association between blue and sadness in color symbolism. Blue is often used in design to convey a sense of tranquility and stability, but when used in combination with other colors or design elements, it can also evoke feelings of sadness. For example, when paired with grayscale or muted tones, blue can create a somber and melancholic mood. Similarly, when used in conjunction with soft and flowing shapes, blue can convey a sense of introspection and contemplation. Overall, sadness, represented by the color blue, is a complex emotional state that can be expressed through color theory and color symbolism in design. Blue is a cool color that is often associated with calmness and stability, but it can also evoke feelings of loneliness and sorrow. By understanding the nuances of color and its symbolic associations, designers can effectively use blue to convey and evoke a sense of sadness in their creative work.

Safety (Green)

The color green is associated with safety in the context of color theory and color symbolism in design. This association is rooted in both psychological and cultural factors. Psychologically, green is often perceived as a calming and soothing color. It is commonly associated with nature and the outdoors, which can create a sense of tranquility and peace. This calming effect can contribute to a feeling of safety and well-being. Green is also considered to be a restful color for the eyes, making it less likely to cause visual fatigue or strain. In this way, green can promote a sense of physical comfort and safety.

Saturation

Saturation refers to the intensity or purity of a color in the context of color theory and color symbolism in design. In color theory, saturation describes how vivid or dull a color appears. It is determined by the amount of gray present in a color. A color that is fully saturated appears rich and vibrant, while a color with reduced saturation appears more muted or desaturated. Saturation is determined by the proportion of pure hue (the basic color) to neutral gray in a color. A fully saturated color contains no gray, while a desaturated color contains a higher proportion of gray. Saturation is often represented as a percentage, ranging from 0% (completely desaturated) to 100% (fully saturated). In design, saturation plays a crucial role in creating visual impact and conveying emotions or messages. Highly saturated colors tend to be attention-grabbing and energetic, while desaturated colors can evoke a more subdued, calm, or sophisticated mood. Color symbolism also associates different levels of saturation with specific meanings or emotions. Fully saturated colors are often associated with energy, excitement, vibrancy, and youthfulness. They can be used to create a sense of dynamism or to draw attention to specific elements in a design. On the other hand, desaturated colors are often associated with subtlety, elegance, or seriousness. They can be used to create a more refined or sophisticated visual aesthetic. Understanding saturation is critical in color theory and design because it enables designers to effectively communicate and convey specific messages or emotions through color choices. Whether it is for branding, advertising, or creating visual compositions, the careful consideration of saturation allows designers to manipulate the impact and visual weight of colors. In conclusion, saturation in color theory and design refers to the intensity or purity of a color. It describes how vivid or muted a color appears, with fully saturated colors being vibrant and attention-grabbing, and desaturated colors being more subdued or sophisticated. Saturation is an essential element in color symbolism and plays a significant role in creating visual impact and conveying specific meanings or emotions in design.

Secondary Color Creation Tools

Secondary color creation tools in color theory and design refer to techniques and methods used to combine primary colors in order to produce secondary colors. Primary colors, such as red, blue, and yellow, are the fundamental building blocks from which all other colors are created. In color theory, secondary colors are derived by mixing two primary colors together in equal proportions. For example, mixing red and blue creates purple, while combining blue and yellow produces green. The secondary colors, along with the primary colors, form the basis of the traditional color wheel. Understanding how to create secondary colors is essential for designers, as they are critical in achieving effective color palettes and conveying desired meanings and emotions. Secondary colors play a significant role in color symbolism, where different colors carry cultural, psychological, and emotional associations. Color symbolism in design relies heavily on the use and combination of colors to evoke specific responses or convey desired messages. Secondary colors can enhance the visual impact of a design and evoke particular emotions or associations. For example, orange, a secondary color created by mixing red and yellow, is often associated with energy, enthusiasm, and creativity. By using orange strategically in a design, designers can elicit these desired emotions or associations in the viewer. Various tools are available to aid in the process of creating secondary colors. Traditional tools such as a color wheel, which displays the relationship between primary, secondary, and tertiary colors, can be used to determine which colors to mix. Modern technology has also provided digital color palettes and software applications that allow designers to experiment and find the perfect combination of primary colors to create the desired secondary color. By leveraging secondary color creation tools, designers can effectively use color theory and color symbolism to enhance their designs and create visual experiences that elicit specific emotions and meanings from viewers. Using secondary color creation tools in the design process adds depth and complexity to visual compositions, allowing designers to communicate more effectively and engage their audience on a deeper level.

Secondary Color Creators

Secondary Color Creators refer to colors that are created by combining two primary colors in equal proportions. In color theory, primary colors are said to be pure and cannot be created by mixing other colors together. The three primary colors are red, blue, and yellow. When equal parts of two primary colors are combined, they create secondary colors. Secondary colors are orange, green, and purple. Orange is created by mixing equal parts of red and yellow, while green is created by mixing equal parts of blue and yellow. Purple, on the other hand, is created by mixing equal parts of red and blue. These secondary colors are often used alongside the primary colors in design to create visually appealing compositions.

Secondary Color Picker Apps

A secondary color picker app is a tool used in the field of color theory and design to identify and select secondary colors. Secondary colors are the hues created by mixing two primary colors together. In the RGB color model, the primary colors are red, green, and blue, while in the subtractive color model (used in printing and painting), the primary colors are cyan, magenta, and yellow. Color theory is a fundamental concept in design, as colors play a crucial role in evoking emotions, conveying messages, and creating visual harmony. While primary colors can be powerful on their own, secondary colors provide additional depth and variety to a design. Secondary color picker apps typically include a color wheel or spectrum that allows users to choose a primary color and then select the desired secondary color based on their preferences. By adjusting the slider or dial, users can mix the primary colors and observe the resulting secondary colors in real-time. Furthermore, color symbolism is an essential aspect of design. Different colors can evoke different emotions and have various connotations. For instance, red often represents passion, love, or danger, while blue is associated with tranquility, trust, and stability. By understanding color symbolism, designers can effectively communicate their intended messages and create meaningful experiences for their audience. Secondary color picker apps enable designers to explore different color combinations and understand how secondary colors can enhance their designs. By experimenting with various hues and saturation levels, designers can create harmonious or contrasting color schemes that resonate with their target audience. Overall, secondary color picker apps offer a valuable resource for designers seeking to incorporate secondary colors into their projects. With the ability to select and mix primary colors, understand color theory, and utilize color symbolism, these apps provide the tools necessary to create visually appealing and emotionally impactful designs that resonate with viewers.

Secondary Color Pickers

A secondary color picker refers to a tool or mechanism used in color theory and design to select and create secondary colors. In the context of color theory, secondary colors are those that are formed by mixing equal amounts of two primary colors. The primary colors are red, blue, and yellow, and the secondary colors are green, orange, and purple. In color symbolism, each color carries its own meaning and significance. The secondary color picker allows designers to choose and manipulate secondary colors to evoke specific emotions or convey certain messages in their designs. By understanding the psychological and cultural associations of secondary colors, designers can create visually appealing and meaningful compositions.

Secondary Colors

The secondary colors, in the context of color theory and color symbolism in design, refer to the colors that are created by combining two primary colors. These secondary colors are orange, green, and violet. In color theory, primary colors are considered the building blocks of all other colors. They cannot be created by mixing other colors, but they can be used to create secondary colors. By combining equal parts of two primary colors, we can obtain the secondary colors. Orange is created by mixing red and yellow, green is created by mixing blue and yellow, and violet is created by mixing red and blue. These secondary colors often evoke specific emotions and have symbolic meanings in design. Orange is commonly associated with warmth, energy, and enthusiasm. It can be used to create a sense of excitement and playfulness in design. Orange is often used to draw attention and is commonly seen in call-to-action buttons or elements meant to stimulate action. Green is frequently associated with nature, growth, and harmony. It is soothing and calming, symbolizing balance and renewal. Green is often used in designs related to sustainability, health, and the environment. It can also be used to create a fresh and relaxing atmosphere. Violet is often associated with creativity, spirituality, and luxury. It has a mysterious and luxurious feel and can stimulate imagination and artistic expression. Violet is commonly used in designs related to beauty, art, and high-end products.

Security (Brown)

The color security, in the context of color theory and color symbolism in design, refers to a hue that is associated with feelings of stability, resilience, and safety. In color theory, security is often represented by the color brown. Brown is a warm, earthy tone that is created by mixing red, yellow, and black pigments. It is commonly found in nature and is often associated with the ground, wood, and soil. When used in design, the color brown can evoke a sense of security and stability. It has a grounding effect and is often used to create a sense of reliability and longevity. Brown is often used in logos and branding for companies that want to convey a sense of trustworthiness and dependability. In addition to its association with stability, the color brown can also symbolize resilience and strength. It is often used to represent endurance and the ability to withstand challenges. In this sense, it can convey a sense of security and safety. While the color brown is primarily associated with security, it is important to consider its context when using it in design. The shade and intensity of brown can greatly influence its symbolic meaning. Lighter shades of brown may convey a sense of warmth and approachability, while darker shades can be more serious and formal. In conclusion, the color security, represented by the color brown, is associated with stability, resilience, and safety in the context of color theory and color symbolism in design. It is often used to create a sense of reliability and trustworthiness, and can also symbolize endurance and strength.

Security (Olive)

Security, in the context of color theory and color symbolism in design, refers to the psychological and emotional associations that the color olive evokes in individuals. Olive is a hue commonly associated with the color green, and as such, it inherits some of the meanings and symbolism associated with green, but with specific nuances and connotations. Olive is often perceived as a color that represents security and stability. It is commonly associated with feelings of peace, tranquility, and harmony. The color olive is known to have a calming and soothing effect on the human mind, which can help create a sense of security and safety. It is commonly used in design to evoke a feeling of stability and reliability.

Sensitivity (Lavender)

Sensitivity (Lavender) is a color commonly associated with calmness, femininity, and relaxation. In the context of color theory and color symbolism in design, sensitivity lavender represents a delicate and gentle characteristic. It combines the calming properties of blue with the feminine energy of pink, creating a tranquil and soothing sensation. In color theory, lavender is classified as a cool color, as it is made by mixing blue and red. The presence of blue in lavender gives it a calming effect, promoting peace and tranquility. This makes it an ideal choice for creating a serene and harmonious atmosphere in design. Lavender is often used to invoke a sense of relaxation and serenity, making it suitable for spas, bedrooms, and other spaces that aim to create a peaceful ambiance.

Sensuality (Crimson)

Sensuality in the context of color theory and color symbolism in design refers to the quality or characteristic of a color, specifically crimson, that evokes feelings of passion, desire, and sensuousness. This deep shade of red is associated with intense emotions and is often used to create an atmosphere of seduction and romance. Crimson, a hue that is predominantly red with hints of blue, is known for its ability to grab attention and create a sense of drama. It is a color that demands to be noticed, and its boldness and richness often make it a symbol of power and strength. In the realm of design, crimson is commonly used to command attention and create a focal point within a composition.

Sensuality (Magenta)

Sensuality is a concept derived from color theory and color symbolism in design, specifically when referring to the color magenta. In this context, sensuality refers to the emotional and sensory experiences evoked by the color magenta. Magenta is a vibrant and intense color that sits between purple and pink on the color wheel. It is often associated with passion, desire, and romance, making it a highly sensual color. The color magenta is known to stimulate the senses, triggering feelings of intimacy, warmth, and sensuality.

Serenity (Blue)

Serenity (Blue) is a color that holds significant meaning in color theory and symbolism in design. In color theory, Serenity is a cool, calming shade of blue that is often associated with tranquility and peace. It is a lighter and softer tone of blue, evoking feelings of relaxation and serenity. In design, Serenity is often used to convey a sense of harmony, stability, and clarity. It is a versatile color that can be used as a primary color or as an accent color, depending on the design's purpose and desired effect. Serenity is often combined with other hues, such as white or gray, to create a soothing and serene atmosphere. Symbolically, Serenity is associated with qualities such as trust, loyalty, and wisdom. It represents a sense of stability and reliability, making it a

171

popular choice in corporate branding and professional environments. Serenity is also associated with the sky and the ocean, and it can evoke feelings of expansiveness and freedom. In color psychology, Serenity is believed to have a calming effect on the mind and body. It is often used in environments that require focus, concentration, and relaxation, such as bedrooms, meditation rooms, and spas. Serenity can help create a serene and peaceful atmosphere, promoting a sense of balance and well-being. When using Serenity in design, it is important to consider its context and intended message. While it is a soothing color, it can also appear cold and distant if used in excess or without careful consideration. It is important to balance Serenity with warm and inviting colors to create a harmonious and inviting design. Overall, Serenity (Blue) is a color that represents tranquility, harmony, and stability. It is a versatile color that can be used in various design contexts to evoke a sense of peace and calm. By understanding its symbolism and psychological effects, designers can effectively utilize Serenity to create visually pleasing and emotionally impactful designs.

Serenity (Indigo)

Serenity (Indigo) is a color that is often used in color theory and color symbolism in design. It is a shade of blue that is known for its calming and soothing properties. In color theory, Serenity (Indigo) is categorized as a cool color, along with other shades of blue and green. Cool colors are typically associated with feelings of calmness, tranquility, and relaxation. When used in design, Serenity (Indigo) can evoke a sense of peace and serenity. It is often used in spaces where a calm and peaceful atmosphere is desired, such as bedrooms, spas, and meditation rooms. Serenity (Indigo) can also be used to create a sense of depth and stability in designs, as it is a darker shade of blue.

Serenity (Lilac)

Serenity, also known as lilac, is a color that holds significant meaning in color theory and is widely used in design for its symbolic value. In color theory, serenity/lilac is classified as a pastel shade of purple. It is created by mixing blue and red pigments, with a higher presence of blue resulting in a cooler and more serene tone. Serenity/lilac is often associated with tranquility, peace, and calmness. It represents a harmonious balance between the energy of red and the stability of blue. When used in design, serenity/lilac can evoke a sense of relaxation and mindfulness. It is commonly used in spaces where tranquility is desired, such as bedrooms, meditation rooms, and spas. The color's soft and delicate nature creates a soothing atmosphere and promotes a feeling of serenity. Serenity/lilac is also known to have a feminine and romantic quality. It is often used in wedding designs, as it symbolizes love, innocence, and purity. The color's association with femininity makes it a popular choice in fashion and beauty industries. In addition to its calming and romantic symbolism, serenity/lilac holds cultural significance in various countries. In some Asian cultures, lilac is associated with spirituality and is believed to bring peace and healing. In Western cultures, the color can represent sensitivity, sophistication, and grace. Overall, serenity/lilac is a versatile color that can be used to evoke a range of emotions and symbolize different meanings in design. Its soft and tranquil nature makes it a popular choice for creating peaceful environments, while its cultural and symbolic associations add depth to its significance in various contexts.

Shade

Shade, in the context of color theory and color symbolism in design, refers to the darkened version of a color produced by adding black to it. It is one of the crucial aspects of understanding color and its psychological impact in design. A shade is created by reducing the lightness or brightness of a color, ultimately resulting in a darker tone. In color theory, shades are commonly used to create depth, contrast, and dimension in designs. They help to establish hierarchy, define focal points, and evoke certain emotions or moods. By manipulating the shade of a color, designers can create different visual effects and convey specific messages to the audience.

Simplicity (Beige)

Simplicity (Beige) in color theory is a light, warm, and neutral hue that represents minimalism, purity, and understated elegance. It is a versatile color that can be effortlessly incorporated into various design styles and aesthetics. As a neutral color, beige is often used as a base color in design, providing a calming and balanced backdrop for other colors and elements to shine. It has the ability to create a sense of space and openness, making it an ideal choice for small or cluttered environments. Beige is often associated with simplicity and unpretentiousness, evoking a feeling of serenity and tranquility.

Simplicity (Gray)

Simplicity (Gray) Gray is a neutral color that is often associated with simplicity in color theory and color symbolism in design. It is created by mixing equal parts of black and white, resulting in a balanced and timeless hue that exudes a sense of calmness and minimalism. In design, gray is often used as a backdrop or base color due to its ability to enhance other colors and provide a sense of cohesion. It has the unique characteristic of complementing both warm and cool tones, making it a versatile choice for various design applications. Symbolically, gray represents simplicity, elegance, and sophistication. Its neutral nature allows it to blend seamlessly with other colors and create a harmonious visual experience. Gray is often associated with professionalism and formality, making it a popular choice in corporate branding and communication materials. Gray is also commonly used to create a sense of balance and stability. It can have a calming effect on the viewer, evoking feelings of serenity and tranquility. This makes it an ideal choice for spaces that require a peaceful and uncluttered atmosphere, such as healthcare facilities and spas. Furthermore, gray is often used to convey a sense of timelessness and longevity. It is a color that does not easily go out of style, making it a safe and reliable choice for long-term design projects. Its simplicity and versatility allow it to adapt to various design trends and aesthetics, ensuring its continued relevance and appeal. In conclusion, gray is a neutral color that symbolizes simplicity, elegance, and stability in color theory and design. It serves as a versatile backdrop, enhances other colors, and evokes a sense of calmness and minimalism. Whether used in branding, interiors, or visual communication, gray adds a touch of sophistication and timelessness to any design.

Simplicity (White)

Simplicity in the context of color theory and color symbolism in design refers to the use of the color white. White is often associated with purity, cleanliness, and simplicity. It is considered a neutral color and is frequently used as a background color in design projects. White is known for its simplicity and its ability to create a sense of calmness and clarity. It is a versatile color that can be used in various design styles, from minimalist to modern to traditional. White is often used to create a sense of balance and harmony in a design, and it can help to highlight and emphasize other colors or elements in a design.

Sincerity (Peach)

Sincerity, when depicted in the form of the color peach, is a hue that embodies authenticity, genuineness, and transparency. It is a gentle and warm shade that evokes feelings of honesty, openness, and sincerity. In the context of color theory, peach falls under the orange color family. It is created by mixing shades of orange with small amounts of white, resulting in a soft, slightly muted tone. This combination gives peach a delicate and approachable appearance, making it a popular choice for design projects that aim to convey sincerity and trustworthiness.

Sleekness (Silver)

Sleekness is a characteristic or quality often associated with the color silver in color theory and color symbolism in design. In the context of color theory, silver is considered to be a metallic hue that reflects light and is often described as having a smooth and polished appearance. When applied in design, silver can bring a sense of elegance, modernity, and sophistication to a composition. Its sleekness can create a visually appealing and refined aesthetic, imbuing the design with a sense of luxury and high-quality craftsmanship. Additionally, silver's reflective properties can add depth and dimension to a design by capturing and interacting with ambient light.

Socialization (Orange)

Socialization, in the context of color theory and color symbolism in design, refers to the psychological and emotional effects produced by the color orange. Orange is a warm, energetic,

173

and vibrant color often associated with enthusiasm, creativity, and sociability. It is a combination of red and yellow, which gives it a harmonious balance between the passionate and energetic qualities of red and the joyful and uplifting qualities of yellow. As a result, orange is often used to evoke feelings of excitement, positivity, and social interaction.

Software For Color Analysis

Software for Color Analysis refers to computer programs or applications that are specifically designed to analyze and interpret colors in the context of color theory and color symbolism in design. These software tools are used by designers, artists, and other professionals who work with color to understand and make informed decisions about color palettes, combinations, and meanings. Color theory is the study of how colors are perceived and how they interact with each other. It encompasses concepts such as the color wheel, color harmony, color temperature, and color psychology. Color symbolism, on the other hand, is the use of specific colors to convey or evoke emotions, meanings, or associations. For example, red may symbolize passion or energy, while blue may symbolize calmness or trust. Software for Color Analysis provides functionalities that can help users in various aspects of color theory and color symbolism. These functionalities may include: Color Palette Creation: The software enables users to generate harmonious color palettes based on color theory principles, such as complementary, analogous, or triadic colors. It allows users to explore different combinations and variations to find the most visually appealing or conceptually appropriate palette. Color Symbolism Reference: The software may provide a database or reference guide that associates specific colors with their symbolic meanings in different cultures, contexts, or industries. This can help users in choosing colors that align with their intended messages or resonate with their target audience. Color Analysis Tools: The software may offer tools for analyzing the properties of colors, such as their hue, saturation, and brightness. Users can compare and evaluate different colors or color palettes based on these quantitative measurements to make informed decisions about their visual impact. Overall, software for Color Analysis serves as a valuable resource for professionals involved in design, marketing, advertising, and other creative fields. It empowers them to create visually stunning and meaningful designs by leveraging the principles of color theory and color symbolism.

Software For Color Conversion

Software for color conversion refers to a specialized tool or application designed to convert colors from one color space or color model to another. Color theory and color symbolism play significant roles in design, and the ability to convert colors accurately and efficiently is essential for creating cohesive and meaningful visual compositions. Color theory is a field of study that encompasses the principles and guidelines for combining colors harmoniously and effectively in various design applications. It explores the relationships between colors, considering their properties such as hue, saturation, and value. Color symbolism, on the other hand, explores the emotional and cultural associations attached to different colors. These associations can vary across cultures and contexts, making it crucial for designers to consider the intended message or meaning when selecting colors. Software for color conversion enables designers to convert colors between different color spaces or models, such as RGB (Red, Green, Blue), CMYK (Cyan, Magenta, Yellow, Key/Black), and HSB/HSV (Hue, Saturation, Brightness/Value). This is particularly useful when working with different devices or applications that use different color models. For example, a design created on a computer screen may need to be printed using a printing press, which typically uses the CMYK color model. By using color conversion software, designers can ensure that the colors they choose on-screen will approximate the desired appearance when printed. Accurate color conversion is critical for maintaining the integrity of a design's visual impact and conveying the intended symbolism. By using software specifically tailored for color conversion, designers can ensure that their color choices align with their vision and effectively communicate their intended message. This software often provides options to adjust and fine-tune colors during the conversion process, allowing designers to achieve the desired results more precisely. Overall, software for color conversion is an indispensable tool in the field of design, enabling designers to convert colors between various color spaces or models accurately and efficiently. By utilizing this software, designers can harmonize colors, consider their symbolic implications, and ensure their designs convey the desired visual and emotional impact.

Software For Color Extraction

174

Color extraction software refers to a specialized tool used in the field of design to identify and extract colors from various sources such as images, websites, or digital artwork for analysis and application. Rooted in color theory and symbolism, this software aims to provide designers with a means to discern the significant hues present in these sources and utilize them effectively in their creative endeavors. Color theory, a fundamental aspect of design, explores the principles and interactions of colors. It delves into the various color properties, such as hue, saturation, and value, as well as the psychological and emotional effects different colors can evoke in individuals. By understanding these concepts, designers can make informed decisions when selecting and combining colors, effectively communicating messages and generating desired responses. Color symbolism, on the other hand, focuses on the meaning and associations attached to specific colors. Different cultures and contexts attribute various interpretations and emotions to particular hues, enabling designers to use colors to convey specific ideas or elicit certain reactions from viewers. For instance, warm colors like red and yellow often evoke feelings of energy and excitement, while cool colors like blue and green convey a sense of calmness and tranquility. In this context, color extraction software plays a crucial role in assisting designers in accessing and utilizing colors effectively. By analyzing images or digital artwork, the software identifies the dominant colors, their combinations, and other relevant color information. Designers can then extract these colors and incorporate them into their creative projects with ease. This software also aids in color palette creation, where designers can extract a range of complementary or harmonious colors for a cohesive visual experience. By integrating the extracted colors into their designs, designers can evoke specific emotions, convey ideas, or establish brand identities more effectively. In conclusion, color extraction software encompasses specialized tools rooted in color theory and symbolism in the design field. By identifying and extracting colors from various sources, these tools assist designers in making informed decisions regarding color selection, manipulation, and overall composition. By understanding the significance of colors and their impact on visual communication, designers can create captivating and purposeful designs that resonate with their intended audiences.

Software For Color Visualization

Software for Color Visualization refers to computer programs or applications that enable designers and artists to explore, analyze, and interpret colors in the context of color theory and color symbolism in design. Such software tools provide users with a visual representation of colors and their relationships, allowing for better understanding and utilization of color in various creative processes.Color theory, rooted in the principles of physics and human perception, examines how colors interact with each other and how they are interpreted by the human eye. By considering factors such as color harmony, contrast, and balance, designers can create aesthetically pleasing and effective color schemes. Software for color visualization assists in this process by providing tools to explore different color combinations, assess their visual impact, and make informed decisions based on color theory principles.

Sophistication (Black)

Sophistication (Black) is a color that holds a significant place in the realm of color theory and color symbolism in design. In the context of color theory, black is often considered the absence of color or the darkest shade, representing the absence of light. It is often associated with the concept of void or nothingness. In the realm of color symbolism in design, black is often denoted as a color that exudes sophistication. It is commonly utilized to portray elegance, formality, and luxury in various design contexts. Due to its association with power, black is frequently used to create a strong and authoritative presence.

Sophistication (Lavender)

The color lavender is often associated with sophistication in color theory and color symbolism in design. Lavender is a pale shade of purple that combines the calmness of blue with the energy of red. It is considered to be a color that evokes elegance, grace, and refinement, making it a popular choice for creating a sophisticated and luxurious atmosphere in various design contexts.

Sophistication (Silver)

Sophistication, in the context of color theory and color symbolism in design, refers to the visual attribute and symbolic representation associated with the color silver. Silver is often perceived as a sophisticated color due to its unique characteristics and cultural connotations. In terms of color theory, silver is considered a neutral color. It falls within the grayscale spectrum, positioned between gray and white. The color silver is achieved by mixing gray with a small amount of white, resulting in a muted, metallic appearance. This cool, metallic quality contributes to its association with sophistication in design. Symbolically, silver is commonly associated with elegance, luxury, and modernity. It is often used in high-end branding and packaging to convey a sense of sophistication and refinement. The reflective quality of silver further enhances its symbolic representation of opulence and exclusivity. Traditional associations with silver include notions of wealth, prestige, and success. In various cultures, silver is used to symbolize purity and wisdom. It is also associated with futuristic or technological themes, which align with its sleek and modern aesthetic. In terms of color psychology, silver is believed to have a calming and soothing effect on the mind. It is associated with clarity, intuition, and introspection. This makes silver an ideal choice for designs that aim to evoke a sense of sophistication while maintaining a serene and harmonious atmosphere. When used in combination with other colors, silver can have different effects. It can add a touch of sophistication and refinement to darker, earthy tones, creating a harmonious contrast. Conversely, when combined with brighter hues, silver can help to balance and tone down their intensity, while still maintaining a sense of elegance.

Sorcery (Purple)

Sorcery, represented by the color purple, holds great significance in color theory and symbolism in design. In color theory, purple is considered to be a secondary color, created by mixing the primary colors of blue and red. It is often associated with power, luxury, and royalty. Purple has a strong presence and stands out among other colors, making it an ideal choice for creating a sense of sophistication and elegance in design.

Spectral Color Measurement Tools

Spectral color measurement tools are devices or instruments used in color theory and color symbolism in design to accurately measure and define the spectral properties of colors. These tools are designed to capture and analyze the wavelengths of light that are emitted or reflected by different colors. Color theory is the study of how colors interact and are perceived by the human eye. It is a fundamental concept in art and design, as different color combinations can create different moods, evoke emotions, and convey symbolic meanings. Understanding the spectral properties of colors is crucial in color theory, as it enables designers to make informed decisions about color choices and combinations. Color symbolism, on the other hand, explores the psychological and cultural associations that people have with different colors. Certain colors are often associated with specific meanings or emotions. For example, red is commonly associated with love or danger, while blue is often associated with calmness or sadness. By accurately measuring the spectral properties of colors, designers can ensure that they are using colors that align with the desired symbolic meanings or emotional responses. Spectral color measurement tools typically use spectrophotometry, a technique that measures the intensity of light at different wavelengths. These tools can provide precise measurements of a color's spectral reflectance or transmittance, which refers to how much light of each wavelength is absorbed or transmitted by the color. By analyzing this data, designers can determine the exact wavelengths of light that contribute to a color's appearance, allowing them to recreate or match specific colors accurately. Some common examples of spectral color measurement tools include spectrophotometers, colorimeters, and spectroradiometers. These devices can vary in complexity and functionality, but they all serve the purpose of accurately measuring colors in terms of their spectral properties. By utilizing spectral color measurement tools, designers can ensure that the colors they choose align with their intended meaning and evoke the desired emotional response in their design work.

Spectrophotometers

A spectrophotometer is an instrument used in color theory and color symbolism in design to measure and quantify the color properties of an object. It measures the amount of light absorbed or transmitted by a substance at different wavelengths, providing a detailed analysis of the object's color spectrum. Color theory is an essential aspect of design, as it influences the overall

176

aesthetic and emotional impact of a visual composition. Spectrophotometers play a crucial role in this field by providing objective measurements of color, enabling designers to make informed decisions based on accurate data.

Spectrophotometry Devices

Spectrophotometry devices are instruments used to measure the intensity of light at different wavelengths. In the context of color theory and color symbolism in design, spectrophotometry devices play a crucial role in accurately determining and reproducing color. Color theory is the study of how colors interact and how they can be combined to create harmonious or contrasting palettes. It helps designers understand the visual impact of color and make informed decisions when choosing colors for their designs. Spectrophotometry devices are used to precisely measure the spectral properties of colors, including hue, saturation, and brightness. By analyzing the wavelengths of light reflected or transmitted by an object, these devices provide designers with objective data about the color composition. Color symbolism, on the other hand, explores the meaning and interpretation of colors in different cultural and social contexts. Colors can evoke emotions and convey messages, making them powerful tools in design. Spectrophotometry devices ensure that color choices accurately represent the intended symbolism. For example, if a designer wants to use the color red to convey passion and power, spectrophotometry devices can help ensure that the specific shade of red chosen aligns with these symbolic associations. With spectrophotometry devices, designers can measure and compare the colors of different objects or materials. This allows for precision in color matching, important in fields like graphic design, printing, and fashion. By using spectrophotometry devices, designers can achieve consistency in color reproduction across multiple media and materials, whether it's printing a brochure or manufacturing a product. In summary, spectrophotometry devices are essential tools in color theory and color symbolism in design. They provide objective data about the spectral properties of colors, helping designers make informed decisions and achieve accurate color reproduction. Whether it's creating harmonious color palettes or conveying specific symbolic meanings, spectrophotometry devices play a crucial role in ensuring the visual impact of color in design.

Spirituality (Blue)

Spirituality in the context of color theory and color symbolism in design refers to the emotional and psychological associations that the color blue can evoke in a person. Blue is often associated with feelings of calmness, serenity, and tranquility, making it a popular choice for representing spirituality. The color blue has long been associated with the sky and the vastness of the ocean, both of which can evoke feelings of awe, wonder, and a sense of something greater than oneself. This connection to the natural world and the sense of vastness can contribute to the perception of spirituality.

Spirituality (Lilac)

Spirituality can be represented by the color lilac in the context of color theory and color symbolism in design. Lilac is a pale shade of purple that combines the calmness of blue with the energy of red. It is often associated with serenity, introspection, and spiritual enlightenment. In color theory, purple is known as a color that stimulates imagination and creativity, making it a suitable choice for expressing spiritual concepts and ideas.

Spirituality (Magenta)

Spirituality, in the context of color theory and color symbolism in design, can be represented by the color magenta. Magenta is a vibrant and intense shade that is often associated with spiritual and mystical experiences. It is believed to open up spiritual pathways, promoting a deeper connection with the divine and the higher self. The color magenta is often used in religious and spiritual artwork, representing a transcendent and sacred energy.

Spirituality (Purple)

Purple is a color that holds significant symbolism in the realm of spirituality. Representing the intersection of red and blue, purple embodies a harmonious balance between two opposing forces. Its association with spirituality stems from its deep connection to introspection, intuition,

177

and higher consciousness. In color theory, purple is often associated with the crown chakra, which is believed to be the gateway to spiritual enlightenment. This chakra is located at the top of the head and is associated with universal knowledge and divine connection. The color purple is used to activate and balance the crown chakra, facilitating the opening of one's spiritual awareness.

Spirituality (Teal)

Spirituality, represented by the color teal in color theory and color symbolism, encompasses a variety of beliefs and practices that relate to the connection between individuals and a higher power or divine energy. It is often associated with a sense of transcendence, inner peace, and personal growth. Teal, as a color, is a combination of blue and green. Blue traditionally represents calmness, serenity, and spirituality, while green symbolizes growth, renewal, and balance. The blending of these two colors in teal creates a hue that embodies both emotional and spiritual aspects.

Spirituality (White)

The color white is often associated with spirituality in color theory and color symbolism in design. It represents purity, light, and transcendence. In the context of spirituality, white is often seen as a symbol of divine presence and purity of the soul. It is associated with the highest level of consciousness and enlightenment. White is also commonly associated with peace, harmony, and unity. It is the color of spiritual awakening and represents the connection between the physical and spiritual realms.

Split Complementary Colors

Split complementary colors are a concept in color theory that refers to a color scheme made up of three colors. This scheme is created by choosing one dominant color and then selecting the two colors that are on either side of its complement on the color wheel. In color theory, the color wheel is a visual representation of the relationships between different colors. It is made up of the primary colors (red, blue, and yellow), the secondary colors (orange, green, and violet), and the tertiary colors (yellow-green, blue-green, blue-violet, red-violet, red-orange, and yellow-orange). The color wheel helps designers understand how colors interact with each other and how they can be combined to create harmonious or contrasting color schemes. Complementary colors are pairs of colors that are directly opposite each other on the color wheel. When these colors are placed next to each other, they create a strong contrast and can be used to add visual interest and depth to a design. However, using complementary colors exclusively can be overwhelming or visually exhausting. This is where split complementary colors come in. Instead of using just two complementary colors, split complementary colors involve selecting one main color and then choosing the two colors adjacent to its complement. This color scheme offers a more subtle and harmonious alternative, as it incorporates colors that are harmonious with the dominant color while still providing contrast. For example, if the dominant color is red, the two split complementary colors would be yellow-green and blue-green, as they are on either side of red's complement, which is green. By incorporating these split complementary colors into a design, a designer can create a more balanced and visually appealing composition. The use of split complementary colors in design can convey different moods and messages. For instance, a combination of blue as the dominant color, with orange-red and orange-yellow as the split complementary colors, can evoke a sense of calmness and tranquility, reminiscent of a serene sunset. On the other hand, a dominant green with split complementary colors of purple and pink can create a vibrant and energetic atmosphere, ideal for designs related to nature or youth. In conclusion, split complementary colors are an effective color scheme in design that offers a balanced and harmonious alternative to using just complementary colors. By selecting one main color and two colors adjacent to its complement, designers can create visually appealing compositions that evoke different moods and emotions. Understanding and utilizing split complementary colors can greatly enhance the effectiveness and impact of a design.

Stability (Blue)

The stability (blue) in color theory refers to the psychological and emotional response elicited by the color blue in design. It symbolizes tranquility, calmness, and serenity. Blue has a soothing

178

effect on the mind and body, evoking a sense of peace and harmony. Its association with the sky and the ocean creates a feeling of expansiveness and openness.

Stability (Brown)

Stability, in the context of color theory and color symbolism in design, refers to a characteristic of colors that evokes a sense of balance, steadiness, and permanence. It is one of the fundamental principles used in the creation of visual compositions to elicit specific emotional responses and convey intended messages. Colors that exhibit stability are typically perceived as calm, soothing, and reliable. They have a grounded and composed presence, often creating a sense of order and harmony in design. These stable colors are commonly found in nature, such as earth tones, deep blues, and shades of green.

Stability (Olive)

Stability in the context of color theory and color symbolism in design refers to the visual perception of a sense of calmness, steadiness, and reliability that certain colors can evoke. It is an important element in design as it helps to create a balanced and harmonious visual experience for viewers. Olive, as a color, is often associated with stability. It is a muted tone that combines the characteristics of green and yellow, symbolizing nature and growth, as well as warmth and vitality. Olive can bring a sense of calmness and grounding to a design, making it suitable for creating a stable and balanced visual composition.

Steadfastness (Beige)

Steadfastness, represented by the color beige in color theory and color symbolism in design, refers to a quality or characteristic of remaining firmly fixed or unwavering in one's purpose, belief, or loyalty. In the context of color theory, beige is often associated with this concept due to its perceived neutral and stable nature. The color beige is commonly described as a light, pale, or sandy shade of brown. It is often praised for its calming and soothing qualities, evoking a sense of tranquility and stability. Beige is a versatile color that works well as a neutral backdrop, allowing other colors and elements to stand out. Its subdued and understated appearance conveys a sense of steadiness and reliability, making it an ideal choice for creating a sense of comfort and consistency in various design applications.

Steadfastness (Copper)

Steadfastness, in the context of color theory and color symbolism in design, refers to the use of the copper color to convey a sense of unwavering commitment, loyalty, and determination. Copper, as a warm metallic hue, holds symbolic meanings that can be incorporated into various design elements, such as logos, branding, and overall visual compositions. Copper, with its reddish-brown hue, is often associated with attributes such as strength, resilience, and reliability. It exudes a sense of stability and durability, making it an excellent choice for design elements that aim to communicate steadfastness. This color can be utilized to evoke a feeling of trustworthiness, dependability, and confidence in a brand or product.

Stop (Red)

The color red holds significant meaning in color theory and color symbolism in design. In color theory, red is classified as a primary color, along with blue and yellow. As a primary color, red cannot be created by mixing other colors together. Instead, it is used to create secondary and tertiary colors. In terms of color symbolism in design, red is a vibrant and intense color that is often associated with powerful emotions and concepts. It is commonly used to symbolize love, passion, and energy. The color red can evoke strong feelings and create a sense of urgency or excitement.

Strength (Bronze)

Strength (Bronze) in the context of color theory and color symbolism in design refers to the symbolic representation and emotional impact associated with the color bronze. Bronze, a metallic color often characterized by shades of brown or amber, is commonly associated with strength, durability, and reliability. In color theory, bronze is considered a warm and earthy hue.

179

It is created by combining various shades of brown with hints of orange or gold. The rich, deep tones of bronze can evoke a sense of solidity and stability, making it a popular choice for conveying strength in design.

Strength (Maroon)

Strength (Maroon) is a color that belongs to the red color family in color theory and color symbolism in design. It is a deep, rich shade of red that is associated with power, determination, and passion. In color theory, the color red is often associated with strong emotions such as love, anger, and energy. Maroon, being a shade of red, embodies these qualities but with a deeper and more intense tone. It is a color that commands attention and conveys a sense of authority and strength. When used in design, strength (maroon) can be a powerful tool to create visual impact and communicate specific messages. In branding and marketing, it can be used to convey confidence, reliability, and leadership. Its deep and bold nature can make a design appear more sophisticated and elegant. Furthermore, strength (maroon) can also be used to create a sense of warmth and comfort in interior design. When used in furniture or decor, it can add a touch of luxury and create a cozy and inviting atmosphere. In color symbolism, strength (maroon) is often associated with traits such as resilience, resilience, and determination. It is a color that symbolizes endurance and the ability to overcome challenges. In this context, it can be used to represent strength of character and the willpower to persevere. Overall, strength (maroon) is a color that represents power, determination, and passion in the realms of color theory and color symbolism in design. It is a color that demands attention and conveys a sense of authority. Whether it is used in branding, marketing, interior design, or symbolic representation, strength (maroon) is an effective tool to evoke strong emotions and communicate specific messages.

Strength (Red)

In the context of color theory and color symbolism in design, the color red represents strength. In color theory, red is classified as a warm color, along with yellow and orange. Warm colors are associated with energy, power, and intensity. Red is particularly powerful and intense, often associated with strong emotions like passion, love, and anger. Red is known for its ability to grab attention and stimulate the senses. It is a very dominant color and is often used to create focal points in design. Because of its energetic and attention-grabbing nature, red is commonly used in advertising and marketing to evoke emotions and draw in viewers. In terms of color symbolism, red can also convey strength and power. It is often associated with courage, bravery, and determination. Many cultures and societies have used red to signify authority and leadership. In flags and national symbols, red is often used to represent a country's strength and resilience. Red can also have negative associations, such as danger and warning, due to its connection with fire and blood. However, even in these contexts, red still conveys strength and intensity. When incorporating red into design, it is essential to consider its psychological and emotional impact. The strength and intensity of red can be overwhelming if not used strategically. It is often recommended to use red as an accent color rather than as the dominant color in a design. By carefully balancing red with other colors, designers can effectively harness its power and create visually appealing and impactful designs.

Strength (Salmon)

Strength is a characteristic of the color salmon in the context of color theory and color symbolism in design. Salmon is a hue that is often associated with strength. In color theory, hues can evoke certain emotions or qualities, and salmon is no exception. It is a warm color that falls between pink and orange on the color spectrum, and it carries with it a sense of power and resilience. In design, the color salmon can be used strategically to convey strength in various ways. It can be used to signify physical strength, such as in sports-related designs or branding for athletic teams. The vibrant and energetic nature of the color makes it an ideal choice for designs that aim to convey an active and powerful message. Furthermore, the color salmon can also symbolize emotional strength. Its warm and soothing tones can evoke feelings of comfort and stability, making it an excellent choice for designs that aim to convey resilience in the face of adversity or emotional challenges. It can be used to create a sense of support and reassurance, offering a feeling of strength and empowerment to viewers. When using the color salmon to convey strength in design, it is important to consider its context and the overall design

180

composition. Pairing salmon with complementary colors, such as blues or greens, can enhance its strength symbolism. Additionally, considering factors such as lighting, texture, and contrast can help further emphasize the strength qualities of the color. In conclusion, in the realm of color theory and color symbolism in design, strength is a characteristic associated with the color salmon. Its warm and vibrant nature makes it an ideal choice for conveying physical and emotional strength in various design contexts.

Subtlety (Beige)

Subtlety, represented by the color beige in color theory and color symbolism in design, refers to a quality of delicate, understated, and quiet elegance. It is a neutral, muted tone that evokes a sense of softness and sophistication. The color beige is often described as a pale, light brownish color with warm undertones. It is created by combining white with a small amount of various colors, such as yellow, red, or gray. This blending of colors results in a hue that is neither too bright nor too dark, conveying a subdued and gentle appearance.

Success (Gold)

Success (Gold) in color theory refers to a shade of gold that symbolizes achievements, prosperity, and triumph. It is a hue that represents the fulfillment of goals and the attainment of success. In the context of color symbolism in design, the color gold is often associated with wealth, luxury, and success. Its warm and radiant appearance makes it an attention-grabbing choice, often used to convey a sense of elegance and sophistication. Gold is commonly used in branding and design to evoke feelings of prestige and excellence.

Sunny Disposition (Lemon)

Sunny Disposition, also known as Lemon, is a bright and cheerful color in color theory and is often associated with positive emotions and energy. Lemon is a shade of yellow, which is considered a warm color along with red and orange. It is created by adding small amounts of green to yellow, resulting in a hue that is vibrant and refreshing. In color symbolism, Lemon or Sunny Disposition represents happiness, joy, and optimism. It is commonly used in design to evoke feelings of positivity and to create a lively and energetic atmosphere. Lemon is often associated with summer and sunshine, bringing warmth and light to a design composition.

Sunshine (Gold)

The color sunshine (gold) refers to a bright and vibrant shade commonly associated with the color of the Sun when it is shining brightly. In color theory, it falls under the category of warm colors, which are typically associated with energy, warmth, and positivity. In design, the color sunshine (gold) is often used to evoke feelings of happiness, optimism, and warmth. It is a color that can instantly grab attention and create a sense of luxury and elegance when used correctly. This color is commonly seen in various design elements, such as logos, packaging, and advertisements, to convey a sense of richness and excellence.

Sunshine (Yellow)

According to the principles of color theory and color symbolism in design, sunshine yellow is a vibrant and radiant hue that is often associated with feelings of happiness, positivity, and warmth. As one of the primary colors, yellow holds a significant place in the color spectrum and conveys a range of emotions and meanings when used in design. In the context of color theory, yellow is considered a warm color, as it is often associated with the sun and light. It has a high visibility and can attract attention, making it an excellent choice for elements that need to stand out in a design. Yellow is commonly used to create contrast and draw focus, whether it is in the form of text, graphics, or backgrounds. From a psychological perspective, sunshine yellow is closely linked to feelings of joy, energy, and optimism. It can evoke a sense of happiness and cheerfulness, making it a popular choice for designs aimed at creating a positive and uplifting vibe. Yellow is often used in marketing and advertising to catch the eye and create a sense of excitement or happiness around a product or brand. Just as yellow is associated with positive emotions, it is also connected to caution and warning. The color yellow is often used in traffic signs and safety equipment to alert people to potential hazards or dangers. This dichotomy between happiness and caution is an important aspect to consider when using sunshine yellow in design, as it can convey different messages depending on the context. Furthermore, yellow is frequently used in combination with other colors to create specific moods or convey particular messages. For example, when paired with blues and greens, it can create a peaceful and relaxed atmosphere reminiscent of a sunny day. On the other hand, when used with black or grey, it can add a touch of sophistication and elegance. In conclusion, sunshine yellow is a vibrant and versatile color that can evoke feelings of happiness, positivity, and warmth in design. Its association with the sun and light, as well as its psychological impact, make it a powerful tool for capturing attention and creating an uplifting atmosphere. However, it is essential to consider the context and pairing of yellow with other colors to effectively convey the desired message or mood.

Swatches Of Color Samples

A swatch of color samples refers to a small patch or strip of different colors that are used in color theory and design to analyze and compare various color options. These swatches are typically created by grouping together different shades, hues, and tones of colors to visually represent the range of possibilities within a specific color palette or scheme. In the context of color theory, swatches of color samples help designers and artists understand the principles of color harmony, contrast, and balance. By arranging and studying different color swatches, individuals can observe how colors interact with each other and how they can be combined to create different moods, emotions, and visual effects. In color symbolism, swatches of color samples play a significant role in expressing meaning and conveying messages in design. Different colors have symbolic associations and cultural connotations, and by using swatches of color samples, designers can explore the psychological and emotional impact of different color choices. For example, warm colors such as red and orange are often associated with passion, energy, and excitement, while cool colors like blue and green are linked to calmness, harmony, and tranquility. By comparing and analyzing swatches of different warm and cool colors, designers can make informed decisions about the color choices that will best communicate the desired message or evoke a particular emotional response in their design. Swatches of color samples can also be used to create color palettes or schemes that are aesthetically pleasing and visually balanced. Designers may use complementary colors (colors that are opposite each other on the color wheel), analogous colors (colors that are next to each other on the color wheel), or monochromatic color schemes (using different shades and tones of a single color) to create visually cohesive and harmonious designs. In conclusion, swatches of color samples are a valuable tool in color theory and design. They provide a practical and visual means for exploring, comparing, and selecting colors based on their symbolic associations, emotional impact, and visual compatibility. By utilizing swatches of color samples, designers can create meaningful and impactful designs that effectively communicate their intended message.

Sweetness (Pink)

Sweetness (Pink) is a hue that falls within the spectrum of colors derived from the primary color red. It is characterized by its light tint and delicate, pastel-like appearance. In color theory, pink is created by adding white to red, resulting in a softer and more subdued tone. In the context of color symbolism in design, sweetness (pink) is often associated with feminine attributes and conveys a sense of gentleness, delicacy, and romance. It is commonly used to represent love, compassion, and tenderness, making it a popular choice in designs related to relationships, weddings, and Valentine's Day.

Technology (Silver)

Technology (Silver): In the context of color theory and color symbolism in design, the color silver represents the concept of technology. Silver, often associated with metallic elements, embodies the modern and sleek aesthetic commonly associated with technological advancements. It is a color that exudes a sense of sophistication and innovation, making it a popular choice in design projects related to technology, electronics, and futuristic themes.

Tenderness (Peach)

The color tenderness, also commonly referred to as peach, is a warm and soft hue that falls under the orange color family. It is a pastel shade with a delicate and gentle appearance, often associated with feelings of sweetness, femininity, and innocence. In color theory and color symbolism in design, tenderness or peach is often used to create a sense of warmth, harmony, and tranquility. It has a calming effect on viewers and can evoke feelings of comfort and serenity. Its soft and subtle nature makes it an ideal choice for creating a soothing and peaceful atmosphere in a design.

Tenderness (Pink)

Tenderness, in the context of color theory and color symbolism in design, refers to a shade of pink that embodies a sense of softness, delicacy, and nurturing. Pink is often associated with femininity, as well as with qualities such as love, compassion, and empathy. Tenderness, as a specific hue of pink, can evoke feelings of warmth, comfort, and vulnerability. It is a color that is often used to create a sense of intimacy and emotional connection.

Tertiary Color Code Converters

Tertiary colors are a set of colors that are created by mixing equal parts of a primary color and a secondary color. In color theory, primary colors are the building blocks of all other colors, and secondary colors are created by mixing two primary colors together. Tertiary colors, therefore, are a further blending of colors to create a wider range of hues. In design, color symbolism plays a crucial role in conveying meaning and evoking emotions. Each color carries its own symbolism and can be used strategically to create a desired effect. Tertiary color converters are tools that assist designers in identifying and selecting appropriate tertiary colors for their design projects.

Tertiary Color Editors

Tertiary colors editors are tools or techniques used in color theory and color symbolism in design to create and refine tertiary colors. Tertiary colors are the result of mixing a primary color and a secondary color together. They are located between the primary and secondary colors on the color wheel. In color theory, primary colors are considered the building blocks of all other colors. They cannot be created by mixing other colors together and include red, blue, and yellow. Secondary colors, on the other hand, are created by mixing two primary colors together. These include green (a mix of blue and yellow), orange (a mix of red and yellow), and purple (a mix of red and blue). Tertiary colors are created by mixing one primary color with one adjacent secondary color on the color wheel. The resulting colors are considered more complex and nuanced than primary or secondary colors. For example, mixing blue (a primary color) with green (a secondary color) creates the tertiary color blue-green. Tertiary color editors allow designers to have more control over the creation and adjustment of tertiary colors. These tools often come in the form of software applications or interactive color wheels, where designers can select and adjust different colors to create their desired tertiary colors. They provide options to mix specific amounts of primary and secondary colors, allowing designers to achieve the exact shade or hue they envision. In the context of color symbolism in design, tertiary colors can be especially valuable for conveying specific meanings or moods. Each color carries its own symbolic associations, and tertiary colors offer a wide range of variations and combinations to evoke different emotions or convey different messages. Designers can use tertiary color editors to fine-tune their color palettes and choose the most impactful colors for their intended design goals.

Tertiary Color Pickers

Tertiary color pickers are tools used in color theory and design to create and select colors that are derived from the combination of primary and secondary colors. In color theory, a tertiary color is created by mixing equal amounts of a primary color and a secondary color that are adjacent to each other on the color wheel. These color pickers allow designers to explore and experiment with a wide range of colors, giving them more freedom and flexibility in their color choices. By using tertiary colors, designers can add depth, richness, and complexity to their designs, as well as create harmony and balance between different color elements.

Tertiary Colors

Tertiary colors are the colors that are created by mixing equal amounts of a primary color and a secondary color together. In the context of color theory, they are the result of combining a primary color (red, blue, or yellow) with a secondary color (green, orange, or purple). The combination of these colors produces six tertiary colors: red-orange, yellow-orange, yellow-green, blue-green, blue-violet, and red-violet. In color symbolism within design, tertiary colors are often used to convey a sense of depth, complexity, and balance. They are considered to be more sophisticated and nuanced than primary or secondary colors. Tertiary colors can evoke different emotions and reactions depending on the specific combination of primary and secondary colors used. For example, red-orange can symbolize passion, energy, and enthusiasm, while blue-green can represent calmness, harmony, and tranquility.

Tetradic Colors

Tetradic colors, also known as double complementary colors, are a set of four colors that are evenly spaced on the color wheel. In color theory, a color wheel is a visual representation of the colors arranged in a circular formation according to their chromatic relationships. These relationships are based on the principles of color harmony and can be used to create balance and visual interest in design. The tetradic color scheme is formed by choosing two sets of complementary colors. Complementary colors are those colors that are directly opposite each other on the color wheel. For example, red and green, blue and orange, and yellow and purple are complementary colors. In the tetradic color scheme, two sets of these complementary colors are selected to create a harmonious composition. The result is a vibrant and energetic color combination that provides a contrast of warm and cool tones. Tetradic colors are often used in design to create a visually appealing and well-balanced composition. The contrasting nature of the complementary colors provides a sense of harmony and tension at the same time. This can be used to create focal points and emphasize certain elements in a design. By using the tetradic color scheme, designers can create a dynamic and exciting visual experience for the viewer. In addition to their aesthetic appeal, tetradic colors also have symbolic meanings in design. Each color has its own associations and can evoke different emotions or convey specific messages. For example, red is often associated with passion and energy, while green is associated with nature and growth. By using tetradic colors strategically, designers can leverage these symbolic meanings to enhance the overall message and impact of their design.

Timelessness (Gray)

Timelessness (Gray) refers to a specific shade of the color gray that is associated with a sense of enduring elegance and classic sophistication. It is a color that transcends trends and is considered to be everlasting in its appeal. In the context of color theory, gray is often referred to as a neutral color that is created by mixing black and white. It is considered to be a versatile color that can be used as a backdrop or a foundation in design, allowing other colors to stand out or harmonize with it. Timelessness (Gray) takes this neutral quality of gray and adds a specific undertone that enhances its enduring and timeless qualities.

Tint And Shade Editing Software

A tint and shade editing software refers to a computer program or application that allows designers and artists to manipulate and adjust the colors of their designs by modifying the levels of tint and shade present in the selected colors. In the context of color theory and color symbolism in design, "tint" and "shade" are two important terms used to describe variations in color. Tint refers to the lightening of a color by adding white to it, while shade refers to the darkening of a color by adding black to it. These two elements play a crucial role in creating visual hierarchy, establishing mood, and conveying meaning in design.

Tint And Shade Editors And Generators

Tint and Shade Editors and Generators are tools used in color theory and design to create variations of a specific color by adjusting its brightness and saturation. Tint refers to a color that has been lightened by adding white, while shade refers to a color that has been darkened by adding black. In color theory, colors are often represented on a scale called the color wheel, where the primary colors (red, blue, and yellow) are positioned equidistantly. By mixing these primary colors together, secondary and tertiary colors are created. Tint and shade editors and generators allow designers to manipulate these colors to create a desired effect or convey a specific mood in their designs.

Tint And Shade Editors

Tint and shade editors are tools used in color theory and design to adjust the brightness and darkness of a color, respectively.In color theory, a tint refers to a lighter version of a color, while a shade refers to a darker version. Tint and shade editors allow designers to modify the brightness and darkness of a color by adding white or black to the original hue. These tools are commonly used in graphic design, painting, and other visual arts to create a desired effect or convey specific meanings.In design, color symbolism plays a significant role in conveying emotions, messages, and meanings. Each color carries its own symbolism and can evoke different feelings or associations. Tint and shade editors provide designers with the ability to manipulate colors and create variations that can enhance or alter the intended symbolism of a design.For example, in branding and logo design, the choice of colors can greatly impact how a brand is perceived by its target audience. By adjusting the tint or shade of a color, designers can create variations that evoke different emotions or convey specific qualities. Darker shades of a color may be associated with elegance, sophistication, or power, while lighter tints may create a sense of freshness, purity, or playfulness.Tint and shade editors also serve practical purposes in design by helping to create contrast and balance within a composition. By adjusting the brightness and darkness of colors, designers can create visual interest, hierarchy, and depth. Additionally, tints and shades can be used to create harmonious color schemes or highlight specific elements within a design.In conclusion, tint and shade editors are essential tools in color theory and design. They allow designers to modify the brightness and darkness of colors, creating variations that can evoke specific emotions, convey meanings, and enhance the overall visual impact of a design.

Tint And Shade Tools

Tint and Shade Tools are an essential aspect of color theory and color symbolism in design. These tools allow designers to manipulate and understand the various shades and intensities of colors, enabling them to create harmonious color schemes that convey specific emotions or messages. Tint refers to the lightness of a color, achieved by adding white to the original hue. By gradually increasing the amount of white, designers can create a range of tints that range from pale and delicate to bright and pastel-like. Tints are often associated with feelings of purity, innocence, and freshness. They are commonly used in designs that aim to evoke a sense of serenity or calmness, such as in healthcare or wellness-related projects. Shade, on the other hand, refers to the darkness of a color, achieved by adding black to the original hue. By gradually increasing the amount of black, designers can create a spectrum of shades that vary from rich and deep to muted and somber. Shades are often associated with feelings of mystery, sophistication, and depth. They are frequently used in designs that aim to convey a sense of elegance or luxury, such as in high-end fashion or interior design projects.

Tint

Tint, in the context of color theory and color symbolism in design, refers to a variation of a color achieved by adding white to it. It lightens the original color and creates a soft and delicate appearance. Tints are often used to evoke feelings of purity, innocence, and tranquility. In color theory, a color wheel is commonly used to understand the relationships between colors. It consists of primary colors (red, yellow, and blue), secondary colors (orange, green, and violet), and tertiary colors (mixtures of primary and secondary colors). By adding white to any of these colors, tints are created.

Tints And Shades

Tints and shades are two important concepts in color theory and color symbolism in design. In color theory, a tint is created by adding white to a hue, resulting in a lighter version of the original color. Tints are often associated with feelings of brightness, lightness, and purity. They can create a sense of openness and expansiveness in a design, and are commonly used to convey a sense of innocence, simplicity, and clarity. Tints are commonly used in backgrounds or large areas of a design to create a sense of space and airiness. On the other hand, a shade is created by adding black to a hue, resulting in a darker version of the original color. Shades are often associated with feelings of depth, heaviness, and mystery. They can create a sense of drama and intensity in a design, and are commonly used to convey a sense of sophistication, elegance,

185

and formality. Shades are commonly used for text or smaller elements in a design to create contrast and emphasize importance.

Tools For Accessible Color Design

One of the crucial elements in design is the use of colors to evoke certain emotions and convey meaning. However, it is also important to consider the accessibility of color choices for individuals with visual impairments. Accessible color design refers to the practice of selecting and combining colors in a way that ensures readability, comprehension, and inclusivity for all users, including those with color vision deficiencies. In the realm of color theory, accessible color design takes into account the principles of color contrast and harmony. Contrast is the difference between two colors, and it plays a vital role in legibility. High contrast between text and background colors ensures that text is easily readable for all users. It is important to maintain a sufficient level of contrast to accommodate individuals with visual impairments, especially those with color blindness. On the other hand, color harmony emphasizes the cohesive and pleasing combination of colors. Different color schemes, such as complementary, analogous, or triadic, can be used to achieve harmony and ensure that color choices work well together. Color symbolism is another aspect that plays a significant role in design, as different colors often carry specific meanings or associations. Accessible color design considers the cultural and psychological implications of color symbolism, ensuring that color choices are both meaningful and inclusive. For example, red is commonly associated with passion and excitement, while blue is often associated with calmness and serenity. However, individuals with color vision deficiencies may perceive colors differently, so it is important to select colors that convey the intended meaning across different visual abilities. In order to facilitate accessible color design, various tools are available to assist designers in making informed color choices. Color contrast checkers enable designers to test the contrast between text and background colors and ensure that they meet accessibility standards. Additionally, color blindness simulators allow designers to view their designs as individuals with color vision deficiencies might see them. These simulations aid in identifying potential issues and making necessary adjustments for a more inclusive design. In conclusion, accessible color design involves selecting colors that provide sufficient contrast and harmonious combinations while considering color symbolism and implications for individuals with visual impairments. By utilizing various tools specifically designed for assessing color contrast and simulating color vision deficiencies, designers can create more inclusive and meaningful designs for all users.

Tools For Color Conversion

Color conversion tools are software or programs designed to facilitate the process of converting colors between different color models or color spaces. In the context of color theory and color symbolism in design, these tools are essential for achieving accurate and consistent color representation across various mediums, such as digital displays, printing, and web design. Color theory is the study of how colors interact with each other and the visual effects they produce. It classifies colors into different models or color spaces, such as RGB (Red, Green, Blue), CMYK (Cyan, Magenta, Yellow, Black), and HSL (Hue, Saturation, Lightness). Each model represents colors in a different way and is used in specific applications. Color symbolism in design refers to the use of colors to convey certain meanings, emotions, or messages. Different colors are associated with different meanings in various cultures and contexts. For example, red is often associated with passion or anger, while blue is associated with calmness or sadness. When using colors in design, it is important to understand the intended symbolism and ensure that the chosen colors accurately represent the desired emotions or messages. Color conversion tools play a crucial role in color theory and color symbolism in design by enabling designers to convert colors between different models or color spaces. For example, a designer may need to convert an RGB color to CMYK for printing purposes. Without a color conversion tool, achieving accurate color representation would be challenging and could result in undesired color shifts or inconsistencies. Furthermore, color conversion tools also allow designers to explore different color combinations and variations. By converting colors between different models or color spaces, designers can more easily experiment with color palettes and choose the most suitable colors for their design projects.

Tools For Color Simulation

Color simulation tools are digital instruments or applications used in the field of color theory and design to imitate, represent, or replicate specific colors in a controlled environment. These tools are indispensable for designers, artists, marketers, and other professionals who work with color and require accurate visualization and manipulation of colors. In the domain of color theory, color simulation tools play a vital role in understanding the scientific principles of color. As human perception of color varies, color simulation tools aid in providing a standardized and objective approach to color analysis. By utilizing these tools, designers can assess the impact of different color combinations, gradients, and variations to achieve harmony or contrast in their design compositions.

Tools For Correcting Colorblindness

Colorblindness is a condition in which an individual has difficulty perceiving certain colors or distinguishing between them accurately. In the context of color theory and color symbolism in design, colorblindness can present challenges as it can affect the way individuals perceive and interpret colors, potentially leading to miscommunication or misinterpretation of intended messages. To address this issue, various tools have been developed to assist individuals with colorblindness in perceiving colors more accurately. These tools aim to enhance color differentiation and improve the overall visual experience for colorblind individuals. One such tool is colorblind filters, which are features commonly found in digital design software or applications. These filters simulate the perception of individuals with different types of colorblindness, allowing designers to visualize their work as colorblind users would see it. By previewing their designs through these filters, designers can identify and rectify any potential issues or color combinations that may be problematic for colorblind individuals. Another tool is the use of colorblind-friendly palettes or color schemes. Designers can select colors that are more distinguishable for individuals with colorblindness, taking into consideration the types of color deficiency that affect the target audience. For example, using high contrast color combinations or incorporating different hues that are easier to differentiate can help ensure that the intended information is conveyed effectively to colorblind users. Additionally, designers can employ alternative means of conveying information instead of relying solely on color. This can be achieved through the use of different shapes, patterns, or text labels to represent or differentiate elements typically identified by color alone. By using these supplementary cues, designers can help colorblind individuals understand and interact with visual content more easily. In conclusion, tools for correcting colorblindness in the context of color theory and color symbolism in design are essential for ensuring accessibility and inclusivity in visual communication. By utilizing colorblind filters, selecting colorblind-friendly palettes, and employing alternative means of conveying information, designers can effectively address the challenges faced by colorblind individuals and ensure that their intended messages are accurately perceived and understood.

Tools For Predicting Color Trends

Color trends are an essential aspect of design, as they reflect societal preferences and influences within a given period. Predicting color trends involves the use of various tools and techniques that aid in determining the colors that are likely to be popular in the future. These tools provide designers with valuable insights for creating visually appealing and impactful designs. In color theory, color trends are influenced by several factors, including cultural, social, and psychological aspects. Understanding these factors helps in predicting upcoming color preferences. Additionally, color symbolism plays a significant role in design, as different colors convey different meanings and evoke specific emotions. Designers can leverage these symbolic associations to create visually engaging and culturally resonant designs.

Tradition (Gold)

Tradition refers to a color that is commonly associated with deeply rooted customs, rituals, and beliefs. In the context of color theory and color symbolism in design, gold often embodies the concept of tradition. Gold is a warm and metallic color that is frequently used to evoke a sense of heritage, heritage, and time-honored practices. It is deeply rooted in cultural symbolism and has a significant historical significance in many civilizations. Gold is often associated with wealth, prosperity, and power, reflecting its historical use in jewelry, architectural accents, and religious artifacts.

Tranquility (Teal)

Tranquility (Teal) in color theory refers to a specific shade that falls within the blue-green spectrum. Teal is created by combining equal parts of blue and green, resulting in a hue that is calming and serene. This particular shade of teal, known as tranquility, is often associated with peacefulness and tranquility. In the context of color symbolism in design, tranquility (teal) is often used to evoke a sense of relaxation and calmness. It is frequently utilized in spaces that aim to create a peaceful environment, such as bedrooms, meditation rooms, or spas.

Triadic Colors

Triadic colors, within the realm of color theory and color symbolism in design, refer to a specific color scheme consisting of three colors that are evenly spaced around the color wheel. These three colors are selected based on their equal distance from each other, creating a harmonious and balanced composition. The concept of triadic colors stems from the fundamental understanding of the color wheel, where colors are organized in a circular format. The color wheel is composed of 12 hues, with primary colors (red, blue, and yellow) forming the foundation. By selecting any one of these primary colors and jumping three spaces in either direction on the color wheel, we arrive at two additional colors that, when combined, create a triadic color scheme. Triadic color schemes are associated with a vibrant and energetic aesthetic, making them ideal for creating attention-grabbing designs. The contrast between the three colors in a triadic scheme adds visual interest and complexity, while maintaining a sense of balance and cohesion. In the realm of color symbolism, the three colors in a triadic scheme often possess their own individual meanings and associations. For example, the primary colors themselves hold significant symbolism. Red is commonly associated with passion, energy, and power. Blue is often linked to calmness, stability, and trust. Yellow is often associated with happiness, optimism, and creativity. When combined in a triadic scheme, these colors can convey a range of emotions and messages. Designers utilize triadic color schemes to evoke specific moods or emotions in their creations. It offers a dynamic and lively visual experience, attracting viewers' attention while maintaining a balanced composition. Triadic colors can be used in various design fields, such as graphic design, interior design, and even fashion design, enabling designers to create impactful and visually striking compositions.

Trust (Blue)

Trust is a color in the realm of color theory and symbolism in design. It belongs to the blue color family, which is characterized by its soothing and calming qualities. Blue is often associated with trust, reliability, and security. Blue is a color that tends to evoke feelings of peace, tranquility, and stability. It is often used in design to create a sense of trust and dependability. The color blue has been found to have a physiological effect on the body, slowing heart rate and reducing blood pressure. This calming effect contributes to its association with trust.

UI Color Design Guidelines

UI Color Design Guidelines refer to the principles and guidelines used in the field of color theory and color symbolism to determine the appropriate colors for user interface (UI) design. These guidelines take into consideration the psychological and emotional impact of colors on users, as well as the functional and aesthetic aspects of the UI design. The purpose of these guidelines is to create visually pleasing and user-friendly interfaces that effectively communicate the intended message and enhance the overall user experience. In color theory, different colors have been associated with specific emotions and meanings. For example, blue is often associated with trust and calmness, while red is associated with energy and urgency. UI Color Design Guidelines ensure that colors used in UI design align with the desired emotions and meanings associated with the brand or the purpose of the interface. This helps to create a consistent and cohesive visual language that resonates with the target audience. Moreover, these guidelines also take into consideration the functional aspects of UI design. For instance, certain colors may be used to highlight important elements or calls to action, while others may be used for background or text to ensure readability. The guidelines suggest appropriate color combinations, contrasts, and hierarchy to ensure that the UI design is both visually appealing and functional. Consistency is another important aspect of UI Color Design Guidelines. Consistent use of colors throughout the interface helps users to establish a mental model of the UI, reducing cognitive load and enhancing usability. The guidelines provide recommendations on the use of color schemes, color palettes, and color harmonies to maintain consistency and coherence across different UI elements. In summary, UI Color Design Guidelines provide a framework for selecting colors in UI design based on color theory and color symbolism. These guidelines ensure that the chosen colors align with the intended emotions and meanings, while also considering the functional and aesthetic aspects of the interface. By following these guidelines, designers can create visually appealing and user-friendly interfaces that effectively communicate the desired message and enhance the overall user experience.

UI Color Guidelines Documents

UI Color Guidelines Documents are formal documents created by designers or design teams to provide guidelines on the use of colors in user interface (UI) design. These documents are based on color theory and the understanding of color symbolism in design. Color theory refers to the principles and guidelines that govern the use of colors in art and design, while color symbolism refers to the meanings and associations that colors evoke in people. In UI Color Guidelines Documents, designers outline the appropriate use of colors in different UI elements such as buttons, backgrounds, text, and icons. These documents provide guidance on color combinations, contrasts, and harmonies to ensure a visually pleasing and effective user interface. For example, they may recommend using complementary colors (colors opposite each other on the color wheel) to create visual interest and balance. Designers also consider the psychological and emotional impact of colors on users. For instance, warm colors like red and orange may evoke feelings of energy and excitement, while cool colors like blue and green may elicit a sense of calmness and trustworthiness.

UI Color Guidelines

UI Color Guidelines are principles and recommendations used in design to help create visually appealing and effective user interfaces. They are based on color theory, which is the study of how colors interact and affect the human perception and emotions. In the context of design, colors have symbolic meanings and can communicate specific messages or evoke certain emotions. Each color has its own psychological and cultural associations, and understanding these associations is essential in creating meaningful and impactful user experiences.

UI Color Pickers

A UI color picker is a tool used in design that enables users to select specific colors for their digital creations. It is an interface element that allows users to choose colors from a predefined color palette or create custom colors using various color models. In the context of color theory, a UI color picker provides users with a range of colors based on the principles of color harmony, contrast, and balance. Color theory is the study of how colors interact with each other and how they can be combined to create visually pleasing designs. It helps designers understand the emotional and psychological impact of colors and how they can influence user experience. Color symbolism is the notion that colors have symbolic meanings and evoke certain emotions or associations. Each color has its own psychological and cultural significance, and understanding color symbolism is crucial in design to convey the intended message or evoke a specific response from the audience. A UI color picker allows designers to explore different color options and select the most appropriate colors based on color theory and symbolism. It typically consists of a color wheel or a spectrum of colors, where users can click or drag to select a specific hue. Additionally, it may include sliders or input fields to adjust the saturation, brightness, or transparency of a color. The color palette within a UI color picker often includes a variety of color schemes, such as complementary, analogous, or triadic colors. These color schemes are based on the relationships between colors on the color wheel and can help designers create harmonious and visually pleasing compositions. By using a UI color picker, designers can ensure that their color choices align with their intended design objectives, such as creating a calming and serene atmosphere with cool blue tones or conveying energy and excitement with vibrant reds and oranges. It allows for experimentation and exploration, helping designers to find the perfect color combinations that resonate with their target audience. In conclusion, a UI color picker is an essential tool in design that facilitates the selection of colors based on color theory and symbolism. It empowers designers to make informed choices and create visually appealing designs that convey the desired message and elicit the desired response from users.

189

UI Color Picking Tools

A UI color picking tool is a software or online tool that enables designers and developers to select and choose colors for their user interface (UI) designs. It provides a convenient and efficient way to explore and find the right colors that align with color theory and convey the desired symbolism in design. Color theory is the study of the ways different colors interact and how they can be combined to create harmonious and visually appealing designs. It encompasses principles such as color harmony, contrast, saturation, and hue. Applying color theory principles helps designers create designs that evoke specific emotions and effectively communicate messages.

Valor (Bronze)

Valor (Bronze) is a color that falls into the category of warm and earthy colors in color theory and is often associated with strength, stability, and dependability. It is a shade of brown with red and orange undertones, giving it a rich and deep appearance. In the context of color symbolism in design, Valor (Bronze) is often used to convey a sense of tradition, reliability, and resilience. It is commonly associated with qualities such as steadfastness, grounding, and a sense of permanence. The warm and earthy nature of this color evokes a feeling of warmth, comfort, and stability, making it a popular choice in design contexts where these qualities are desired.

Value

The value in color theory refers to the lightness or darkness of a color. It is the level of brightness or richness that a color possesses. The value of a color is determined by how much black or white is added to the pure hue. When black is added to a color, it becomes darker, and when white is added, it becomes lighter. In design, the value of color plays a crucial role in creating contrast, depth, and hierarchy in visual compositions. By adjusting the value, designers can create visually balanced and harmonious designs. High value contrast can create emphasis and draw attention to particular elements, while low value contrast can be used to create a more subtle and serene atmosphere.

Vibrance

Vibrance, in the context of color theory and color symbolism in design, refers to the intensity or strength of a color. It is a measure of how vivid or bright a color appears, and it often contributes to the overall impact and visual appeal of a design. In color theory, vibrance is closely related to saturation and brightness. Saturation determines the purity or depth of a color, while brightness refers to the lightness or darkness of a color. Vibrance, on the other hand, focuses specifically on the strength of a color's appearance.

Vibrant Color Editors

Vibrant Color Editors refer to individuals or tools that possess the ability to manipulate and enhance color in the field of design, particularly in relation to color theory and color symbolism. Color theory explores the principles and guidelines for creating harmonious and visually appealing color combinations, while color symbolism examines the meaning and association of different colors. When it comes to color theory, vibrant color editors play a crucial role in helping designers achieve a desired aesthetic by adjusting and fine-tuning colors. They provide a range of tools and techniques to alter the hue, saturation, brightness, and contrast of colors. By using vibrant color editors, designers can enhance the intensity and vividness of colors, creating a sense of energy and excitement in their designs. These editors allow designers to explore various color harmonies, such as complementary, analogous, and triadic, to ensure a balanced and visually pleasing composition. In addition to color theory, vibrant color editors also make it possible for designers to work with color symbolism. Color symbolism involves the use of specific colors to convey emotions, ideas, or messages within a design. Vibrant color editors enable designers to manipulate the psychological impact of colors by adjusting their vibrancy, saturation, and tonal values. This flexibility allows designers to evoke specific emotions or associations through the use of color. For example, vibrant reds may be used to evoke passion or excitement, while calming blues can create a sense of tranquility or trust. In conclusion, vibrant color editors are essential tools for designers who seek to create visually stunning and meaningful designs. Through their capabilities in color theory and color symbolism, vibrant color editors enable designers to manipulate and enhance color in a way that creates harmony, intrigue, and engagement.

Vibrant Color Tools And Software

Vibrant Color Tools and Software are a set of digital resources used to explore, manipulate, and enhance colors in the context of color theory and symbolism in design. These tools and software provide designers with the ability to create visually appealing and harmonious color palettes that effectively communicate the desired message or evoke specific emotions. In the realm of color theory, these tools and software enable designers to understand the relationships between different colors, such as complementary, analogous, and triadic color schemes. By allowing the exploration and visualization of these color relationships, designers can make informed decisions about color combinations that create balance and harmony in their designs. Additionally, vibrant color tools and software provide various features to manipulate and adjust colors, including hue, saturation, and brightness. Designers can easily tweak the intensity and vibrancy of colors to suit their design goals and convey the desired emotions. With these tools, it becomes possible to experiment with different color variations and find the perfect balance that enhances the overall visual impact. Furthermore, vibrant color tools and software play a crucial role in color symbolism within design. Colors hold significant meanings and can evoke specific emotions or associations. These tools offer an extensive range of color palettes and libraries that are curated based on their symbolic representation in various cultures and contexts. Designers can leverage these pre-established associations to effectively communicate their intended message and elicit the desired response from their target audience. In conclusion, vibrant color tools and software are indispensable resources for designers, providing them with the means to explore, manipulate, and enhance colors in the context of color theory and symbolism. By utilizing these digital tools, designers can create visually appealing and emotionally impactful designs that effectively communicate their intended message and resonate with their audience.

Vibrant Color Tools

Vibrant Color Tools refer to a range of resources and techniques used in color theory and color symbolism within design. These tools help designers explore and implement vibrant and impactful colors in their works, ensuring that the message and visual impact of their designs are effectively communicated to the intended audience. Color theory is a field of study that examines the ways in which colors can be combined, contrasted, and harmonized to create visually appealing and balanced compositions. Vibrant Color Tools facilitate the application of this theory by providing designers with ways to experiment with different color combinations and variations, enabling them to make informed decisions about which colors to use in their designs. These tools include color wheels and charts, which help designers understand the relationships between different colors and how they can be manipulated to achieve desired effects. By using these tools, designers can determine complementary, analogous, or triadic color schemes, ensuring that their designs have a harmonious and balanced color palette. Additionally, Vibrant Color Tools encompass resources such as color swatches and palettes, which offer pre-selected sets of colors that work well together. Designers can use these palettes as a starting point or source of inspiration, ensuring that their designs are visually appealing and consistent in their use of vibrant colors. Color symbolism, on the other hand, explores the meaning and associations that different colors hold in various cultures and contexts. Vibrant Color Tools assist designers in effectively communicating specific emotions, themes, or messages by incorporating colors that carry symbolic significance. These tools provide designers with a comprehensive selection of vibrant colors that are associated with particular meanings or evoke specific emotions. By understanding and leveraging color symbolism, designers can evoke desired responses from the audience and create designs that are visually impactful and conceptually meaningful.

Vibrant Colors

Vibrant colors, in the context of color theory and color symbolism in design, refer to shades that are bold, intense, and eye-catching. These colors are highly saturated and possess a high level of brightness and luminosity. They command attention and exude energy, making them a powerful tool in visual communication and design. Vibrant colors are often associated with positive emotions such as joy, enthusiasm, and excitement. They have the ability to evoke strong reactions and create a lively and stimulating visual experience. These hues can instantly grab the viewer's attention and create a dynamic focal point in a design composition.

Victory (Bronze)

Victory (Bronze) - In the context of color theory and color symbolism in design, victory (bronze) is a color that represents strength, perseverance, and accomplishment. It is a warm, earthy tone that is commonly associated with success and triumph. Bronze, as a metallic color, embodies qualities of durability and resilience. It is often used to convey a sense of achievement or victory in various design applications. The color bronze is derived from a mixture of yellow and red pigments, creating a hue that exudes energy and power.

Vintage Colors

Vintage colors refer to a palette of hues that were popular during a specific era in the past, typically around the 1920s to 1970s. These colors evoke a sense of nostalgia and are often associated with retro or antique aesthetics. In color theory, vintage colors can be represented by muted tones, earthy tones, and warm neutrals. In design, vintage colors are used to create a sense of history or to convey a certain mood or emotion. Each vintage color carries its own symbolism and meaning, which can vary depending on cultural context or personal associations. For instance, soft pastels like blush pink or mint green are often associated with femininity, innocence, and romance. Earthy tones such as mustard yellow or olive green can represent a connection to nature, grounding, or a rustic charm.

Vitality (Gold)

Vitality in color theory refers to the quality or state of being full of energy and life. In the context of color symbolism in design, the color gold represents vitality. It is a color associated with success, achievement, and abundance. Gold is often used in design to evoke feelings of optimism, positivity, and vigor. It can be used to create a sense of energy and enthusiasm in various visual elements, such as logos, typography, and illustrations. The brightness and shine of gold can attract attention and make a design appear lively and vibrant.

Vitality (Mint)

Vitality, in the context of color theory and color symbolism in design, refers to a specific shade of green known as Mint. This color is characterized by its pale and light appearance, resembling the color of mint leaves. Mint green is often associated with freshness, youthfulness, and a sense of rejuvenation. In color theory, Mint falls under the green color family. Green is widely regarded as a color that symbolizes balance, harmony, and growth. It represents nature, vitality, and fertility. Mint, as a specific shade of green, carries all these qualities but with a softer and more delicate touch.

Vitality (Orange)

Vitality, also known as orange, is a color within the color theory and color symbolism in design. It is a warm, vibrant, and energetic hue that often evokes feelings of enthusiasm, excitement, and creativity. Orange is a secondary color, created by mixing equal parts of red and yellow. It falls between red and yellow on the color wheel, and its intensity can range from a fiery, intense orange to a softer, more muted shade.

War (Maroon)

War (Maroon) is a deep, rich shade of red that falls within the warm color family. It is often associated with strength, power, and passion. In color theory, maroon is seen as a variant of red that has been darkened, creating a sense of intensity and seriousness. In design and art, maroon is a versatile color that can be used to evoke a wide range of emotions and convey different meanings. Its association with war symbolizes courage, bravery, and determination. It is a color often used to represent militaries, soldiers, and related themes in visual communication.

192

War (Red)

War (Red) is a vibrant and intense color that holds great significance in color theory and color symbolism in design. It is often associated with strong emotions, power, energy, and passion. In color theory, red is classified as a warm color along with yellow and orange. It has a high wavelength and is visually stimulating, making it one of the most attention-grabbing colors. Red can evoke a sense of urgency and excitement, drawing people's focus and creating a sense of importance. It is often used to highlight important elements or to grab the viewer's attention in design compositions. Red is also deeply rooted in symbolism. In various cultures, red is associated with different meanings and emotions. In Western cultures, it is often associated with danger, power, and aggression. It can convey a sense of warning or alertness. Red is also closely tied to love and passion, representing desire and intense emotions. In this context, it is commonly used in romantic or intimate designs. In design, the use of red can greatly influence the overall perception and impact of a composition. When used sparingly or as an accent color, red can create a focal point and add a sense of energy and excitement to a design. It can be used to emphasize important information or to create a sense of urgency. However, excessive use of red can be overwhelming and distracting, so it is important to use it judiciously and in balance with other colors. Red is a versatile color that can evoke a wide range of emotions and messages depending on how it is used. It has the power to attract attention, convey intensity, and elicit strong emotional responses. With its rich symbolism and energetic qualities, red is a valuable tool in design for creating impact and communicating messages effectively.

Warm Color Generators Online

Warm color generators online refer to digital tools or applications that assist in generating warm colors based on color theory and color symbolism in design. These generators provide a platform for designers, artists, and anyone working with colors to explore and create warm color palettes for various purposes. Color theory is a field that studies how colors interact and how they can be combined to create different moods and effects. Warm colors, including hues like red, orange, and yellow, are often associated with feelings of warmth, energy, and positivity. They can bring a sense of excitement and liveliness to designs when used appropriately. Color symbolism in design refers to the meaning or associations that certain colors evoke in viewers. Warm colors can symbolize various things depending on the context. Red, for example, can signify love, passion, or danger, while orange may represent enthusiasm and warmth. Yellow is often associated with happiness and optimism. Warm color generators online enable individuals to experiment with these warm hues and discover pleasing color combinations. They offer functionalities such as color wheels, sliders, and swatches that allow users to select and mix warm colors according to their preferences. The generators often provide predefined warm color schemes or palettes to inspire users. These schemes are designed based on color theory principles and can be useful for designers who may need inspiration or are looking to create a cohesive color palette for their projects. Furthermore, warm color generators online may offer features to adjust the saturation, brightness, and contrast of warm colors to achieve desired effects. Users can explore variations within warm color schemes, creating subtle or vibrant combinations to suit their specific design intentions. Overall, warm color generators online serve as valuable tools for designers to experiment, discover, and create warm color palettes that enhance their designs. These tools empower individuals to utilize the power of warm colors and tap into the psychological and emotional impact they can have on viewers.

Warm Color Generators

A warm color generator is a tool used in color theory and design to create and identify warm colors. Warm colors are a group of colors that evoke feelings of heat, energy, and warmth. They are typically found on the red, orange, and yellow side of the color wheel. In color theory, warm colors are believed to advance or come forward, making objects painted in warm colors appear closer to the viewer. They have the ability to create a sense of excitement and stimulate the senses. Warm colors are often associated with strong emotions such as passion, happiness, and energy. They can create a lively and inviting atmosphere when used appropriately in design. Warm color generators are online tools or software that help designers choose and create warm colors for their projects. These generators allow users to explore various shades and combinations of warm colors, helping them to find the perfect color scheme for their design. By inputting specific color values or using sliders, designers can easily generate warm colors that

193

match their desired aesthetic. Understanding the use of warm colors and their significance in design can greatly impact the message and emotional response of a design. For example, using warm colors in a restaurant logo can stimulate appetite and create a welcoming atmosphere, while using warm colors in a bedroom design can evoke feelings of coziness and comfort. In addition to their emotional impact, warm colors can also create a sense of depth and dimension in design. By using warm colors in the foreground and cooler colors in the background, designers can create a sense of balance and harmony in their compositions. In conclusion, warm color generators play a crucial role in color theory and design by enabling designers to create and identify warm colors. These tools help designers evoke specific emotions and create visually appealing compositions. By understanding the significance of warm colors and their impact on design, designers can effectively use warm color generators to enhance their creative projects.

Warm Color Palette Generators

The warm color palette generators are tools or algorithms that assist designers in creating a collection of colors primarily consisting of warm hues. In the context of color theory and symbolism in design, warm colors are typically associated with energy, excitement, passion, and intimacy. These colors evoke sensations of heat, warmth, and brightness similar to those produced by the sun or fire. Warm color palette generators utilize various techniques to generate a harmonious combination of warm colors. These tools take into consideration principles such as color harmony, color temperature, and color psychology to create visually appealing palettes. Color harmony refers to the arrangement of colors in a way that is aesthetically pleasing and balanced. It can be achieved by using complementary, analogous, or triadic color schemes, among others. Color temperature plays a significant role in warm color palette generation. Warm colors, such as red, orange, and yellow, are considered to have a higher color temperature, as they are associated with heat and warmth. These colors can be used to create a sense of energy and intensity in design. Warm color palette generators may use algorithms that calculate color temperature or suggest colors that have a similar temperature to ensure a cohesive and harmonious palette. Color symbolism is another important aspect of warm color palettes in design. In many cultures, warm colors are associated with specific meanings and emotions. For example, red is often associated with love, passion, and excitement, while orange can represent joy, enthusiasm, and creativity. Yellow is commonly associated with happiness, energy, and warmth. By incorporating these symbolic meanings into a design, designers can create a visual language that communicates the desired message or emotion to the audience. Warm color palette generators provide designers with a convenient and efficient way to explore different combinations of warm colors. These tools can assist in creating visually appealing designs that evoke specific emotions or convey particular meanings. By utilizing the principles of color theory and symbolism, designers can leverage the power of warm colors to create engaging and impactful designs.

Warm Colors

Warm Colors are a group of colors that are perceived as being warmer in comparison to cool colors. They are typically associated with elements such as fire, sun, heat, and warmth, and include hues such as red, orange, and yellow. In color theory, warm colors are positioned on one side of the color wheel, opposite to cool colors. In terms of color symbolism in design, warm colors evoke various emotions and have different connotations. They are often associated with energy, passion, and enthusiasm. The use of warm colors in design can create a sense of warmth, coziness, and intimacy. They can evoke feelings of excitement, optimism, and creativity. Warm colors are known to stimulate appetite, which is why they are commonly used in the food industry, particularly in restaurants and food packaging.

Warmth (Apricot)

Warmth (Apricot) in color theory refers to a specific shade within the warm color family that evokes a sense of heat, energy, and intensity. It is a vibrant hue that lies between orange and pink, taking on the appearance of a ripe apricot fruit. Color symbolism plays a crucial role in design, as different colors evoke various emotions and associations. Warm colors, including warmth (apricot), are often associated with feelings of passion, enthusiasm, and creativity. In the color spectrum, warm colors are located on one side, opposite to the cool colors. Warmth (apricot) carries a strong sense of heat and intensity that can convey these emotions in design.

Warmth (Beige)

Warmth (Beige) in color theory refers to a pale, soft, and light hue that falls within the neutral color palette. It is often associated with warmth, comfort, and a sense of coziness, resembling the natural tones found in earthy materials such as sand, wheat, or desert landscapes. Beige is created by combining varying amounts of yellow, white, and sometimes a hint of red or orange. In design and color symbolism, Warmth (Beige) is commonly used to evoke feelings of relaxation, subtlety, and understated elegance. Its neutrality makes it a versatile color that pairs well with a wide range of other hues without overpowering them. It serves as a calming and grounding presence, creating a warm and inviting atmosphere.

Warmth (Brown)

Warmth (Brown) is a color within the context of color theory and color symbolism in design. It falls within the warm color category and is characterized by its associations with earthiness, stability, and warmth. In color theory, warmth is associated with colors that evoke a sense of heat and coziness. Brown, specifically, is often referred to as a warm color due to its connection to natural elements such as wood, earth, and soil. It is created by combining different amounts of red, yellow, and black pigments. Brown can range from light tans to dark chocolates, and each shade carries its own symbolic meaning.

Warmth (Gold)

Warmth (Gold) is a color found in color theory and used as a symbol in design. It is a hue that falls within the warm color spectrum, which includes colors such as red, orange, and yellow. Warm colors are associated with heat, energy, and positivity. When used in design, Warmth (Gold) can evoke a sense of luxury, wealth, and power. Gold, in particular, has long been associated with these qualities due to its rarity and historical use in ornamental objects. It is often used to add a touch of elegance and sophistication to designs.

Warmth (Orange)

Warmth (Orange): In the context of color theory and color symbolism in design, warmth refers to a perceived sensation of heat or the illusion of warmth elicited by the color orange. Orange is a secondary color that combines the energetic qualities of red and the joyousness of yellow, creating a hue that symbolizes feelings of warmth, comfort, enthusiasm, and vibrancy. Orange is often associated with the sun and fire, linking it to concepts of energy, creativity, and passion. It can evoke feelings of excitement, enthusiasm, and a positive outlook. Its warm undertones can promote a sense of happiness, joy, and an overall uplifting atmosphere. This makes orange an ideal choice in design where the goal is to create a visually stimulating, lively, and engaging environment.

Warmth (Peach)

Warmth (Peach) is a color that is categorized within the warm color family and is often associated with feelings of comfort, softness, and nurturing. It is a shade of orange that has a high level of red undertones, resulting in a subtle, delicate, and slightly muted appearance. In color theory, warmth is one of the fundamental characteristics used to describe colors and their emotional impact. Warm colors, including Warmth (Peach), are known to evoke feelings of energy, passion, and positivity. They are often associated with fire, the sun, and warmth itself, which in turn create a sense of coziness and welcome.

Warmth (Yellow)

Warmth (Yellow) is a color that represents energy, optimism, and happiness in the context of color theory and color symbolism in design. It belongs to the warm color family and is associated with the sun and light. Yellow is often used to convey warmth, light, and positivity in design. In color theory, yellow is classified as a warm color due to its ability to evoke feelings of heat and energy. It has a high wavelength and is perceived as one of the brightest colors. Yellow is often used to grab attention and create a sense of urgency or excitement. It has the power to uplift the mood and stimulate mental activity. Yellow is also associated with gold, which symbolizes wealth and success.

Water (Blue)

Water (Blue) is a shade of blue commonly associated with the color theory and color symbolism in design. It is a hue that often represents the natural element of water and is frequently used to evoke feelings of calmness, serenity, and tranquility. In color theory, blue is classified as one of the three primary colors, alongside red and yellow. It is situated on the cool side of the color wheel and is considered a "cool color." Blue evokes a sense of calmness, stability, and introspection. It is often associated with feelings of trust, reliability, and loyalty. As water is crucial for life and sustenance, the color blue can also symbolize purity, cleanliness, and renewal.

Wealth (Gold)

Wealth (Gold) is a color in the context of color theory and color symbolism in design. It is a shade of yellow that is associated with opulence, prosperity, and abundance. In color theory, gold is often considered a warm color due to its connection with the sun and its shining and radiant appearance. It is seen as a color that evokes positive emotions and carries the connotation of luxury and richness. Gold is often used in design to convey a sense of wealth and prestige. It is commonly associated with high-end products and services, such as luxury brands and exclusive events. The color gold is used strategically to attract attention and create a sense of extravagance and glamour. Its use in design can create a feeling of elegance and sophistication, appealing to a target audience that desires and appreciates luxury.

Web-Safe Color Code Converters

Web-Safe Color Code Converters are tools used in the field of color theory and design to convert colors into the web-safe color palette. In web design, the web-safe color palette is a collection of 216 colors that are consistent across all operating systems and web browsers. These converters ensure that the colors chosen for a website or digital project will appear the same on different devices and platforms, maintaining the intended visual impact. Color theory plays a crucial role in design as different colors evoke different emotions and convey distinct messages. Understanding color symbolism is essential to effectively communicate a desired message to the audience. Colors have the power to influence moods, emotions, and behaviors, making it vital to choose appropriate colors for specific design purposes. The web-safe color palette was developed in the early days of the web when display systems could only render a limited number of colors. This palette consists of 216 colors that were considered "safe" because they were consistently displayed on both PCs and Macs at the time. However, modern software and devices can display millions of colors, rendering the web-safe palette somewhat obsolete. Web-Safe Color Code Converters provide a solution for designers to ensure their chosen colors translate accurately across different platforms. These converters convert the colors chosen by the designer into the closest web-safe color equivalent. For example, if a designer selects a shade of blue that is not part of the web-safe palette, the converter will find the closest web-safe blue and provide the corresponding color code. The color code is a combination of numbers and letters that represents a specific color within the web-safe palette. The most common format for the color code is the hexadecimal system, which uses a combination of six characters to represent the intensity of red, green, and blue (RGB) in the color. For example, the color code for the web-safe blue could be #0000FF, where FF represents the maximum intensity of blue and the absence of red and green. By using a web-safe color converter, designers can adhere to the web-safe color palette, ensuring consistent color reproduction across platforms. This helps to maintain the integrity of the designer's intended color scheme, as well as the overall visual impact and message conveyed by the design. In conclusion, web-safe color code converters play a vital role in color theory and design by ensuring consistent color reproduction across different platforms. They help designers adhere to the web-safe color palette, maintaining the intended visual impact and message of their designs.

Web-Safe Color Editing Tools

Web-safe color editing tools refer to software applications or online tools that allow designers to

196

modify or adjust colors while adhering to the web-safe color palette. In the context of color theory and color symbolism in design, web-safe colors are a restricted set of colors that can be accurately displayed on computers with limited color capabilities, typically 256 colors or less. The web-safe color palette was popularized in the early days of the internet when computers and monitors had limited color rendering capabilities. In order to ensure consistent and reliable color display across different devices and platforms, designers had to choose colors from a specific set that were defined as web safe. These colors were chosen to align with the limited color capabilities of monitors at the time. Color theory is an essential aspect of design that deals with the visual and psychological effects of color on human perception. Different colors evoke different emotions and can communicate various meanings or messages. Color symbolism is the study of how colors are culturally associated with specific meanings or concepts. Web-safe color editing tools are designed to assist designers in creating harmonious and visually appealing color compositions while ensuring the compatibility of colors across different devices and browsers. These tools typically provide a palette of web-safe colors and various editing functions to adjust hue, saturation, brightness, and other color properties. By using web-safe color editing tools, designers can select colors that align with their design goals, taking into consideration the psychological and symbolic associations of different colors. They can experiment with different color combinations and fine-tune the color palette to create a visually cohesive and meaningful design. In summary, web-safe color editing tools are software applications or online tools that enable designers to modify and adjust colors while adhering to a restricted set of colors known as the web-safe color palette. These tools are essential in color theory and color symbolism, allowing designers to create visually appealing and consistent designs that communicate specific messages or evoke desired emotions.

Web-Safe Color Editors

Web-Safe Color Editors are tools that allow designers and developers to select and work with colors that are considered to be "safe" for the web. In the context of color theory, these tools help ensure that the chosen colors can be accurately displayed across different platforms and devices. Color theory is the study of how colors interact with each other and how they can be used to convey certain emotions or messages. It plays a crucial role in design, as colors have the power to evoke emotions and shape the overall perception of a website or application. Color symbolism, on the other hand, is the concept of associating specific meanings or emotions with certain colors. For example, red is often associated with passion or danger, while blue is often associated with calmness or trust. Understanding color symbolism can help designers effectively communicate their intended message to the audience. Web-Safe Color Editors take color theory and color symbolism into consideration by providing a curated selection of colors that are known to display consistently across different browsers and operating systems. These editors typically present a grid or palette of colors with their corresponding hexadecimal codes. Hexadecimal codes are a standard way of representing colors in web design. By using a Web-Safe Color Editor, designers can be confident that the colors they choose will be accurately displayed on various devices, ensuring a consistent and cohesive user experience. Moreover, these tools can save time and effort by providing a pre-selected range of colors that are known to work well together. In summary, Web-Safe Color Editors facilitate the application of color theory and color symbolism in web design by providing a curated palette of colors that can be relied upon to display consistently across different platforms and devices.

Web-Safe Color Pickers

Web-Safe Color Pickers are tools or applications that help designers select colors that are consistent and compatible across different web browsers and operating systems. These color pickers are specifically designed to offer a limited set of colors that are safe to use on the web, ensuring that the chosen colors will be displayed consistently on all devices. Color theory and symbolism play crucial roles in design, as they help convey meaning and evoke emotions through the use of color. Web-Safe Color Pickers take these principles into account by offering a range of colors that are universally understood and accepted in the digital realm. In color theory, colors are often categorized into primary, secondary, and tertiary colors. Primary colors, such as red, blue, and yellow, are the building blocks of all other colors. Secondary colors, such as orange, green, and purple, are created by mixing two primary colors together. Tertiary colors, such as yellow-green or red-violet, are a result of mixing primary and secondary colors. Color symbolism, on the other hand, refers to the cultural associations and meanings that different

197

colors hold. For example, red is often associated with passion, love, and energy, while blue is commonly associated with calmness, trust, and stability. By understanding color symbolism, designers can effectively communicate their intended message through their color choices. Web-Safe Color Pickers provide a limited color palette that consists of 216 colors, commonly known as the web-safe palette. These colors were selected to ensure compatibility across various platforms and devices, as earlier versions of web browsers had limited color capabilities. Each color in the web-safe palette is defined by a combination of red, green, and blue (RGB) values, using only a limited number of possible combinations. By employing a web-safe color picker, designers can ensure that the colors they choose will be displayed consistently for all users, regardless of their device or browser. This is particularly important in web design, where color consistency can impact the overall user experience and the perceived professionalism of a website. In conclusion, Web-Safe Color Pickers are essential tools for designers to select colors that conform to the limited color palette recognized by all web browsers and operating systems. By adhering to the web-safe palette, designers can guarantee color consistency and compatibility across different platforms, ensuring their intended color symbolism and design concepts are effectively communicated to their audience.

Web-Safe Colors

Web-Safe Colors are a set of colors that are considered to be universally consistent across different computer platforms and web browsers. In the context of color theory and color symbolism in design, using web-safe colors ensures that the intended color scheme and symbolism of a design are accurately represented and preserved when viewed on various devices and browsers. Web-safe colors are limited to a palette of 216 colors, which are defined by a combination of 216 indexed colors in the 8-bit color depth. These colors are standardized and recognized by all major web browsers, guaranteeing that the colors will display consistently across different platforms. The use of web-safe colors is particularly important in web design, as inconsistent color rendering can lead to variations in the visual appearance of a website and potentially affect the user experience. Color theory plays a crucial role in design, as different colors evoke different emotions, convey meanings, and elicit specific responses from viewers. By adhering to web-safe colors, designers can ensure that their chosen color schemes accurately convey the desired symbolism and impact of their design. For example, if a designer intends to use the color red to evoke feelings of passion and intensity, using a web-safe shade of red guarantees that viewers across platforms will perceive the intended emotional response. Similarly, color symbolism in design refers to the cultural or psychological associations and meanings associated with specific colors. For instance, blue is often associated with tranquility and trust, while yellow evokes feelings of cheerfulness and optimism. By using web-safe colors, designers can maintain the intended symbolism across different platforms, allowing viewers from diverse backgrounds to interpret the design consistently. Overall, the use of web-safe colors in color theory and color symbolism ensures visual consistency and accurate representation of a design's intended message and emotional impact in web design. By using the limited palette of 216 standardized colors, designers can create harmonious color schemes that communicate their desired symbolism effectively, regardless of the device or browser used to view the design.

Websites For Color Combinations

A website for color combinations is a platform that provides designers and artists with an assortment of colors to help them effectively choose and use colors in their designs. These websites are based on color theory and color symbolism, which are important concepts in the field of design. Color theory is the study of how colors interact with each other and how they can be combined to create harmonious or contrasting effects. It helps designers understand the relationships between colors, such as complementary, analogous, or triadic color schemes. By using color theory, designers can create visually appealing and balanced compositions that evoke specific emotions or convey a particular message. Additionally, color symbolism refers to the cultural associations and meanings assigned to specific colors. Different colors can evoke different emotions or convey different ideas and concepts. For example, red is often associated with passion and energy, while blue is associated with calmness and trust. Color combination websites typically offer a wide range of color palettes, schemes, or gradients that designers can utilize in their work. These platforms often provide color tools and generators that allow users to experiment with different color combinations and see how they interact. Some websites even offer predefined color schemes based on color theory principles, making it easier for designers to choose a harmonious set of colors for their projects. These websites also consider color symbolism and provide information on the meanings and cultural associations of different colors. This can help designers in selecting colors that align with the intended message or theme of their design. By understanding the symbolic meanings of colors, designers can create more impactful and meaningful visuals. In conclusion, websites for color combinations are invaluable resources for designers and artists. Through the use of color theory and symbolism, these platforms offer a variety of color options and tools to assist designers in creating visually appealing and conceptually meaningful designs.

Websites For Color Exploration

A color exploration website is a digital platform that provides resources and tools for understanding and exploring color theory and color symbolism in the context of design. These websites offer a range of information and interactive experiences to help designers and artists make informed choices about color usage in their creations. Color theory is the study of how colors can be combined and arranged to create aesthetically pleasing and visually balanced designs. It explores concepts such as color harmony, contrast, and the emotional impact of different colors. By understanding color theory, designers can effectively convey messages and evoke specific emotions through their use of color. Color symbolism, on the other hand, is the attribution of particular meanings or associations to different colors. Different cultures and contexts may have varying interpretations of color symbolism. For example, red may symbolize love and passion in one culture, while it may connote danger or warning in another. Color symbolism is often used in design to reinforce or enhance the message or mood of a design. Color exploration websites provide various resources and features to facilitate the understanding and application of color theory and symbolism. These include: - Color wheels and palettes: These tools showcase different color combinations and allow users to experiment with different hues, saturations, and brightness levels. They help designers understand how colors interact with each other and find harmonious combinations. - Tutorials and guides: Websites may offer step-by-step tutorials and guides on color theory and symbolism, providing examples and explanations of different concepts. These resources can help users deepen their knowledge and gain practical insights into applying color principles in design. - Case studies and examples: Color exploration websites often showcase real-world examples and case studies that demonstrate effective color usage in various design contexts. These case studies may analyze the color choices and their impact on the overall design and user experience. - Psychological and cultural associations: Websites may provide information on the psychological and cultural associations of different colors, helping designers understand the potential meanings and interpretations that colors can evoke in their target audience. By providing these resources and tools, color exploration websites enable designers to expand their understanding of color theory and symbolism, make informed design decisions, and create visually compelling and meaningful designs.

Wholeness (Turquoise)

Wholeness, also known as turquoise, is a color in the context of color theory and color symbolism in design. It falls within the blue-green color family, being a hue that is reminiscent of a mix between blue and green. Turquoise is often associated with the gemstone of the same name, which has been revered for its beauty and healing properties throughout history. In color theory, wholeness represents a balance between the serene calmness of blue and the energetic freshness of green. This creates an overall feeling of harmony and tranquility. Turquoise is often referred to as a color of balance, as it combines the calm of blue with the vitality of green.

Wisdom (Blue)

In the context of color theory and color symbolism in design, wisdom is represented by the color blue. Blue is often associated with qualities such as intelligence, knowledge, and insight, making it a suitable color to symbolize wisdom. The color blue is known to have a calming and soothing effect on the viewer, which can evoke a sense of tranquility and peace. This attribute of blue makes it an ideal choice to convey a sense of serenity and clarity, both of which are closely related to wisdom. Furthermore, blue is often associated with depth and stability, which are important components of wisdom. Just as wisdom implies a deep understanding of complex concepts and situations, the color blue can convey a sense of depth and complexity. In addition

199

to these inherent associations, the use of blue in design can also elicit specific cultural and psychological responses. For example, in Western cultures, blue is often associated with trust, reliability, and loyalty. These positive connotations can further enhance the representation of wisdom when blue is used in design. On the color wheel, blue is considered a cool color that is often associated with water and the sky. These natural elements can also contribute to the symbolism of wisdom, as they represent vastness, expansiveness, and infinite possibilities. Just as the sky seems to have no limits and holds endless knowledge, the color blue can provoke thoughts of limitless wisdom and understanding. Overall, in the realm of color theory and symbolism, blue embodies wisdom through its association with intellect, stability, calmness, and trustworthiness. By incorporating blue into design elements, one can effectively convey a sense of wisdom and intelligence to the audience.

Wisdom (Indigo)

Wisdom, also known as indigo, is a hue that holds significant meaning in color theory and color symbolism in design. It is a deep, dark shade of blue with a touch of violet. In the color spectrum, indigo falls between blue and violet, representing a bridge between two colors associated with calmness and spirituality. Indigo is often associated with wisdom and intuition. It is believed to stimulate the mind and encourage deep thought and introspection. This color is commonly used in designs that aim to evoke a sense of mystery and depth, as well as to convey a feeling of wisdom and knowledge.

Wisdom (Purple)

Wisdom (Purple) Wisdom is a color within the realm of color theory and color symbolism in design. In color theory, purple is a secondary color created by mixing blue and red. It sits on the color spectrum between blue and magenta. Symbolically, purple is often associated with wisdom.

Wisdom (Yellow)

The color yellow, specifically represented by the term Wisdom in the context of color theory and color symbolism in design, symbolizes various concepts and emotions in different cultures and contexts. Yellow is often associated with positivity, happiness, and enlightenment. It has the ability to stimulate mental clarity, creativity, and logical thinking. In this sense, Wisdom represents the color yellow's capacity to mentally stimulate and promote intellectual growth.

Workshops On Color Theory

Color theory is a fundamental aspect of design that explores how colors interact with each other and how they can be used to evoke specific emotions and convey messages. It encompasses the study of color harmony, contrast, and symbolism. Workshops on color theory aim to educate and guide designers in understanding the principles and applications of colors in design. These workshops delve into the impact of colors on the visual experience, highlighting the psychological and emotional effects that different hues can have on viewers. Through the exploration of color harmony, participants gain insights into combining colors effectively to create visually appealing and balanced compositions. By understanding the principles of color contrast, designers can learn how to leverage the differences in coloring to make elements stand out or create depth and dimension in their designs. The workshops also emphasize the importance of color symbolism in design. Colors can carry cultural, historical, and personal significance, and being able to interpret and use these symbolic meanings can add depth and meaning to design work. Participants will learn about the symbolic associations of different colors, such as how red can symbolize passion or danger, while blue may evoke feelings of calm or sadness. They will also examine the cultural variations in color symbolism, as colors can carry different meanings in different cultures. Through practical exercises and hands-on activities, workshop attendees will have the opportunity to apply their knowledge of color theory and symbolism to create their own designs. They will explore the impact of different color choices on the overall visual communication and how colors can enhance or detract from the intended message. These workshops aim to empower designers with a deeper understanding of colors, enabling them to make informed decisions about color palettes and effectively convey their desired meanings and emotions through their designs.

Youth (Green)

Youth (Green) - In the context of color theory and color symbolism in design, youth green refers to a specific shade of green that is often associated with concepts of youthfulness, growth, and vitality. This particular shade of green is typically bright and vibrant, reminiscent of the lushness and freshness of nature. It carries a sense of energy and renewal, symbolizing the beginning or early stages of life. The use of youth green in design can evoke feelings of optimism, enthusiasm, and the promise of new beginnings.

Youthfulness (Lilac)

Youthfulness (Lilac) is a color that holds significant meaning in both color theory and color symbolism in design. In color theory, lilac is considered a variation of purple, which is a secondary color created by blending blue and red. It is typically associated with creativity, spirituality, and luxury. Lilac is often described as a light shade of purple with a slight blue undertone, giving it a delicate and airy quality. In the context of color symbolism in design, lilac is commonly associated with youthfulness. This is due to its soft and feminine nature, which evokes feelings of innocence, playfulness, and freshness. The lightness of lilac creates a sense of light-heartedness and optimism, making it an ideal choice for designs targeting a younger audience or promoting youthful qualities.

Youthfulness (Peach)

Youthfulness (Peach) is a color within the color theory and color symbolism in design that represents the vibrant and energetic nature of young individuals. A shade of orange with hints of pink and yellow, it exudes a sense of freshness and vitality. In color theory, youthfulness is often associated with the color peach. This warm and inviting hue is reminiscent of the softness and delicacy of a ripe peach fruit. It is commonly used to evoke feelings of innocence, playfulness, and optimism.